THE IMPROVISATION GAME

CHRIS JOHNSTON

Chris Johnston trained at the Drama Centre, London, before working in small-scale theatre as a writer and director. He has created performances in a wide range of venues, has taught extensively and recently completed a Fellowship in Creative and Performing Arts at the University of Warwick. He is currently Co-Director of Rideout and Director of Fluxx.

by the same author

HOUSE OF GAMES

Making theatre from everyday life

THE
IMPROVISATION
GAME

DISCOVERING THE SECRETS
OF SPONTANEOUS PERFORMANCE

Chris Johnston

NICK HERN BOOKS

London

www.nickhernbooks.co.uk

A NICK HERN BOOK

The Improvisation Game
first published as a paperback original
in 2006 in Great Britain
by Nick Hern Books Limited,
14 Larden Road, London W3 7ST

Cover design: www.energydesignstudio.com
Cover photo: Darren Robb/Stone/Getty Images

British Library Cataloguing data for this book
is available from the British Library
ISBN-13: 978 1 85459 668 0
ISBN-10: 1 85459 668 3

Typeset in Monotype Ehrhardt by
Country Setting, Kingsdown, Kent CT14 8ES

Printed and bound in Great Britain by
Cromwell Press, Trowbridge, Wilts

Play what you hear, not what you know.

Miles Davis

For Robin

ACKNOWLEDGEMENTS

I'd like to acknowledge the support and advice of Nick Hern and his colleagues in preparing this book. I'd also like to thank all those hundreds of creative practitioners – actors, dancers, musicians and others – who engaged in improvisation projects with me in the UK and beyond. Many of these were risky, exciting, rewarding and joyous. Some were just plain daft. Also to those such as Alan Rivett, Colin Ellwood, Mark Evans and Adrian Heathfield, I'd like to extend my thanks for helping to organise, facilitate or make possible these projects. A good number of these events, and indeed the writing of this book, were supported financially by the Arts and Humanities Research Council, to whom I am extremely grateful. My thanks also go to Maggie Gordon-Walker whose affection, advice and encouragement ensured the book did finally get completed.

I'd also like to thank the following for giving their time in interviews. All quotes from the following people are from these interviews, unless otherwise indicated: Gaby Agis, Danielle Allan, Robert Anderson, Joe Bill, Jo Blowers, Alison Blunt, Sally Brookes, Pete Brooks, Andrea Buckley, Annie Castledine, Guy Dartnell, Jennifer Ellison, Matt Elwell, Tim Etchells, Simon Fell, Kevin Finnan, Martin Glynn, Tony Guilfoyle, Don Hall, Paula Hampson, Adrian Heathfield, Saul Hewish, Kate Hilder, K.J. Holmes, Rex Hossi Horan, Wendy Houston, Keith Johnstone, Jonathan Kay, Mark Long, Kate McCoy, Phelim McDermott, Sue McLennan, Neil Mullarkey, Rick Nodine, Deborah Paige, Mary Prestidge, Eddie Prévost, Sten Rudstrom, Peter Sander, Nancy Stark Smith, Mark Sutton, Sandy Van Torquil, Keith Whipple, John Wright.

CONTENTS

INTRODUCTION

This book aims to provoke the future endeavours of improvisers everywhere – in theatre, dance, music, live art or any uncategorisable mix of these. Most improvised work is considered as a sub-section of an art form; here I'm trying to look at improvisation as a core discipline, the fundamentals of which exist within all the separate genres. I concentrate chiefly on improvisation within theatre, but dance and music practice are also considered where they share elements or problems. The geographical orientation is primarily the UK, with some reference to the USA, and a few inadequate nods towards work elsewhere.

Let's define improvisation for our purposes here as:

The spontaneous invention of words, behaviours, sounds, or movement within a context understood as fictional, aesthetic or representational.

There are others . . .

SOME HISTORY I

In the beginning, when clouds were God's breath, and buffaloes roared without fear, and time was uncounted except by death and birth and the sky darkening, there was performance. And it was never counted as special or apart because it was and it was what happened and without it we thought there would be drought and insufficiency and possibly war when you wanted peace, or peace when you wanted war. So we moved and shook and spoke in sequences of unidentified languages and evoked harmony in ourselves and terror in our enemies. And we urged ourselves good fortune and bonded with each other and reinforced ourselves as tribe of reindeer or mountain or lyre bird.

And we took no photographs nor did we issue a press release quoting what a famous critic had said about our previous triumph nor was there a Channel Four documentary team turning our fiction into reality or our reality into fiction. Nor was anyone writing a postdoctorate thesis arguing about physicality in a pre-mediatised society but still there was performance. And the sun cooked our heads until our minds swam with imagined victories. And we roared our affirmations while our children cried in awe and uncertainty and sickness and we looked to see if spirits had entered them. And amongst us in the flames there were one or two who leapt and spiralled with a kind of fever that is a sure sign of possession and so they were listened to for their wisdom, for if we failed to heed them then our wombs might be empty and snakes might carry off our young. And this was performance. But no researcher came with notebook or camera and there was no criticism of how the plot perambulated or the set shook or the actress faked it. For this was performance and improvisation, and it happened and it happened often and it was at the heart of things.

SOME HISTORY II

A PARTIAL ACCOUNT

15th–17th centuries
    Commedia dell'Arte
1843   UK Theatres Act, making improvisation illegal
1879   Birth of Jacques Copeau
1920   Jacob Moreno explores the use of improvisation in therapy
1952   John Cage premieres *4'33"*
1960   Improvisational workshops start at Second City
1961   Lenny Bruce performs at Carnegie Hall, New York
1963   Viola Spolin publishes *Improvisation*
1966   *Trio A* performed in New York by Rainer, Gordon and Paxton
1968   The abolition of theatre censorship in the UK
1968   Living Theatre premieres *Paradise Now*
1970   Scratch Orchestra perform at the Royal Albert Hall
1970s   Theatre Machine on tour
1972   Performance of Steve Paxton's *Magnesium*
1970s   Afrika Bambaataa forms Zulu Nation
1979   Keith Johnstone publishes *Impro*
1997   First Chicago Improvisation Festival
2004   Improbable Theatre present *Lifegame* at the National Theatre, London
2006   *The Improvisation Game* published
2006   Shifti, the first mixed-art form improvisation festival, at Warwick Arts Centre.

PART ONE

THE WHY

THE WHY

Why are we improvising? Why use improvisation rather than tennis, carpet-weaving or opera? Improvisation tends to be used primarily in pursuit of one of four aims:

- As RESEARCH into ourselves to increase self-knowledge, perhaps sharing the results of this research with others as performance.

- For LEARNING better how to communicate with each other, manage emotions or improve life skills.

- To understand, manage or reconcile CONFLICT. This work is sometimes associated with programmes for social change.

- To create ENTERTAINMENT without necessarily any recourse to a higher purpose, unless you see laughing as a higher purpose, which you might.

I

RESEARCH

'Contact Improvisation is not just another dance technique or discipline. It's a form for discovering who we are beneath our skins. It is a place where our self-concept is questioned. Who am I? What is the shape of my fear? To what degree am I present? What particular trance am I in at the moment? What dialogue is running in my mind? What ghosts gnaw at my soul?'

Ken Martini

'Having worked at the characters for ages, the actors can go into character and do a wonderful improvisation that might go on for one or two hours non-stop. That doesn't give you a scene. That merely suggests a scene. My job is to distil that into something that happens in a few minutes and says just as much. And indeed says more, because obviously my job is also to inject things into it and edit things out, and to open up stuff that's dormant . . . Very little of what you've seen in my films is actually being improvised on camera, 99.9 per cent of it is very, very highly rehearsed and scripted down to the last word. But it's evolved from improvisation . . . ' Mike Leigh

'The aim of improvisation in training actors in rehearsal, and the aim of exercises, is always the same: it is to get away from Deadly Theatre.'

Peter Brook

Improvisation is a research tool, widely used by artists from all disciplines. It's a staple procedure in creating performance. While more cerebral exercises such as writing or composing allow for greater control over decisions, improvisation can deliver the shock material. With its spontaneous, unpredictable processes, improvisation can deliver the right-brain gifts that sneak in under the radar. It's arguable that improvisation is in fact inseparable from the creative process, even when the artist is writing or composing. It's arguable that improvisation is the first artistic medium of all. The very best kind of research. Within music composition for example, Peter Sander argues, *'You cannot be a composer if you can't improvise.'* For even there, with the artist alone, improvisations are taking place within the mind of the individual. Without improvisation, neither composition nor choreography nor performance can truly exist – unless perhaps the piece is delivered to you in a revelation. That does happen, and followers of Mohammed and Moses and Dylan argue it. But most artists work improvisationally, testing and trying out ideas until something fits just right. Increasingly it's used in television too, with shows from *Curb Your Enthusiasm* to *The Thick of It* having actors improvise around basic scenarios. The artist who consciously uses improvisation benefits from conjunctions, associations, accidents and impulses that might otherwise be checked or censored. I might be tempted therefore instead of asking 'Why improvise?' to ask 'Why should we not improvise?' After all, the skills involved have application almost everywhere – certainly beyond the arts. You might argue they're wasted on the arts. As Joyce Piven said on stage during the seventh Chicago Improvisation Festival, calling out to the political world, *'We've discovered so much – why don't they come talk to us?'*

THE SELF

The medium of improvisation, properly handled, has the capacity to show us to ourselves. It can reveal the shadows, surprising us horribly. While travelling to a familiar place, it can trip us up and demonstrate we're not who we thought we were. And if we're honest enough in that moment, we can get to appreciate that we don't know the world or ourselves that well. This is the moment of potential research. At that moment, the old knowledge is found lacking. There is another self to be seen, and improvisation is the conjuring excercise.

There's a problem-solving exercise called the Newspaper Game popular in prison drama. Several sheets of newspaper are laid on the floor. The group is asked to work out how to get into a position where everyone is touching the newspaper and not the furniture or the floor. Dutifully, everyone stands on the newspaper. Mission accomplished. Then the quantity of newspaper is reduced. Again, people stand on it and mission accomplished. It's reduced again and again. Each time, as the paper acreage reduces, the group will perform a range of dangerous and time-consuming acrobatics rather than abandon this previously successful strategy. Eventually someone will say 'Maybe we should think about this differently' – and finally the group will realise that the best way to solve the problem is for everyone to hold the paper and jump into the air. What's interesting is how the 'old knowledge' is hung on to for so long. Keith Johnstone has observed how in tests, children will abandon a trail that has run out, but adults will persist with it way beyond the moment when it's realised the trail is going nowhere. It sounds familiar. Frustrations set in. You feel like you've made an investment in a particular strategy, so you'll be damned before giving it up. There's a reluctance to abandon the old knowledge *even when it's proved not to work*.

The reason is, it's quite simply a hard thing to be constantly adjusting to new knowledge. Most of our core activities run on old knowledge. This is certainly true for adults, who get reluctant to change routines. When new knowledge hits us, we start to accommodate ourselves so we have a relationship with it no longer based on its immediacy, its newness or its presence as a discomfort. In a sense, we institutionalise that new knowledge and take the spark out of it. We absorb it within 'the familiar', change gear by a fraction, and carry on. As we get older, there's less and less enthusiasm for adapting. Some are better at recognising the importance of the new knowledge than others. They are the ones who recognise the need to keep learning, keep changing. These are those who start as mavericks, jeered at by society, and end up being applauded as visionaries.

> 'It's all right letting yourself go, as long as you can get yourself back.'
> Mick Jagger

Whoever thought that getting computers to talk to each other was ever going to succeed? And part of that project is recognising that what is changing is not just the exterior world, but also ourselves. Improvisation can be a tool with which to research our individual selves. It can help to make us aware of what is happening within the body, mind and emotions. It seeks out newness, it's a natural digging tool, its radar is always searching for something that's never been seen or heard before (if we can let it). So it's a good device for challenging the old knowledge and digging up what's changed within us.

Improvisers are constantly discovering more about themselves if they stay open to the messages that come through. Arnold Mindell in his Dreambody work got patients to identify what was physically wrong and to exaggerate the symptoms in front of him. In the process

> 'Action Theatre makes you confront yourself. Some people may not like that.'
> Sten Rudstrom

of exaggeration, the patient often experienced new insight into the causes of the problem. By going into the new, difficult, problematic, disabling symptom, knowledge is found about how to cure it. If improvisers work together, they are banging up against their own deficiencies, and these rear up in the consciousness. They can be identified in part through the responses of others. Through discussion and feedback, individuals can learn more about their defaults with each other and what they need to do to become more communicative, more social or more effective as performers. Improvisation practice inevitably segues between communication issues and artistic issues. This is one reason why issues of structure and conventions are so important, because by addressing these, participants are able to create safety for themselves in their explorations. In turn, these structures and conventions allow more unconscious play to emerge. This is one reason why improvisation has the role it has within drama therapy, psychodrama and Process Work. In the moment of staging, there is a chance that the unconscious may be tricked or encouraged to show itself, making self-discovery more likely.

Contrary to popular belief, improvisation is not some casual exercise. It's not just about 'adlibbing'. While the spirit behind it is often deliberately casual and throwaway, the practice itself does involve a conscious organisation of resources within a context established for that purpose. It needs time and space for its expression. It needs, or at least can benefit from, forms and structures that permit this impulsive freedom that is so beneficial. If you're going to walk off into space, you need to be confident someone will catch you *if it is just space down there*. If you're going to open your head and respond impulsively for the first time, ensure there are those in the room who can put your random, sciatic doodlings into some meaningful context. And while there are parallels with the kind of improvisation required for 'getting through the day', it really is not the same. The cliché that 'everyone improvises from the moment they get up' is only true in a very partial, and perhaps unhelpful way. Improvisation requires a degree of consciousness which involves the performer being 'at one remove' from real life – yet crucially attached to it. It involves both detachment and engagement, a balancing act that is hard to get right. Those coming to it for easy answers might be better tackling a more short-term career path, like astrophysics. It takes a while to become versed in the patterns and protocols of dramatic improvisation, whether you follow a comedic, therapeutic or any other kind of impro path. Not that it can't be treated casually or indulged in occasionally, of course it can. But a casual acquaintanceship won't allow many secrets to be discovered.

To discover something new about the self necessarily involves trying to avoid the familiar. The mind will tend to seek after the familiar, the old knowledge, because in a sense it's more comforting. The process therefore depends significantly on allowing the voices that are turbulent, difficult or incorrect in the self, to come through. Keith Johnstone writes clearly about the importance of not censoring ourselves for this reason. He stresses the importance of being unafraid to face our own demons. For if, as he argues, we are to deny the power and inclinations of our own imagination, then we begin to stunt our own creativity. *'My feeling is that sanity is actually a pretence, a way we learn to behave. We keep this pretence up because we don't want to be rejected by other people – and being classified insane is to be shut out of the group in a very complete way . . . The stages I try to take students through involve the realisation (1) that we struggle against our imaginations, especially when we try to be imaginative; (2) that we are not responsible for the content of our imaginations; and (3) that we are not, as we are taught to think, our "personalities", but that the imagination is our true self.'*[1]

> 'Everyone can be a great improviser in their bathroom.'
> Wendy Houston

This last is a huge and very significant claim, and although I read it years ago in *Impro*, I'm still not sure I've absorbed its significance yet. If my imagination is my true self, then to reject what my imagination offers is to reject my true self. That's the logic. So how is it possible that I can start to be open to my imagination? When it first comes to you, this notion about the primacy of the imagination is both truly frightening and truly exciting. It's one reason why so many students come back from reading *Impro* claiming it's the 'best book ever'. But it's also the reason they put it away and never open it again because they might just be asked to go on the journey that Johnstone outlines. His thesis has been proved correct a million times: if the improviser is open, then ideas and images will come through – unbidden. At first glance this looks and feels illogical. How can ideas and images come through unbidden? Surely you have to go in search of them. Well, yes, possibly. But they may just come through anyway – given one thing: that the improviser is awake: listening, watching and paying attention. If the watcher is asleep when the signal comes, then quite likely the improviser will answer to the teacher afterwards – 'I wanted to have an idea, but nothing came to me.' Instead you have to be like the character Nakata in Murakami's *Kafka on the Shore* who believes that when he gets to the place he is going, he will know what to do – rather than deciding what he wants to do and then going to a place to achieve it. In this extract, Hoshino is asking his friend Nakata about how he, Nakata, is going to 'open' the Entrance Stone, as they've been instructed to do. Hoshino has just carried this large, heavy stone up to their apartment on his friend's instructions:

Can I ask you something else?

Yes.

If you do open the Entrance Stone here, is something amazing going to happen? Like is what's-his-name, that genie, going to pop out like in *Aladdin*? Or will a prince that's been turned into a frog French kiss me? Or else will I be eaten alive by Martians?

Something might happen, but then again maybe nothing. I haven't opened it yet, so I don't know. You can't know until you open it.[2]

A computer can't really improvise. Mine can, because it suddenly does things that aren't commanded and aren't required. Which is a kind of improvising. But arguably this is just technical erraticism. If it could improvise as part of its function, then its operating system would be the imagination. The improviser sets off towards self-knowledge by booting up the imagination. It's not about being wilful, being driven or having a clear goal. It's about shaking hands with the devil then inviting him to sit down and tell his story. Why the devil? Because imagination, left to its own devices, is likely to go its own devilish way. As dreams do. So let the imagination do its worst. Open the Entrance Stone and trust that something will emerge. Or as Guy Dartnell put it to me: *'You're trying to become a channel for something. Rather than your having to involve yourself in a lot of effort, mental or whatever, to come up with stuff, you try and welcome or attract something to you . . . Instead of the audience watching your effort, they go on the dream.'* In this way, the self is more acted upon than acting. It's the inverse of a traditional idea of research which is that you go out in search of something, find it and bring it home for inspection. Here, you stay still, allow something to come to you, then try and express it before it leaves again. Hence the quite legitimate claim that improvising is rather like becoming a medium for spirits.

THE GROUP

Improvisation can go further to bring forward themes and images arising from a group working together collaboratively. Arguably there is a connection here with the notion of a collective unconscious, the existence of a body of shared psychic material that becomes apparent only in its expression. The notion holds particular appeal when a group of people with similar backgrounds commit themselves to an imaginative exercise. The material emerging from their endeavours can often be identified as saying something about the predicament or life situation of that group. Their commonality as individuals helps to pool experience and more easily mesh together dramatic material of substance. It may be that a story emerges that seems to encapsulate or mirror the experience of all. Again, it's as much a question of allowing material to emerge imaginatively, as it is about going in search of something. Although paradoxically one has to have first a searching, enquiring mind for this to occur.

Augusto Boal refers to a process that he calls 'pluralisation', in which a group who share similar circumstances adopts one person's story because that particular story has a certain resonance, an ability to speak for all who recognise its truth. The selection of such a story then underpins a piece of performance. While Boal's work directs itself towards the articulation and correction of social injustice, improvisational research is not confined to the territory of Theatre of the Oppressed. It can and is used widely by artists in every art form to devise resonant material for future performances. It's hard nowadays to find a company that doesn't in some way or other use improvisation as a tool to dig up stories, imagery and elliptic material to use for performance purposes.

I was working in a UK adult–male prison where there is a therapeutic community. This means that the prisoners there have elected to commit themselves to a daily regime of meetings in which experiences and feelings are analysed. As Rideout, we were making a devised play with a group of about ten men. Several days into the process, we were stuck. Various exercises had been run and some material had been gathered, but it wasn't anchored. We needed a different kind of exercise – one that cut through the nonsense and gave us some essential imagery the group would take ownership of. We wanted something to 'come through'. So I asked one of the men to come on to the stage and to sit in a chair. Then I asked him to take an attitude towards his surroundings. This meant him taking a stance towards the space. He understood that he was playing a character in a scene, although we didn't define who that was and I didn't ask him. I did ask him to stay still for the duration of the exercise. Then I asked the remainder of the group a series of simple questions. So nobody moved in the exercise, we quite deliberately just opened the doors and trusted that inspiration would arrive. That the Entrance Stone would open. The process went something like this, with answers being called out randomly by different group members:

This character on the chair. What can he see?

The floor.

Describe the floor.

It's dirty. There's rubbish on it. There's a pizza box with cigarette ends in it.

Where is he?

In his room.

Which room?

Living room.

Is he alone?

Yes / No.

How is he alone and not alone? Is someone with him?

No.

So who or what is with him that he's not alone?

He's got a dog with him.

Is it his dog?

Yeah.

What kind of dog is it?

It's a big dog. It's a mongrel. Yeah, and it's dangerous.

How is it dangerous?

It bites people.

Including him?

No, he's the only one it doesn't bite. (Laughter)

Who has it bitten in the past?

Loads of people. Shopkeepers. Strangers, friends, everyone. That's why he keeps moving.

What do you mean, moving?

He has to keep moving from place to place. Keeps switching homes. Because of the dog. He keeps moving on. Or he gets kicked out. To avoid having the dog taken away and locked up. It's his best friend, see . . .

Once we had the dog and the moving on, we knew we had our story. It had been the right exercise at the right time – for a change. It was a question now of elaborating and developing this initial premise. What was particularly intriguing was the moving on, and the willingness to move on rather than deal with the difficulties caused by the dog. Why was the character making these kinds of priorities? What had occurred to force him to move on? Now we could split into sub-groups and get some different answers to these questions. Each group was given different questions to answer, by improvising and discussing further amongst themselves. How was the dog acquired? (Unsurprisingly, it was rescued.) How did he survive, always moving on? (He took the dog to dogfights for money). How did he deal with the dog's victims? (He tried to elicit sympathy for the previous maltreatment of the dog!) The final play had the dog owner as a central character, coming into town and making friends and enemies. The dog served well, if one chose to look at it that way, to represent that part of the offender self that was beyond rehabilitation. We had tapped into a significant truth about this group that might have been denied within ordinary conversation: that this part of the self was, despite the therapeutic context, beyond therapy. It was a case for them now of wild dog management.

INSTANT THEATRE

I borrowed this questioning technique from a theatre form called Instant Theatre, developed by Word and Action. Instant Theatre is a participatory exercise that might be described as a king of divinatory acupuncture. It uses questioning to pierce into the spirit of the group – or audience – and draw out its character as answers, in the form of a mythic story. This story has the same relationship of a dream to the dreamer; its narrative crossed through with illogical elements, inconsistencies and wild juxtapositions. Yet this mish-mash of narrative elements is as fair a summary of that group's preoccupations as you might find, mythologised admittedly. The making of the dream/story is achieved through a question and answer process not dissimilar to the example above. It depends for its success on the correlation of two key elements: the insistence on strict rules being adhered to, and the absolute freedom of the imagination permitted by the exercise of the rules. Some people assume that strictness of theatrical protocols only restricts the freedom that participants have to imaginatively express themselves. The reverse is the case. Imaginative freedom is only really achieved within a context of absolutes. So as the performers ask questions of the group (or audience), it is ensured that no censorship operates on any answers given. Every answer is accepted, irrespective of vulgarity, potential for libel or likelihood to cause offence.

The actor in the role of a questioner asks questions to elaborate a story, much on the model of 'What happens next?' Care is taken to ensure that all questions are open not closed, so they make no assumptions about the answer. The question asked is 'What is the priest doing when the tower falls?' rather than 'Is the priest praying when it falls?' The role of the questioner is to be honest to the narrative momentum created by the audience. The questioner aims to be a lightning conductor, a conduit for whatever flashes of inspiration or disquiet emerge from the answerers.

The resulting narrative is usually a quirky and eccentric mix of the contemporary and the mythic, the surreal and the prosaic, laced

'When a group assembles to create a piece of Instant Theatre it abandons (intellectual) knowledge, effectively putting itself into a state of innocence. What grows through the question and answer process is a fabulous knowledge, long-since abandoned by the authoritarian group-principle as too dangerous. The fabulous disturbs the undisturbed, finding unknown answers in everyone's shared dark ... by the end of the play, the whole has been melded into a kind of word-tapestry, whose reverberations stay active for those who care to continue listening.'

R.G. Gregory, *The World of Instant Theatre*

together by the storytelling convention. Once it's created, the company acts it out with the audience participating. Subsequent to the enactment, it becomes raw material for any further number of expressions for example through visual arts work or the writing of poetry.

In terms of its potential as a research tool, Instant Theatre is unequalled in its democratic spirit of enquiry and its consistency of formal processes. These ensure – as far as possible – that individual egos cannot dominate. The story performs its divinatory function most effectively when the audience is distinguished by homogeneity of age, class or creed, for then the spectators' narrative impulses tend to coalesce. Spectators can be heard calling out similar suggestions, or there is loud approval of suggestions just made. Gregory comments: '*Instant Theatre, in effect, is Campbell's* Hero with a Thousand Faces [the book by Campbell articulating the key stages of the myth of the hero]. *Each time it dips into the unknown, and comes up with a treasurable statement, offering through its collection of individual shards, the glimpse of a culture the group very often doesn't even know it shares. An Instant Theatre performance may register at the time as a random, corny, crudely-brought-together piece of nonsense; something for the moment but nothing more. Yet its residue, the story, may yield to pages and pages of dream-interpretation.*'[3] It's as close as one might get to the audience improvising its own show about itself.

DEVISING

Most companies' research takes place privately, within what's understood as a devising process. In this context, themes, ideas and narratives are improvised to generate material for the coming show.

They get to be dug up from the group or some raw material is used to provoke reflections on that material. Devising is almost inseparable from the practice of improvisation: taking an idea, trying it out, assessing the value of the emerging material, and saving or deleting accordingly. *'It's not absolutely necessary for someone to come along with some deeply thought-out notion or criteria or idea. Devising can be down to a group of people from day one. Usually people are very inhibited if they don't have the big idea – they feel that there should be something of enormous importance here. Something we're going to dedicate our lives to, for the next x weeks. Having said that, I do think it's important that during the process of creation, the group does start to realise that notion, and does start to dedicate its life to it. And if you've got the right kind of trust, the big idea does evolve.'* (Mark Long of the People Show.) To take this view is to accept that ideas will 'come to the surface' once the devising process is engaged. The skill lies in recognising them, harpooning them and reeling them in. That makes it sound simple, but of course it isn't. It's very easy to get lost in the devising process, perhaps ending up with too much or too little material, or material in which no one has confidence. Or perhaps again, the popular variant: material about which everyone disagrees. There are essentially two approaches to devising, although it's really impossible to pursue one exclusively. The two approaches are more or less co-dependent. The first is methodological. By this means, the devisers follow a set path of procedures or exercises. The process is divided up into different packages of time with set objectives for each stage of the process. For example, first the world, then the characters, then the story. Each section will involve games, improvisation or discussion. The second approach is inspirational; the devisers simply following hunches, moving zig-zaggedly through a process of association, looking for what inspires.

THE FISH

After devising many shows and then being asked to share something of that process in a teaching context, I tried to carve out a few methodological principles from what had been a pragmatic, hit-and-miss affair more often than not. The method involves identifying key stages of the process while allowing different freedoms within each section. So it's a combination of the two procedures outlined above. I hit upon the fish as a means of explaining this. Or perhaps I should say

The Fish. This is a diagrammatic interpretation of the process that begins with a blank canvas or a room full of no ideas, and ends with something that's as tight as a script from Harold Pinter. The fish looks like this:

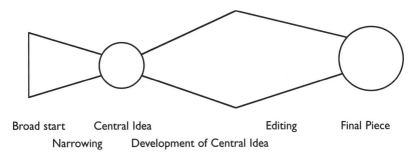

Broad start   Central Idea   Editing   Final Piece
        Narrowing   Development of Central Idea

At the beginning, we have no idea at all what to make a show about. (If you already know what you want to make a show about, jump ahead to the second part of the process.) So you're at the wide tail. You're looking for a central notion; a theme, a relationship or an image perhaps. This central notion will serve to anchor the work. The first stage is often the most inventive and playful part of the process because it's wide open. It's comparatively easy for a director to lead a process like this, using a range of exercises that have the capacity to generate material. After all, there are no prior obligations. Exercises might range from the simple – a game like Boal's

Completing the Image

The group sits in a circle or faces one way. One person gets up, makes a still shape. Another adds himself to the image. The first person sits down. A third gets up, and so on. By watching this process over ten or fifteen minutes, once the bravado has ebbed away, the group's themes begin to surface, more and more clearly as time goes on.

Completing the Image can be played with almost any group – to the more complex like The Gate in which any number of watchers direct any number of improvisers, using a process of freezing and reanimating to move the narrative along. A number of exercises are given at the end of this book that can be used in this way. It's useful to adopt a range of *different kinds* of exercises to generate material. This is because each kind of exercise will tend to generate its own kind of material. If for example you want to discover something about the *world* of the piece or about a central *relationship* within it, the exercise needs to prompt the performers to be creative within one of those two areas of definition.

Once sufficient material has been generated in this first stage, there needs be a narrowing down, a selecting out of preferred material. This process might take place within the group or alone by a director. Once a central notion (or two) is found as a result of this narrowing, this redefined material will become the source material of the second stage of improvising. Now this core idea – or ideas – can be kicked around all over town, to see what emerges. Get the core idea wrong, and no one is animated in the second stage. Get the core material right, and everyone is animated. This core material could be of any kind, it could be about:

- A world (the piece will be set in a café or someone's memory or a wood)
- Relationships (it's about a relationship between an old woman and a young man)
- A theme (jealousy or the struggle for independence from family or the lure of fashion)
- An image (of children in a war zone)
- A piece of narrative (how a girl from a rich family slides into drugs and prostitution)

Whatever it is, the subsequent work will be about imaginatively filling in the blank spaces around that central idea. If the piece is set in a wood, who goes there? Who owns it? What does it represent? There's a thousand and one improvisations to be constructed as part of the second stage, where the fish widens from the tail towards the body.

Alternatively, you start with a notion already in place. So the 'tail' section of the work just doesn't happen. John Wright told me that his company Told by an Idiot has at different times started with – variously – the character of Tartuffe, the story from *The Time of the Gypsy* (a Yugoslav film), the story of Bligh from the *Bounty* and the image of a woman dying of Alzheimer's. In any of these examples, following the fish, the group skips the first stage of play/research, and moves on to this second stage: exploring that given material through improvisation.

'When you make a piece, you ask every possible question you can ask of the piece, and answer it, and if you're looking for an idea, you ask every possible question of what that idea has to do. And what you do is eliminate lots and lots of stuff until that creative part of your brain that's looking for ideas is looking in a smaller and smaller area so it's not grasping at anything – you're not saying it could be a rock musical or the answer could be Cliff Richard – no, the answer is a lift.'
Pete Brooks, talking about the devising of *L'Ascensore*, created by Insomniac Productions

So what's involved in this second stage? Let's take an imaginary example: the story of an older woman who lived through two world wars. She lost a son and a brother, but through these tragedies she found a new way of life that better suited her independent nature. This is the story the group wants to work with. What happens then is the improvisations all become geared towards an elaboration of that woman's story – her relationships, dreams, accidents, psychological standpoint, and so on. You 'ask questions of it' as Pete Brooks argues in the quote above. As already indicated, it's my argument that all useful dramatic material can be considered under one of five headings. The function of this typology is to help identify what does emerge, and where the work needs to move next:

- THEME – the ideas or issues that are explored
- WORLD (AESTHETIC) – the dominant location or the conventions governing the production
- NARRATIVE – the evolving story or sequence of causative shifts
- IMAGERY – the shapes and images – what the spectator witnesses
- RELATIONSHIPS (or ROLES) – relationships of characters or the roles played by performers in relation to each other.

These are the significant, essential components of any performance, although clearly any one piece might rely more heavily on certain elements than others. It can be used as something of a check list to manage the devising process. Once this stage of improvisations has been completed and you know more than anyone would wish to about the woman who lived through two world wars, then comes the business of narrowing down again. (There's a kind of honeymoon period with all material. After a certain point, it fails to imaginatively provoke and inspire in the way it did before. Time to move on.) This is the editing process (and the forming of the fish-head). You decide to keep the visit of the woman to the graveyard where she finds out she doesn't cry, but you reject the incident where she empties her son's room. And so on. Material is selected in this way, perhaps negotiated over with the group, until you have a relatively fixed sequence of scenes that will make up the show. The next task is probably rehearsals.

FINDING THE FRAME

One secret of devising is knowing at any point where you are in the process. To find yourself asking fundamental questions of the material a few days before the show opens may be invigorating or perhaps an indication that you didn't ask them early enough. So it's useful to know the right questions at the right time, although it's hardly an exact science. Tim Etchells talked to me about Forced Entertainment's approach to devising that echoes some of the distinctions made above. *'The first kind of improvisation is where we're basically looking for ideas, looking for something to do. These are big, general diggings or explorations. We might have a few costumes and props floating around, or maybe a single half-baked idea for what might happen and on this quite slender basis we'll get on our feet and start playing. This can be very productive but it's so open (and so sink or swim!) that it often leads nowhere – so I guess none of us really likes to do it this way. It's like you're looking for something but you have very little clue what it is.*

'Often, a bit further along in a process, we'll look for new stuff by improvising in reaction to the material that we've already developed. This is a slightly less blind process – in that material we've already generated at least sets up some frames and expectations to work with or against. So for example, we might have what we think is the first forty minutes of a show, and we'll be trying to extend that, to see what might happen next. In a case like this we might run through the material we do have and then simply try to continue to jump off the end of the known material and see what happens.

'A third kind of improvisation comes for us at a later point where we might know for sure that there is a section of a show that will comprise a certain activity, or a certain kind of text or combination of the two. In this case you may have a structure and key elements of the scene in question

already and your job is simply to find more good stuff along similar lines.
This part of the process is about asking "What we can do within a frame?"
rather than "Can we find a frame?"'
The notion of the 'frame' is like a container ship for the material.
Once found, there is a clarity about the devising task. In a one-man
show called *Jackson's Way* developed by Will Adamson, which won the
Perrier Award at the Edinburgh Festival in 2004, the dramatic frame is
a motivational speech by a life coach, played by Adamson. Within this,
the contradictions and absurdities of life coaching, gurus, motivational
practices and other lifestyle delusions are satirised. My guess would be,
the idea for the frame came early. What makes it work so well is the tension between the performance frame, i.e. the 'life coach session', and
the actual content of what is said, namely that all actions are pointless
and it's pointlessness you need to embrace. *L'Ascensore*, the show
created by Pete Brooks and Insomniac Theatre some ten years previously, was set entirely in a lift. This was the holding frame as well as
being the location. Playing only to a small audience by intent, the lift
doors opened, a scene was shown, and then they closed again. When
they opened once more, we were on a different 'floor.' When a frame is
literal and physicalised like this, it both anchors the improvisations and
creates a kind of funnel through which all the creative ideas have to
squeeze.

When Mark Sutton and Joe Bill from the Annoyance Theatre in
Chicago developed *Bassprov*, a two-person impro show set in a fishing
boat, they tried initially to incorporate flashback scenes. They wanted
the show to focus on the relationship between these two different
characters. By using flashbacks, they could take audience suggestions,
jump out of the boat, act the flashback scene, and jump back in. But
after a while they realised a key lesson from sitcom: that a situation
where people can't escape often generates stronger material. So they
dumped the flashback scenes. Now they never get out of the boat.
They found that the tighter the frame, the more effective the
improvising. *'We put ourselves in the bear trap and spend the hour trying
to get out.'* (Mark Sutton.)

Almost anything can function as a frame that holds a piece together
conceptually. In a show I made with Simon Balfour, Bibe Lille-West
and Sophia Kingshill about Sid Vicious and Nancy Spungen, we knew
the holding frame at the start: this was the couple's comeback
interview. Sid and Nancy had come back from the dead to relaunch

their careers. So all material developed out of improvisation had to fit into that. We took one major excursion out of the frame, a flashback scene at the Chelsea Hotel just before Nancy died, but otherwise everything happened in front of a 'studio audience'. Without such a frame, the piece may have had a looser structure. Sid and Nancy's comeback interview gave us the opportunity to explore both the conflict between the two primary characters (he, obsessed with lifestyle issues, she determined for success), as well as contemporary obsessions with fame. A good decision about a frame can realise weak material strongly, while a poor decision can make even interesting material pale. There's a desired tension between form and content which in the best productions sees them pulling against while simultaneously complementing each other.

One way to create a frame might be the definition of a world. By defining a world, certain kinds of dramatic exploration are ruled in and certain ruled out. Parameters are set. In Ricky Gervais and Stephen Merchant's *The Office*, the title gives the world of the show. That world is hardly ever left. If it were left for more than a scene or two, its greenhouse effect would start to diminish. The situation comedy follows in the steps of many others whose location has been essential; *Fawlty Towers* and *Steptoe and Son*, for example. Lindsay Anderson's film *If . . .* is set entirely in a public school except for one scene. In that one scene the rebel public school boys go to the local café, meet a girl, and as a result their behaviour shifts and the visit triggers the denouement of the film. What the excursion does also, is cinematically reinforce the closed, secretive and authoritarian world of the school they've just left. It strengthens the absurdly gothic and repressive nature of that regime and so increases a sense of justification for the violent rebellion that follows.

DIFFERENT FRAMES

In Kevin Finnan's work with Motionhouse Dance Theatre, an equivalent of a theatrical frame is supplied by the shape and substance of the physical set. There's a comparison with *L'Ascensore*, mentioned above. This may even be constructed before any choreographic work has commenced. What the set does is to define the physical parameters for the improvisations to come. The design brief will encompass not just the conventional set but also the surround: the floor, the walls and the ceiling. The design of the set is informed by the themes chosen for the show, but significantly it doesn't assume any choreography. *And where does the [design for the] space come from? It comes from the research into what we think might be the content of the show, the theme we're going into. For example, this current show: we wanted to explore the issue of an urban experience of life and communication, so in order to do that, the environment needed angles, geometric shapes, steps, chairs. Then, as the Russian Constructivists did, you can create everything else with your body actions.'* (Kevin Finnan.)

One reason to fix the set design early is pragmatic as well as artistic. Since the company tours to so many different locations, it constructs a set that can be erected within any space it has to go, interior or exterior. This means the choreography, once devised, never has to adapt. *'So now, our set goes in, we do our show. And it's a narrow space, but still we hang from bars upside down, we climb, we fly, we swing. We explore the whole space.'*

Having built the set under Finnan's guidance, the company explores the themes through improvisation. And Finnan leaves the dancers to play and improvise on their own – *'and I go off on holiday.'* He returns to shape and give a journey to the material the company has developed in his absence. A central focus for this part of the process becomes rhythm. *'What makes our shows work is . . . the rhythm of the whole show. It's like making a film. When a filmmaker makes a film, there's a real focus on the rhythm of the shots because he understands that it's all a time-based thing . . . In a theatre you can afford to have someone walk into a beautiful, empty, black space and take maybe two minutes and then walk over and pick up a glass of water down stage right, and it can be riveting. But if you do that in a shopping centre, it's not going to hold the same attention. However, if before you've done it, you've had a blinding punch of energy, with people flying across the air – and then bang! It stops, and suddenly someone walks across to the glass of water – then you'll watch . . . So whereas I used to spend ages worrying whether it should be this move or that move or this elbow should be up or down, now I realise what's most important is working out the rhythm of the scenes as they occur.'*

It may be useful to take a look at how composers of music approach this issue of form/frames and content. Peter Sander is a composer and improviser who won't mind me saying that his approach leans towards a respect for the classical rules of composition. In contrast to contemporary composers who argue that free music has redefined composition, Sander holds fast to a distinction between structure and content, and to the practice of composition *through* structure. What is implied is that the composer begins with a sense of the inherited form, rather than, as in Finnan's case, a structure that is built from scratch. Nevertheless, the principle is the same: first build (or borrow) your frame. *'Structure is the vessel into which you pour your ideas, be that tunes, rhythms, textures . . . and if you write something which is stylistically rooted in the European 16/17th century onwards . . . then you have to fulfil those grammatical rules, those vocabulary expectations. Writing a piece of music is a piece of communication. I write a piece of music for an audience to understand. If I write in a language they don't understand, I might as well not write it.'*

Sander talks about two different approaches – instinctive and cerebral. If you're writing anything more than a tune or 32-bar song, then you have to make a structure. He has little time for contemporary music, which, pace Schoenberg's twelve-tone system, has continued, in his view, upon an increasingly intellectual path to the point in the fifties and sixties that *'a roomful of computers would have had an orgasm'*. He cites Boulez, claiming that Boulez would argue, *'Anything that had a human element is bad – that everything had to be mathematical.'* Sander maintains that the avoidance of traditional structures has led in contemporary music to an emphasis on intellectuality that, perversely, reduces the content. Since it is the function of the content to facilitate the empathic communication between composer and audience, this has now been lost. It's possible that free improvisers might agree with his hypothesis, if not with the argued consequences. As Eddie Prévost, AMM's drummer, writes, *'The structure becomes the content: dialogue as interaction, the end as well as the means.'*[4] Simon Fell argues that the rejection of traditional musical structures and the success of free improvisation, has in fact led to a crisis in composition: *'Composers are wandering about a bit at the moment. I just think there's so much energy and so much truth in improvisation that it doesn't need composition; but that composition needs improvisation to renew itself, or to go back to some of the principles which inform improvisation.'* It would appear then that musicians from different positions are recognising the same thing; that there is something approaching a loss of confidence within music composition practice, although clearly quite different strategies are urged as solutions.

FINDING THE CONTENT

Once a central notion or frame is in place, the emphasis moves from the macro to the micro. John Wright is a director who uses games in a variety of ways to develop material. Initially his work with Trestle Theatre involved masks that were made by the actors and employed to generate characters. As in the approach of Motionhouse, the set was sometimes built first. *'In one project we did –* Plastered *– the first act was set in a pub, the second in a hospital. So we got the designer to build a set before we made the play. And then we added all these different masks we'd made. Then I got them to improvise . . . so we had 'the regular' in the pub, 'the barmaid' and 'the barman' – and the family who were treating the son on his birthday to his first drink . . . It was pure trial and error.'* While John's approach has developed considerably since these early productions, his emphasis on the importance of the micro moment has remained. He describes his role as a director as being one of 'not getting in the way'; instead nudging the actors to make bigger choices. Later, John set up Told by an Idiot with Paul Hunter and Hayley Carmichael. This company allowed him to work on a bigger canvas and to reach far beyond what he identifies as the primarily 'psychological realism' that was the trap that Trestle fell into. *'In the '80s I thought it was all about making action. In the '90s, I came to the conclusion that it was about playing – that playing* initiates *action.'* His work with TBAI has concentrated on what he identifies as four areas: unconscious play, conscious play, closed games and open games. These are the four strategies that facilitate devising. The games, he says, can be anything. *'I generate action by using these tiny little open games – and it could be anything. Often actors come up with them . . . Paul Hunter and Hayley Carmichael played one where one couldn't look the other in the eye – this game could be developed into a whole emotional score.'* John would refer to the Alphabet Game as a closed game: where each player (of a pair) would have to start the next sentence with the next letter of the alphabet. An open game – and John acknowledges Keith Johnstone's development of these – would for example be an actor putting a hand into a pocket and pulling out something to trigger the next scene. *'So even if I was doing Hamlet or Chekhov, we'd be looking for tiny games to make it alive – but without the audience knowing this is going on.'* Keeping the audience's eye pointed in a different direction is part of the benefit of such games. For *'It's nothing to do with the text. The written text is*

*everything written down, while the performance text is everything that we
find in the room at the time. The motor of that is play and improvisation,
that is unique to that group of people. And I'm constantly trying to get one
text to inform the other.'*

The wonderful benefit of these open or closed games within the
devising process is that once found, they anchor the action in sequences that can be repeated, in the way that a children's game can be
repeated. If the game is about avoiding eye contact, or trying to stop
someone sitting on a chair, this game has a structure that is easier to
recall and re-find than *what is generated by it*, that is the feelings involved. When the game is re-played, the feelings are more likely to be
found again organically. So games like these help when fixing the work.
And after all, fixing improvisations and making them set, is one of the
most problematic areas of devising. *'There are three areas to an action
which I think are important to structure: one, the anticipation that something is going to happen – two, knowing where you are in the scene – the
relief when it is happening – and three, at the end it's the pay off. You feel
differently to how you feel at the beginning.'* John acknowledges that he
learnt this way of structuring in part from Yoshi Oida.

Open or closed games help to create the colours and rhythms of the
devised piece. Once in place, they can function to bring the production
alive each time it plays because they function as triggers to generate
playful re-enactment. It's never the same as it was the first time, but the
revisit can still be playful and innovative in its own way.

THE WORLD

Beyond the finding of frames and development of content, improvisation is used to help actors research the world of the production and
bring that world alive on stage. The world of any production is a
notion that embraces everything really significant about it – that *isn't*
the narrative. It concerns the atmosphere in the space, the culture or
behaviour of the characters, their linguistic references and the use of
theatrical language to express these aspects. It's an integral, elemental
part of the process, which if not addressed, may cause a performed
play to default into an easy psychological naturalism. If the play itself
aims for that, which arguably is not what theatre does best, then an
inattention to the world can mean the piece becomes asocial and
ahistorical. It loses power and resonance just where it hopes to be

effective. To avoid this, directors use improvisation to bring the actors to a point where they can absorb something of the mores of the time. A director such as Robert Lepage uses improvisation to interpret the themes, images and behaviours that are specific to the concerns of the production, as means to provide access to the world. When Tony Guilfoyle joined Robert Lepage's theatre company, Deus Ex Machina, to play Frank Lloyd Wright in the production *Geometry of Miracles* and to take Lepage's role in *The Dragon's Trilogy*, he entered into a process of improvisation despite the fact that both shows had been made earlier. Lepage *'sets up a rehearsal world you feel secure in'*, says Guilfoyle; *'and so you don't get the tensions you get in other situations.'* With his Drama Centre training, Guilfoyle prefers to be given an objective in the improvisation and *'an idea of activities that this character might use.'* For him as an actor he found the process *'liberating'* by contrast to a situation *'where you have a director who says "let's improvise" without any idea of where it's going or what the possible conflicts are.'* Again, there was study and research in both productions, with Tony absorbing a bulk of information about Lloyd Wright and his architectural ideas and outputs. But without a flexible rehearsal process that allowed an improvisational grounding of the information, the study material could only remain cerebral. Tony found Lepage setting up just such a process.

There was a scene in *Dragon's Trilogy* that set out to explore a family's responsibilities in a situation where the child gets ill. It looked at how the parents' coping mechanisms were influenced by the social expectations of the time. *'It was a scene about a Chinese man who worked in a shoe shop and his wife, who was Quebecois. It was set in the '30s. Their daughter gets meningitis. The man wants his wife to stay at home and look after the child rather than the child being institutionalised.'* Under Lepage's direction, the group started to rehearse. *'It was extraordinary, but very simple . . . We did a scene and a lot of it was archaeology, pulling stuff out of the ground, using videos of the previous production . . . As he says himself quite often, he* [Lepage] *works in quite a naturalistic fashion so it can be a bit soap-like sometimes . . . We did the scene several times, it was OK, but it was just soap, quite simple and not theatrically very interesting. So he started to have the husband move chairs from around the room into the table, to create a home situation. That made it a bit more interesting. He* [the character] *would be talking and doing that at the same time . . . '* So the group carried on working on the scene until Lepage suggested the Chinese man play the scene by first coming to the shoe shop run by Guilfoyle's character – set up at the other end of the stage area – and telling him, the shopowner, about the daughter's situation. And while describing her predicament, the actor was asked to '*take the four chairs from the shop space and walk them up the other end of the stage and place them around the familial table. The last chair which he takes, which I had been sitting on, he places under his wife's behind, so she's seated semi-forcibly, as if by an enthusiastic waiter, so suddenly she's caged . . . and it works extremely well.*' What Lepage therefore does is use this stagecraft to bring home to the audience the power of the husband in the situation, and the husband's ability to force his views on to the wife. At the end of the scene, the wife is caged. Such were the mores of the time.

Developing the characterisation of a real person is now a frequent task within film, television and theatre practice. You can hardly turn on the television without seeing an actor portraying a dead politician, rock star or celebrity. It's a truism that to understand the celebrity you need to understand that individual's world. When I was working with Simon Balfour and Biba Lille-West to realise the roles of Sid and Nancy, it was the chance to research contemporary documents that helped create the seedy, introspective twilight of the pair. We studied grimy talk show footage from the States, photographic stills from the Chelsea Hotel, eyewitness accounts of their drug consumption, the book written by mother Deborah Spungen along with police reports of Nancy's murder. Then the actors would improvise characterisations. Biba's approach was more determined by a focus on the psychological aspects while Simon started with the externals, on the assumption that adoption of the body shape, manner and tone of Sid would start to generate the sensations and attitudes that the man held internally. The process of assimilation was made easier for both by our shared decision to have the Sid and Nancy 'come back from the dead' to relaunch their career. This relieved us from having to recreate scenes that punk historians would take us to task over. This decision also allowed the actors to develop their own text. The characterisations proved so successful that we began to see rather too much of Nancy Spungen offstage as well as on.

I went to talk to Max Stafford-Clark about how he used improvisation when the script was already very well set. '*I use improvisation quite a lot to fill in details of the backstory, once the script is there. For example, in* Duck, *the play I've just been working on, there's a relationship between a young woman and the man she's been living with. They've been together for a year, and the play catches them having rather a bad time. But in fact over that year they've had very good times. So I'd do improvisations around, for example, Christmas, where she's opening her present from him – or something that makes the emotional story much clearer . . . Another example in the same play might be when the young woman, Cat, comes in to see her girlfriend. She has just been down to the police station to give evidence about why a jeep has been blown up. In fact, she did it. And she's full of relief and quite excited, because they don't suspect her at all . . . So in order to get the excitement of that, we did set up (and play) the interview and gave the actors playing the police specific leads and so on – it made the scene when she comes in afterwards much more alive. . . . '* The use of improvisation to play out scenes referred to in the script but not enacted, has become something of a staple strategy. Working on *Duck* by Stella Feehily, Stafford-Clark's company Out of Joint were also given digital cameras, taken to the city and let loose to wander the city's streets. The taking of photos helped the actors to absorb a sense of the physical environment of that city. Soon after, the references in the play to travelling around the city came alive. But Stafford-Clark doesn't confine the use of improvisation just to contemporary plays. He's used it with *Three Sisters* and other pieces, including Timberlake Wertenbaker's much-performed piece about convicts in Australia in the eighteenth century:

'When I did Our Country's Good, *at first the improvisations were hopeless because the actors didn't have enough information about the eighteenth century . . . but gradually the actors become more informed. There were two specific improvisations, which helped the text: one was by an actor who'd read Albert Pierrepoint's book about hanging. He came in and gave a lecture about how to hang someone; "The weight ratio to the drop: if you have a heavy man, he'll drop further . . . and you have to be careful you don't pull the head off because it's a public spectacle . . . The skill of it is in getting the hood over the head. A good death is about fifteen seconds, a bad one is when he's dangling and dancing on the end of the rope for four or five minutes." These hideous details.'*

A more radical means to bring home the world of the piece is to extend the research into the fabric of the rehearsal process itself. One of the more striking examples can be found in the Living Theatre's practice while working on *The Brig* in 1963. This play by Kenneth Brown depicted life in a marine punishment block in the USA. As John Tytell outlines in his book on the company, *'The action of* The Brig *was simple, repetitive, and hellish. Its emphatic point was that sane prisoners had been conditioned to behave like madmen. Implicitly, it suggested that the world was a prison.* Kenneth Brown showed the progress of a day from *sunrise to bed-time, arranging the action in a series of dehumanising episodes where the excruciatingly boring routine of the prisoners was interrupted by the torture of the guards.'* Judith Malina's solution for the problem of realising this Artaudian hell was in part to structure the rehearsals along similar lines. *'Judith realised that the free and easy spirit of spontaneous invention that had previously characterised the company during rehearsals could only work in contrast to the mood of absolute tyranny that she wanted to suggest with* The Brig. *She scheduled long rehearsals, usually lasting seven hours, forbidding any lateness, conversation, joking, or eating in the theatre, with smoking restricted to a particular area. Lapses would be penalised by work details.'* This was all in addition to more orthodox research; learning the Guidebook for Marines, learning to march in step and chant in metre, to crawl, to take measured steps, to turn corners squarely and all other behaviours associated with this camp of hell. The resulting performance was considered a close approximation of the kind of theatre Artaud had imagined.

It's hard, although possible, to feign emotional honesty in improvisation. For the enquiring mind therefore, the craft of improvisation offers a means to discover material that may not have emerged via other routes. So many productions of the last twenty years by companies such as Motionhouse, Improbable, Told by an Idiot, Shunt, Forced Entertainment, The People Show, Insomnia, to mention just a few referenced here, would not have been possible without this special facility.

CODA

FORCED ENTERTAINMENT'S WEBLOG – AN EXTRACT:

And then, somewhere between all these things above – a piece of practical work:

'Robin vs. Jerry competing to be the narrator of the show which each claims is the story of his life. Barging each other out of a single spotlight. John and Terry joining in to illustrate scenes (fucking in a meadow, a wedding?, a murder . . . All very unclear but not in a bad way). Robin illustrating

Jerry's narrational sections with the signs "LAUGHTER", "BORED RIGID", making "wanker" gestures behind Jerry's back . . . All the time assuring him that it's good and he should carry on. Combination helpful/ aggressive. Music – apparently helping the narrative along – Mulholland Drive score, Peaches Felix Parts, some instrumental stuff from 21 Grams, Booker T Bootlegging, The Eagles of Death Metal Already Died. John phoning Jerry onstage on his mobile to tell him that they are about to enact the fucking scene he described earlier. (Jerry is about two metres away). The tinsel curtains wheeled in to make the scene "complete", blown "tastefully" by an electric fan that Richard has imported from the disabled toilet. Claire sat at the side. Also claiming that this (all that we are watching) is the story of her life – the gunshots in particular. Then telling us that she is not in it and that we should ignore her. Then announcing that she is in it again. Robin asks what she's doing "in it". Claire says she's texting Cathy. Robin says "What?" Claire says "It's private". Music drowns out the narration – more or less continuous, from Robin and Jerry in alternation/competition. Robin – "All this happened a long time ago. Obviously things have changed – I don't look like this anymore . . ." He's in a suit with a wild afro wig. Jerry announcing that the next scene happens sometime after Robin died. Robin looks vaguely nonplussed, takes a sip or two of beer and then ducks himself under the long ragged bit of white gauze that Terry has been pretending is a wedding dress. So Robin is a ghost under the train of Terry's dress. Terry speaking inaudibly to Rob, obviously telling him that it's her dress and he shouldn't do that. Robin stood next to Jerry as Jerry continues to talk, Robin a ghost still under the gauze. Jerry – a eulogy to Robin. Claire chiming in from the side "Robin was a cunt". More music. Claire with the sign that says "DISGUST". John gives up and comes to sit outside and watch. Jerry still talking. Claire throws cola all over Robin, who starts to man-oeuvre an entire dustbin full of water across the stage in search of revenge. Given the amount of electrical stuff in play, the fact that it's nearly 5pm and the fact that Claire's wearing her own clothes I call a halt to the proceedings.

'Inevitably, since this is the longest running, most complex and probably most interesting thing we've done in three weeks, the video camera was not running during this improv. So it's already consigned to speculation and version. Each of us doomed to remember something entirely different. And no chance to go back and check the tape.'

Tim Etchells, Forced Entertainment weblog, 23 February 2005

2

LEARNING

'In its most archaic sense, theatre is the capacity possessed by human beings – and not by animals – to observe themselves in action. Humans are capable of seeing themselves in the act of seeing, of thinking their emotions, of being moved by their thoughts. They can see themselves here and imagine themselves there; they can see themselves today and imagine themselves tomorrow.'

Augusto Boal

Improvisation is not only about a culture of research. Especially in a community context, it offers tools for individual and group learning. Through its exercise, a range of skills – social and personal – can be enhanced. Dramatic improvisation is best placed to achieve this because of its capacity to replicate social life.

SPONTANEITY

Viola Spolin's work on theatre games, often cited as the primary source for dramatic improvisation practice, already contains these precepts about learning through drama. Her work began with children and immigrants in the 1930s. And while the theatre games were fun, they aimed also to be educational. This work chimed with that of Iona and Peter Opie who in their observation of children's playground games identified the capacity of these to improve the players. It led them to write a series of books extolling the benefits of organised play, for children's development. Spolin argued that what was crucial about the theatre games was spontaneity. *'Through spontaneity we are re-formed into ourselves. It creates an explosion for that moment, it frees us from handed-down frames of reference, memory choked with old facts and information and undigested theories and techniques of other peoples' findings. Spontaneity is the moment of personal freedom when we are faced with a reality and see it, explore it and act accordingly. In this reality the bits and*

Facing

Two performers face each other. One makes a gesture to the other. The other's task is simply to reply in any way he or she likes, but without copying. Everything is allowed. There are no obligations other than the obligation to respond. Variation: the first makes a sound, the responder must make another sound, not the same one. Repetition should be avoided. It should be played slow at the beginning, then faster.

---

pieces of ourselves function as an organic whole. It is the time of discovery, of experiencing, of creative expression.'[5]

Clearly the 'spontaneous' moment, in which the player is at his most receptive and open, unencumbered with obligation, is identified as the 'learning' moment, where a shift or an insight can occur. Although these words were written some considerable time ago, long before most of our present-day companies were formed, they have a contemporary resonance. They echo for example in a definition of 'liveness' offered to me by Adrian Heathfield who co-directed the 2004 Live Culture event at Tate Modern in London. *'It's to do with opening oneself to that moment, to the live moment, the moment when meaning is in question. It's the moment when meaning falls apart.'* This is in direct contrast to what was surely the prevailing wisdom at the time of Spolin's writing. The key learning moment then would have been identified as the moment when wisdom was 'received from another', probably the teacher. This certainly corresponds with the experience of Keith Johnstone who observes, *'My teachers had felt obliged to destroy our spontaneity, using techniques that had proved effective for hundreds of years.'* His rejoinder to this is simple: *'So why not reverse their methods?'* He argued to me: *'Education is not meant for the child, it's meant for the teacher. You don't want to educate people really, because they might ask questions. You want them to stack shelves . . . Normal education makes you afraid of failure, so you try to avoid it. However, you can teach people that when they fail, they don't have to punish themselves.'*

The spontaneous moment feels risky because the player is opening himself up to the unknown. Let's say that player is me. It's not *the unknown* that's dangerous in this context, rather I've learnt to treat *all unknowns* as dangerous, for my own protection. The anxiety involved is part of my personal early warning system. If I didn't look left and right crossing the road, I might be killed. So thinking about possible consequences is a very useful tactic in many, many situations. There's no question about that. However, now that I've learned to 'think ahead', can I also unlearn it in order to confront spontaneity? I have to learn to close down these defence mechanisms or at least not respond when I have the desire to flinch. It takes practice. I can see my one-year-old child is fearless and I envy that. He's perpetually 'in the present' and is incapable of taking offence in the way adults do. But his fearlessness has no consciousness, and I want both. Practice is really the only way. Practice familiarises the self with the imagined dangers of this alarming world and slowly reduces them. Similarly, good facilitation helps to ensure that the judgement of others is not allowed to shame the risk-taker. If these conditions apply, I will inevitably emerge with a heightened confidence and a greater understanding of what learning spontaneity can bring.

In the spontaneous moment, essential social and communication skills can be practised. This is because spontaneity opens up a gap between the past and the future in which impulses can be followed. Drama operates using a gestural and verbal language that is shared with the culture of social interaction, so it's particularly useful for re-imagining social interactions. Improvisational role-play has become a staple of work in schools, colleges, prisons and educational institutions where interactive skills need be improved. It's particularly useful with young people drifting towards a position on the edge of society where they're vulnerable to drugs, crime or manipulation. Perhaps formal education has failed them. These kids are not necessarily consciously rejecting the social reality they see around them in creative protest; they may just be experiencing a social alienation that's a consequence of feeling let down. Through drama's ability to re-stage the act of living, it becomes possible to test hypothetical, imagined, alternative realities. It becomes possible to develop different selves.

'Carol never realised how she looked until others told her. Following the exercise, others in the group described and then demonstrated her behaviour back to her. They showed how she stood when she was on the station platform, and how she reacted to the teacher who came up to her. Carol was shocked. She never thought she appeared that aggressive. She immediately wanted to go back and do the exercise again, to show that she was capable of managing her own emotions.' (Sandy Van Torquil.)

WORKING WITH PRISONERS

Saul Hewish works with me in Rideout, an organisation running pro-jects within UK prisons. The organisation's remit is to engage prison-ers with a learning process that employs imagination and spontaneity, rather than reading or writing, to illuminate and solve problems. The kinds of problems we're talking about are those dealing with the individual's relationship to family, culture, authority and self. To what extent have these relationships been damaged by the decisions or behaviours of the individual? Or are these dysfunctional relationships the cause of the offending behaviour or the consequence? Dramatic improvisation practice can be employed to help answer these questions. We can start to put the default behaviour of the offenders under the spotlight a little. We can set up triggers to this behaviour and by watching it, discuss it with the individual, assessing how it might damage him or her – or others. Perhaps the behaviour is partly unconscious. The only way to find out is to put the individual in some imagined social situations and ask him or her to respond as he or she would in real life. Then we can jointly speculate. A discussion can be had about real-life incidents from that individual's path. Was the behaviour we've just seen characteristic?

With others watching, some assessments can be made. The Prison Fellowship uses the image of a large object thrown in a pool of water. It only takes a moment for a throw but anyone standing nearby, gets wet. The effects of any crime ripple outward in ways not necessarily perceived by the criminal. It's possible that neither the root causes nor the consequences of the offending behaviour have been fully considered by the offender. By improvising situations, it's possible to reflect back our observations as watchers, and those of the group to increase the self-awareness of the individual who is acting them out. In this work, therefore, there's a process of:

- RESEARCH through improvisation
- Articulation of what is discovered through FEEDBACK AND DISCUSSION
- Setting of NEW CHALLENGES for the participant
- Further FEEDBACK AND DISCUSSION

Grandmother's Footsteps

Running it in prison shows up quickly some elementary truths about the players. Who runs to grab grandmother? Who hides behind someone else? Who plays a long, slow, waiting game?

1 The research stage involves learning about the group and the individuals within it. It means getting them to play simple games where their default behaviour will be displayed. It could be simple theatre games like Fruit Bowl (adapted to Football Teams) or games where objects are concealed by one part of the group from the other.

Problem-solving exercises might be used. Two players are given a simple conflict between them. Two chairs are placed on the stage area, and two players invited to sit down. One is to be the taxi driver, another is the customer. This is the end of the journey. It turns out that the fare exceeded the estimated fare given and the customer has no more money. The aim is to find a compromise. How do the players resolve the problem? The solution lies not in one being either generous or the other aggressive, but in finding a compromise by which both benefit – or suffer – equally. How are the participants able to cope?

2 Never mind if they don't succeed, we can observe how the participant deals with the problem and then feed back to him the spectators' observations. There can be discussion around the default impulses of the participant and of any alternative choices that might have been available.

3 Once material has been gained about the group, the facilitators are more familiar with the participants' strengths and weaknesses. It becomes possible to set up role-plays or exercises in which individuals are challenged to extend their skills. This might include practice of different kinds of behaviour, e.g. to use negotiation skills to take the heat out of a potentially violent situation. Two friends have fallen out over their car that's been broken into. Each blames the other for leaving it open. How to reconcile them? The challenge is to make decisions out of awareness and choice rather than habit.

Rideout recently worked with a group of young offenders at HMYOI Swinfen Hall. One of the young men in the group was

worried about going back home where he believed certain individuals were waiting for him. He believed they were going to attack
him. He was sure he'd retaliate. In his mind there was no other
choice. We ran an exercise in which we established a rectangle of
chairs. He was placed in the middle, given no instructions whatsoever except to deal with the situation as best as he could and not
leave the rectangle if at all possible. The two actor-facilitators came
in and out of the circle, one threatening him with violence if he
didn't leave the area, the other telling him he was a coward not to
lamp the guy who was threatening him. He stayed the course and
resisted both sets of provocations.

4 Feedback and discussion allow for the player's choices to be
examined. What decisions were taken and how did they work out?
How did these differ from those employed in the early exercise?
Hewish argues: *'The act of improvisation for offenders is such that they
are able to practise – or withhold – a degree of spontaneity which a lot of
them don't have control of as part of their day-to-day coping
mechanisms. Improvising in a structured context means that they can get
immediate feedback on how they're operating . . . The survival strategies
that a lot of men have developed; the ability to talk one's way out of a
situation, to lie, to con, or to lie and believe the lie – I remember doing
that as a child: if I tell myself enough, it* will be true *– come under
examination here.'*

There are several reasons why this process can work better than sitting
around a table doing problem-solving exercises using a pen and paper:

- The work is rooted in play and imagination
- The exercises and role plays can draw on the vernacular of the participants
- The exercises use an oral storytelling tradition in which it's likely
  the young men are well versed
- There is little reading or writing, so non-literacy is not a disadvantage

Very often young men (for it largely is men that Rideout work with) are
aware that they have a default set of responses to certain situations,
often conflict situations, but feel trapped within these. They feel it is

inevitable that if certain conditions are in place, they cannot react except with violence, as in the case above. They find it difficult to make a distinction between reaction and response. Drama's ability to slow down action, analyse and examine sequences of thoughts and actions, enables discussion about this distinction. Men in prison are also sometimes reluctant to test out other ways of coping because of fearing a loss of face should it not come right.

'It's not true of all offenders but for some, the act of doing this improvisation workshop or performance helps them with issues of confidence and a sense of self, so that means that possibly they don't have to use old, more dysfunctional coping mechanisms.'

Saul Hewish

Testing out strategies in a room away from actual conflict, enables them to mitigate such a fear. Such life rehearsal is a matter of understanding both cognitive and affective processes, and in particular how they relate. Rideout takes the view, not always supported within the criminal justice system, that development of *cognitive skills* is inadequate without equal emphasis on the behaviour of *affective skills*, in other words the management of feelings. Without such a recognition of the role of feelings – linked more directly as they are to unconscious drives – finding cognitive solutions to life's problems can appear superficially easy. Many important life decisions are made under pressure or under the influence of powerful emotional states. To test an individual's ability to cope means drawing uncompromisingly on drama's ability to provoke and disturb.

To some degree, what happens here is a reversal of impro training with actors. There, the emphasis is on releasing spontaneity – acting before you think. Here, it's the opposite, thinking before you act. The learning focus is placed on the usefulness of deliberation and reflection. The spontaneous moment in this context therefore invites a different response. Is the participant able to bring care and thought to bear in that moment?

Let's imagine another challenge exercise, something more concrete. We'll imagine the participant is called John. We already know that one of John's issues is he goes for short-term solutions when he meets difficulties. He doesn't think ahead to consequences. He takes wild short cuts when he should be circumspect. (We discovered this in the early part of the work.) John goes out of the room while the exercise is set up and then returns once the 'set' has been 'built' and once the actors are prepared. John is told he's running a burger bar at a weekend festival. Another member of the group (who was involved in the preparation) is working as his assistant. The improvisation begins. Other members of the group, in role as festivalgoers, come and buy burgers (props are used). Then we tell him that as a result of so many customers, he's running low in burgers. His assistant offers to get some from a friend who works in wholesale. This is the first challenge. Does he ask for information about this food source? Assuming the assistant goes to buy, we later establish that customers are complaining about the standard of these new burgers. They taste like . . . cardboard/shit/ goat's testicles. This is the second moment of challenge. How does he deal with the complaints? Offer money back?

Finally, a 'health inspector' arrives, probably played by one of the facilitators. A customer whose son was taken ill has 'contacted' the inspector. This is the third moment of challenge. How does the player cope? If he deals with the problems well, it won't be particularly dramatic. Does that matter? Not at all. But the facilitators might heighten the level of challenge. If, for example, he closes down the stall early on when he initially runs out of food, then peer pressure is created by a group of 'friends' who magically arrive – and are hungry. John's self-image, known to be a weak spot, is prodded.

At the point of feedback, his behaviour can be mirrored back to him. If he did well, then what he did is identified and named. If he didn't do so well, the group is there to point out how and why. Prison inmates are usually pretty frank with each other. And following the discussion, John might be ready to run the gauntlet again, this time adopting a different stance. So that *'within the group process there is involved the practice of a number of (less familiar) strategies.'* (Saul Hewish.) Perhaps John discovers that taking short-term solutions actually piles up more problems in the end. Maybe he finds that keeping up appearances can take a greater toll than admitting mistakes early.

THE FALSE AND THE REAL

It's possible and often happens that John complains during feedback he'd never have acted like that in real life. After all, he'd say, 'real life' and 'improvisations' are completely different. He'd be right in one way.

In another way, he'd be wrong. For while in a role-play, he would understand cognitively that the situation is *not* real, his or her involuntary physical/emotional responses still become activated *as if it was real*. Should John or anyone, myself included, be called stupid or arrogant within an exercise, we would likely have an involuntary response that the brain will not be able to completely over-ride. This is because such provocations come in under the radar. The brain knows the situation is false, but has no easy mechanism to prevent the emotional/physical impulse of anger or hurt being experienced. So we tend to act *as if* the situation was real. Experienced actors and professional communicators will have the experience to help them 'switch off' or manage the feelings that are provoked. But participants in a prison context will be less defended. In fact, if a participant were to completely shut out the causative triggers, he would need to close both his eyes and ears. For the eyes pick up signals that are taken straight to the nervous system. If you want proof of this, find an escalator that isn't working. Your brain will tell you that as you get on to the escalator, it won't move. However, your body won't accept this. The eyes have put together information that this is an escalator and therefore it's going to move. So your body expects movement. As you step on the machine, your body will generate counter-balancing impulses in anticipation of movement. So you will feel even more disorientated than you would have done, had it been moving. Not only has the sense memory of a moving escalator kicked in but also the mind becomes confused when the anticipated movement doesn't happen.

REDISCOVERY

Kate McCoy works with prisoners and drug users, making shows and creating workshops as part of TIPP – Theatre in Prisons and Probation. She observes how drug users find a benefit in improvisation because it allows them to reclaim lost selves. Here, the work is less about resisting impulses than about rediscovering responsiveness. *'Drug users have to be experiential learners. Because they took the drugs and found they didn't work, they have to learn from that. So part of the recovery involves cocaine and heroin users realising that they have had no actual real emotions for maybe fifteen or twenty years. And they've become completely shut off. Theatre is about reawakening those emotions – trying out the new parts of "you". Improvisation can work in at least two ways to do that. One is discovering the parts of you that you haven't been able to express, the other way is trying out the parts of you don't even believe exist, but you want to* make *exist. We're doing this devised play at the moment, and the group were having a discussion about what they were doing when they were acting. Some in the group were saying "I want to rediscover bits of me", yet others were saying "I want to try out something that is unlike me." They view this project as an important part of their recovery. They say in reference to the Drama Day, "That's where I come alive again."'*

The spontaneous enquiry can therefore be directed either towards something new or towards something lost. It can be about finding a new response to override reactions, or it can be about bringing to the surface feelings that have been buried.

Sometimes the mask plays a part in this kind of work, because it makes tangible the external self. It gives concrete form to the part of the self that has been developed as a result of drug or crime dependency. The mask *makes concrete* the idea that one's external self is *not* one's real self. Such a mask can be put on and taken off just like a 'front'. (It's extraordinary to see the lengths that some young men will go to in order not to have their 'front' taken away. I remember a probation client who used to arrive to the group session in a white Mercedes that he left parked outside so he could keep an eye on it. He argued he had nothing to do with crime any more and said he saw no problem in being poor. But when we staged an imaginary Christmas Day and told him in role that he couldn't afford presents for his son that year, he disintegrated. The truth was, his self-image was entirely built on wealth.)

> **Triggers**
>
> A group sits around on chairs, in a circle. Each has a newspaper or magazine. Each chooses an article or a picture to tell the others about. Does the story trigger any associations? If so, these should be articulated? What feelings are provoked? What memories? It doesn't matter if everyone talks at the same time. Immediately afterwards, the group is invited to make a series of still images based on that conversation.

LIFTING THE MASK

If the socially acquired mask-self is simply the front, then the 'real' self is something closer to that mutable flux of feelings and contradictions felt internally. The real self is closer to the emotional core where those feelings exist. Whilst the offender might believe these feelings should never be shown, they are perhaps a truer indicator of the individual's core identity. There will be benefit in understanding the distinctions. The theatre company Geese, both in the USA and in the UK, have developed a set of masks to help make this distinction between self and front, more tangible. The masks are called 'fragment masks'. Each one embodies a particular stance. 'To lift the mask' therefore becomes a metaphor for telling the truth, for speaking from the heart, for saying what one really feels. Sally Brookes, a former director of Geese UK and a mask-maker herself, outlines this. *'The masks are looking at "front".* *They're looking at the external, the evident behaviour. This allows you to* *look also underneath the mask, at what's happening internally – and this is* *often much more emotional, and a contrast to the behaviour. And these* *coping strategies that are employed, are not just to do with their offending –* *they've probably employed them since childhood, having learnt to be quick* *on their feet, being vigilant and so on.'* Within Geese sessions, participants often relish using the set of masks because they recognise them. Admittedly they are faster to recognise the behaviours in others than in themselves, but this is still an impulse that the facilitator can build on. The most commonly used fragment masks are:

- THE JOKER – this role is about making light of everything, making a joke of everything, taking nothing seriously so that any more serious questions can be batted away with a gag.

- THE VICTIM – this role is about playing the part of someone who has been unfairly treated by the world. Everything bad that's happened is the fault of other people.

- THE RESCUER – this role is about putting the focus on to other people, calling for help to be given to someone else, possibly The Victim. This way the spotlight on the self is avoided.

- THE FIST – this role presents an overt or covert threat to anyone who challenges the wearer. It's instinctively aggressive and hopes to keep things under control by using the threat of violence.

- THE GOOD GUY – this role pretends to be innocent. It involves appearing to be unknowing about the causes and effects of any incident. In reality, the Good Guy knows quite well what's going on.

- THE MOUTH – this role likes to talk its way out of situations, saying anything at all, even complete rubbish, rather than have the focus of enquiry more meaningfully directed.

- MR COOL – this role likes to take a laid back approach to life, essentially articulating an arrogance that makes a mockery of any challenge.

- THE BRICK WALL – this role specialises in 'stonewalling' – it refuses to make any contribution to the interaction. It is the archetypal 'no comment'.

The Geese facilitator will preface the use of masks with a discussion about their use in history, and in everyday life. The discussion moves on to the notion of 'front', not implying that there is anything intrinsically wrong with it, on the contrary, but rather that it's important to understand the front/mask is not the real person. Then the facilitator demonstrates the point by showing in a short devised scene how a young man in a pub gets into an argument. Sally Brookes would, for example, play the role of the young man entering the pub.

S/he walks in, masked, stops just inside the doors and looks around defensively. He approaches the bar and buys a drink. He looks around again and then acknowledges someone with a nod of his head. He takes a seat in the corner of the pub. He walks over to the pool table and puts a coin down and then returns to his seat. He waits. He becomes agitated as he repeatedly glances over at the pool table. Suddenly he gets up and walks back to the table. He appears to be engaged in a heated exchange for a matter of seconds before taking a pool cue and lifting it above his head.

After the scene, the group would be asked to try and externalise some of the thoughts and feelings of the man in the scene. What might be going on in his life? What had been going on that day? The answers will give the facilitators information about that group's preoccupations and view of the world. After this, the fragment masks will be presented. Then the group may be divided into sub-groups which are invited to devise a short scene that shows the masks in action. These might be with the real masks, or, once the metaphor has bedded in, mask behaviour without the artefacts. The sub-group might come back with, for example,

- A domestic scenario
- One that involves an authority figure, perhaps a policeman
- An argument between peers over drink or cars

While a scene is being acted out, the facilitator might invite a mask-wearer to 'lift the mask' and share the true thoughts and feelings of the character. The learning therefore continues to centre around this idea that the image you present to the world is not always an accurate reflection of your personal feelings. The correspondence between the image and the self is a matter for negotiation that the individual can make their own decisions about.

> 'I stopped him. I explained that if he turned from the window, looked at his father and didn't move his head, then he'd experience exactly the sensations he was trying to avoid. I said that he mustn't try to suppress the head movements but to be aware when he does them.'
>
> Keith Johnstone

LIFE SKILLS

There's a further role for improvisation, which evolves from how its practice calls upon life skills. Through improvising, the player is forced to engage certain 'muscles', certain ways of establishing relations. Saul Hewish: *'While one doesn't "teach improvisation" with offenders, nevertheless the learning of improvisation does involve the acquisition of particular skills: listening well, supporting others, being flexible, asking questions, empathising with others and – if you're working with characters – existing in the role of the character while also existing at a meta-level in terms of where the improvisation is going.'* This ability to function on two levels simultaneously is a skill worth acquiring for those whose response to provocation is simply to express the immediate impulse. When the reflective imagination is bypassed, the individual defaults to a more primitive kind of operating system: early software that can't hold more than one idea in memory. The same applies sevenfold when the improvisations are leading towards a production. For then not only does the participant have to develop basic impro skills, but teamwork skills are challenged through the collaboration to realise the event on stage. The offender is probably unfamiliar with acting in front of an audience. It can be daunting. It makes demands on offenders in ways they don't expect. In front of an audience, the offender is asked to become transparent and to acknowledge a mastery of role. If the individual is still offending, this is a rite of passage almost impossible to navigate. On two occasions I've known offenders to bottle the performance at the very last minute – in both cases we discovered that the individuals in question were still secretly engaged in criminal behaviour.

One case was particularly startling. The individual was maintaining the front of an 'ex-offender', while in his secret life it was a very different story. He was extremely adept at this duplicity. He performed in two shows with a particular company that specialised in working with ex-offenders on probation. In both he shone, bringing what seemed like personal honesty to the stage. As a result, he was asked if he would like to develop a one-man show based on his experiences. It came to be called *Breaking the Pattern*. The central character was an offender, determined to change his life. The show was developed up until the final scene which was to be the key scene in which the criminal pattern of the fictional character was finally broken. But the actor and director couldn't make progress with this final scene. So they took a break from working, even though the first night was just a week away. Then after a few days, the company's administrator took a call from the police. The actor in the one-man show had been arrested. He had been caught behaving oddly in an art gallery, which was being visited by a group of schoolchildren. He was put in a cell overnight. In the morning, he was offered a caution and told to leave. But he said he had something to confess. The police listened to him. His confession involved telling of several rapes he'd committed over the recent period. He had – finally – found an ending to the play. However, he had found it in reality, not within the fiction of the drama. The show, unsurprisingly, never played.

TRANSFERABILITY

When I met Keith Whipple in Chicago, who uniquely among my interviewees works in both drama therapy and comedy impro, he gave me a list of Spolin's Seven Aspects of Spontaneity. He wanted to demonstrate how these comedy impro skills were fundamentally no different to the life skill set which the psychoanalyst Erik Erikson developed in 1956. He wanted to show how the practice of impro skills works in many different contexts. The learning dimension, he argued, exists equally for the offender, the errant child or the actor. While the uses differ to which these different individuals put the benefits, they are essentially wrestling with the same process. Mastery of the skill set enables Keith to operate simultaneously at the Institute for Therapy through the Arts as a drama therapist, and on stage at the Comedy-Sportz Theatre as an improviser.

Spolin's key principles are:

1 Play a Game

2 Go Beyond Approval/Disapproval or Right/Wrong Thinking

3 Express as a Group

4 Physicalise

5 Practise Varied Techniques for Direct, Dynamic Awareness and Communication

6 Involve your Audience

7 Carry the Learning Process into Daily Life

Erikson's Eight Stages of Psychosocial Development are so called because they characterise the learning stages necessary for the personality to develop into a mature human being. Failure to pass through any of these stages can leave the individual with needs or deficits that may leave them at a disadvantage in terms of negotiating his or her position in society. Keith argues that by working on your improvisation skills, you are already addressing what Erikson describes as the key learning required for a mature adulthood. Whipple argues: *'Look down the list and they're all words you'll hear in improvisation training.'*

Erikson's Eight Stages are:

1   Learning Basic Trust versus Basic Mistrust (Hope)
2   Learning Autonomy versus Shame (Will)
3   Learning Initiative versus Guilt (Purpose)
4   Learning Industry versus Inferiority (Competence)
5   Learning Identity versus Identity Diffusion (Fidelity)
6   Learning Intimacy versus Isolation (Love)
7   Learning Generativity versus Self-Absorption (Care)
8   Learning Integrity versus Despair (Wisdom)

Whipple goes on to add, *'Most people would say, "Wait a minute, improvisation – that's all about anxiety, getting over fear and stage fright" and in a way that's true – in therapy it can be very successful if it's structured right, because it's about engaging and mastering oneself and one's social interaction with others –* during that anxiety. [my emphasis] *There's a need for us to overcome that anxiety because we are the creatures that can envision things that aren't there. The deer has to have a direct stimulus to think there's a wolf in the bushes. We on the other hand can imagine there's something there. Which creates . . . anxiety, unless we create structures to manage that anxiety.'* The point about fear and anxiety is significant. We are tempted to think anxiety and fear are simply to be avoided, and the more successful the avoidance, the better. But another way to look at this is to say that anxiety and fear are in our blood/genes/race memory. So to be constantly subject to fears – even when there isn't a wolf in the bushes – is not abnormal. When London suffered the bomb attacks in July 2005, a huge campaign was launched to demonstrate that 'We Are Not Afraid', as if

> **On the Bus**
>
> 'is not about one person standing out from the rest of the group. It's about one person being accepted by the group . . . You're on the bus, and every new person that gets on the bus comes on as a character. But when they get on, the entire bus takes on that character. So it's an impro game but it deals with social acceptance. "I'm gonna do what you come on with." Then you can sidecoach that.'
>
> Keith Whipple

fear itself was a sign of weakness. Surely the inverse is the case. To recognise the value of fear and act on it may be more useful than putting away the idea that fear itself disables us. Fear can help us survive. (This connects directly with the points Phelim McDermott makes later in this book about 'hotspots' – those points occurring in improvisation we instinctively steer away from, because we're anxious about the consequences of going there. Perhaps instead of avoiding these hotspots, we should go there and learn from them. After all, our fears are only amplified by our avoidance. My own mother, for all her many qualities, was constantly sidestepping the hotspots at the dinner table – and there were a good many of them to be avoided. Her well-meaning avoidance only increased our fearfulness.)

Whipple's argument by inference is that by improvising, you are compelled to 'grow up.' You cannot evade engaging with others, as you can do in everyday life. The practice prompts you to find ways to establish relationships of mutuality. He uses a game called On the Bus, which is similar to games elsewhere. He might choose it in preference to other 'guessing' games because his group, 11–13 year olds with behavioural issues, don't want a spotlight on them. A spotlight can make them feel awkward or less able. On the Bus is about generating a sense of social acceptance – making everyone feel OK about who he or she is. Such exercises are set up deliberately to engender pro-social feelings and sensations. In this case, it's about building empathy. Kate McCoy uses an exercise with ex-drug users that has a similar aim. It involves each participant improvising different moments from the different stages of their lives. Each player devises a series of short scenes. In the first, the player is ten years old, the second fifteen, the third twenty, and so on. What emerges? To what extent are there similar experiences shown? Does it tell the group anything, either about similar journeys or about the triggers involved in drug addiction? Perhaps the work will move on to explore imagined or idealised experiences. Again the aim is to find connections and reduce a sense of separateness – separate individuals having nothing in common with each other.

By these means, experiences can be manufactured that assist the process of maturation indicated by Erikson. Should one wish to, it is possible to set up quite difficult challenge exercises that purposefully engender in the participants mistrust, shame, guilt, and so on, precisely in order to trigger the coping strategies that will override or manage these feelings. In struggling to overcome the negative energy, the individual finds new resources within. An example would be that given earlier with the young prisoner fearful of returning home. Provoked to aggression, he overcame the aggressive impulses by using reason.

BEYOND DRAMA

While drama is the natural explorer of social behaviour, it's not true that a learning focus can't prevail within other art form improvisation work. After all, the essentials of drama – teamwork, creativity and spontaneity – are the staples of many other programmes. Music projects challenge participants to master rhythm, co-ordination, listening and an awareness of form. Dance or movement projects call for self-discipline, understanding of impulses, physical contact and work on gravity, weight and balance. Organisations such as the Irene Taylor Trust and Live Music Now! run music projects over days or weeks in UK prisons.

The aims of such projects go beyond the artistic, and might include the improvement of relationships between inmates, or between inmates and staff. Kevin Finnan, Artistic Director of Motionhouse Dance Theatre, leads movement projects in male prisons drawing from Contact Improvisation, contemporary dance and aikido. I had originally met Kevin Finnan at a weeklong workshop led by Augusto Boal in the late eighties. Ten years later he was leading a programme at HMP Dovegate, a privately run prison in the English Midlands where Rideout was also working. It was interesting to see how he'd brought some Boalian ideas about social change into a dance/movement context. As expected, the prisoners in HMP Dovegate had had no prior contact with contemporary dance practice. So there was no virtue in trying to impart a stylistic orthodoxy. *'We take understandings from all that came out in the '50s and '60s in America . . . Rather than saying "You've all got to learn to be like me". we're simply extending what your body range is doing. What's important is how expressive or communicative you are with your body.'* Finnan stresses the importance of the pace and energy of the project, not giving the men too long to think about the implications of what they're getting involved with. It's important they *'don't know where they're going . . . It's like a river, you pick them up and put them down before they have time to reflect.'* The team teaches a range of skills: how to roll, fall, catch and be caught – with safety. There are never less than two facilitators. Before long, there's dialogue, communication and crucially – sacrifice. What helps to make it familiar to the men, and something they can stick with, is the fact that it's task-based. There's a clear instructional element, and within these tasks there are challenges to be met and overcome. Men in prison are more comfortable with task-based work. You know where you stand.

Where the *learning* takes place is in two areas particularly. The first involves recognising and working with the feelings that are generated by the work. If these are noticed by the participant and spoken about either privately or within the group, the individual can acquire some personal insights about the self. *'If you understand that the mind is part of the body, as opposed to Descartes' governance, what happens is, once you're really working the body and you're using it to express yourself, then its limitations become shown to you, and to others, and your aspirations are being shown to others. You're releasing all sorts of connections that you hold within yourself: memories, associations. You create this flux, this turmoil. It may make you joyful or it can give you stuff to deal with. Sometimes it makes great art, and sometimes it just makes for a great experience.'* The second area is that of skills and abilities learnt, which are acquired as it were by default because of the nature of the challenges. Driven by the enthusiasm to engage with an art form, individuals are forced to collaborate with others and respond to others' feelings in ways that elsewhere they might consider a sign of weakness. *'If you can communicate with others within the exercises, take responsibility for yourself and for someone else – and let responsibility go – these are the lessons you need to learn in life, and society.'*

A particular example of this would be the male inmates' attitudes to women. It wouldn't be stereotyping male prisoners to say that traditional attitudes towards women tend to predominate. Certainly the notion that women might compete physically on an equal footing with men, will earn a few smug grins around the room. But this is where the men's worldview lets them down. Movement improvisation doesn't follow the same precepts as football or weight lifting. *'Women in the room make an enormous difference. They subvert the expectations of the men. The men are all there; a bit nervous about whether they should do this. So then I just get one of the girls to pick one of the men up. So then you've got this great big bloke up in this small woman's arms and they think – "How on earth did she do that?"'*

Through its ability to replicate social interactions and through its gentle pressure on participants to communicate, improvisation practice is particularly useful for engaging with a study of social relations. Just as gravity pulls us to earth, so the practice of staging fictional interactions calls from us a recognition that while there are differences that need be recognised, our similarities – in terms of what we dream about or for – may ultimately be more distinct.

One Two Three

1. The set up is the same as for 'One Two' – the group should be seated in a circle.

2. Begin with the first person saying 'One'. The next person says 'Two' thereby setting the tempo, and the next person says 'Three' maintaining the same speed.

3. The fourth person to join in says 'One' at the same time as the first person repeats their 'One.'

4. Continue going around the circle in this way until everyone is saying One, Two or Three. There should be an overall even pulse.

5. When ready, change directly from your beat to the next one. If you are on One, the jump will be to Two, if on Two the jump will be to Three, and if on Three, jump back to One.

Adapted from *Search and Reflect* by John Stevens

CODA

CHILDREN

While this chapter has concentrated largely on adult learning, it's time to acknowledge the appropriateness of these strategies for children. Spolin's work started with children. The adults who would benefit from the improvisation practice described are sometimes merely 'catching up' on learning they missed in early life. One of the more dynamic and influential teachers of children who used role-play extensively was Dorothy Heathcote. Her use of dramatic role to present challenges to her children ushered them into an experiential form of learning not possible within the education practice of her time. There is a story, possibly apocryphal, of her entering a class of children who were all rebelliously keeping their coats on. 'Ah, I see you've got your coats on. That's good', began Heathcote 'because where we're going is very cold . . . '

'So I now reach my main question. Do you think this "trapping of people within a life situation", however small or lengthy (because drama can be two seconds or it can be two months) has anything to offer you in the teaching concerns you have? Can it help you to draw attention to something? You have to answer it for yourself. And try, if you can, to put aside fear. Drama is such a normal thing. It has been made into an abnormal thing by all the fussy leotards, hairdos and stagecraft that is associated with it. All it demands is that children shall think from within a dilemma instead of talking about a dilemma. That's all it is: you bring them to a point where they think from within the framework of choices instead of talking coolly about the framework of choices. You can train people to do this in two minutes, once they are prepared to accept it.

Do you think this thing called drama offers you anything? Can it help you to extend the understanding about something by thinking from within a framework? Do you believe it might help you to help your classes bring about any behavioural change? It might be the behavioural change of "stop chucking the books about", or it might be the behavioural change of "notice the archaeology of the architecture a bit more". These are all different aspects of behavioural change, for they are the beginning of perceptive changes. Do you think it is valuable to help you extend with your classes the range of attitudes they are capable of examining, and do you think it would help them to develop ordinary gumption?'

Dorothy Heathcote, *Drama as a Process for Change*,
published privately by Cleveland State University
and reprinted in Dorothy Heathcote:
Collected Writings on Education and Drama, TSP, 1984

3
CONFLICT

'Theatre is conflict and life is conflict. Oppression exists in the relationship between two persons, when dialogue becomes monologue. The aim is to become human again by re-establishing the dialogue.' Augusto Boal

'If I go to struggle with you, we can improvise around struggling, but in such a way that I'm not forcing you to struggle with me. I'm inviting you.'
Sue McLennan

Is the function of performance simply to reflect and argue about what is happening below the topsoil of social change, or can it be interventionist? In a way the question proceeds from a dichotomy that is artificial. Like light, performance both reflects and changes our perception of what it falls on. The argument that it can intervene rests on two ideas. First, that plays and performances force audiences to confront uncomfortable truths. Second, that on a micro-social level, performance can apply its tools to situations of social conflict where mediation and understanding are required. This chapter looks at how improvisation can be used in these latter cases to 're-establish the dialogue', as Boal says. You'd need a much, much larger book to explore all its possible uses, from work with gangs on urban street programmes in New York, to negotiating law programmes in the Brazilian Parliament as Boal has done or taking theatre into war zones in Sri Lanka as James Thompson has done. But

> **Boxing Match**
> 'Two people standing several metres apart must react immediately to blows doled out by their partner. This works best if one person beats up the other, then the roles are reversed – it is difficult to react to imaginary blows and dole them out at the same time. we would usually close this exercise with gestures of tenderness, or by moving on to the "lovers" variation which follows.'
>
> Augusto Boal,
> *Games for Actors and Non-Actors*

we can at least demonstrate the instrumentality of improvisation, and articulate how practitioners have developed conventions around this particular use.

FRAMING CONFLICT

Improvisation, because it offers a flexible, malleable, mutable system of tools, can be applied to situations of dispute in order to analyse, deconstruct, represent and re-imagine the constituent elements. In the previous chapter, this usage was outlined in terms of objectives that were more personal. The objectives lay in effecting change at an individual level, and through that at a social level. This chapter is primarily but not exclusively concerned with conflict between groups. The art of dramatising conflict does a number of things; it begins to marry conflict with play, it takes some heat out of the conflict through the use of contracts and it gives the participants some distance on their behaviours. Facilitators are able to put frames around those energies, enabling discussion and speculation. Further, these energies are not dissipated by the use of the frames – which might disqualify the exercise – but can be expressed just as strongly. This is possible because of the nature of the (literal or metaphoric) mask that allows for emotions to be expressed fully, while the consequences of their expression are confined to the exercise. The use of a mask even heightens the passions involved since the projection of these passions is not compromised by the presence of any literal danger.

The conscious artificiality of any event which stages improvised conflict aids in raising consciousness about the factors involved in causing it, since the distance between the 'real' social world and the 'demonstrated' aesthetic world, encourages a mental reckoning. These factors start to be seen in a different light, as Bertolt Brecht argued should happen within performance, and as Augusto Boal has arguably demonstrated within his Theatre of the Oppressed. The corralling of conflict into the territory of play is not inappropriate given the nature of play itself. *'Play can be everywhere and nowhere, imitate anything, yet be identified with nothing . . . Play is the supreme bricoleur of frail transient constructions, like a caddis worm's case or a magpie's nest,'* writes Victor Turner[6] in *Body, Brain, Culture*. In a straight fight, play can take on conflict, wrestle it to the ground and make it laugh. Of the different art forms, arguably drama is better positioned as a medium within which to posit such conflict exploration because of its use of spoken language, its use of a defined (rather than abstract) aesthetic and its representational vocabulary. However, before looking at examples of this work, it's worth noting briefly how performance has traditionally acted as a mediational conduit for the progressing of social reconciliation or change.

CUTTING IT

Since the early days of human society, groups used dance and music as means of self-assertion, to enhance a sense of identity and to display strength to other groups when there was a need to symbolically challenge for superiority or territory. Performance was a means by which these impulses were expressed, managed and symbolised. The world was viewed as an arena of conflict within which each separate group needed to make alliances – with nature, spirit and other groups – to sustain itself and grow. Ritual provided a conduit through which these aspirations and reconciliations could take place. By means of ritual, groups could grow stronger through the creation of alliances with spiritual powers and with each other. With this assistance, they would find the means to enforce the defeat of those that threatened the health of their community.

'The dancer's swift transition to the role of the monstrous Mahish – Durga's powerful challenge – and the battle dance, alternating the roles of the two combatants (danced to sabdas accented on drums) carries the dramatic sequence to the supreme climax – the final victory of the Goddess Durga, worshipped (in a still pose) with chants of praise and waving of lighted lamps.'
Regini Devi,
Dance Directors of India,
Delhi and London, 1972

In the late twentieth century, within the ghetto areas of Los Angeles, USA, we can see examples of how urban youth culture has developed and popularised dance forms that transform the conflict impulse into a different vocabulary that still has echoes of an early, pre-Christian, tribal society. The use of dance and rhythm bear characteristics of early ritual in which enemies, represented within the ritual, were defeated. '*1969 in Los Angeles was the year that Afrika Bambaataa started organising ghetto youth into one of the first breakdance crews, the*

Zulu Kings. The Zulu Kings won contests and talent shows. They performed their moves at dance clubs. Bambaataa recognised the potential for acrobatic dancing, and he encouraged young people to stick with it. But most people thought the Zulu Kings were just another gang. However, when a rival street gang challenged the Zulu Kings, they called for a break in the usual street warfare and suggested that the two groups fight with steps rather than weapons. Sure enough, the rival gang was just as ready to square off with dance steps as they were with knives and chains. Afrika Bambaataa's followers grew into the Zulu Nation. The kids in the Zulu Nation would rather dance than fight, and breakdancing (a term invented by Afrika Bambaataa) became an integral part of hip-hop. These dance battles gradually evolved into a highly stylised form of mock combat called "Uprock". In an uprock battle, a dancer would lose if he actually touched his opponent."[7]

This formalisation and transubstantiation of conflict in which virtuosic superiority is pursued has also become professionalised by musicians. The 'cutting contests', from a generation prior to Bambaataa, offer an example. This rivalry found its outlet in formalised game-competitions in which issues of status became resolved. The aim was to blow the other performer off the stage, to cut him down, to establish a greater ability in the eyes of the audience. It's argued that jazz itself has had its character altered by notions of professional rivalry between performers, as Ted Goia writes: *'Under the inspiration of James P. Johnson and others, the world of stride piano developed a macho, competitive ethos that has since come to permeate the jazz world as a whole. This overlay of artistry and combat remains an important – and often overlooked – tradition in African-American culture. In later years, the cutting context – a jam session in which outplaying the other participants ("cutting" them in jazz jargon) – became an important part of jazz pedagogy and practice, and the most crucial rite of passage for a young player . . . When Art Tatum travelled to New York for the first time "he found himself escorted to a Harlem nightspot where the greatest masters of stride – including Fats Waller – were ready to do battle." When it came to Tatum's time to play, he let loose with a dazzling "Tea for Two" full of dense harmonies and sweeping runs and arpeggios that left the audience speechless . . . "That Tatum, he was just too good," Waller later recollected.'*[8]

It's arguable that both traditions outlined above fed into and informed the more contemporary 'rap contests' between artists as represented in Eminem's film *8 Mile* and now widely seen in a range of venues and on a variety of media. The 'rap contest' traditionally gives rappers a chance not just to flex their word skills against each other and to raise the standard of the art form in so doing but to compete and gain ascendancy. The inherent boastfulness and demonstration of rhyming skill that's involved in rap, works to provoke and antagonise the opponent. Audiences show their appreciation for the performer who uses the form most inventively, aggressively, rhythmically, harmonically. The spectacle has many of the essential ingredients of an improvised theatre form; stylisation, word play, demonstration. We can see many examples of similar competitiveness in plays where characters verbally joust for advantage, for example in the 'duel' fought with rhyming couplets in *Cyrano de Bergerac*. Within contemporary rapping, it's the allegedly sexist and homophobic content within the provocations, assert critics, that has led to arguments about the cultural value of the art form. It's a popular target for liberal commentators who maintain that its relish for violence, rather than diminishing and transforming the conflict, actually feeds it. But what's evident is that the form has resonance for its audiences because it offers a means for them 'speak through' the artists. For while the individual rapper launches himself or herself into rhyming patterns of what appear to be simply individual assertiveness and self-aggrandisement, it's the resonance these outpourings have for the spectators that creates meaning for them, echoing the role of the shamanic individual who carries with him or her, the power of the group/gang/tribe.

Moving from a predominantly black to a predominantly white context, to understand the energy behind contemporary American comedy improvisation, you might do worse than consider the phenomenon as a further development of the same professionalised, competitive game-playing. Actors, performing with an ensemble around them, vie for audience approval through the use of wit, physicality and verbal flair. The ruthless pursuit of audience laughter and the emphasis on individual skill has long been a feature of the American scene. It's not so markedly different in spirit from a rap contest with different groups rooting for their chosen favourites. The 'stars' are often identified and given prominence in the billing. Verbal dexterity and wit remain, despite all the talk of 'group mind', perhaps the most highly valued accomplishment. US comedy impro often does come across as a cutting contest for comedians.

RITES OF PASSAGE

Martin Glynn is an artist-facilitator of African descent who works with black youth in prisons and other criminal justice contexts. He became interested in searching within African-American traditions for forms and structures that worked to ameliorate the conflict between young black men and the civic state they found themselves in. He started to search for where the tradition of 'rap' had come from. In her book *Rap Music and Street Consciousness*, Cheryl L. Keyes identifies the origins of rap in the African bardic tradition, the bard being a storyteller-singer who chronicles local history and transmits cultural traditions through performance. Glynn observes that it was the African-American traditions such as 'the dozens' – a game of exchanging insults, field hollers and toasts – that were crucial in the cultural development of rap. *'The [notion of the] dozens derives from rejected slaves – those who were considered not fit to work, who were separated and put into groups of 12 – the dozens . . . and it was their way of communicating with each other which led to the term.'*

Glynn's work, using music and drama in prisons, consciously taps into this African-American culture of using rhythm, movement, gesture and verbal dexterity as a means to forge identity. His particular focus is on encouraging the young men he works with to see these cultural traditions as advancing them emotionally, psychologically, culturally – without this journey necessarily involving conflict with the authorities. In other words, he advocates, rather than an anti-Babylonian stance, a pro-cultural stance that seeks respect from and accommodation with white society through the adoption of a creative, modern, African culture.

He became interested in the prison context specifically after working with Afro-American activists in the States, and with young black men confined there. He was led to the perception that young prisoners had 'missed' any grounding experience that gave them a legitimate place within the host society. *'As I started to investigate, I discovered that the drama of initiation is the basis of rites of passage. How you come into manhood, how you define your manhood, your place in the community . . . So I started to look at African ritual theatre. But of course today you can't go out and kill a lion or like a Native American dig your own grave. So I studied African-American psychologists who'd developed psychological rites of passage around identity formation, using cognitive shifts. And I found a philosophy called "negressence" that is the five stages of developing black consciousness . . . Growing up in this country, you're brought up on* Beowulf, *the* Iliad *and other epic narratives that we weren't part of . . . And the interesting thing about Western mythology as opposed to African mythology is, a lot of the former hinges around the notion of the reluctant hero. The hero was physically bigger at the end of it. In African mythology by contrast, it was a human being who transcended himself and became a divine being. And I realised that in the work I'd been doing, I'd been replicating more a Western idea.*

'*So when I did a project a couple of years back and took a group of offenders through a course, I placed it within an African mythic structure. By building in the spiritual element, for men over a certain age who were very dissatisfied internally, I'd found a mechanism not to just go through the mind and body, but the mind, body and soul, so it was holistic. So it was more about how to develop a divine approach to personal transformation, as opposed to it being about just the tests and ordeals. Because prison itself is also a rite of passage – in four stages: preparation, separation, transition and reincorporation. The preparation is badness on the street, the separation is prison, the transition is in prison and the reincorporation is when you go out*'.

Glynn's use of a rite of passage/journey structure within projects of this kind gives him an authority and a sense of role that might otherwise be absent, or might not otherwise earn the respect from the youth he's working with. At the start of a project, there'll be a 'grounding ritual'. Although that's not a term he uses in the room, that's what it represents to him. It gives him the scope to introduce issues of belief and values that many facilitators might shy away from. While he'd recognise that the course structure he's most likely working within won't recognise these terms of reference, and therefore there's a tension between the cultural stance and the cultural context, Glynn nevertheless seeks opportunities to interpret group dynamics in ways that accord with a rites of passage template. '*I'll give you one example of a real rite of passage that took place. There was a guy on the project who was a dancer. He wanted to dance. But he knew the opposition he would get from the rest of the group. Because they associated contemporary dance with being gay. So about halfway through, the other inmates got together and said "No, he's not doing it." We were going to do a live performance. They didn't want him to dance in front of them and they be associated with it. Psychologically, the young man was devastated. So going back to this idea of a journey, the first stage was the call to adventure. The call was "I want to dance." Then to the second stage which was refusal of the call: "You can't do it. The guys don't want you to do it." Third stage, crossing of the threshold. He was encouraged by the mentor, which was me. Then he faced threats from the group. But eventually he came to the point of no return, and he was ready to do it. But it was like in the horror films, just when he was ready to do it, the beast came back: "You will not do it." So then I had to come in. And I did a dance. And I said to the guys in the group "Are you saying I can't do it?" So then he did the performance.'*

DRAMATISING THE CONFLICT I

Augusto Boal is probably the major exponent of the use of 'applied drama', as it's now called, to situations of conflict. His work draws on the prior cultural education work of Paulo Freire who perceived that by encouraging reading and writing amongst the peasant population of Brazil, there was an additional increase in the peasants' ability to empower themselves in their relationships with landlords and police. It's possible to see Theatre of the Oppressed as a direct continuation of this project: the promotion of a theatre vocabulary in order that groups and individuals can better express their felt injustice. Forum Theatre is essentially a Marxist structure, echoing in what some might argue is a simplistic way, the struggle between classes. Its purpose is to dramatise a social conflict and explore through improvisation how the victimised or damaged party might learn better how to fight back. These improvisations function as a kind of rehearsal of (or consideration of) possible strategies that might be used by the oppressed group or individual in the world beyond.

A scene is staged in which the protagonist – the character representing the oppressed group – experiences difficulties as a result of actions taken by the antagonist. In the days in which Boal and his colleagues were developing Forum Theatre, the antagonist might be a policeman or a landlord, the protagonist a peasant or young person. The end result of this short play is that the protagonist is defeated. The peasant might be evicted or the young person sacked. The question is then opened up to the audience, 'How can this character fight back more effectively than we saw here?' 'What could this character do differently?' There's no assumption that this is direct rehearsal for political action outside rather that it's a debating chamber in which experiments can be tried and evaluated. Once the play is done and the problem put, members of the audience – spect-actors to use Boal's word – are invited to come forward to try out in practice any suggestions for 'different' actions the protagonist might have taken. Improvisations are then conducted to explore how defeat for the protagonist might be avoided.

For the Forum Theatre actor, the skills involved are quite subtle, representing a distinct variation on the conventional. This is improvisation with a particular set of protocols. The actor playing the role of the oppressor/antagonist needs to be careful. While it's important to be constant and faithful to what is known of the antagonist's likely behaviour, she or he must perform with the same spirit of enquiry and determination to find solutions as that driving the spectator playing the protagonist. After all, they are both colleagues in the same investigation. The aim is to be truthfully engaged in a search for solutions, while at the same time 'playing' on one side or the other. Furthermore, the performer will likely need to 'play against' any number of spectactors who emerge to play the role of protagonist. This calls for a flexibility of playing coupled with a holistic view of the purpose of the enterprise that many performers find elusive.

In the improvisations with the audience member, the improviser-antagonist hopes to provoke the volunteer into discovering strengths of character and ingenuity that illuminate the potential, possibly hidden, weapons of struggle that might be used by someone 'like' the protagonist in the world outside. In other words, s/he aims to be difficult and bloody-minded precisely in order to be more comprehensively defeated. S/he has to operate on the spectrum between two compelling desires: the obligation to present a realistic and strong antagonist, and the desire to 'accede' to the protagonist in order that the hero/ine triumphs and the participant feels vindicated. This calls for a need to work at the meta-level of the improvisation as well as the real, physical, moment-by-moment level. The role of the Joker (facilitator to the exercise) is to monitor and manage all this, ensuring that the playing of conflict is truthful and realistic without it descending into real conflict. The task echoes that of the facilitator working with offenders. Too much pressure and the participant is unnecessarily defeated; too little and nothing is really achieved. What the Joker needs to do most particularly is ensure that the spectator is not granted an 'easy victory' in the interests of everyone having a good time and getting a (false) sense of achievement.

Let's consider a landlord/tenant example in more detail. There's an improviser-antagonist playing the landlord, and his rival, the protagonist, is a female tenant. After the play has been presented (in which the woman is evicted from her home), a woman has come up from the audience to make the landlord see sense. She is motivated by an identification with the tenant and believes she can do better than the character in the drama. The following is an imagined improvised dialogue between the improviser-antagonist and the spectactor. The spectactor's initial idea is to put off the problem by telling the landlord to come back another day.

LANDLORD: You have to leave. You haven't paid the rent.

WOMAN TENANT: *I'm waiting for my husband to come back from abroad. I can pay you then. Come back another day.*

So your husband's away?

Yes, but when he returns he will be able to pay you everything we owe up to this point.

But you're late in paying.

What else can I do? I'm not earning.

So what are you suggesting?

I am appealing to your sense of fair play, to your humanity. You know that you have a right to kick me out, according to the contract. You also know that it will be difficult for me to find somewhere else without a deposit.

When is your husband returning?

I don't know.

Tomorrow?

Maybe.

The Joker moves the scene on to the next day, and again the landlord has returned.

LANDLORD: Is your husband here?

WOMAN TENANT: *No, he hasn't returned.*

You said he would be here today.

No, I didn't.

You did. But we'll overlook that. Come here and sit down on the bed.

Fuck off.

OK, no problem, just an idea. (*The landlord goes.*)

In this work-through, the actor playing the landlord lets the spectactor off the hook. By so doing, he fails to maintain what would be a consistent antagonist-strategy, thereby giving the woman an artificial 'victory'. He does it because he's fearful of the implications of using sexual blackmail. But in backing away, he's perhaps inadvertently given the impression that being aggressive to the landlord was an effective tactic. His anxiety about playing a sexual blackmailer has led to this. Perhaps he was worried that if he started making aggressive, verbal sexual demands within the improvisation, this might discomfort the spectactor to the point where she couldn't continue.

The key to Forum Theatre improvisation may lie in an appreciation of the difference between blocking and resistance. In other words, being able as an improviser to provide resistance to the spectactor while holding within that assertiveness a yielding quality. In this way, as in martial arts, there is in the playing a combination of lightness and flexibility on one hand, with determination and combativeness on the other. It's about knowing the difference between 'I daren't go that way so I'm going to block you' (blocking) and 'Come on, wrestle me for it' (resistance). And making this emphasis public to the audience. So there's a Brechtian sense of distance between the players and the material. If this spirit had been applied, the dialogue might have gone as follows:

LANDLORD: You realise, don't you, that I have the power to make you leave?

WOMAN TENANT: *But you're not going to do that.*

You hope. Look. I'll make it plain. If you haven't found the money by tonight, then your husband will come. That is, I will be your husband. Just for an hour or so. Then because your husband has arrived and gone again, we can consider the rent has been paid. Do you understand what I'm suggesting? You have until tonight to think about it. If you lock the door on me or you're not in, I shall arrive tomorrow morning with the bailiffs. Good day. (*The landlord goes.*)

At this point, probably the Joker would step in to ask the spectactor how she would like to continue the improvisation. What does she want to put in place before the night comes? Or does she want to pick up the scene at the time of his next visit? Or does she want to retire? Now the problem has been put back on the audience member for her to strategically think through the options, without feeling personally coerced.

The distinction between resistance and blocking is discussed elsewhere; without it, narrative or thematic development is always held hostage to the anxieties of the improviser. Forum Theatre relies on improvisers practised in the form, genuinely committing themselves to the exercise without either predetermining loyalties or being afraid to behave as characters wilfully subjecting others by force of their position or power. One of the more effective pieces of Forum Theatre I experienced was within the Greek Cypriot community, where the shared desire to pursue solutions to issues relating to national identity and the question of relationships with Turkey engaged everyone present. Both actors and audience were so engaged that the exercise was shot through with an emotional commitment and an honest search for solutions. It was this that grounded in everyone's mind an overall understanding of the exercise's purpose. Actors had no problem playing any number of unpleasant roles because this sense of collective purpose was so visibly evident.

BOAL IN THE WEST

Boal's work thrives especially well where the issues under deliberation have clearly articulated lines of conflict. This isn't always the case within the West, so he consciously shifted the focus of his own approaches as a result of his contact with Western culture. As he says: *'Before coming to Europe, I had done a lot of Forum Theatre in a number of Latin American countries, but always in "workshop" situations, never as a "performance" . . . In Latin America, the audience was generally small and homogenous, the spectactors almost always being the workers from one factory, the residents of a particular neighbourhood, etc. Here, besides that kind of "workshop" forum, I have also done shows for hundreds of people who didn't know each other at all.'*[9]

Europeans have a different set of issues, he observed. Instead of cops on the street arresting you without cause, these cops were 'in the head'. Oppressions had been internalised, allowing the overt state security system to rely on psycho–social imperatives to operate in place of a visible and aggressive police force. Boal's subsequent elaboration of his methodology, written up as *The Rainbow of Desire*, articulates a more complex set of strategies that starts to share many features with drama therapy. Forum Theatre however, remains the most distinct expression of his ideas, and its technique of juxtaposing expressions of disempowerment with images and actions of resistance rumbles under most of his work.

FORUM THEATRE / NOT

In the years since Boal came to Europe and he extended his range of techniques to suit the angst–ridden climate of the West, practitioners have taken and adapted many of his techniques. As a result, some of the initial emphasis on empowerment and social change has been lost. Boalian ideas have been taken by artists and others and applied to a range of situations, many of which have nothing to do with fighting oppression. People glibly refer to doing Forum Theatre without having any of the understandings of its roots and purpose. This was brought home to me clearly in Tel Aviv when I found myself chatting to a man at a British Council drinks party. He proudly announced he had been running Forum Theatre for several years. Which group was he currently working with? *'I have been working with Israeli Generals'*, he explained. *'What is their particular concern?' 'They have many.' 'For example?' 'For example, what to do when a General gives an order to a subordinate and that order is not carried out. It's a problem.'* Yes, I thought to myself, remembering Tom Hurndall, killed by Israeli soldiers. I was amazed just how far the idea of Forum Theatre had travelled. I speculated idly what Augusto Boal would say, were he able to join the conversation. One thing was certain: this had as much to do with Theatre of the Oppressed as Sudoku has to do with combating AIDS in Africa.

> 'Forum Theatre is a sort of fight or game, and like all forms of game or fight there are rules. They can be modified, but they still exist, to ensure that all the players are involved in the same enterprise, and to facilitate the generation of serious and fruitful discussion.'
>
> Augusto Boal

Another popular act of theft is to take the principles of Forum Theatre and apply them to business contexts. The explosion of business training courses within the UK has led to actors and directors scrabbling around for games and exercises to please first-class carriage loads of business executives who want to give better speeches and get their staff working more productively. You can earn a fair living running your own corruption of Forum Theatre in this way. But we should be clear that this has little to do with social change, and a great deal to do with making a profit-making organisation more effective in its management.

Not all Boal's children are quite so recalcitrant and self-serving that his legacy in Europe is not beneficial. Many theatre companies in schools, prisons and other establishments continue to explore his work. Boal himself is frequently a visitor to UK shores, usually as a guest of Cardboard Citizens, a company of homeless and ex-homeless who tour Forum Theatre to a wide range of establishments.

DRAMATISING THE CONFLICT II

Coming from a different perspective to that of Boal, Amy and Arnold Mindell use dramatic processes to engineer conflict resolution where groups or individuals have become set against each other. Rather than explore conflict with the antagonist-oppressor absent, Process Work aims at having the parties in conflict engage in the same event. While its background is in more conventional therapeutic techniques, *'Process Work moves beyond the parameters of traditional psychotherapy, extending into such areas as conflict resolution with groups, institutions and communities, addressing social issues and ethnic and national conflict; organisational development in business; educational work with children in schools; creativity and the arts (theatre, music, visual/tactile arts, writing); the environment and spirituality. Its orientation towards research, to practical and direct application and to becoming widely accessible to people world-wide, places Process Work beyond the usual definitions of psychology.'*[10]

Phelim McDermott, a performer and director with Improbable Theatre, discovered an interest in this area through studying Mindell's written work. As a result of a fellowship from the NESTA Foundation, he's studied how drama, politics and philosophy combine within this system. Attending 'worldwork' seminars, he observed how individuals and groups bring issues of conflict into the Process Work arena. In any conference, different issues will come to the surface. '*In Athens, homophobia was a major issue . . . People vote in some way on what issue we're going to work on. There are a number of facilitators. There will be a big group process . . . There will be a space – a circle – in the middle where the conflicts get processed, and an outside space where people watch. You can step in and become part of the process, and the process involves enacting those roles in that issue . . . Within that process, they're looking for hotspots, moments when things are said and then get passed over, moments like in a dinner party conversation when someone says something and everyone pretends it didn't happen. So they have to go back and find what's within that hotspot . . . In the enactment of the roles, people will play the roles and try to get to the truth of it. Someone may play George Bush. They talk about ghost roles, figures who are mentioned in the conflict but aren't present. Bush might be one of them. It might be the warlords, who are profiting from the war, or people who are watching the war on the television. The Indian community did this process, which was earth shattering – it was like the best theatre you've ever seen. It was around this guy being an Untouchable – and how he was badly treated because of this. And he started*

Conflict Resolution Exercise

1 Choose a friend to help you with the exercise.
2 Describe a real conflict with a real opponent you have in your life right now.
3 Have your friend play the opponent.
4 Take your own side strongly.
5 Notice when you are uncomfortable with your position and either become neutral or take your opponent's side.
6 Go back to your original role and notice if things have changed or continue until the conflict disappears or until both sides feel they have won.
7 Add new methods and steps to the work and write me about it.'
                        Arnold Mindell, *The Leader As Martial Artist*

shaking – people were holding him. It was like an extraordinary chan-
nelling. It was like one of those dragons that had entered into him. It was
like a moment that had come from the centre of the earth. And I thought
"That's what I want to see on the stage!"'

Process Work continues to grow in influence as activists and therapists
seek out new ways of struggling with issues of community and world
conflict. As in drama therapy, drama's protocols offer a language by
which it's possible to externalise and represent these conflicts, reducing them to proportions that allow discussion and representation. At a
time when information about the world's conflicts reaches us in searing
detail and in fulsome description, it becomes increasingly difficult for
us as individuals to process much of this information usefully.

'SPIRIT'

In 2003, Phelim McDermott took some of the Mindellian ideas about
conflict resolution into Improbable's show *Spirit*. The company
wanted to explore the theme of conflict on a global scale but instead the
show became about how to realise and explore conflict between the
performers. Such an idea offers a clear challenge to more conventional
theatre where the story of the performers putting on the show is
hidden from the audience as far as possible. Improbable wanted to
bring this element to the fore. As the company says in an interview with
Ginnie Stephens on its website, *'There are two stories in our shows: the*
story the performers are telling and the story of the performers putting on
the show. This second story is the most important to us. If it is not present
then the telling of the story will be pointless.'[11]

So for *Spirit*, the company built into the structure of the show a
means to 'out' any conflicts or disagreements that the actors (Phelim
McDermott, Guy Dartnell, Lee Simpson) were experiencing. The
body of the show concerned three brothers who were bakers. The
army had called one of them up but another brother went in his place.
As this story was told/enacted, there would be moments when any
simmering disagreements between the actors might be externalised. At
particular points, improvised conversations would break out. And
they'd get personal. The night I saw the show, one actor was accused of
never having any ideas, another of being bossy, another of being vain.
Guy Dartnell recognises that the show wasn't always equally

entertaining. He acknowledged that the issue of how to incorporate the conflict remained one to work at. But he does consider that both the enterprise and the results, took Improbable's work into a new area.

'When Improbable made Spirit, we directly wanted to look at that issue (actors in conflict) because we came from a tradition of improvisation in which you tried to accept anything that anyone did. So even if you didn't like it, you followed it, because that was the technique. And then gradually we realised that the question is always there, "What happens when you're at loggerheads with each other?" You're in conflict. Generally in that tradition, at that point everything breaks down. You have two people on stage who just argue . . . The thing is, we could only go down this road by having someone there to facilitate that. And Phelim had this inkling that Process Work as a form for people to work with their issues, had similarities with the practice of improvised performance. And he came across Arlene Audergon, who was not only a Process Worker but had also worked artistically. And when you find someone who has bridged those worlds within themselves, then you have the possibility of someone who can work with people both artistically and therapeutically . . . So instead of having people come down from the stage (to have arguments) to have them on the stage and work at those things . . . But it was also about people being able to say what they really liked about each other. Because when you get into conflict, you get into an area of intimacy . . . There were shows when we really argued, and people got upset in the show – but because we'd practised that technique (and you can't "make" conflict happen) people expected it, so there was the possibility of it staying light, and it didn't exclude the audience . . . The arguments could be about anything – the venue, the town you were in, about the performance, about the people in the audience, the stakes on stage, the build-up of something over a number of performances . . . Things would come up on stage and they wouldn't necessarily be referred to offstage – you might leave it on the stage as part of the show . . . Sometimes we'd create a conflict that wasn't really there. But we certainly got hold of something and the main thing was, we made a vehicle that could include conflict, conflict between ourselves, conflict with the audience – and it would be part of the show.'

BEYOND

The example of Spirit shows a way of reducing the vastness of the issue of conflict to something that three actors can engage with in a room, and then share with audiences. Likewise, successful political activism often works by reducing large issues to bite-sized, newsworthy proportions. When Bob Geldof bangs the table and demands that people give money for the famine in Africa, or when Jamie Oliver presents the UK Education Secretary with the actual meal eaten by children in UK schools, issues like famine and food come alive. Theatremakers in the early 21st century, following a period when political theatre was thought to be either redundant or pretentious, are trying in all kinds of ways to wrestle with this problem of making work relevant on a global scale, without falling into the traps that some fell into thirty years ago when it was believed that to 'tell it how it was' would be sufficient. Gone are most former assumptions about efficacy of pure agitational practice and instead, strategies of both guerrilla activist theatre (as recounted in Jan Cohen Cruz's book *Radical Street Performance*, 1998), new political writing (as championed by companies such as the Red Room amongst others), and the application of theatre to situations of conflict are investigated instead.

For the latter, projects such as In Place of War aims to '*research, link, debate and develop the practice of performance in sites of conflict – bringing together theatre makers and scholars who practise performance: in place of war.*'[12] In Place of War was developed initially by James Thompson perhaps partially in response to the parochialism of much theatre practice in the UK. Rather than explore notions of conflict at home, this initiative goes to sites where conflict has led to war and that war is current. In his book, *Digging Up Stories,* Thompson recounts some of the difficulties involved when a theatre practitioner with a Western, academic, research sensibility takes himself off to Sri Lanka and lends support to theatre initiatives there. His journey, fascinatingly recounted in this book, appears to lend further support to the notion that all theatre practice must bend and lean in favour of the dictates of the context it travels to, perhaps even dissolving and reassembling itself. He suggests that we are yet at the beginning of a learning curve in which Western practice adapts itself to situations of extreme conflict. This is particularly proved to be the case where the local context is characterised by a theatre practice that cannot easily be recognised as anything other than traditional – by the visitors. Furthermore the sometimes easy distinctions that tend to be made in the West about different 'kinds' of theatre, are rendered far less significant here. As he writes in the conclusion of his book, '*Travelling through a war zone has made me question the possibilities of applied theatre, at the same time as struggling with the performative in the setting. If applied and social theatre are opposed to either a non-applied or an aesthetic alternative, a binary is made inevitable by these terms that cannot be sustained in zones of crisis or ongoing violence . . . Anyone brave, inspired, committed, reckless or fearless enough to create theatre in a moment of war cannot have their practice reduced to the non-applied or the applied: the entertaining or the efficacious. This work can simultaneously be done because of and in spite of the conflict:*

- *A distraction from and a reaction to horror*
- *A flight from and a confrontation of painful memories*
- *A celebration of resistance and mourning of its futility*
- *A plea for peace and a call to arms* [13]

With the world riven by conflicts at global, national and local levels, to take the art of play into the darkest, most despairing arenas can do no worse than assist in relaxing the authoritarian grip of zealotry where it is found, and introduce play-bound procedures where otherwise fanaticism might go unchallenged. Unlike the football games in No-Man's-Land during World War One, the aim is not simply to resume hostilities at the next sunrise.

CODA

'The philosopher Hegel replies: "The essence of theatre is the conflict of free WILLS". *That is to say: a character is a will in flux, a desire in search of its satisfaction, but it does not obtain its object immediately: it is the exercise of a will which collides and conflicts with other, equally free, but contradictory wills. Nothing more than this is essential to the theatre: not sets, nor costumes, nor music nor buildings – without all of these, theatre can still be made, even without a theatre, but not without conflict. All these other elements can strengthen and intensify, they can embellish the theatre, which simply would not exist without the conflict of free wills and, adds Brunetiere,* "wills which are free, and conscious of the means they will employ to attain their goals".

And even this definition is too ample and inclusive. Within it can be included a dialogue by Plato or a boxing match: in both cases the characters exercise free wills to defeat their opponents, whether by means of reason or by force. The Law of Conflict *is the first law of dramaturgy. Coincidentally, it is the first* "law of dialectics".'

Augusto Boal, *Legislative Theatre*

4
ENTERTAINMENT

'The National Circus of China used to tour with a show where everything was so perfect that they had a man each night would go round to see the artists and say to one: "You fall tonight", otherwise people are bored. You have to remind them "It's not TV you know, it's the real thing."

Robert Lepage

IT'S NOT THE PLAYING:
IT'S THE WINNING AND LOSING THAT COUNTS

The reason Keith Johnstone borrowed a sports construct and used it in the theatre is this: we don't just want to watch perfection. We want to watch failure as well – mistakes, pratfalls, accidents. In sport, goals are scored but there are also near misses. Moments of terrible despair. Moments in which everything is in the balance for both players and watchers. Moments of human failing. But it doesn't follow we want to see the inevitability of disaster. We want to see the struggle of two teams desperately trying to engineer a result over the other. This struggle is an essential point of focus for us as audience. This is one reason why improvisation as performance exists; because we enjoy the uncertainty of struggle, watching things emerge. The audience is complicit with the performers in not knowing the outcome. It's uncertain, unpredictable, occasionally heart-wrenching and also sometimes disappointing. But because of this, it is somehow closer to our day-to-day, moment-by-moment experience of life. If the improviser can find a way of celebrating failure as much as success, then extraordinary entertainment can be created. The attempt to achieve something impossible is always engaging. For the imagination does not know 'impossible'. *'I asked the group to improvise a scene on the beach. It was interesting. I asked the group to improvise a scene on the moon. It was predictable. I asked the group to improvise a scene set in the future, when brains had been replaced by empathic computers. It was remarkable.'* (Sandy Van Torquil.)

Improvisation as performance covertly legitimises what we believe already: that life consists of triumph and disaster, connectedness and disconnectedness, success and failure. A key to successful improvising, as with successful living, is to treat these two impostors the same. For the improviser, this means that she or he must learn to swim in shark-infested waters, be cheerful about reaching land, but stay cool about being eaten occasionally. Must in other words, become comfortable about being *transparent*. The greater the degree of transparency, the less that is hidden of our creative process during the event. And the more engaging is the improvisation. Or as Ruth Zaporah, the architect of Action Theatre argues, *'The job of Action Theatre improvisers is to manifest their moment-to-moment experience – not just what they're doing but how they are experiencing what they're doing: either its meaning or how it feels or both.'* A conventional theatregoer would probably reject this mission statement on the grounds that he's not interested in seeing the craft at work, he wants only to see the results of that craft. He wants circus without mistakes. But when Penn and Teller went on national television and started demonstrating the secrets of the Magic Circle, they got themselves into big trouble – but only with other magicians, not with their audiences. Never mind the Magic Circle, these are the magicians we need: those who do the trick first, then show you how it's done.

Whatever your viewpoint, there is transparency in the way that a great footballer's skills are evident to anyone who watches him play. If the improviser is comfortable with showing vulnerability, is prepared to invite the spectator in to observe private emotional processes at work, the chance is there to build an exciting relationship with the audience. You could argue this is a technique. But it's not a technique like learning chord changes on a guitar. It's an attitude of mind. Nor should it *become* merely a technique like chord changes, for the emphasis on technique simply leads to virtuosity, which isn't what the theatre does well. It should be about being comfortable with processes of chance, and sharing the emotional journeys arising from these with an audience.

LEGACY OF THE SIXTIES

Arguably this contemporary idea of improvisation as subversive, radical entertainment, sits in a continuum where earlier experiments of the '60s and '70s would also appear. The work of John Cage and Merce Cunningham used chance and randomness to inform when particular dance or music events were to be performed. Dice or I Ching sticks were thrown to make the choices. In this early work, it was understood that what was important was the transparency that showed how certain *choices* were made in respect of the delivery of that material. The presence of this decision-making created a kind of 'liveness' within the performance, which lent it a unique flavour. You had to be there, to see that version. With the influence of Dada in the background, artists wanted for each particular event to be removed from any sense of there being a production line in which repetition of experience and conformity of product were the goals.

Julian Beck and Judith Malina's Living Theatre performances also involved shifting away from the practice of rehearsing the show into creating an event that was simply not possible without the presence of an active, participating audience. The Living Theatre allied notions of improvisation with political agitation, using dialogue with the audience as a means, for example in *Paradise Now*, to agitate for radical social changes around issues of the Vietnam War and drug use. Joseph Moreno carried out parallel but complementary experiments within a more deliberately therapeutic context where improvisational ideas were employed in governance of the relations between practitioners and audiences. In the United Kingdom, Cornelius Cardew and collaborators such as the music group AMM, took the cue from Stockhausen (to whom Cardew was briefly an unhappy apprentice) and began to freely improvise without the constraining orthodoxy of regular chord progressions or tonality. They arrogated to themselves a freedom to move sonically across the

> 'There are, of course, no traditional roles in AMM music. There are no soloists or leaders, and no rhythm section. Decision-making and identity comes from the manner in which AMM treats its own history. It is beholden on each player to find a role within AMM. No specifics of performance are ever discussed.'
> Eddie Prévost

available sound fields, allowing the audience to simply drop in, watch the experimentation and leave again. The Scratch Orchestra, led by Cardew, created events in a range of locations deliberately inviting non-musicians and other artists to participate.

The notion of improvisation as entertainment has grown since then but there are sharp differences between the statuses of different improvising art forms. Since the 1920s, jazz has been consistently recognised as an established art form and more recently, even non-idiomatic free improvisation has achieved some measure of recognition. At the 2006 Shifti Improvisation Festival in the Midlands, UK, the London Improvisers Orchestra, still with a hint of the Scratch Orchestra about them, earned themselves a five star review in a national newspaper. This kind of recognition is unusual but not remarkably so. Dance improvisation however, remains very much a minority interest. Dramatic improvisation likewise struggles in the West for recognition as a mainstream art form, although comedy impro has had considerable success in the States and to some extent in the UK also, although still only to a fraction of the extent. Our Western culture, predicated on notions of consumerism, prefers the neatly packaged, previously honed, crafted and reviewed product to be set before them. This is a society that prizes commodity above process and literacy above the image. Improvisation as performance struggles as a result.

In the East, there are contrasting examples; Indian music and Khatak dance both draw on improvisation practice and are arguably positioned within the mainstream. Flamenco, the dance-drama form, is similarly established, although not without achieving a history of accommodation. *At its most elemental, flamenco will be performed spontaneously, in a family gathering or in the back room of a bar, or under a shady tree in a village square, anywhere where a group of gypsies might gather to chew the fat and sing or dance or play guitar for pleasure and sweet pain. It was with mixed feelings that the Gypsy families shared with non-gypsies an art form that reflected their deepest roots – a bit like "selling the family silver" (this partly explains the "mystery" that Gypsies have conjured up, so as to keep the "payos" ("non-gypsies") coming back for more, making them pay for any revelation, sometimes embroidering on the truth and misleading the "tourist"!'* (Danielle Allan.)

COMEDY IMPRO

Within the orbit of theatre, we have to turn to comedy improvisation for the practice that has had the greatest impact commercially. The comedy and comedy impro industries are closely linked, with performers often entering the latter to get a toehold in the former. The comedy industry, with its landscape of TV and film, can offer lucrative financial and status rewards to successful individuals. In the States this is particularly clear, with many performers seeing comedy impro as an audition opportunity – there's always the hope that someone, a producer, a director or a writer from Mad TV, is in the audience. Despite this careerist edge to the impro industry, it's true to say that the bastard children from the marriage of comedy and improvisation have rocked – or gently nudged at least – the cultural status quo in several Western countries. Some performers have become very good at this kind of performing. We in the UK have the Comedy Store Players with their various offshoots (Paul Merton and his Impro Chums, Stephen Frost and the Improvisers) while in the USA, following the lead set by Second City and ImprovOlympic, there are a considerable number of troupes, schools and clubs devoted to the form. Chicago itself has four full-time drama schools delivering impro courses, before we even begin counting the troupes. Why is Chicago the centre of the US impro world? No easy answer suggests itself. When I asked Chicagoan improvisers that question, they answered predominantly in terms of the legacy of Spolin and Sills, Close and Halpern, and how these great teachers lived or worked in the city.

Except for Don Hall who, with his musical background, answered, *'If you want to see where the future of impro lies, look at the Chicago jazz scene. Theatrical improvisation is behind the times – it's really a later incarnation of the same thing. Only it's just not musical. Everybody loved jazz because you could dance to it. But after a while, a clutch of intellectual black musicians were tired of having the music co-opted, and they created be-bop. That was a much more complicated, multi-layered kind of thing. It was much more improvisational, and could be compared to long-form improv. There's more of a narrative and it's a little harder to follow.'* The comparison between dramatic improvisation and jazz is often made, but then the comparison between jazz and almost any lively art form is often made. However, Hall's point has to be broadly correct: in many ways the two share a similar spirit, and the point that impro is simply an historically later manifestation, needs be taken seriously.

JOHNSTONE AND SPOLIN

There were two contemporaneous developments that are generally referred to as seeding the spiny monster that is comedy improvisation. The first was Chicagoan in origin, involving Second City Theatre Company and later ImprovOlympic. The second was Keith Johnstone. Second City was formed in part by Paul Sills, whose mother was Viola Spolin. Her work is largely credited as providing the storeroom of ideas and exercises that have allowed what is now several generations of improvisers to step out on stage without a script. Spolin's work began with children and refugees in a Chicagoan Recreational Project some twenty years prior to the forming of Second City. *'The games emerged out of necessity,'* she has said. *'I didn't sit at home and dream them up. When I had a problem* [directing], *I made up a game. When another problem came up, I just made up a new game.'*[14] In 1946 she founded the Young Actors Company in Hollywood. Children six years of age and older were trained through the medium of the still-developing Theatre Games system, to perform in productions. This company continued until 1955, when Spolin returned to Chicago to direct for the Playwright's Theater Club and subsequently to conduct games workshops with the Compass, formed by her son, the country's first professional, improvisational acting company that led to Second City. From 1960 to 1965, still in Chicago, she worked with Paul Sills as workshop director and continued to teach and develop Theater Games theory. As an outgrowth of this work, she published *Improvisation for the Theater* (1963), consisting of approximately two hundred and twenty games/exercises. It has become a classic reference text for teachers of acting, as well as for educators in other fields. However, Second City's luminous sketch comedy was only developed through improvisation. It took the later innovations of Chana Halpern and Del Close working at ImprovOlympic to take Chicagoan improv into an established practice of performing comedy improvisation on stage. For those interested in the details of this history, there are several books available which tell

> 'Almost everything we teach or practice at Second City can in some way be traced back to Viola, either through her seminal book . . . or through those she trained.'
>
> Anne Libera,
> *The Second City Almanac of Improvisation*

the story more interestingly and more fully than can possibly be done here, in particular Anne Libera's *Second City Almanac* and Rob Kozlowski's *The Art of Chicago Improv: Short Cuts to Long-form Improvisation*.

Chronologically, Keith Johnstone's work, while having many similarities, started later. Johnstone says he was actually unaware of the Spolin work on theatre games, developing his own approach independently. But the synchronicity is quite striking. In the early 1960s, the Royal Court (then the only theatre in London committed to new writing) set up a Writers Group to encourage would-be playwrights. It explored ways to seed new narratives that might get turned into plays. Keith introduced games and exercises to help create material. *'Dramatic action is where one person changes another – most plays I was reading failed to do that,'* he wrote later in his book, *Impro*. Johnstone's drive was always towards narrative – the games were a means to realise that, reflecting in part his own interest in playwriting. Later, he set up Theatre Machine and the company starting to 'borrow audiences' from other productions currently running, to try out these game-based exercises in front of them. The success of this work led to the company touring small theatres within the UK and Europe. Subsequently Johnstone moved to Calgary in Canada and went on to develop a range of improvisation formats for performance, including *Gorilla, Lifegame, Maestro* and others that in both spirit and execution shared much with the Chicagoan tradition – albeit with some important differences. As Johnstone explained to me, *'In 1966 I found Spolin. Someone in the audience said you must know of her work. I said I'd never heard of her. Someone gave me her book. There wasn't much I could use. It seemed very competitive. But there were some nice things like physical contact . . . The Who What Where stuff really worried me. It seemed they were trying to produce normal theatre by improvised means. I was trying to invent things that hadn't existed before.'*

Certainly many American improvisers would see his work as closer to their own than these comments suggest, especially after the development of Theatresports. After all, that form invites a quasi-competitive element into the space, much as the early experiments of Del Close had done. However, it has been acknowledged by Anne Libera that the emphasis on status was largely absent from Spolin's work, perhaps not surprisingly given the less class-conscious nature of American society. Certainly there's little or no mention of status in

Spolin's book. Similarly, Johnstone's work on masks and his emphasis on narrative also provide something of a distinction. Keith is pretty scathing about American comedy impro, seeing it as chasing the laughter much of the time, and lacking some of the more important thematic elements that make theatre come alive, such as the role of the hero and the exploration of family life. He considers that given the Chicagoan tradition was largely about *'entertaining people who were drinking'*, his impression was that they *'abandoned storytelling as too difficult.'* There's some confirmation of this in Rob Kozlowski's book when he writes that much Chicagoan improvisation work in the '90s was simply about being funny. *'Much of this is the paradox of having to perform in a cabaret or bar environment where the patrons are often loud and obnoxious and the performers sometimes have to match their level of hysteria in order to even be heard.'*[15]

Probably many in Chicago would argue rightly that the situation has changed since that time, especially given the new emphasis on long-form improvisations: shows that use one theme or narrative for the whole evening. But Johnstone's observation that *'the difference between my work and Second City's is I don't think they could go round Europe and play to people who didn't know English'* is probably incontestable. In the context of this discussion, it should probably also be mentioned that Keith's awareness of current impro practice is limited by the fact that he tries whenever possible to avoid going to the theatre, and especially to comedy improvisation.

THE LONDON CONNECTION

Interestingly, what is the UK's finest comedy-impro company, the Comedy Store Players, was informed at its crucial stage of development not by Keith Johnstone but by Mike Myers out of Second City. It's also one of the few ensembles this side of the Atlantic that has achieved continuity of personnel over a long period. I had the good fortune to check the Players' history with Neil Mullarkey, who obviously teaches elephants how to remember things. *'I was at Cambridge University . . . and found myself a member of the Footlights . . . While doing a show called* Get Your Coat, Dear, We're Leaving *at the Gate Theatre in Notting Hill, I came across a man called Mike Myers who was sitting in a wheelchair, hunched up, because we'd used all these wheelchairs on stage. He was selling tickets and had painted our set. And we got talking.'*

The talking led on to the two of them appearing at Jongleurs Comedy Club and later the Edinburgh Fringe as Mullarkey and Myers. Then later still, when the idea for the Players was mooted, Myers along with Kit Hollerbach were leant on to provide the exercises. *'Kit Hollerbach of the Comedy Store, had done a lot of impro in San Francisco with Robin Williams and others; she taught us the games, as did Mike . . . A few weeks later we did the first version of our show; the first half was stand-up, the second half was impro, because you'd never get people to pay money when we had no idea what we going to say, and it went on from there.'* The games they taught have remained staple to the Players' shows at the Comedy Store ever since, with very few variations. There's Freeze Tag otherwise known as LA Switch, then Die, Three-Headed Expert, EMO (changing emotions mid-scene), Film or Theatre Styles and the final sketch, which is triggered simply by a request for a Title. Mullarkey says that while the group has tried changing the games or introducing new ones it's felt a bit like *'trying to rewrite the Bible'*. In terms of the Anglo-American comparisons, he also comments that *'I've guested at Second City and at the Groundlings in LA. In LA there are more people on stage and they play the games much quicker. I felt hurried all the time.'* And the Players are not exactly slouches.

One quality that makes the Players so entertaining may have something to do with their skill at finding what Mullarkey would call 'the game of the scene' – an idea familiar to American improvisers as well as to students of John Wright and Keith Johnstone. One example of such a game within the Players' performances might be the 'game of breaking the rules'. Mullarkey explained: *'We know each other and trust each other so we can do all the bad things . . . sometimes the game is to be naughty, to not give offers, to do all the things you shouldn't do. As long as you know what the game is – Gaulier talks about Le Jeu where the game is to follow what the other person is doing – then we're OK.'* The Players have one or two conventions in performance that are particularly distinctive and create quite hysterical moments. There is something particularly English about the one that always strikes me which usually (I believe) happens in the middle of a song. Neil Mullarkey: *'We never plan it, but it's been such fun. It's so coarse, so unoriginal, so old-fashioned but incredibly funny. Somebody goes, "I went out the front and I saw a –" and at that point Richard Vranch will stop playing, we'll all stand up as one, as if horrified . . . Then to whoever was threatening to say this word, we say, "Come on, behave yourself, you can't say that." And he says,*

"OK, I'm sorry, I won't do it again, I promise I won't do it again, I really promise I won't do it again" – and of course then he goes and does it again. And then suddenly there's "anchor" or "china" or whatever – and they are increasingly rude words they're heading for. And the NOT saying the rude word is the funniest thing. Saying a rude word would not be funny at all.'

Within both the USA and the UK, the exploratory shift from shorter, sketch-based comedy to longer formats, has inevitably thrown up issues of structure, tone and theme that give practitioners plenty to work on. Companies and individuals such as Improbable, Forced Entertainment, Fluxx, The Spontaneity Shop and Kevin Tomlinson in the UK and many more in the USA are making this journey. Some of these explorations are discussed in the chapter on Structure below.

IMPROVISATION ON TV:
IT'S ONLY A GAME SHOW / NOT

Perhaps the biggest explosion of improvisation in any kind of popular context has been on television. There's no space here to deal with the infiltration of improvisation into sitcoms and comedy dramas although it's a significant and considerable phenomenon. In part influenced by *Curb Your Enthusiasm* in the USA, shows like *Green Wing*, *The Thick of It* and others in the UK allow actors to improvise around a basic scene template. The good stuff is extracted during the editing. A show like *The Thick of It* actually films four times as much material as is required to allow for this reduction process. But there's more to it than just cutting off more cloth than you need in the shop and cutting it to size back home. The show deals with political machinations much in the way that *Yes, Minister* did. There's a synchronicity going on here. Alan Yentob put it this way in his own programme on BBC2, *A Funny Thing Happened . . . 'The show uses improvisation in order to mirror the improvisation of political life.'* Because politicians are forever making stuff up in the face of adversity, the television cameras or both, it's only fitting that their counterpart actors should be thrown into a similar predicament. Improvising with a comic rather than political sensibility, they play out similar scenes, which quite unaccountably begin to appear just a little absurd.

The other area of development has been reality television, its very name hiding the conceit of its manipulations. *Big Brother* was developed initially in the Netherlands, building on shows like *Survivor!* and has since swept all before it. It may be argued that reality TV has no place within a discussion of improvisation since the 'performers' have effectively no control over the operating structures of the 'improvisation'. However, the fundamental relationship of performer and audience still prevails. Participants enter the house (or the island or the jungle or the castle) as performers, contracted to remain visible to the audience throughout the exercise. It's part of the game that these performers are not professional actors so their 'performing' is expected to be revealing precisely because they lack 'performer selves'. They have various tasks to fulfil and relationships to negotiate, and while they don't expect for the most part to play a character or demonstrate any artistic ability, they are nevertheless – in all but name – performers under contract. (In the first series of *Big Brother* in the UK, it was alleged by someone I know working at Endemol, the show's producers, that the most animated discussion amongst the housemates was about these very contracts – but these discussions were unsurprisingly never aired.)

Once an individual has knowingly contracted in, they give over a certain power to the producers in the hope of power in the life after the event. The variant situation, that of the individual who is filmed secretly – see *Punk'd* or *Fantasy Island* – and subsequently gives their approval, involves a fundamentally different relationship. For in *Punk'd*, at the time of 'performance', there is no knowledge or awareness of the audience. There is no knowledge or awareness of performing even. So the absence of any complicity with the rules of the exercise debars it from being a performance in the sense we traditionally understand that term. Where the contract is knowingly entered into, what follows is essentially a long improvisation during which the performers have no control over the governing structures. As widely recognised, this is a convention that is open to abuse. Hence much reality TV is inseparable from the idea of cruelty. There's a subtextual agreement between the production company and the audience that what we'll see is suffering along the way. It's a relationship between a corporate dominant and a willing team of submissives in which the submissives create an assertive mask for the occasion that is necessarily, because of their lack of training and the unfamiliarity with the exercise, lightly worn. How much cruelty and humiliation is engineered is a matter entirely for the company but given this is a competitive world, there's no point in generating less than the prevailing norm and a great deal in favour of doing more. In other words, the level of humiliation needs to be racked up each time the series airs, otherwise the audience is disappointed. *'Viewers overwhelmingly believe that people overact for the camera, and part of the appeal of the reality TV experience is waiting for the mask to slip, in moments of stress and conflict, revealing the concealed "true self" or "real face" of a contestant. In their hunger for occasions when anger flares and performance gives way to authenticity, we see the audience's fascination with a gaudy, demonstrative selfhood, and a boundless curiosity for the shadowplay of false and real selves.'*[16] This comment picks up a number of themes already floated in this book: the search for vulnerability, the relationship between the mask and the actor, and the exploration of conflict (in this context staged) as a means to reveal something of our shared nature. At its heart, then, there are many similar currents running here as there on the improvisation stages. Albeit with one very big difference.

When the production company Endemol found itself in court in Holland as a result of one of its series, the company's defence team stated that part of its raison d'etre was *research*, the kind of research that was comparable to the Stanford Prison Experiment. It was an interesting choice of comparison. The Stanford Experiment involved a group of volunteers recruited by Philip Zimbardo who signed up to play the parts of guards and prisoners within an elaborate role play. *'It was a time (1971) when social psychology had taken on a distinctly situationist character, with leading researchers producing experimental scenarios similar to the reality shows that would emerge some twenty years later . . . an environment was contrived to elicit, record and interpret responses.'*[17] However, there was no legitimate basis for the research and no quantitative measures could be applied to the results. What happened was more surprising to the organisers than they expected, although looking back on it one would have to say, the results should have been anticipated. *'On the second day, the prisoners rebelled. They barricaded themselves inside their cells and hurled insults at their jailors. The guards . . . called three officers on leave and rushed the cells with fire extinguishers, blasting inmates off the barricades with streams of CO_2 . . . Almost immediately, the atmosphere of play-acting turned into something more sinister . . . The period after the rebellion saw the guards grow more brutal, and the stress this placed on inmates began to appear dangerous; after thirty-six hours, one prisoner lapsed into a state of high trauma and had to be released. Inmate 8612 presented textbook symptoms of incipient nervous* *collapse, crying uncontrollably, with intermittent fits of rage and disorganised cognition . . . All of the volunteers could at any time cry "Stop" or "I quit", but in the course of six days, none of them did so . . . On day six of an intended two-week run, Zimbardo aborted the experiment. The inmates were evincing signs of concentration camp or gulag inmate behaviour – turning on any of their number who the guards singled out as 'bad', showing decreasing levels of concern for one another . . . and in many cases exhibiting . . . hysterics. . . . The guards, meanwhile, showed signs of enjoying their power, and capitulated to the wild joy of sadism.'*[18]

One could argue that it will be only a matter of time before such experiments represent the mainstream fare of reality TV, if we hadn't already seen a show on BBC2 which in many ways replicates the Stanford experiment called, with a flair for imagination, *The Experiment*. While viewers weren't treated to a repeat of the same descent into violence, it was evident again, not least because of a similarly premature end, that removed from the normal routines that reinforce selfhood and given an alternative set of routines and responsibilities, the sense of identity that informs ethical and rational decision-making disintegrates faster than Clint Eastwood spits tobacco. In such a context, performers start to behave according to the mask that they have been given, for that is the only reality consistently reinforced. With their familiar, self-imposed boundaries absent the performer finds himself in a space without an ethical floor. It therefore becomes possible to fall far and fast into behaviour that lacks any of the ethical checks and balances normally present. It's a *Lord of the Flies* scenario in which the participants 'forget' – such is the hypnotic power of the exercise – they can summon up an escape chopper any time they like. Professor Wilson is a professor of criminology who was employed as a consultant on *Big Brother*. His resignation was *'prompted by the refusal of its creators, Endemol, to listen to any advice I gave them about what would happen if they put back into the main house two contestants who had been separated from the remainder, but allowed to hear and watch everything that was said about them. Anyone with the slightest knowledge of human behaviour – never mind a background in psychology and criminology – would know this was a recipe for disaster. But stupid me, I understood too late that disaster was what the programme makers wanted.'*[19]

It's one thing to mimic the authoritarian routines of your subject matter within rehearsal procedures as the Living Theatre did, or to devise shows during the night instead of the day as Pete Brooks'

Insomniac Theatre did; it's quite another to remove from the performers any contact with the controlling formalities of their own exercise. When this happens, the performer no longer has contact with the 'self' who signed up for the exercise in the first place, so it comes as a great surprise to that individual just how destructive the exercise can be. It remains a 'role play' certainly, but *the awareness of playing a role does not occlude the possibility of one's actions and feelings within that role being as authentic as any other; the game is not removed from life: for its duration it is life, both a pretend world and the real world.*[20] Or as Caroline O'Shea, a performer in the UK's first series of *Big Brother* in 2000, said, *'It was the cruellest experience of my lifetime.'* Although many go into *Big Brother* with the professed intention of 'learning about myself', the performer runs the risk of discovering neither herself nor 'what is real' in any conventional sense of the term. Rather, what is discovered is just how very tenuous is the dependency that a sense of selfhood has on any prevailing reality, and in particular how quickly that sense can slip away within a regime of moving mirrors.

> 'It might be argued that the public engagement in such performances indicates a tendency to believe that the cameras will reveal what people are "really" like, but in fact it is the contradiction between the ways of seeing an individual that seems to be enjoyed. It is the uncertainty, the undecideability, which, like the banality of these shows, fascinates.'
>
> John E. McGrath, *Loving Big Brother*

TRANSPARENCY AND LIVENESS

We end where we started: with an idea about transparency. Unlike the authoritarian procedures of reality television which aim to enforce transparency under duress, improvisation practice, whose protocols are organised by its practitioners, presents an alternative idea. This is the possibility of voluntary revelation with the minimum artifice. While comedy impro continues to thrive, other initiatives are emerging that re-orientate practice around non-virtuosic explorations of human vulnerability and exposition. Adrian Heathfield makes a useful distinction between *an emphasis in certain kinds of impro . . . on the virtuosity and skill of the performer that overrides other kinds of meaning . . .*

and the emphasis in improvisational performance practice where the energies are directed more towards meaningful play.' He argues that it is not enough to proceed merely from the idea that creativity itself *'is something laudable.'* The performer needs to allow this creativity to reflect back on preoccupations in a way that avoids the simple invitation to applaud the bravado. Can this be entertaining? Is this sufficient? These are questions that are not necessarily apolitical. Heathfield sees the exercise of meaning-determined performances as antithetical to a performance culture that is rooted in play and in an examination of relations. He argues that his interest is rather in seeing performance that *'instils in the audience an inclination to question, and the potency and force of that, as opposed to delivering or illustrating ideas. This would be an inclination to question meaning and authority and power.'* He argues that the issue of politics is tied to that of liveness, and hence to the structures that govern performance at its time of event. *'The liveness provides a point of entry for the spectator into the felt experience of the moment – those terms "felt" and "experience" are very politicised for me.'* The performance therefore *'concerns itself not with the idea of life but life itself.'*

These comments echo what Julyen Hamilton has observed, coming from a dance background and using improvisation extensively within that tradition. *'My work is about opening up moments so they don't need to be quickly or narrowly concluded. So you can see the many levels in there, the different points of view, the subtexts.'*[21] Adrian Heathfield points to the work of Karen Finley, the American performance artist, as an example of performance that is effective in the terms that he describes, where performance offers a challenge to the dominance of *'rational thought and its relationship to male thought and power.'* He argues, *'If you think about Karen Finley, liveness and improvisation form an important part of the politics of that work. She is obviously generating a stream of consciousness poetics that gives her access to sets of feelings and expressions of relations that would be completely inaccessible from a rational, masculine perspective. That is the politics of her work. She is able to speak a kind of feminine language that addresses questions of masculine power and abuse in both society and relationships. The political capacity of the work comes from its form. The force of her open associative writing is doubled in the live performance, which is more like channelling or a ritual incantation.'*

Performance that relies largely or exclusively on improvised elements is still a comparatively rare creature when seen alongside the flocks of well-trained, well-disciplined, regular birds. Unpredictability is both the charm and weakness of such practice. Operating within a commercial context where spectators choose from a long list of possible delights, entertainment that denies reassurance at the level of either form or content, inevitably in our UK climate, struggles for the same level of popularity. Yet ultimately it may be the audiences themselves, those who prefer different stories differently told, who become the triggers to an unsettling of mainstream culture. For it may be they who, in increasing numbers, start to alter patterns of theatre-going through their rejection of more time-worn, less immediate entertainments. In time they may turn in more significant numbers towards more explosive, unpredictable, event-driven phenomena. The circus performer who deliberately falls, as mentioned by Lepage at the top of the chapter, may become the star turn rather than the excitement at the edge.

CODA

'On hearing meta-music for the first time some people are confused. A noise is presented to them that does not conform to their previous ideas about the nature of music. Two kinds of negative responses prevail. Anger (in various shades) that this experience has been visited upon them. And disbelief that the musicians are serious about their work. But others take to it like a duck to water. For them the experience is one of relief. They feel vindicated by the freedom exhibited by such music. It relieves them from an alienation they had felt from established or commodity musics, which education and the market place had thrust upon them.'

Eddie Prévost, *No Sound Is Innocent*

PART TWO

THE WHO

I

THE IMPROVISER

'The most important thing about improvisation is to make it as easy as possible.'   Guy Dartnell

'Your job as a performer is to make your life more difficult for yourself.'
Wendy Houston

'The gold can be anywhere . . . where you least expect. I think the biggest thing that I learned even before Improbable, and I think every artist discovers it somewhere down the line, is that the best stuff is in the mistakes. And really creativity is not about how many ideas you can have, but kind of how receptive to that notion you are. And I think that's just a life thing, and I'm amazed they don't teach it in school because it's absolutely universal. You read it everywhere . . . anyone who's creative, you read that same thing; whether it be couched in different terms . . . but it's well known that most discoveries happen outside the laboratory.'
Julian Crouch

JOURNEY

When you go on stage as an improviser, you're looking to make a journey. You're looking for a moving current that will carry you on that journey. You're looking for a current stronger than your 'good ideas'. If your good ideas have walked you out into the water, you want a current that's stronger than walking. You probably can't see the current from the beach. It's beneath the surface, an undertow. And part of the self will always want to resist this sense of being pulled away. This is one of many paradoxes: the aim is to make a journey, yet for this to happen you need to abandon the self-protections that are so useful in the rest of life. In the rest of life certain skills serve you to keep you still, balanced and directed. Here, they may prevent you from becoming truly engaged. For these skills in self-protection can hide the vulnerability that is perhaps your most useful ally.

Furthermore, what makes the work interesting and absorbing for an audience, is seeing these self-protecting resistances overthrown visibly, right there in front of it. Spectators like to see the performer being moved or carried away in a manner that's unexpected and to some extent unwished. It's risk-taking by proxy. If the performance lacks any sign of resistances overcome by a greater force, then performers leave themselves open to being asked the question, 'Why not do a different kind of performance where there is no struggle, no indeterminacy about outcomes?'

The performer hopes to leave behind the familiar protocols of everyday behaviour and enter a different world. An awkward dream life for the duration. Some find it easier than others to leave offstage behaviours behind. Some improvising musicians talk of making this journey without any effort at all. They find such a rapport with their material, they're gone in a moment. Chuck Israel for example, comments, *'No matter what you're doing or thinking about beforehand, from the very moment the performance begins, you plunge into that world of sounds. It becomes your world instantly, and your whole consciousness changes.'* [22] The comment suggests an easy transition. But for dramatic improvisers, this kind of immersion into 'that world' is something that doesn't come so easily. Many different pressures impinge on the improviser's consciousness. There's no script to lean on, no previously fashioned boat that will take you out into the water. So the protective barriers are up. After all, these are strangers out there, watching. So, there's nothing for it. At the risk of taking the metaphor too far, the performer has to build a boat right there and then, in front of the audience, if there's to be any travelling.

Thinking about what the improviser does in terms of a *journey* has several advantages. Firstly, the metaphor crosses over between art forms. Within jazz it's often drawn on: *'Despite the difficulties of verbalising about essentially nonverbal aspects of improvisation, artists favor two metaphors in their own discussions about the subject that provide insight into unique features of their experience. One metaphor likens group improvisation to a conversation that players carry on among themselves in the language of jazz. The second likens the experience of improvising to going on a demanding musical journey. From the performance's first beat, improvisers enter a rich, constantly changing musical stream of their own creation . . .'* [23]

Dancers use it also, as the following discussion with the Liverpool Improvisation Collective indicates. For the dancers in this group, what is often a key determinant in the evolution of any dance piece, is the personal relationships existing between the improvisers. For anyone who witnessed Kirstie Simson and Julyen Hamilton improvise together for the first time after a break of fifteen years at the Shifti Festival in 2006, the case is evident. A close personal alliance had been broken over that time, and their reunion on stage crackled with an extraordinary resonance. Especially if the dancers are working without any predetermined score, then relationships are profoundly influential in determining moves, gestures, use of space and quality of energy – the articulation of the journey made.

PAULA HAMPSON: *'I have a track or journey through it, even if it jumps off. There's something about the idea of journey that helps me mentally.'*

JO BLOWERS: *'When you don't know where you're going, don't you pay attention a lot more? And don't you remember where you went? I know I do. If I'm just a passenger in a car or if I know the route very well . . . I don't pay attention very well.'*

MARY PRESTIDGE: *'I feel like I'm going on an expedition.'*

PAULA: *'It's what you said before, when you've done a performance you remember certain flavours. The word journey is quite prominent for me as I do like to have a sense. If I'm in a quartet and you're doing a solo, there's something about that bridge from solo to meeting to a duo or trio . . . I don't know if I see it as a travelling journey.'*

JO: *'For me, compositionally there's always a strong sense of beginning, middle and end. I rarely forget how something started . . .'*

PAULA: *'Or you're so clearly in the moment that you've brought the beginning with you.'*

JO: *'We do take time to stop – or we try to. Everything from nodding off for a moment, to visiting a motorway caff . . . That's what's so interesting about the journey metaphor – it's not a linear thing.'*

In my interview with the group, Jo Blowers pointed out that it's precisely this opportunity to work in a non-linear way and follow digressions that makes improvisation so fascinating. You acquire permission 'not to be in control'. You get carried in different directions rather than consistently feeling obliged to 'make things happen.' There is still a sense of a task of course, and this involves concentration and responsiveness. The mind and body are anchored by that sense. But this doesn't have to involve any kind of 'trying to achieve something'. If you try to achieve something, the body resists usually. The body moves forward through space of its own momentum, asking questions of itself continuously. However, it's the sideways trajectories, the digressions, the detours that give the performance its quality of spontaneity and chance. Not that this means abandoning the central journey. Julyen Hamilton talked about this at the Shifti Festival: *'I like the linearity of intent, of consequence (a story, theme or phrase) leading you to somewhere you weren't aware of beforehand . . . getting into a "groove" reflecting the "zapping" nature of humans . . . like animals ranging hugely in their perceptions . . . constantly navigating . . . an attitude I like to be in the piece. If you range too much, you lose the line but if you stick in the groove you get stuck! There is a constant tension between these two intentions and necessities. I'm constantly trying to stretch both. It's architectural somehow.'*[24]

So the metaphor of journey is useful in distinguishing the relationship between forward motion – or 'advancing', to use dramatic improvisation terminology – and exploring tangentially, that is downwards or sideways. When the motion is forwards, it's the story, the principal narrative that's being extended or developed. When the exploration is sideways, linear momentum is abandoned while the constellar circularity of the moment-just-arrived-at becomes the point of absorption. Nancy Stark Smith refers to such moments as 'gaps'. In such moments, there is neither future nor past, only the stickiness of the present. The story is suspended. In this moment can be generated a game, a

'Where you are when you don't know where you are is one of the most precious spots offered by improvisation. It is a place from which more directions are possible than anywhere else. I call this place the Gap. The more I improvise, the more I'm convinced that it is through the medium of these gaps – this momentary suspension of reference point – that comes the unexpected and much sought after "original" material. It's "original" because its origin is the current moment and because it comes from outside our usual frame of reference.'

Nancy Stark Smith

joke or a repetition. The moment might be comic, bizarre or sad. It might involve a reflection, an observation or an aside. It's a moment of fooling which although it doesn't advance the forwardness, does the job of signposting other, more incidental but no less important elements of material. Does this take us closer to the unconscious? Possibly. Once the game-moment is completed, the resumption of that more deliberate excursion, the main journey, is given sharpness and clarity through the completion of the digression.

Theatre since the Greeks has largely relied on this idea of linear narrative, of events unfolding through a beginning, middle and end, to give audiences a clearly recognisable way to understand the event. A time line orders the dramatisation. Within it, points of character or incident are offered to the audience. The audience is comfortably engaged in speculation around 'what happens next'. It's a linear progression, hence the phrase 'dramatic line'. Macbeth begins as the Thane of Glamis, becomes the Thane of Cawdor and eventually ends of King of Scotland, before being killed. Events proceed chronologically. However, present-day dramatic practice recognises the insufficiency of this linearity to always convey contemporary insights. Other protocols are sought in order to extend ideas of how emotions, sensations and memories operate within the psyche. To some extent the notion of 'the gap' or 'the digression' is elevated to a status equal to or greater than that of the journey. Or else the notion of journey is redefined so it becomes no longer reliant on a chronological sense of time unfolding. As a result, alternative models of time-construction are built on the sites of what are perceived as outmoded chronological orthodoxies.

Pinter's *Betrayal* runs backwards. In *Waiting for Godot*, 'nothing happens, twice' (untrue and a cliché but signposting the unorthodoxy). In time-based and performance work, this deconstruction of linearity is taken further. Time stops, moves backwards, forwards again, becomes cyclical through repetition. In Station House Opera's *Roadmetal Sweetbread*, the real self co-exists with the filmed self simultaneously. In the durational performances of Forced Entertainment, narrative line is neglected entirely in favour of an excursion into possibilities presented by a single dramatic situation. In *Quizoola!* three performers change roles while the format is unchanging: a question and answer session, improvised from a book of 2,000 questions. In *12 a.m. and Looking Down*, the performers simply present themselves again and again to the audience, using clothes and placards. It's an ever-changing image, each one with its own juxtapositions and resonances. The notion of time is disrupted both by the length of time the piece runs (anything up to 24 hours) and by the avoidance of any narrative intent. There is however, still an *'agenda of forwardness'*, as the musician Charles Hayward would say, but one created from a different, perhaps more musical energy – of exploration around and within a single point. The comparisons with free music improvisation practice are legitimate because free music traditions discard orthodox notions of 'progression' and 'momentum'. Instead of linearity, *'the music spreads out sideways'*, as Simon Fell argues. There's no driving beat or evident tonality, no *'dead hand of harmony'*, yet there is still that journey being made through changes in tempo, texture and intensity.

EMOTIONS AND FEELINGS

How then does the dramatic improviser learn to be sufficiently open yet balanced to ensure a journey does still evolve, albeit one redefined outside a conventional chronological orthodoxy? How does he or she create an engagement with the audience that doesn't rely on speculation around 'what happens next'? That allows for spontaneity without generating simply a random, chaotic sequence of material bits and pieces that never connect? The answer lies to some extent in the pursuit of emotional engagement. If you as an improviser are engaged emotionally, then you are better placed to get into a kind of groove, providing a respect is kept for the emotion that's driving the energy.

'Well, it's always very difficult to say what prompts anybody to do anything, let alone getting underwater and teaching ravens to fly. But I think it probably all dates back to a very early age, when I was quite a young fellow. My mother, Lady Beryl Streeb-Greebling, you know the wonderful dancer – a hundred and seven tomorrow and still dancing – she came up to me in the conservatory – I was pruning some walnuts – and she said "Arthur" – I wasn't Sir Arthur in those days – she said, "Arthur, if you don't get underwater and start teaching ravens to fly, I'll smash your stupid face off," and I think it was this that sort of first started my interest in the whole business of getting them underwater.'

Peter Cook
as Sir Arthur Streeb-Greebling

It's a question of the improviser resigning control to some extent and trusting that emotions have an intelligence worth sharing. Guy Dartnell: *'You're trying to become a channel for something . . . Rather than your having to involve yourself in a lot of effort, mental or whatever, to come up with stuff, you try and welcome or attract something to you. The easier you can be, the less effort is required. Instead of the audience watching your effort, therefore, they go on the dream.'* This statement can be set alongside similar comments by the musician Eddie Prévost: *'In the midst of performing you can only wait for the sounds to arrive. The momentum of playing takes control of the musician; for once committed to making the music he is no longer free. All thoughts about structure and emotional content become inadequate to the task of improvising once the first note has been sounded. Thereafter the total being of the musician is involved; involuntary responses meld with overt technique; the mind scurries unsuccessfully to keep up with the unconscious. The musician, if he is lucky, is reduced/devolved to an observer, while the music flows. He can only watch hands move across keys-frets-skins. He is possessed.'*[25]

Both Dartnell and Prevost are talking about reactiveness – the ability to 'be moved' by the circumstances. It becomes a matter of holding on to the fin of the plane as it carries you. Is this then what creates the journey? Simply emotional reactiveness? If so, then to what? Largely, it's reactiveness to whatever stimuli are placed in front of the improviser; be that another improviser, an object, the suggestion from the audience, the challenge presented – the possibilities are many. So does that mean it's all about concentrating on feelings? To some extent yes, but that doesn't mean you rush around 'being emotional'. Guy Dartnell: *'What I mean is not something that's clearly emotional . . . rather, that if you can lock into that emotional flow, the emotions will tell you what to do. They will tell you whether to speak, and what to say. And when you switch from speaking to singing, they will tell you how. There's a hand of intelligence operating at a feeling level in a person.'* Experienced improvisers will acknowledge this – that a point in the journey comes when there's a clear imperative to speak or not speak, or sing or leave the stage. True, it's largely nurtured by experience but that sense is there even in beginners if they listen to it. Perhaps it has an innate quality.

This very much connects with the emphasis within Action Theatre practice, the drama/movement system developed by Ruth Zaporah, on recognising that 'improvisation is not about making things happen – it's about growing what is already happening'. In other words, working out of the reactiveness that is constantly occurring. The improviser is allowing an internal circuitry – which never stops (until you're dead, and some say not even then) – to become the *body of instruction* for the event. The improviser's task is to take these instructions – messages from within – and act on them. But this sets up another question. If this is about recognising and acting on your feelings – and improvising musicians would identify this too, since their criticism of composition is that the written score cannot adequately incorporate the emotions of the player in performance – then surely all that's involved is sharing your emotions with the audience. Not so. That would be interesting, but only as much as watching a trapped dog in a cage is interesting. What is more interesting for the audience is seeing the emotional journey being given shape and definition.

If the reactiveness has no sense of accumulation, it becomes a randomness that consistently betrays the past and the 'journey' never develops any sense of form. In effect, there's no journey. Without intelligence existing at a meta-level in which a sense of form is maintained, then it is all merely randomness. Once an initial reactiveness has been articulated and given shape to something, this is the start of a journey. The improviser needs to remember each significant decision made along this route. By so doing, the journey achieves coherence, at least in its own terms. Reincorporation becomes possible, perhaps essential. With this task in mind, the implications of journey begin to impose themselves on the improviser, even if that becomes awkward and the improviser's 'preferred' material has to be abandoned because

'I look across the stage. As I do that, another improviser walks on to it. She's walking towards me with a kind of voracious, predatory look – but affectionate. I read that in an instant. I figure she's after me, she's chasing me. My reaction is to flinch, and also to laugh. So that's it then. I'm not afraid of her, this is some kind of play, but at the same time, to enhance the interaction, I'm going to back away from her, also in the spirit of a game. Then we'll find out who we are to each other.' In this way we've established the beginning of a journey, and the audience has witnessed it. Whatever happens subsequently, these qualities of flirtation, chasing and dominance/submission exist in our relationship – they may change but we can never pretend (as actors) that they never existed.'

Sandy Van Torquil

of obligations accepted. That might feel embarrassing. But the point is not to avoid embarrassment, it is to become embarrassed.

This shape of the journey is the result not only of the improviser's feelings responding to the evident provocations from external sources, but also other factors such as the memory of the journey so far and an overall sense of dramatic form. The search for form cannot be underestimated as a factor. It's a hard lesson to learn, the lesson of how to realise formal shape from raw material, especially outside of a relatively easy construct like the comedy sketch, and it's why some improvisation companies lean on tight structures to help them.

The performer is therefore not simply being invited to 'be indulgent' – which is the classic criticism of improvisation ('Great fun for the actors, but what about the audience?'), she or he is instead trying to become a conduit for feelings and sensations that grow up or 'cook up' in the individual as a result of the performer's relationships to the dynamics and material of the event. And then for these feelings to be articulated in such a way as to craft a shape or a journey that does the business of 'making sense' of them for an audience. (This is where the training comes in: learning to understand emerging sensations and feelings as improvisatory material and then working them not unlike a sculptor who works with clay.)

A DIGRESSION ABOUT FEELINGS

As an aside, there may be a useful distinction to be made between feelings and emotions – terms that are often loosely interchangeable within improvisation teaching. This is the distinction made by Antonio Demasio: *'I have proposed that the term feeling should be reserved for the private, mental experience of an emotion, while the term emotion should be used to designate the collection of responses, many of which are publicly observable. In practical terms this means that you cannot observe a feeling in someone else although you can observe a feeling in yourself when, as a conscious being, you perceive your own emotional states. Likewise no one can observe your own feelings, but some aspects of the emotions that give rise to your feelings will be patently observable to others. Moreover, for the sake of my argument, the basic mechanisms underlying emotion do not require consciousness, even if they eventually use it . . . To be sure, at this point in evolution and at this moment of our adult lives, emotions occur in a setting of consciousness: We can feel our emotions consistently and we know we feel them.'*[26] For our purposes therefore, emotions are our visible responses to what happens around us while feelings are what are experienced internally and involve mental awareness. Feelings come and go. They are inevitable, and so deserve respect. Ruth Zaporah has also written about this distinction: *'Feeling states may look like emotions but the improviser's relationship to the experience is quite different . . . Feeling states rise spontaneously and linger until replaced by another. The shift from one feeling state to another is determined by the content and musicality of each moment of the improvisation, as sensed by the improviser. Unlike emotions, feeling states are unnameable.'*[27] It's clear from this that, like Damasio, Zaporah sees the feeling states as transitory, fundamental and linked to consciousness. Looking at this proposition in the context of our earlier argument about the need for transparency, the improviser therefore would be aware of looking to make his or her emotions – rather than feelings necessarily – visible to the audience. The improviser then would be better placed to make decisions, not only about how to make emotions visible to the audience but about what behaviours to put on top of these. After all, complete transparency is impossible. There is always a disjunction between what is felt and what is seen; the point is to be looking to close the gap even though, in a way, that's impossible.

Within dramatic improvisation, this scope for decision-making might mean having the character take an attitude towards the event occurring that was in contrast to the emotion felt and seen. In other words, 'feeling' that I have anger, it's possible then to smile. 'Feeling' that I am pleased, I choose to appear sad. Within character-driven improvisation, this kind of choice can be highly effective. It sets up a tension within the individual, and generates a subtext. It's almost as if the performer enters into a conspiratorial relationship with the audience in which the audience sees the true but *hidden* emotions.

Some performers, beginners especially, but by no means all, just find the whole business of managing feelings very difficult. This is often because what they feel is simply plain fear. So the characters played become frightened and incidents enacted all about self-immolation. *'The scene becomes about vomiting because the actors are afraid.'* (Keith Johnstone.) I'm not sure that there's any fast-track solution to this, outside of practice. To deliberately conceal your emotions from yourself and the audience leads to a kind of dishonesty. Besides, it becomes harder then for other emotions to come through. The overall effect is for the improviser to become emotionally blocked. Better to express the fear, and once expressed, discover different feelings made possible by the giving away of fear. One key to this process of staying 'open' is the avoidance of getting into judgement. That is, judgement of self or others around you. Easy to argue, difficult to accept. But what judgement does is begin the blocking process. Ruth Zaporah has written about how true improvisation avoids judgement. For the improviser, she writes, *'There is no judgement or evaluation, nothing is good or bad.'*[28]

BEGINNINGS

Before walking on stage, the improviser has to prepare. Even if he or she consciously avoids preparation, there's still a decision being taken to avoid it. Which is a kind of preparation in itself. Keith Rowe, a co-founder of the improvising band AMM, looks at the issue of preparation like this: *'How do you prepare for a performance? I think you prepare by preparing yourself. The difficulty is not in the manipulation of the instruments; it's in the perception of how you view performance. For me, I put the guitar on the table, I get it all working, I go off and do something, and then it's eight o'clock and it's time to play. I look at the guitar in absolute horror at that point. I really don't have a single idea. I'd go further and say that when my hand descends to play the very first notes of the performance, I still don't have any ideas. As the hand or the fingers are just beginning to touch the strings, ideas begin to come – and then you take it from whatever happens at that stage. I think the only way for me, preparing for a performance, is through observation, observing the world around: that means listening, paying attention, focusing. What a performance is, is basically focusing on what is happening in front of you – in order to focus and have something worthwhile within you, to be reflected. That comes from constantly observing what's happening around you.'*[29] It's interesting how this musician observes his own processes much in the way that a dancer or actor might. There are no structural preoccupations, it's just the listening and the observing that's important. This gives him all that he needs since the externals in turn provoke feelings and sensations within. They are observed *'in order to focus and have something worthwhile within you.'* His comments also highlight the importance of being *in the present*, rather than for example thinking about previous performances or anticipating too carefully the performance to come.

To begin the journey then, the improviser reacts. But what if the improviser is simply carrying onstage feelings that have nothing to do with reaction but are consequent on other, earlier events? Some improvisers find that at the beginning of the show, a pressure to 'perform' is at its strongest. That's when fears are magnified. It's why bullying, cowardice and other demonstrations of negative behaviour can appear early during shows – these emotions surface in character that really belong to the performer. It's certainly been my unconscious default on a number of occasions: to play a bullying character. In this way, I unconsciously I think I'm solving the problem of the scene. But if I can bring more awareness to that impulse, and focus more consciously outward at the onset of the journey, then maybe I'm not that fear's slave.

What to react to externally? The question is particularly pertinent in solo work for the evident reason that there's basically no one else on stage to react to. There's simply the improviser, the space and the sounds within the space. So the problem is condensed. In Sten Rudstrom's solo performance at Greenwich UK in 2004, as he moved on to the stage he heard a child whispering in the audience. To him it sounded like a mouse. So the first word he said aloud was 'Mouse.' It gave him the start he needed. The start came from his listening. This was his equivalent of a first note played on a piano – immediately setting parameters for what was to follow musically. If the improviser is open, is open to be moved by what he sees, touches and feels, it won't take long before he starts to engage with something. He might feel there should be a 'correct' starting point, and that something like a child whispering in the audience is evidently not that 'correct' start point. He might be tempted to keep looking. The problem is, you can look for ever, and since he's alone, who is to agree with him that one start point is better than another? Maybe in a group show, it would have been right to ignore the mouse-whisperer. There might be other signals more important coming from the other players. But in Rudstrom's case, he felt that to ignore that sound would have been a mistake at that point in time. In fact, responding to that sound becomes an act of incorporation.

'One of the things I work on in teaching, is stopping the dancers just wandering around the space, looking for the next idea.'

Sue McLennan

As the dancer and teacher Sue McLennan observes in the quote alongside, you can't be searching around for too long. The tendency of the mind to go constantly picking things up and putting things down inhibits engagement. The improviser should be operating out of courage and trust. Supporting the early decision as far as possible. However, to return to the anxious improviser referred to earlier, if that person's mind is solely preoccupied with judgement, then that judgement can't be ignored. So best for that improviser to go with it, and accept it. As Rudstrom advises, *'Alright, here comes this "judgement" – say hello to it – then use it as material.'*

BOLD CHOICES

This argument about being positive indicates a strong case for the dramatic improviser to make a *bold choice* at the top of any scene. If this is made on the back of a reaction, then that reaction is given clarity, purpose and forcefulness. The improviser has committed to something – it almost doesn't matter what – and that choice transmits to the audience the idea that there is something at stake here. Something matters. If the improviser is on stage alone, then the reaction has to come from engaging with the space. But that's no less a case for making a strong start. To hesitate around it, to do the equivalent of making a mark on the blackboard and then crossing it out, simply signals indecisiveness and lack of confidence to the audience.

A strong start also does something else crucial: it makes the possibility of later dramatic shifts more likely. This is particularly the case when there are two or more improvisers on stage. Let's take an example. If two performers walk on stage, look at each other, then move rapidly around the space constantly with fast, dynamic movements, this sets up a fierce, energetic pattern. Any sudden alteration of that pattern will create an impact, a sharp bend in the road. If, for example, they suddenly drop to the floor and become almost still, it creates a terrific effect. Maybe they don't even 'know' what they're doing – it doesn't matter. They're doing something and in time we'll find out whether or not it has some defined meaning. The initial offer or idea – fast movement – has been developed sufficiently that it's a shock to suddenly leave it behind. This is a shift: a break with the past. The movers have given themselves something to *move on from*. If they'd just come in and wandered about aimlessly, hoping that something would turn up ('Throw something at me – I'm great at reacting'), they would be in a less strong position to make a shift. It's something you see frequently both in workshops and on the stage, this dilatory vacillation:

> *A single male actor enters, picks up a hairbrush, makes a face, puts it down again. He looks out of the window, waves to someone. Actor sits down and looks at newspaper. Puts down newspaper, goes to the edge of the stage, calls to second player offstage. 'How are you getting on in there?' 'I'm fine.' (Because the other player is also afraid of committing to anything.) 'Where were you?' 'I was mucking out the pigs.' (That's something defined.) 'I'm glad I didn't have to do that.' Comes back. Picks up the newspaper again. And so on . . .*

Mick Napier and colleagues at the Annoyance Theatre have made something of an issue out of this business of starting scenes boldly: *'As an individual when you start a scene, it's about whether or not you create a point-of-view for yourself, a character for yourself, an emotional base or whatever the fuck that thing is, if you create that for yourself it creates a roadmap for the rest of the scene . . . For me, improvisation's mainly about that.'*[30] As Yat Malmgren famously used to observe to his students at the Drama Centre, *'Nothing comes from nothing.'* Now of course some improvisers rightly point out that something can come from nothing if you make the 'nothing' the 'something' that is sought. In other words, rather than avoid the sense of there being nothing there, and looking around and so on, you externalise the sensation of 'having nothing' – and hence it becomes something.

But let's go back to the idea of the strong start, a reaction to something within or around you that will give the journey a beginning. If the improviser is sharing the stage with other improvisers, there may be a temptation to avoid a strong choice. It might be the fear of 'boxing in' your colleague to a particular idea that makes the improviser hesitate. 'I'd bet-

> 'All thoughts about structure and emotional content become inadequate to the task of improvising once the first note has been sounded.'
> Eddie Prévost

ter not be too strong because that will take away my partner's choice.' In fact, your partner may be only too grateful that you've narrowed the field a little. It's true in music as in drama. If someone starts strongly, probably the others will be happy. 'OK, we're in the key of B flat, I can go with that.' 'OK, that's a four-three rhythm, I can go with that.' 'Oh, we're meeting in a mortuary, I can go with that.' 'Oh, we're singing in B flat in a mortuary, I can go with that.' By stopping ourselves over-protecting others on stage, we set up something interesting. Napier in his book argues clearly the importance of not acquiescing to a phoney kindness towards others: *At the top of an improv scene, in the very beginning, take care of yourself first. That's right, be very selfish at the top of your scene. Do something, anything for yourself first. You'll have plenty of time to "support your partner" later . . . I only feel supported by my partners if they make a move, if they do something. If they just stand there and look at me thinking about supporting me, I am absolutely unsupported. The more powerful a choice they make, the more I am supported.'[31]

This also connects with what is sometimes referred to as the point-of-view of the character. Or I might call it the stance. It's about the way the performer playing a character looks at the world in that moment. What is the attitude towards the surrounding space? Contemptuous? Proud? Excited? The stance embodies both the drive (motivation) of the character as well as the world-view. It has a certain energy that won't be dropped whatever you throw at it.

A: I love this place! I want to buy this place.

B: *You're trespassing.*

A: Great! So you have rules about strangers being here. I like that!

B: *No, I'm just a big guy who likes threatening people.*

A: When I buy this place I'm going to employ you.

B: *You can't buy me, buddy. I'm my own guy.*

A: That's the spirit. Unconquerable. Now we're going to play a game. I'm going to put down money here and when it gets to the sum you like, you're going to tell me who owns this place and what their weak spot is. (*Gets out wallet.*)

In this example, a strong positive stance helped the improviser drive through a scene that the colleague is threatening to halt in its tracks. Matt Elwell of Comedy Sportz might describe such a trajectory as 'achieving full extension'. He argues that the task of the improviser is to extend as fully as possible the material that is present. As Napier describes, there is a great temptation for improvisers to bale out on these early decisions. As soon as a conflict starts to build or some new information intrudes, an anxiety about conflict starts to play in the mind, and the improviser gives in unnecessarily. Doubtless this will be way too quick for the audience, who were just appreciating the contest.

A: I love this place! I want to buy this place.

B: *You're trespassing.*

A: OK, take it easy . . . I'll be going in a minute.

I think this has to do with a latent fear of violence. There's an anxiety that conflict situations can't be explored. They'll end in violence and we're improvising here, for Christ's sake. Anything could happen. People might get hurt. Perhaps there's an unconscious association between vulnerability and aggression. 'If I am seen as aggressive, I may become vulnerable. Or you may.' There's also the legacy of Johnstone-itis, a false belief that good improvisers always and only say 'yes' to things. Which means 'Do you want to fight?' only has one answer. In this corruption of Johnstone's approach the idea of 'acceptance' is taken literally. It's taken to mean that you have to say 'yes' to everything and not argue, otherwise you're breaking a fundamental 'rule.' It's hog-wash and turns improvisers into performers who can't handle conflict. Should any improvised scene develop to violence, then so be it. There are a thousand ways to express that violence gesturally, symbolically or representationally. Improvisation training should encourage learning about inventiveness so situations such as these can be negotiated with ingenuity. The audience doesn't mind any kind of technique employed in the moment; slow motion, punching the air, sudden jumps of time. What they do want to see is the performers going for something and making that something work. If the performers are comfortable with each other and there's complicity, they will find a way to explore the conflict in the scene. After all, it's likely that within that conflict the real secrets of the relationship will come to the surface.

So the important thing is to respect your first decision and hold to it long enough for any shift to come about organically rather than out of a felt sense that you need to shift because things might turn ugly later. Having said that, the opposite is probably also true . . .

THE GROOVE

Once the journey has begun, the improviser is looking for that current under the surface, waiting for the undertow or force of possession discussed earlier, to take hold. When it comes, it's not dissimilar to what musicians refer to as 'the groove'. *Among all the challenges a group faces, one that is extremely subtle yet fundamental to its travels, is a feature of group interaction that requires the negotiation of a shared sense of the beat, known, in its most successful realisation, as striking a groove. Incorporating the connotations of stability, intensity, and swing, the groove provides the basis for everything to come together in complete accord. "When you get into that groove," Charli Persip explains, "you ride right on down that groove with no strain and no pain – you can't lay back or go forward." That's why they call it a groove. It's where the beat is, and we're always trying to find that.'*[32] The notion of the groove may be useful to dramatic improvisers if one considers who in the jazz band is most expected to contribute to the creation of the groove. *'Although potentially involving all band members, the groove depends especially on the rhythm section's precise coordination, the relationship between drummer and the bass player usually being the most critical.'*[33] So what would be the equivalent in dramatic improvisation? Who would provide the rhythm? I'd have to say that the closest equivalent might be the improviser who is generating either a definition of what's happening, or bringing some emotional clarity to the situation. It's the improviser who is saying implicitly, 'This is what's happening here. We're interrogating this prisoner / trying to escape from this castle / doing a folk dance from an imaginary culture / phoning each other on stage.' It's the individual who's creating a momentum in the scene around which others can gather. This has to do with role, and the different roles that improvisers can adopt with each other. If two or three people are all providing an equivalent momentum, the same job is being repeated unnecessarily. So there's possibly an unrecognised and unhelpful conflict, just as if two members of Roadside Assistance were both trying to sit in the same driving seat of the stopped car. Once the groove is happening, then other improvisers need to get behind it, in a way that's complementary. If this happens, then someone else repeats the interrogative questions / sees imagined windows or doors / dances alongside / responds to the phone call. If someone else is providing a counterpoint, then that player is saying, 'This prisoner is innocent, let her go' / 'I like

it here in this castle – why try to escape?' / 'All folk dancing is reaction-
ary and counter-revolutionary.' / 'My phone's run out of juice . . . '

To be *not* in the groove is very clear: that's when all the voices are
going simultaneously: 'Let the prisoner go!' / 'She's already con-
fessed!' or maybe 'I want to be the prisoner – tie me up!' Anyone who's
ever improvised will probably recognise this situation. There's argument and competition over where the groove is, and offers to redefine
it are ignored. We also know what it's like when the groove falls away
or someone gives up on it, and there opens out just a big empty space
for everyone to fall into. The more experienced and courageous
improviser will at that point see this merely as an opportunity to create
a new rhythm or a new idea, just as the jazz musician will quickly lay
something else down for others to get involved with. So there's a new
rhythm in charge. The question is then, who'll have the courage to abandon the old one?

In solo improvisation, immersion in the material comes in a
different way, through locking into a groove *within oneself.* This means
finding a stance, an emotional lock-in that subdues judgement and
triggers creativity. As Sten Rudstrom says, *'If it's cranking, then I'm
riding it, there's less of me making the choices.'* What characterises this
state is responsiveness. The improviser is looking for something to respond to, something that triggers the imagination and in turn creates
emotional engagement. When it's happening, the solo improviser
becomes like a detective who's hunting down some quarry. What's at
the end of the search isn't so important, it's the evolution and articu-
lacy of the chase that's important. The trigger could be anything. In
my own solo improvisations, some discovered narrative ideas that
helped me to find a groove were:

- The interview of a hit and run driver

- A British soldier trying to flush out an Iraqi sniper

- A girl on a beach waiting for a whale to get landed

- The doorman at the Ritz speculating on those who passed through

- A man returning from hospital with another man's arms sewn on
  him

- An old woman waiting for an invisible bus

All of these were created in the moment rather than as pre-prepared material. But this is a personal list. The characters and incidents worked on that day, they might not work on another. But the need to identify the equivalent of a groove is always there. Jonathan Kay is an English improviser who has performed solo for years and runs extraordinary workshops for those who want to 'bring more of themselves into the world'. His work centres on the notion of each individual having within them a 'fool' whose emergence both liberates and entertains. Kay posits the existence of a 'fourth dimension' within improvisation that in some ways might be an equivalent of the groove, or even a place the improviser is lifted into by the groove (ultimate grooviness?), a place where narrative, character and literalness of circumstance is left behind. You've done the hard work, you've found the engagement, now you get the chance to play within this archetypal dimension. It's a place where the improviser feels the decisions are being made by a higher intelligence. It's as if the performer has gone through that 'gap' referred to in discussions about journey. Once through the gap, you're in another world where narrative is a lesser concern. There you get spoken to by the imagination and there's no arguing back.

PRESENT TENSE

The improviser's journey in performance takes place in time and is defined by time passing. Yet it involves a different attitude towards *how* time passes. There's not the same sense of time passing as you'd experience going to the shops. If the sense of time feels exactly the same as when you go to the shops, then there's something missing. On stage there is the chance to project yourself into theatre time. There, the hands of the clock are liable to stop altogether, whizz around at seven times the speed or maybe even go for a walk off the clock face. In this theatre time, it's only what's happening right now that's important. The future can take care of itself. Performing with this mindset really is very different. Instead of thinking, 'What shall I do next?', the improviser should be asking, 'What is happening right now?' It's not that easy. The reason is, the mind has learned to habitually operate under 'What shall I do next?' It's been taught that 'What's happening?' is inadequate. Foregoing concern for the future is dangerous. Standing in the middle of the road asking, 'What's happening?' might bring the answer, 'You're about to be run over.' Safety would be sacrificed. Especially when the individual feels under threat, careful planning is essential. If there's a fire in the house, planning the next few minutes is imperative. But in improvising, you really don't want to worry about the future, you want to be living entirely moment-to-moment because it's in that spontaneous present that self-discovery is possible and creativity lives. In that present you are more open to receive signals, intuitions and impulses that would otherwise be relegated by the mind to the status of unnecessary, trivial and slightly dangerous irrelevances.

This phrase 'being in the present' is perhaps unhelpful because we're surely all 'in the present' already. So what's the fuss? Like a lot of impro terminology, it's a bit lame. Perhaps it's best explained through metaphor or analogy. An example might be 'The driver of a car is driving in the dark. Only she's driving backwards with the lights on. But she doesn't look ahead. She only looks behind. So she's looking at the road driven over, but not the road to come.' Ruth Zaporah puts it well by talking about the flow of time within the improvisational event. Someone who is constantly looking ahead will inevitably see time as segmented; the past, the present and the future. It exists in packages. The effective improviser experiences it differently. She writes: '*An improviser follows action as it unfolds, each moment leading to the next within the intent of the improvisation. If I intend a movement improvisation confined to a chair, for example, I follow moments of action while adhering to that intention. The intention acts on the material that surfaces, and vice versa. The intention sets limits on the improvisation. It closes doors, insisting that the improviser search the others that are possibly less obvious, less predictable. What constitutes a moment? What is the form or structure? What is the content, story or meaning? This, of course, is determined by the improviser's perceptions. Action Theatre improvisers, contact improvisers, jazz vocalists, painters and poets all view moments differently because they have different priorities. But, there is an essential condition that is common to all moments – one unfolds into the next: there is no stopping. Actions take place within a flow, a continuum – a stream of movement and stillness, sound and silence – each moment a response to the moment before.*'[34]

Being 'in the present' is a definable yet elusive skill. It can be learned but it's hard to learn because describing it doesn't take the student much closer to an understanding. It's a state best experienced. In many ways being in the present involves a *suspension* of something more than it does an *application* of something. It involves the conscious suspension of these habitual, planning mechanisms. These everyday mental processes we've learned are of course completely vital when crossing the road, but here they're not useful. This is because they involve both *judgement* and *anticipation*, two of the activities which are most inclined to prevent the improviser feeling and responding with openness. By consciously suspending them, the improviser starts to feel adrift. It's uncomfortable and a little disconcerting, but it's a more creative state of mind. 'Do less' is a popular injunction from improvisation teachers, meaning don't engage too much with activity, so that sense of being adrift is allowed to be felt. But like all these teaching injunctions, it has its limitations and can be misused. The difficulty lies, especially for beginners, in identifying what to do less of. I know a charming improviser who likes to start most improvisations by finding a chair, sitting on it, and waiting. For him, it's about doing less. For us, it's about being an unimaginative pain in the ass.

This emphasis on being in the present can't however be taken as an invitation or pretext to avoid an uncertain future. It's not about the improviser *avoiding* something. It's about allowing momentum to take hold. Keith Johnstone has written about this issue of avoidance: *'If great clowns get into a car it will go somewhere. Even if it shakes itself to pieces it will at least have driven around the circus ring a few times before it explodes. But if beginners (or badly trained improvisers) pretend to get into a car some saboteur will say "There's no gas in the tank", or "This car only goes in reverse!" or "We'd better look at the map first!", or "I've left the keys in the house", or "I forgot to tell you – I took the wheels off yesterday!" Even if the car manages to "drive forwards" it'll run over a pedestrian, or get a puncture, or the road will divide and they'll argue about whether to go right or left – anything rather than travel to a destination. Beginners see such behaviour as "being funny", but I see them as protecting themselves from a future in which they might be altered. It's easier to "drive away" than to invent reasons for not driving away, but moving into the future implies the possibility of change. But beginners experience "being changed" while they're being stared at as weakness, as a loss of control. So they conspire to have nothing happen.'*[35] So to enhance this notion of being 'in the present', it can be stated further that it's about a willingness to experience what is happening right now that *includes* allowing oneself to be compelled by the momentum of the present, into an uncertain future.

MEDITATION

Meditation practice offers one way in to an understanding of this altered sense of time. Ansuman Biswas works across the art form spectrum. He studied with Keith Johnstone before going on to do a University Drama degree. It was in a period of dissatisfaction with his academic studies that he got involved in meditation, and found it a useful way in to spontaneous performance. He also took up drumming and Indian music. *'I got into vipassana meditation practice at that time. It was at a pretty low point in my life when I was really confused about everything. So I was working on music . . . and doing this meditation practice. And those two things combined have become the foundation for all my work.'* While being involved in a range of art forms, Ansuman chose music as his primary concern because *'There was something essential about it. It occurs in every human culture and even non-human culture, arguably. It's there in the fabric – of the stuff in the universe. There's something musical there. So I thought, maybe this is what I should be concentrating on.'* And when Ansuman started to meditate, he got a sense that *'this is very clearly the root science of something I'd had an intimation of in music. This meditation practice just went down to the nub of the matter, of how consciousness can be used.'* So combining the meditation practice with the music training, he had then *'a combination of technical skills and guilelessness – two important things that go together. At the simple level, one of the things that meditation gives is the training of oneself to concentrate. And to be focused. And being focused and concentrated, these are transferable skills. Wherever you apply it, it's going to have its benefits. Meditation is a widely applicable root training. It's a bit like laser light. You can do what you want with laser. You can cut metal, you can read a CD, you can light something. You can point to a graph. There are all sorts of applications. But the basic thing is, you're making light waves all point in the same direction. The same kind of thing happens in the mind: you're just training yourself to . . . sharpen the point of the mind so other things drop away. Other distractions get less and less. So the object you're looking at gets brighter and brighter.'* Ansuman argues that this heightened ability has appropriateness for improvising performers working in almost any artistic medium.

Nor is it simply about being able to concentrate better. *'There are other things. It's also about seeing the wider picture. As well as focusing, another skill is to take the attention through the body. To be aware of sensations as they crop up in the body – without reacting. You just acknowledge. So you get this very wide picture of what's really happening – without imagining it. And you're not buffeted by the picture because you also train yourself not to be desperately unhappy when something unpleasant happens or euphoric when something great happens. That is incredibly useful when you're performing. Because you have a very wide awareness of what is happening around you – and at the same time, it just is – nothing is particularly a disaster . . . And at the same time, it just is. Nothing is particularly a disaster . . .*

And then you can choose to respond to what is happening in whatever way is appropriate. You can be more efficient with energy and therefore you have more choices in improvisation.'

Biswas identifies Keith Johnstone as an influence in his approach and it's worth remembering in this context how Johnstone's path was itself informed by his own rejection of teachers who told him above all to 'reject and discriminate'. It was this rejection of pedagogical orthodoxy that led him to develop a range of exercises that liberated actors from the constraints of accessing 'acceptable' material.

> 'If you listen to soap operas on the radio, you'll notice that the conversations are almost never in the present. Characters constantly discuss either something that happened in the past or something that may happen in the future. The effect of this is to lull the listener into a kind of oozy comfortableness in which nothing is felt to be at stake.'
>
> Sandy Van Torquil

Sten Rudstrom's approach to this question of time incorporates recognition of the importance of seeking out the *unfamiliar*. Particularly as a solo improviser, he argues that the *familiar* tends to close down creativity and invites repetition. The unfamiliar kickstarts the imagination and gets the engine turning over. Everything then is as much a surprise to the improviser as it is to the audience. The improviser is more truly living 'in the present'. He told me, *'I'm trying to work with the unfamiliar as much as possible. I'm trying to keep the mind in the unfamiliar as much as it can be. The mind is constantly seeking the familiar – in a story or in a movement quality. I don't know why. It may be genetically part of our survival structure, there's fear built into our survival so, "Let's get out of the unknown, pin it down and name it", and then there's less fear.'* To follow this path involves a constant struggle in getting away from familiar fault lines that perhaps have been used in training situations. Can nothing then be repeated? Is the task of the improviser always about avoiding repetition? What of those situations and themes that keep coming back into the mind? *'There are two schools of thought about repetition. There are probably more. One is, if something keeps coming back, you haven't gone into it deep enough. The other school of thought is, if this thing keeps coming back, then stop doing it. Now if you are in a place that's constantly seeking the unfamiliar, and something repeats, and you investigate it for something that you do not recognise, then it's not a repeat. You're just finding a new thing in it. Do an inventory. What's happening in your mind, what's happening in your body, what's happening in your system? You're going to notice something that's different. Then you're able to craft.'*

So when you're improvising, are you therefore involved in a process of selection? *'Very much so. The whole process about improvisation for me is the difference between reaction and response. Reaction means no choice, response means choice.'* These comments echo the earlier discussion about *reacting* to stimuli in the space, and finding a *response* out of that. It points up something else about the notion of presence. That is, to be spontaneously engaged does not mean that choice or selection is not involved. The limitation of the narrow idea of spontaneity, that it's just about externalising what you feel, becomes apparent once the improviser is aware of several things happening simultaneously. As soon as that level of awareness is reached, it's no longer possible to just externalise the prevailing impulse. You have to get involved in decision-making. Del Close, the influential teacher at ImprovOlympic used to observe that it's your third idea – not your first – that is maybe the one to go with. Of course there's an implicit danger that this process of selection becomes intellectual, which would take one away from engaging with the present. So practice becomes necessary, allowing these decisions to become increasingly intuitive. The improviser 'sees' or 'feels' the options – makes a decision – then immediately 'sees another' set of options. It's like looking into a kaleidoscope. One small turn and immediately the coloured beads create a completely different configuration. The point is not to be dazzled by the new configuration but have the courage to re-evaluate.

SHIFTING

Within any journey, narrative tension and narrative development are paramount. If the story of an imaginary book goes: the journeyman sets off, walks along the road, arrives at his destination, sits down in the cottage, puts his feet up and has a cup of tea, it won't win prizes for surprises. As a play it won't draw audiences, as an improvisation it will leave us puzzled. It's not the journey that counts; it's what happens along the way. As Keith Johnstone says, *'The nature of drama is: something alters.'* To state this is a truism, but finding the narrative shifts organically is one of the biggest challenges. Boal's distinction between quantitative change (increasing pressure but essentially doing the same thing) and qualitative change (doing something radically different) is useful, but Ruth Zaporah's definitions are perhaps more precise. Sten Rudstrom outlined to me how change is conceptualised within the Action Theatre methodology: *'It's all about change: shift, transform and develop. But if you look at it anthropologically, it would have to be develop, transform or shift. Develop is: "I'm doing something and I continue to do it." Develop is as if a photograph is getting clearer, the longer you're there. It gets more detailed. Transform is: "I'm doing something, and it slowly changes into something else." So it's no longer developing in the same pool of colours, but it's transforming from one pool and going into another pool. You can see each step of the process. And Shift is "I'm doing something, then I'm doing something else." '*

Using pure movement, these terms are relatively easy to define:

- DEVELOPMENT would involve the performer stretching out the hand to point at something. She would keep pointing, each time finding more detail. As a result, kinaesthetic understandings would start to resonate. Through repetition, the meaning would start to crystallise and the action would achieve more precision. It would gain a certain charge. It would radiate more. Essentially, however, it's the same action.

- TRANSFORMATION might involve the performer slowly extending the hand further, shifting balance, leaning forwards when pointing and starting to make a circle with the arm.

- SHIFT would involve the performer stopping the pointing then starting to do a completely different action such as hopping or waving.

So to demonstrate this physically is relatively straightforward. But when working with character and narrative, things become trickier. Signals become more ambiguous and more numerous.

For the solo improviser, shifts and transformations are easier to achieve because there is no one else to negotiate with. For the ensemble, there are signals coming at each member of it very fast, multiplied by the numbers on stage. It requires awareness on the part of all present to register each other's shifts and transformations. Often what happens is, an offer to shift is made but is misunderstood by other players. As a result, it's ignored. Then one of the players who did the ignoring makes an offer of a new shift – and now she's ignored because the others are confused – or else the player who makes the initial offer blocks the new one out of spite. What is central to recognise is the need for shifts to emerge organically, that is, accompanied by a sense of inevitability. Improvisers often seek change intellectually and fail to experience the sensations kinaesthetically. When I recounted some of the difficulties I'd experienced working with a group on finding shifts, Sten Rudstrom's answer to my question, 'How do you get people acknowledging each other's shifts and transformations?' was simple: *'Practice, practice, practice, practice, practice, practice, practice.'*

In the face of these difficulties, some companies take the responsibility out of the actors' hands and impose a score that has its shifts predetermined. For example, the improvisation might be built around the defined stages of a pre-existing story. So that each section in the narrative generates a different scene. Following George Lucas, popularisation of Joseph Campbell's work on world mythology, some companies got interested in developing their own version of Skywalker et al. They used the idea of a mythic journey as written up in Campbell's *The Hero Has a Thousand Faces* to build a narrative template that would be interpreted differently each night. Fluxx did this when performing *The Call* in Atlanta in 2004. The US impro group Sheila created *Instant Odyssey* consciously based on the same twelve-step sequence. Kozlowski outlined how it was done in his book on *Chicago Improv*: *'In adapting the structure for an improvised two-act play, the group* [Sheila] *was able to use the concepts behind these beats in building an improvised piece. While they would not necessarily follow the mythic steps to the letter, it created a foundation around which they could create.'*[36] So there's a scene in which the main character 'gets the call but declines it', later there's a 'mentor' scene, a 'testing' scene, a 'road back' scene and so on. In this case, the *score* for the performance does the work of determining where the shifts are going to occur. For example, when the call to adventure, having been initially refused by the hero, is finally accepted, there's a shift. We've seen it in a hundred detective films. The retired detective is coaxed out of retirement for one last case. In the scene he stops saying 'No' and finally says 'Yes'. The improvisers know at that point, when the hero changes his or her mind and agrees to go on the mission, that's a shift.

Sheila's *Instant Odyssey* would be described as an improvisation with a 'closed score'. By contrast, an 'open score' would have no decisions made in advance about narrative. Improvisers have to make decisions about when shifts take place. Made too quickly, the shift has no meaning. Made too slowly, the performance feels stuck. The audience needs and expects development. At some level, they know that one function of performance is the demonstration of the human ability to adapt to circumstances. As a key skill in the task of survival, it has to be up there amongst the most important. So they want to see a demonstration of adaptation on the stage. They want to see the performer changed – by the space, by other performers, by the audience, by accidents, by what happens. The notion of develop/transform/shift offers a methodological template that makes the task of mapping narrative developments more manageable. There's more to be said on this in the chapters on Ensemble and Structure below.

ACCIDENTS

What happens in a shift is that the performer is knocked away from a prior trajectory. For example, the journeyman sets off on his journey then falls down a bear pit. This deflection could be the result of a dramatic development like a pit being dug. But it can also arrive through an unanticipated accident or misunderstanding. Improvisers, by contrast with colleagues working with a written script, welcome accidents. Or they should do. The slip-up may generate the shift that was otherwise elusive. The night I saw *Jerry Springer – The Opera*, there was a technical hitch. The whole show stopped. One of the actors told a shaggy dog story. Sometimes a toilet flushing offstage generates the material. Or the wrong character is introduced. Or the wrong word is said. Perhaps there is even something in the score designed deliberately to encourage mistakes, for example an impossible or unreasonable task. In Improbable's 2004 show *The Hanging Man*, copying tasks were set for one of the performers that left her deliberately struggling to keep up. She got a round of applause on the night I went. Or you set performers at odds with each other so there are deliberate collisions and misunderstandings. Wendy Houston works a lot with this idea of interfering with the performer's preferred activities so there ceases to be a clear distinction between 'the intended' and 'the accidental'. *'I get very tired of people expressing themselves, being original . . . having an interest in your own experience over and above what you're giving to the audience. I like it when people are sidetracked on to another activity . . . I like it when people have their head covered, or are blindfolded, staggering about . . . I give them words to respond to, telling them to follow the rhythm of the word, be obvious. Or one person interviewing another person and someone in the corner, feeding them suggestions. It's about going outside your own choices, not being wilful, but accepting other kinds of suggestions – that's for me what it's about.'*

There are also deliberate subversions by actors of each other, which can have a similar effect. At a recent performance of *Animo*, Improbable's improvisation format using acting and puppets, Guy Dartnell started an improvisation about a temple by remarking on the splendour of it. (A large piece of bendy piping indicated the arch of the temple.) *'Shall we go in?'* he asked Phelim McDermott, pointing. *'We are in,'* Phelim replied. *'That's the way out.'* This deliberate subversion of the acknowledged practice of accepting everything the other improviser creates, makes a small shift and immediately gives Dartnell something to work with; in this case, his 'stupidity' at misunderstanding where the door was. McDermott had played a hand of 'breaking the impro rules'. Now Dartnell has a character idea to work with, he's a stupid Guy. Phelim and Guy remind me a little of Pete and Dud, with Dud/Guy usually landed with the role of being bullied/picked on by Phelim/Pete. I remember much further back, Jim Sweeney and Steve Steen as the Wee Wees asked by the audience to do a sketch about the Chancellor of the Exchequer at the barbers. Jim started by miming a razor being sharpened. 'Welcome, Chancellor . . . ' said Steve.

Accidents and deliberate subversions help to cause shifts in the journey because they induce feeling states. They knock the improviser off balance and if she or he can accept the dislodgement, that shift may create the content of the scene. The accident becomes incorporated and welcomed as much as any deliberate offer. For the remainder of the temple scene, Dartnell will need a bit of extra help understanding some basic things.

Performing in this way, 'mistakes' as such, cease to exist. It's not dissimilar within music practice. Stephen Nachmanovitch writes: *A "mistake" on the violin: I have been playing some pattern: 1, 2, 3, 6; 1, 2, 3, 6. Suddenly I make a slip and play 1, 2, 3, 7, 6. It doesn't matter to me at the time whether I've broken a rule or not: what matters is what I do in the next tenth of a second. I can adopt the traditional attitude, treating what I have done as a mistake: don't do it again, hope it doesn't happen again, and in the meantime, feel guilty. Or I can repeat it, amplify it, develop it further until it becomes a new pattern. Or beyond that I can drop neither the old pattern nor the new one but discover the unforeseen context that includes both of them.'*[37] Freud asserted that accidents, unconscious puns, mistakes, slips of the tongue or 'parapraxes' can illuminate our unconscious. They take us into a deeper relationship with the material, something that is closer to the undertow. Accidents and mistakes are to the experienced improviser material that can set up a line of exploration likely to be revealing, funny and telling. The transparency of the improvisational aspect of the exercise is highlighted. The audience enjoys the joke that is clearly to some extent *on the improviser.*

Alternatively, something happens in the space that needs to be incorporated. The audience have heard the crash of a door somewhere in the building, or the shrill scream of a child outside. Something falls off the wall. There's an implicit challenge to the improviser: make what you can of that. Recently I was improvising a scene as a British soldier, trying to flush out an Iraqi rebel soldier from a house. I'd already established he was upstairs and I was downstairs. Suddenly everyone in the space heard this toilet flush upstairs in the floor above the theatre space. I was blessed. Clearly, the Iraqi sniper was shitting himself . . .

STRONG DECISIONS

The improviser's journey is aided similarly by strong rather than weak decisions, not just at the beginning but throughout the performance. If a strong decision is made on the back of a mistake or subversion, it carries momentum. I was always perplexed by the distinction between strong and weak decisions until I realised that strong decisions were those that created an uncomfortable and uncertain future but nevertheless honoured the past.

STRONG DECISIONS

- Explore complementarities
- Explore contrasts
- Put the maker of that decision at risk rather than others
- Are vivid rather than pale
- Point to something below the surface, a subtext
- Help to define roles
- Advance the narrative (maybe)
- Enlarge or extend the existing material

WEAK DECISIONS

- Repeat something already sufficiently established
- Forgo change for safety
- Put others at risk unhelpfully
- Stay on the surface
- Fill time without using it
- Muddy a sense of your role
- Ask questions to fill time

Strong decisions also advertise a relationship to the structure. They show an awareness of where its pillars are, either by building more pillars or playing around them. And it's very likely in the relationship between structure and journey that the mercurial inspiration for the improviser is to be found.

SOLOING

Solo improvisation presents unique challenges. There's no one there to create offers for you, and no one to take the focus when you die of shame and misery because your brain is suddenly poleaxed. 'You're very brave' is the comment I heard most frequently when I embarked on a series of solo performances, having never done anything remotely similar before. I didn't know what they were referring to at that point. I did later. A while before the first show, I discovered a new psychological condition: pre-traumatic stress syndrome. Nor did the sheer immobilising terror weaken in its intensity as the season of performances continued. I had hoped for some kind of blasé insouciance to become part of my weather armoury, as a result of battle hardening. No, the only reassurance I could clutch at, was the belief – of dubious integrity – that despair was in some way a necessary precondition for a good show. What was almost worse was the comments I received from friends after any show. 'That was really brave,' they said. Clearly they'd forgotten the unspoken but established tradition that compliments after a performance should represent a substantial heightening of those offered before.

Beyond its unique collection of terrors, the soloist, not unlike a man who keeps dangerous dogs in his backyard for fun, can nevertheless have a good time on stage, and not necessarily at the expense of the audience. An early point to be made, and it's not an unobvious one, is about the infinite degree of freedom the form offers. There are no collaborators to whom the improviser need defer. But this freedom is a snare to the beginner. *'Freedom is a very frightening proposition,'* Simon Fell observed to me talking about music, but he might well have spoken of solo dramatic impro. If you've spent years becoming familiar with the wide-open spaces of the solo stage, as Sten Rudstrom and Julyen Hamilton have, to name just two, it holds fewer terrors. But others arriving to it may prefer initially to navigate those spaces with something like a map and compass. 'Something like' is probably an idea about structure. To break the time down into sections and work to create fragments was one of my first notions that proved valuable. As the season progressed, it became easier to enlarge the duration of each section and to play with the connectedness between sections. (I also cheated hugely by inviting guests to play in the spaces between the sections, relying on musicians and dancers who were themselves comfortable with solo performance.)

> 'Always work at the top of your intelligence . . . Try to skip your first impulse to respond, and move on to the next, less obvious one. This is contrary to most academic advice that the first thought is the best one. It just isn't. Sometimes, it's the third thing you think of.'
>
> Del Close

After a while, I could start to appreciate the freedom. Clearly an advantage to the solo improviser is having a vocabulary of expression that is varied. Knowledge and mastery of a range of different modes breaks up the potential sameness that can occur when the event remains within one only. Modes would include:

- STORYTELLING
- COMMENTARY (enacting an image or scene while commenting on it)
- INHABITED SCENE (speaking as the character within the scene)
- MOVEMENT
- ABSTRACT SOUND
- DIALOGUE WITH THE AUDIENCE

It's also possible to mix or segue between different modes. Shifting from one to another can enhance a narrative shift that takes place simultaneously. The great advantage is you need never negotiate over shifts of either mode or content with other performers, thereby increasing the decisiveness of the shift. It's equally possible to develop very much an 'own style' without having to compromise. You get to develop a style full of jump-cuts, allusions, metaphors, conventions and protocols without the burden of teaching them to others or having those others shoot them down. The process of experimentation and selection of successful strategies, and the discarding of the unsuccessful, can furthermore take place within the performance as well as outside.

The downside of the freedom was of course not having collaborators with whom to assess the efficacy of these experiments. After all, reading the eyes and body language of the audience is far harder than reading other performers. You have to learn instead to use not just peripheral vision but also peripheral hearing, sensing and intuiting. The performer needs be mindful that solipsism and indulgence are only a step away. There's a constant need to challenge the evolving practice to ensure that it's not simply comfortable default patterns that make up the journeys of the performances. One way to help this is to get the audience to throw in curveballs either through suggestions, props or other means. Kevin Tomlinson uses a strategy like this in his solo show, *Seven Ages of Man*. Before the show starts, he invites the audience to write down lines of dialogue on small pieces of paper. These are then parked on the stage and used as material by him at different moments, sight unseen. As the character of Old Man, for example, he would recount to another character, memorably played by a tailor's dummy at one point, a story of their previous conversation. 'I remember that time you said to me – ' reaches for scrap of paper with dialogue line – 'My mum was my dad.' The inevitability of non-sequitors is pretty high but the technique shifts Tomlinson's playing so that he's forced to conjure with the consequences. His self-evident confusion creates a warm, empathic relationship with the audience.

In my own solo show I've used a similar convention. I've asked for two members of the audience to secretly steal two props from the props table before we start and then deliver them back one at a time to the stage – during the piece. I made sure not to see what the chosen items were. My task was to incorporate the props as soon as they were delivered. The spectators might either just chuck 'em in at random or wait for a moment when a prop was required. I remember one occasion when I was playing an elderly woman talking to her small niece. I explained to the niece I had a present for her, and asked for the prop. It was so ridiculously apposite. The prop was a doll. Luckily, the doll was battered and smeared with black colouring, permitting a monologue on the struggle of commerce to keep up with commercial opportunities for a mixed-race society. On another occasion it was a pair of swimming goggles when I was talking to my 'mother' about how I wanted to leave him. It became about how my dad – who'd left home himself – used to take me swimming. And then it became about this extraordinary world I discovered underwater.

It's a peculiar thing about props. In a different show, I used a similar technique of asking for two props to be chosen but this time they were kept visible to me. I had then to use them in that scene. To my surprise, what I discovered was that the best way to make a scene in which the props appeared essential and organically linked to the scenic material, was to *ignore* any knowledge I had of them at the outset. In other words, I'd just set off with some mad action or, rather, discovering a situation thoughtlessly. Then some way in, I'd turn back to the prop and decide how it could be incorporated. Now you'd think this would be the wrong way to go about it. You'd think you should take a good look at the prop and build a scene around that. But that way never worked. One time I was given a plastic bird. I started walking and jumping, then waving. It appeared I was waving to a friend who was high on a cliff. How to use the bird? I picked it up. It then became clear. I started demonstrating to my friend that this bird had knocked me off the cliff. And then died as a result of its encounter with my head.

So the later I looked to incorporate, the better. 'Leave your decisions as late as possible' is an adage proved correct in this case. Perhaps this is what they meant when they talked about bravery. Because you do have to trust to some deity to believe that you will come up with something. I remember developing one scene as a lion tamer. I think he was working in a Victorian circus. I spent a long time subduing the lion, played by my guest in the show, the dancer Rick Nodine. Finally he was subdued. I picked up the prop. It was some kind of bendy piping. All I could think to do was shake it over the lion. Then of course the lion revived. The second prop in the same scene was a trumpet and the use of that became valedictory.

Solo work lends itself to crossover practice, to the crossover between dance and theatre or between abstraction and naturalism. The performance with the dancer Rick Nodine assisted this because we each pulled each other away from comfortable, separate art-form safety zones. In such cases, the vocabulary can slip between narrative, image, commentary and movement. With this switching going on, the soloist can move between playing a character *in* an inhabited scene, and story telling *about* the events of that scene. In this way you get different perspectives on the material.

Solo work invariably foregrounds the personality of the soloist. Seeing other performers' solo shows during the Shifti Improvisation Festival in 2006, I could see this borne out. Andy Eninger's *Sybil* format has become rightly legendary within impro circles in the US. It is very much character-based, working outwards from a simple idea to create four central characters whose lives later connect. There are no props as such although objects are mimed. Kevin Tomlinson's *Seven Ages of Man* moves through those ages with a central character for every section, each with a costume and a setting that involves props and stage furniture. A number of conventions are used such as that outlined above, and another using a horn and bell to get an audience member onstage to help define how Tomlinson should play a character known to the audience member (this technique is similar to one developed by Keith Johnstone for *Lifegame*). Sten Rudstrom's show existed more in an abstract realm, relying largely on gestural movement in a half-lit space, occasionally breaking into short monologues without any single narrative being more than hinted at. Of course solo improvisation is really not solo at all, it's a journey made with the audience, whether that's three people or three hundred. To see Julyen Hamilton perform during the same festival, with his vocabulary of movement placing him closer to a dance tradition, was to see how the notion of personality becomes a prism for personal revelation. But of course revelation is only possible if the soloist replaces the challenge offered conventionally by other performers with something else; for example, a challenge made to oneself by self-imposed structures, as in Hamilton's performance about imprisonment entitled *Cell*.

Rudstrom and Hamilton both improvise from within what would be clearly identified as a movement-based practice. The same would be said for another soloist, Andrew Morrish who, while known for his extensive use of verbal language, writes *'It may surprise some who have watched me perform, but I experience my content nearly always as movement first, and language second. Language is fantastic for getting rid of thinking, which is getting in the way of my presence and openness – the fundamental level is sensation and especially the sensation of moving.'*[38] Whereas the playwright will inevitably edit out weak material and everything that 'doesn't fit', the improviser's task is different. It's to build from his or her reactions to the event/material, a journey through the performance that acknowledges not just the shifting patterns of emotions but mistakes, digressions and non-sequitors. To make a success of it calls for courage as well as the willingness to appear foolish, mad, and, especially, transparent. It's as true for the member of the ensemble as it is for the soloist. This is not a journey that can be made without a generous attitude. Nor is it an event that lacks significance. It was a point put to me by two improvisers from Chicago, Don Hall and Jennifer Ellison. In the interviews I conducted, I heard no more inspirational contribution:

DON: *'Even if it's an audience of five, these are people that took the money that they earn, and they want to sit down and have you feed them, give them something they don't have. We're at a point in history where personal communication is at an all-time low. You don't really have to get eye contact and communicate with anybody. But when you get that opportunity, and you have a group of people in the audience, fucking take it seriously. And really make it count. Because you might not get another chance.'*

JENNIFER: *'You'll never get that time back. I've run into improvisers and actors who go "I don't care, I'll open myself up, it doesn't bother me." Well, fine. That may be the case. But still treat it with respect, no matter what it is you're doing because minutes and minutes and minutes and hours and days are flowing by. And you will never get that time back. So treat that sacred moment when you're up on stage and speaking to people, with respect. And that doesn't mean it has to have austerity. But have something to say and have a good time saying it, and just communicate. Have communion with your audience.'*

CODA

Two texts on solo improvisation:

A PERSONAL DIARY ENTRY. 7 JULY 2005

'Amidst the bombs and the Olympic result, I did the sixth show last night. I need to put down some reflections on that. Interesting how the audience warmed to a light, gay, free character whose energy was all up. And when I got to the point in the scene when I couldn't put off picking up the prop any longer and picked it up and held it – still not knowing how it would fit – at that moment when I held it, I found out how it would fit. That old adage of leaving (certain kinds of) decisions till the last minute, proved true again (albeit that you have to box yourself into making them). G pointed out afterwards that I sometimes needed to challenge myself and not drift into non-specificity. He also questioned that the space didn't allow sufficient distance between audience and performer, the kind that allowed a more fulfilled trance state (although I'm not sure he used that phrase). I got myself into some difficulty with a three-person scene where none of the characters were really well defined. Three is really too many unless one is just a sketch. Once again, I needed to take longer to sink into a new character rather than propel him or her into a busy drama. The Dad character suffered in this way. Go back to the identity kit for each – mannerism, energy quality, p.o.v., stance. Don't worry about this being boring for the audience; it's worth taking time. The landlady: didn't know where to take her. Need to concentrate on the energy and dynamic of the relationship – take a pitch at it – e.g. there's someone laughing at him (before we know WHO is laughing). In other words, just concentrate on the opposite quality before going anywhere near defining. It could be a ghost laughing or a child, it doesn't have to be someone who would "logically" be there. Third: old woman falling. Maybe could have explored the "falling" a lot more, e.g., falling at breakfast lunch and tea, different time frames – explore that. In other words use a different kind of frame for the scene. "I always fall . . . in the morning . . . etc." The theme becomes stronger throughout: death, war in the family, belief in spirits. Odd, coming just 24 hours before the terrorist attack on London. Was something coming through?'

STEN RUDSTROM

Finally, here is Sten Rudstrom's retrospective account of a short performance he gave in 2004 at Greenwich, London. It's interesting to observe the decision-making process. Note the emphasis on selection of options within the journey rather than simply following 'whatever idea comes'.

'I start the piece. I extend my hand. And I start sensing what's happening in my hand. And there's a mother and daughter, or someone, in the front row, whispering. Explaining the piece. And I'm thinking, "How long is this going to go on?" So that comes as a message. That this could be a pain in the ass. So it could be a judgement. And I do my best to just accept it as a message — there's somebody whispering — and if it's affecting me, it's probably affecting everybody in the audience. So I do my thing, but that information keeps coming back and it keeps coming back. They are still whispering and acoustically sneaking around. I associate of this: I think, this is just like a mouse. So I say "Mouse". [later] *I lay down. Because I know that it's time. It's time for that mouse development to have some different colours. I'm fully content to lay down there on the edge of that light. And stay there. And I get a message that says "You should do something else." And I say to myself, "That's just a message. I can choose to leave it. What I'm doing now is perfectly fine. It's enough." Then the helicopter comes.* [A sound of a helicopter over the building.] *And I know the audience hears the helicopter and the audience knows I hear the helicopter. And I make a choice. It's stupid to pretend the helicopter's not there. That's a choice I make. I could have behaved differently . . . Later, it occurs to me, this is a huge sound. I'm alone. And I make a choice to use that. Then it occurs to me, I'm in a circle of light. Then it occurs to me – here's the mind seeking the familiar – I'm lost on an island.'*

2

THE ENSEMBLE

'Group dancing . . . requires a shared aesthetic and stylistic unity; or some explicit structure and techniques that facilitate intervention and the development of the dance. For example, Kenneth King's use of grids to organise the space within his dances; Richard Bull's choreographic improvisation techniques based on analogous practices in jazz music and a tremendous variety of dance scenarios; Douglas Dunn's combination of set movement sequences with decision-making by the dancers as to when and where in the space each sequence will occur.' Anne Halprin

'Divorced from reality yet reflecting it, communal theatre carries artists and audience together to a level of universal emotional response, then returns them to quotidian reality with a keener sense of the psychic structures shared by all people.' Philip Auslander

'Sometimes people feel good about a performance when all they've done is articulate their own clichés effectively. Whereas the more interesting performances are the ones where the musicians are ill at ease with the situation, and having to work very hard to try and overcome certain obstacles. That's where improvisation is worth its weight in gold.' Simon Fell

THE IDEA

Not a few times I've thought of giving up on this book, as writing about improvisation can appear arrogant or deluded. I'm trying to speak about processes that are essentially non-verbal, so words can feel like clothes for humans hanging on a horse. It's not surprising that most of what can be asserted rightly remains open to challenge. The opposite of any assertion is usually true in some way or other. Trying to lay down protocols for ensemble work is like trying to knit water into a cardigan. This is certainly evident when talking about the relationship of the individual to the ensemble. If you think the key rule is, 'Listen to your colleagues', you should be reminded that Ornette Coleman instructed his band members to ignore each other in pursuit of their improvised musical journeys. The seminal improvising band AMM took a similar path in their early years, preferring the layered sound of musicians playing simultaneously rather than the practiced complementarity of jazz. *'Part of AMM's philosophy, its ethos if you like, is the idea of concurrent commentary: separate voices speaking at the same time, interweaving and interleaving. But each voice is not atomised or individuated. Paradoxically, it may be that individuality can only exist and develop in a collective context.'*[39] It's no different within the shifting, unstructured dance of Contact Improvisation: individuals make connections with others by looking after themselves first. Mick Napier's assertions about the primacy of self in dramatic improvisation strike a similar note. In all these examples, individualism is asserted as a precondition of collectivity.

The argument isn't saying that competitive individuality is the whole story. If everyone were in service to him or herself alone, the result would be cacophony. What I believe it is saying is that individuality can't be sacrificed to the false good that is some pastiche of collective harmony. That true collective practice relies on individualities working in balance. So how do you find that balance? In his book *Shadow and Act*, Ralph Ellison offers this observation. He's writing about jazz but he might be referring to other art forms: *'There is a cruel contradiction implicit in the art form itself. For jazz is an art of individual assertion within and against the group. Each improvised moment (as distinct from the uninspired commercial performance) springs from a contest in which each artist challenges all the rest, each improvisation represents (like the successive canvases of a painter) a definition of his identity: as individual, as member of the collective and as link in the chain of tradition.'* Try as you might, you can never eliminate the element of contest between improvisers; you can only surround it with checks and balances. The impulse to improvise cannot be divorced from the egotistical drive to shine. On the other hand, if you choose to rely too much on checks and balances, drawing out the competitive edge, then you risk blandness and inefficacy. The resulting work is full of good intentions but those good intentions are all we see. When it comes to ensemble, apparently, we're dealing with paradoxes. We're talking about:

- THE IDEAL VERSUS THE REALITY
- THE INDIVIDUAL VERSUS THE GROUP
- THE WHOLE VERSUS THE PART
- THE PERSONALITY VERSUS THE SERVANT
- ESTABLISHMENT OF IDENTIFY VERSUS LOSS OF IDENTITY

But simply arguing that assertions about good ensemble practice cannot ever be made would be an evasion. It's just useful to remember that those that are made may be valuable only in relation to their *context*. It is context that validates or debunks the validity of any assertion about effective practice.

THE IDEAL AND THE REALITY

The argument runs that when a group works, there's a special kind of consciousness that can grow up, a 'group mind' that is capable of fermenting a peculiar and extraordinary creativity. I believe the important word here is 'can'. Let's consider a quote from a well-respected book on improvisation that has no reservations when it comes to rhetoric: *'The ImprovOlympic workshops constantly prove that a group can achieve powers greater than the individual human mind. Scenes created have turned out to be prophetic, and ESP has actually occurred on the stage. Players are able to speak simultaneously, at a normal rate of speech, saying the exact same thing, word for word. Some teams became oracles on stage, answering the great questions of the universe, one word at a time, leaving audiences chilled and astonished.'* The lines come from *Truth in Comedy* by Halpern/Close/Johnson. I don't know whether Del Close was stoned when he wrote it, but as a manifesto it raises the bar pretty high. Perhaps the crucial word in the quotation is 'workshops'. It's true that without the pressure of spectators, improvisers can relax with each other and generate a complicity between themselves behind closed doors, which is not always possible on the main stage. As Phelim McDermott commented to me, you do see amazing stuff in workshops away from the demanding eyes of strangers. But arguably this private work is not the complete exercise. The real test comes when the ensemble operates in a performance situation with all its attendant pressures.

My guess is *Truth in Comedy* is like the Communist Manifesto for comedy improvisers. It sets out an ideal world in which all comedic improvisers would like to live. But if this is an ideal, what's the reality? It's true that his central assertion is a valid one: that within an ensemble, a spirit of creativity can take hold, which informs the behaviours of the ensemble in such a way that they do achieve an unusual level of mutual understanding. It's what is sometimes referred to as the galvanising of a 'group mind'. Each member of the ensemble operates according to the spirit of the group, and appears to make the right decisions every time. Homogenous material is mysteriously created without single authorship being present. Performers feel 'instructed' but not by any offstage authority. But it's impossible for it always to happen like this. Often the same group of people on the same stage make a hash of it. Perhaps this helps to explain why sometimes Show A is all bad and Show B is all good, rather than both shows being a mixture of good and bad. For in Show A the gods were present and paying attention, and in Show B they had other business. OK, such a theory has the benefit of poetic quaintness but doesn't recognise that Graft and Craft are probably the only two gods involved.

A SPIRIT OF UNITY

Before examining ensemble skills, it may be useful to return to the book's first question. Why improvise? Improvisers often coalesce around a determination to put two fingers up to the offered hand of conventional theatre. They want to spit on the over-produced, mass-marketed entertainment that lulls the soul and reinforces the idea that all's well with the world. And why not? It's easier to be against something than for something. It's as brave a project. Besides which, you soon learn what it is you champion through this rejection. If Julian Beck and Judith Malina's contempt for American capitalism had been any less fierce, they would not have led the Living Theatre around the gaols and theatres of the West with so much consistency of purpose. Their anarcho-libertarian drive to chip away at US imperialism lent them an energy that contemporaries who merely espoused love and peace rarely equalled – irrespective of what critics may say about their output. If Nabil Shaban had found opportunities within the established theatre in the UK in the seventies, he would not have founded Graeae as a means for disabled actors to bring their concerns and skills into a public arena.

Similarly, the Shysters Theatre Company in the United Kingdom led by Richard Hayhow has retained consistency of personnel because of the company's clear dedication to finding a way for individuals with special learning needs to make theatre as others could, only differently. These determinations create a coalescing of intentions that makes a group of individuals bond together; necessary if the challenges of survival are to be overcome.

When Second City Chicago performed in the 1960s, the company was driven by the knowledge that their approach was different, it was exciting, and it was putting the boot into traditional comedy. Improvisation was throwing up material that was more contemporary and had a sharper edge than anything else on offer. The onstage chemistry was more authentic – immediacy was the mission. When Sir Edmund Hillary and his Sherpa came to a performance, that night included a mountain-climbing scene. The spirit of a shared mission helped to put fire into the company. On this side of the Atlantic, the free improvisation music pioneers, such as AMM and SME, set out to reject entirely prevailing notions about the necessity of following jazz templates. They wanted to go further than Coleman and Coltrane and consciously debunk the idea that free jazz was the current avant-garde. Following a time-honoured jazz tradition of deliberately inverting established rules, Cornelius Cardew, Keith Rowe, Derek Bailey and John Stevens set out to orchestrate soundscapes that resisted familiar harmonic patterns, rhythmic clichés and any known compositional structures.

There are other examples of acts of defiance that if strung together would form a paper chain representing the history of live performance. Pity the artist that has no enemy to conquer. She can practise forever, but where are the smiling edifices of vanity to be blown up? As capitalism becomes more adept at enfranchising and ameliorating cultural discontent, artists have to be increasingly fast on their feet to avoid incorporation into the status quo. Once you've been punk'd, before long you'll be *Punk'd*. The resistance of improvisers to be absorbed into product-led consumerism can only help to consistently rekindle the abrasive spirit of a collective, rather than an individual, artistic vision.

CONTINUITY OF PERSONNEL

'What is an improviser? A craftsman? An ensemble player? A versatile unit of production, able to shift into any task? It's clear that Western consumer culture prefers the latter, and encourages it. Transferability is the keynote skill, a willingness to perform in any commercial context according to demand. Product placement. Skill transferability. If you can improvise a tune, ad lib lines for a TV advertisement ... dance in the chorus of a video ... you're an improviser, we want you.'

Sandy Van Torquil

Ensemble practice tends to benefit from continuity of personnel. However, the commercial arts culture of Western capitalism finds the task of promoting individuals a more convenient exercise than that of promoting theatre or dance companies. It's far easier to identify a leader of a group, and fixate on that individual, rather than give equivalent media time to the vision of the entire ensemble. The corollary of this is that there are pressures on the individual artist to define him or herself in that same way. There are pressures experienced from drama school onward, encouraging the individual to perceive herself or himself as an individual entity primarily, who should owe no long-term loyalty to any ensemble. The individual performer is encouraged to think of her or his career first. This is the touchstone of survival within the market: there are no meaningful loyalties except to the self. So the performer is implicitly or explicitly encouraged to do everything from advertisements on television to West End musicals, from understudy work to experimental fringe theatre (protective agent allowing) if it advances the prominence of the individual's name. Inevitably this culture inhibits and atrophies ensemble practice. It's one reason why Peter Brook left the UK for Paris, Keith Johnstone left for Canada and Footsbarn left for Europe. It's why ensembles struggle constantly to hang on to their actors.

Additionally, UK arts funding tends to put pressure on theatre companies in such a way as to militate against the maintenance of ensembles. This situation has prevailed for years, although since the demise of Thatcherism, the Arts Council of England has increased the range of those companies to whom it has granted Regularly Funded

Organisation status. Complicite, Forced Entertainment and Improbable, amongst others, have in different ways benefited from a shift towards the recognition that maintenance of ensembles has to be a funding priority. While Complicite tend to work more as a production company since the period when Marcello Magni, Jos Houben and Simon McBurney were the performers, Forced Entertainment for their part have maintained a consistency of personnel that derives significantly from their forming the company straight out of Exeter University.

Forced Entertainment also gives the lie to the notion that performance training in the UK is entirely weighted against the ensemble idea. Tim Etchells: *'When we started, Impact* [Theatre Co-operative] *was the main influence. They were what we had seen as students. While we were at Exeter we were already a group . . . and we did three or four projects there. The big thing on the course was studio practice. So we did a lot of improvising, a lot of trying things out.'* The practice of maintaining the same ensemble of six has allowed a development of a consistent artistic vision, often not apparent in companies where the Artistic Director changes as the years roll by. Improvisation has been a central part of FE's practice, more usually in the devising work but additionally within long-form, durational pieces such as *Quizoola!* and *12 a.m. and Looking Down.* Improbable have maintained comparable consistency with a smaller group of key players; Phelim McDermott, Julian Crouch and Lee Simpson. The Comedy Store Players have retained the same core personnel since inception: Paul Merton, Neil Mullarkey, Jim Sweeney and others clearly don't find each other's company so awkward that they can't keep coming back. Their work at the Comedy Store, tied into the commercial comedy circuit, and their part-time status, relieve the group of a need for funding. AMM would probably be the stand-out example of a music improvisation ensemble in the UK with longevity. It started life in 1966 and at the time I interviewed founder Eddie Prévost, who was still going in a roughly similar line-up, bar the sad death of Cornelius Cardew. However, at the time of the interview in 2004, Prévost was himself musing about the group's possible termination. When I quizzed him about the secret of their longevity, his answer was simple: *'We didn't play very much.'*

The advantage of consistency is it makes the risk-taking process much less fearful. Quite simply, people know each other better. There is less anxiety over appearing foolish. Company members have already seen you naked, stupid and lost for words. They've seen you destroy improvisations for all kinds of reasons, none of them creditable. They've seen you make demands of others that you failed to fulfil yourself. They have seen you fall over when you should have danced and danced when you should have fallen over. They have seen you succeed but learned afterwards that you cheated. They've seen you improvise well, badly and appallingly badly. Understanding has followed. As a result of all this, you survive. You absorb an understanding of each other's tendencies, predilections, defaults and possibilities. You learn to make offers or provocations knowing how your offers will resonate with others. When I saw T.J. Jagadowski and Dave Pasquesi perform in Chicago, two performers long familiar with each other, they started by staring hard at each other from a close distance. One of them said 'Breathe'. The other breathed out. 'Cake?' said the first. And they were away.

Dance ensembles working together over years internalise each other's weights, heights, and movement patterns. With this knowledge performers can deliberately strategise to take advantage of others' strengths. Against another partner this particular move may be dull or overly passive, but with this dancer, it's going to trigger something vital. Actors can likewise explore conflicts between each other with more intensity and passion with less fear of reproach or misunderstanding. They can take risks with more confidence, knowing the leap won't be ridiculed. Consistency of personnel, assuming the personnel in question retain respect and affection for each other, can be a passport to more engaged, subtle and precise improvisations.

But consistency of personnel has its downsides also. Mark Sutton is a performer with the Annoyance Theatre and Bassprov. I asked him about this issue. *'I think it can be a blessing and a curse. I think that if you're with someone you know and there's nothing you're gonna do that's* not *going to be supported and is* not *going to be "gone along with" then that's a good thing. As long as you don't fall into the same patterns all the time. One of the big challenges of our show* [Bassprov with Mark and Joe Bill], *is to continually break our own patterns. And I think we've been pretty successful in doing that, in that a lot of our show has to do with debate, and so there are times, for example, for two or three shows in a row when I find myself taking the conservative side against his more liberal side, so the next show I make sure that I speak something extremely liberal and force him the other way'.* But Sutton also makes the point that while consistency of personnel does give you these reassurances, *'I also love being on stage with people that I've never been on stage with – because you never know what's coming. And it adds a whole new element of excitement to the show.'* Sutton argues for a balance between familiar and unfamiliar faces. Currently within Chicago there is far more crossing over of performers between companies than there used to be, following an earlier period when Second City, Annoyance, and ImprovOlympic faced off against each other in friendly but earnest turf wars. Continuity of personnel can lead to an artistic stasis where the group just grows stale. John Wright told me he found that his time with Trestle Theatre Company naturally came to an end because the group was resistant to taking in new members. *'It was a closed group that consumed itself in the end.'* If the ensemble doesn't take on new members, it can start to merely recycle the old ideas. Things become predictable. Each improviser simply triggers the others' defaults, because those are comfortable patterns. It's like the Festival jazz band who've been playing together for years and who tick all the boxes in a way that makes the audience idly wonder, 'Is there anything progressive about this jazz any more?' One way to avoid the problems of either a fixed ensemble or a constantly changing line-up is perhaps the establishment of something in between.

The idea of a 'fluid ensemble' echoes what the guitarist Derek Bailey's Company aimed to achieve. He's quoted his own programme notes for a concert: *'For some time it has seemed to me that the most interesting results in free improvisation come from semi-ad-hoc groupings of musicians. There is a growing pool of musicians, in England and in other countries, who work together regularly but not continuously and not on the basis of being members of a set, permanent group. It is this type of ensemble, not fixed in personnel or style . . . that now offers, I believe, the greatest possibilities to be found in free improvisation. Company's structure, such as it is, is based on the idea of the repertory theatre company; a pool of players out of which groupings might be drawn for specific occasions and performances.'*[40] One advantage of this company structure is that performers get pulled into new areas without losing their core identity. When Christine Jeffrey joined Bailey's outfit for a period, Evan Parker described her contribution to the group (himself, Hugh Davies, Jamie Muir, Derek Bailey) by saying *'Christine's effect was, through a combination of trance and whimsy, peculiarly her own at that time. To incorporate her range of expression required that we broaden the emotional continuum of the music considerably.'*[41]

GROUP COMPOSITION / S

Liverpool Improvisation Collective is a group of four women who practise, train and dance together whenever possible. Listening back to the tape of our conversation, I'm reminded of the importance of being inspired by those you're working with. Jo Blowers articulated this in respect of the different histories each performer would bring, intimating an important aspect of ensemble work – that the ensemble is less about imposing some uniform methodology (although there are successful examples of this) but finding a style, a way of working, a vocabulary that integrates the different styles and passions of the separate performers. After all, each made a different journey to be there. Jo Blowers was talking about how Paula Hampson's work with Julyen Hamilton offered a means to the group to expand and enrich its style: *'I'd got really intrigued by what would happen if all four us were in the space and we kept working as a collective, and knowing that one person is actually imprinting a methodology or a perception.'* But it's not only what an individual performer has learnt and absorbed, it's also what he or she carries as a personal style. *'And then I thought, when I watch Mary* [Prestidge] *doing things and I'm not doing it with her . . . I get very intrigued by what it is that Mary does. It's not about any other artist, although all those other artists are in there. It's exactly the same with Andrea and Paula, I'm really fascinated by what I see as very distinguishably what they're doing.'* This must be a universal feature of ensembles that are happy to work together: when personalities complement each other, something extraordinary can occur. As Derek Bailey comments about the improvising band Joseph Holbrooke, *'Amongst the many things enjoyed by that group was the productive contrast between the musical personalities of Gavin Bryars and Tony Oxley. Bryars had a somewhat ambivalent attitude towards the group then, never sure if he should be there at all, but knowing, I think, that it suited his musical position at that time (he subsequently became a composer). Combined as it was with a certain natural anarchic tendency it contrasted sharply with Oxley's direct, totally committed stance. This kind of juxtaposition has the effect of producing a continuous, slight, musical friction which is, I think, very productive in an improvising group.'*

As long as personalities find each other usefully provocative and a stimulus to growth, then it's presumably easier to overcome what may be personality differences. Peculiarly, individuals who are close friends don't automatically work together so well as improvisers, as do two others who are less friends than colleagues. This could lead to a 'Why did the Beatles (or any other group) break up?' discussion. Arguably the personalities involved found that the benefits of collaboration ceased to outweigh the problem of social friction. In other words, George got fed up with Paul's pedantry and bossiness, and John got fed up with . . . Paul's pedantry and bossiness. I guess the Beatles were pretty good for a while at bringing each other down to earth. After all, it was a height to come down from.

In an ensemble, if you're working with a big agenda, you need a survival strategy that encompasses a talent for problem solving. Phelim McDermott and his colleagues in Improbable claim to be very good at ensemble building but I can't tell you their secret. However, they do place an emphasis on getting the group working together well offstage, rather than worrying solely about what they will do on it. They proceed from the idea that if the group is working well offstage, the show will take care of itself – even if it isn't ready. This was born out in New York when the company was presenting *Lifegame*. Lee Simpson: *'I think that . . . if there's a problem, an unspoken "thing" in a group of people, that that is what you have to deal with. It doesn't matter where you're at . . . We cancelled the dress rehearsal before our New York debut, this off-Broadway run of* Lifegame *– because there was a problem in the group. The producers were downstairs waiting for a dress rehearsal and we just didn't do it – it sounds like we all get together and love each other – it's actually more about letting it out. Because that's where the gold is as well – in the problems. In what's unspoken. We'll be so close to shows going on and there's someone in the corner having a cry because we're dealing with something or something has to come out. We've learnt that you can't ignore that stuff.'* Phelim McDermott: *'Well, if you ignore it, it goes on stage . . . and it's invisible but the audience feel it. It's like something that they feel that hasn't been dealt with. Or is waiting to be dealt with. And the audience feel strange because they feel it's their responsibility to deal with it.'*[42]

Any discussion about ensemble has also to reckon with the issue of different challenges at different stages of growth. They are clearly different at the beginning, when you have seemingly unlimited freedom. As you go on, and audiences perhaps get to know you, they have expectations. So those audiences arrive expecting that ensemble to continue the narrative of that company in ways that are familiar. Phelim McDermott: *'When you start out you can invent the rules, because*

*you don't know what you're doing. And then you start to tell a story, which
is the story of your own company. And that initial work gets created as if
during your teenage years . . . Even if you're twenty-eight when you form
the company, there's a sort of story then about "How do you grow up as a
company?" And I think a lot of companies don't keep going, or don't know
how to go through the puberty, or how to become an adult . . . It's the whole
thing of how do you stay spontaneous and irreverent, and playful, when
you've got responsibility – as an adult?'* (www.improbable.co.uk)

Growing up inevitably means changing, experimenting. Consistency of personnel may help the growth. It may also lead to some kind of house style. This can be both an advantage and potentially a dead weight: an advantage if the style and root ideas are sufficiently flexible to allow company development, a weight if it isn't. Chicago has many improvisation companies, and the extent of agreement over conventions within the city is very striking. Many companies within it share similarities in house style. Most of the prevailing conventions in improvisation were forged in the early days of Second City when an accessible, comedic style emerged from a process of combining sketch work with Viola Spolin's theatre games. Conventions taken for granted within the comedic impro tradition include the use of mime, the absence of set, the emphasis on ensemble, the predominance of the short scene, a quest for laughs, the avoidance of costume and, too, the absence of black faces in the cast. This has to stand as a significant failing within a profession that prides itself on its multi-culturalism. After all, the ensemble idea is rooted in an understanding about inclusiveness. Any ensemble building a relationship with its audience needs to be able to reflect that audience back to itself. Mark Sutton comments: '[The impro scene in Chicago] *is pretty white. In ten years of Annoyance Theatre we've had one Afro-American . . . Second City has been trying hard to find performers of colour.'* And he adds: *'If you're a black performer, there's no need to stay in Chicago.'* It's not that there aren't black performers excelling within theatre improvisation, but there aren't many doing it. Companies such as Oui Be Negroes exist, but they are in a minority. Perhaps current practice in the form of the house style is failing to bring in improvisers from the black community because at the beginning, the roots of that style were embedded too well into a certain kind of white culture. After all, the original style was rooted in entertainment that took place in white neighbourhoods and white bars. Maybe that has become more of a weight than an advantage. Maybe that culture has proved insufficiently flexible and malleable to attract individuals outside the constituency of white, predominantly male improvisers. In the UK, the situation is not radically different, albeit the impro scene is one thousandth of the size. Since the shift of gear that took place in the late eighties, black and ethnic minority performers with good improvisational skills have been able to find work perhaps more easily than their white counterparts. This is a reversal of custom and practice over previous periods when black actors were marginalised and their appearance on main stages or television was rare. But those who survived the discrimination along with those just arriving, have found better opportunities commercially. The new work opportunities have tempted them away from long-term involvement in the ensembles.

BUILDING AN ENSEMBLE FROM SCRATCH

It's time to look at how artists and director have gone about creating ensembles. Deborah Paige is a director familiar with the more common practice of working with actors who are an ensemble only for a few weeks or months. There's an immediate challenge of bringing everyone into the same project. Her tactic is sometimes to start offstage. *'One of the reasons I use techniques of exploration, I would say, rather than improvisation, is to try and find an ensemble way in which you are all working in the same world. And given that everyone brings a different imagination to it – and the exciting thing is the combustion points between everyone's imaginations – then what I'm concerned with is making sure our imaginations are all happening within the same field . . . In some ways I'll do things to get that company working physically and mentally, to shortcut the process of working as an ensemble. And that might just be – going for a walk. I will do anything to try and avoid the traditional rehearsal period where you sit down and do a read-through on day one.'* Working on a production of *Blue Remembered Hills* by Dennis Potter, written for adult actors to play the parts of children, *'The bulk of the day was given over to finding out what it was to be six years old. The first read-through wasn't a read-through; it was an action-play-through in the Forest of Dean. That was our first meeting. I got the actors together and got them to devise games for the other actors to play. So they were doing it themselves – not as a character but as themselves . . . I do believe that if you've got your casting right, what everyone brings as themselves is what you want.'* Paige acknowledges that *'not everything will be useful to everyone'* but works from the presupposition that this common experience of improvised play creates a shared pool of understandings.

Phelim McDermott has observed that beginning an ensemble has very much to do with the forging of identity. This approach has some echoes of Paige's. He's looking for a spirit of unity through developing the identity of the group, something that encapsulates the personalities involved and stamps a uniqueness formed from that encapsulation. *'The way that I work and try and help people with their creativity, whatever the environment is – a six-week rehearsal period, a four-week workshop – is to create the myth of that group. And the improvisation and the games for me are ways of making a sort of world, which is their world, our world, which supports and makes the rules of the games clear. Now sometimes those games might be very specific. On the first day this might be a trust game. You get up and lead people around with their eyes shut. But also there are lots of games which come from the edges of the group, which start with in-jokes in the coffee break, jokes about the group, which may be important ways of helping that group be creative.'*

John Wright started his professional life co-founding and directing Trestle Theatre Company in the '80s. He now works with Told by an Idiot, but alongside that project, he jumps around the world creating other productions. John has always placed great emphasis on the use of play and masks to facilitate an ensemble spirit. *'I define different aspects of impro. And if I'm training actors or building an ensemble, it goes through a series of different phases. For example, I'll start always with play. Just straightforward, unconscious play. Which is a bit like doodling or something. I start with a mask: the innocent mask. There are lots of innocent masks. For example, that monkey mask behind you.* [I'm sitting in John's kitchen and he's pointing at a wooden mask from West Africa hanging on the wall.] *You see the raised eyebrows and the little mouth? This mask is just like a monkey. It knows nothing and it learns nothing. It just discovers things every time. And it has no sense of thought. And you find that mask of the innocent crops up in lots of different cultures . . . It's about not thinking but simply reacting at a sensory level. And at a tactile level. And going from one thing to another to another. So I would set up various games. And the very first starting point is to stop people thinking. Stop people making things up and instead get people to react . . . It's completely mercurial, childlike, although not like a child. It's like being an animal, a monkey in fact. And it releases an animal energy, which we can put into different situations. Unconsciously at first. Then we take it to a conscious level where they do it for an audience. I'm not interested in meaning or structure, but an imaginative flow, which is entirely reactive. The most inane thing in front of you is what you're working with. It's like driving a car and only looking at the bonnet. And that's a pretty big lesson to learn, not trying to work out what you're going to do – just trying to react.'*

There's a journey therefore in building the ensemble from unconscious to conscious play. Arriving at the point where the instinctive qualities remain, but where the actor can start to make choices. This is the same point when the actor can start to work with others. *'This is where complicity comes in. It's the real secret behind everything. It combines Stanislavsky's holy trinity – Concentration, Relaxation, Imagination – terribly important for an actor. Complicity combines all these. Complicity is not a unison; it's a kind of "I think you're in charge" and "You think I'm in charge" . . . You have to watch and you have to feed off each other.'* Wright places this idea of complicity at the heart of ensemble practice. It's the *sine qua non* of collaboration. If achieved, it allows for any degree of absurdity or strangeness or individualistic competitiveness to enter the exercise, without alarm from others on stage.

LEARNING THE SKILLS I

One of the first lessons any ensemble member learns is that he or she is not alone. It sounds obvious but it has some unobvious implications. When you leave your front room in which you improvised an extra-ordinary scene between a goddess and Van Morrison, you find the rehearsal room a different landscape. It's no longer a matter of you and the mirror; the collaboration with others changes everything. Group scenes are hard because of their complexity. The *Commedia* troupes operating in Europe in the seventeenth century rarely did scenes with more than two players, simply because this improvisational complexity compromised the dramatic and comedic purity of the drama. (Interestingly, the novice learned *Commedia* not by training but by watching the seniors in action. After he had watched sufficiently, then he performed himself without rehearsal.) After all, if a solo improviser has essentially one relationship operating – between herself and the audience – then a duet will have three. A group of three on stage will have six, or seven if we include the whole group as an entity. It will have ten potentially if we include the possible duets that might be created within the trio. And we haven't mentioned the lighting operator or a musician.

What are the key skills? Perhaps the first is that cited by improvisers across the art form spectrum as the first, last and foremost: *listening*. Neil Mullarkey, who is a member of Comedy Store Players and an occasional teacher of impro in a range of contexts, put it like this: *'When I first did a workshop for non-actors . . . I had the idea of giving them each a bit of paper with "This is the Secret of Impro" on it. On the paper was written one word. LISTENING. And that is the basis of all the teaching I do. And that's also why I teach impro in a corporate context, in terms of communication . . . Listen to the offers being given you. Instead of thinking ahead "What am I going to do next? (I can't*

> **'Yes, and . . .'**
>
> 'Two actors work together. The first says a line, expressing an idea of what the two might do together. This might be a line like 'Let's have a cup of tea.' The other has to start the second line with 'Yes, and . . .' He might say 'Yes, and then we can put loads of sugar in!' The third line along with every subsequent line have also to start with 'Yes, and' so the dialogue builds to a crescendo as every offer is accepted.

listen to what you're saying to me because I've got to BE GOOD, come up with the RIGHT ANSWER), just listen." I just have five rules, really: Listening, Accepting, Giving Offers, Making Assumptions and Reincorporation.'

Listening in this context is much more than just using the ears. It's about listening, watching and sensing, absorbing as much as possible of what is happening in the space. Another way to describe this activity is 'attending' (to what is happening). Exercises to encourage listening would be those like Keith Johnstone's 'Yes, and . . .' in which every line spoken has to be picked up and developed by the other actor.

The second skill is probably something close to what is known as *accepting*. It's the willingness to act on what you've heard, without entering into disagreement about the value of that invented material. If someone calls you Dad, that's who you are. If someone hands you a book and says it's their life story, that's what it is. If someone says they like you, you're likeable. If someone sees a ghost, that ghost exists whether or not you see it as well. Not arguing with fellow improvisers is the first step towards the complicity discussed earlier, which is really

Creating the World

One player goes into the space and tells the audience who or what he is. For example, he's a coalminer reduced to digging coal from his own garden – unsuccessfully. He takes an appropriate position or starts digging. The second player walks on and declares himself the child of the coalminer, who's playing in his room upstairs. The third says she is the postwoman, a gossip who likes to put it about that this coalminer is mad. And so on. The world might also contain ghosts from the past, moods or even established traditions, embodied.

nothing more than acceptance writ large and felt deeply. To refuse to accept others' creativity or to dispute their choices publicly almost always leads the improvisation towards a cul-de-sac smelling of urine. Playing the game of breaking the rules is one thing, but simply refusing to accept sets improvisers at odds with each other. The result is there's no momentum, no narrative and no discoveries. But when improvisers are accepting each other's ideas, then relationships are formed. Exercises such as Creating the World help to nurture acceptance.

The third skill probably involves understanding how to create *change.* This means creating narrative development or shifts. Given the improviser is now aware of others, able to establish relationships and begin an activity, narrative is the next focus. So it echoes the early discussion about Develop, Transform and Shift. Let's imagine the improviser is in a location. It's a clothes shop, for example, holding a mirror up so another character can try on clothes. But this activity can't carry on forever, at some point it needs to transform or shift. The point about change is it needs to emerge out of inevitability. Too often improvisers change for the sake of change, rather than staying with an activity and allowing it to develop its own momentum that will force itself on the improvisers.

- The location is a clothes shop. The male character is trying on clothes while the female character watches. The relationship is defined as brother and sister.

- The mirror-holder might deepen the relationship between the two, defining it more accurately. For example, the sister starts to articulate resentments over the brother's success in television. (DEVELOP)

- Alternatively, the sister might become increasingly playful, moving the mirror around and turning the scene into a baiting game. (TRANSFORM)

- Or the sister might put down the mirror and pick up the clothes and start putting them on herself. The brother then sits down and gloomily offers to pay for her new outfit. (SHIFT)

Keith Johnstone proposes an exercise called 'What Comes Next' to develop understanding about narrative development. Keith Johnstone also suggests that the exercise might be developed so that when there are two improvisers on stage, the men in the audience control the man, and the women control the woman. He adds that a good guideline is, *'The moment your story wipes out, scrap it and start another.'* At an early stage of development, just allowing scenes and stories to die naturally may be useful. Improvisation relies more on lying back than driving through. "Trying hard' is not what it's about, it's not the same as finding momentum. Effort can be turned back into play, but in the early stages of learning ensemble craft, it may be better to walk away from dramatic activity in which no one feels inspired.

'What Comes Next?'
'The hero says, "What comes next?" and is told what to do. Improvisers should return to this game like body-builders to their weights. In its "classical" form only one player is onstage. "Make no decisions for yourself," I say. "Just ask, "What comes next?" and then do what we tell you. If the scene is boring, blame us.'

Keith Johnstone,
Impro for Storytellers

The early improviser tends to separate out feelings and sensations into those that are appropriate for expression, and those he or she believes should be hidden. It's useful for the director or teacher, if this is happening, to encourage awareness and articulation of that process because part of the learning lies in hiding less and less, and showing more and more. And of course the struggle to elucidate or bring to the surface, awkward thoughts and feelings, may assist any scene. Fear and anxiety about self-revelation often causes arguments between performers unfamiliar with the challenges. So another early lesson, perhaps the fourth skill, is about working with *conflict*. In conflict, the body grips and binds itself. If you can 'play' conflict however, then the body remains relaxed, so the improvisers are more 'open' and less worried about 'where the piece is going'. Conflict between the *actors*, in early ensemble training, needs probably to become the conflict between the *characters*. (Another way to untangle ensemble conflict or confusion is to establish a convention in which the performers break off briefly to speak to each other as actors. 'Sorry, why are we having this argument?' Or 'Sorry, I thought we were on a beach.' 'No, we're in an insurance office.')

Because there are quite a few potential pitfalls early on, it's good to develop what might be a fifth skill, which is *problem-solving*. It's useful to learn how to disentangle problems at an early stage. If the actor can become familiar with coping with failure, she or he is in a strong position. Therefore exercises that deliberately invite problems, such as 'I've No Idea What's Going On', can be useful.

'I've No Idea What's Going On'
A player goes into the space and deliberately behaves obtusely, without any clear or consistent idea. Probably this is just a series of physical actions that have no apparent logic. Under normal circumstances the second player should wait until something is defined. However, here a second player goes in and also does something peculiar so that neither understands anything of the other. Then a signal is given and without giving up on their separate projects, both start to find connections. The important thing is to talk to each other. 'Are you on a march?' 'No, I'm phoning my friend.' Without abandoning anything that is determined, the players have to come into the same, defined reality. 'Ah ... I've just lent you my phone and I need it back now ...'

A way to start ensemble work is to work in pairs, to minimise the levels of complexity. And to always *view things holistically* if possible, to bear in mind the bigger picture. This might be considered the sixth skill. It helps to dodge backwards and forwards between being a performer and being an audience member. You want to carry that audience wide-frame perceptiveness with you. That way, you're keeping in mind what the piece requires rather than just 'what it would be fun to contribute'. So what does the big picture need? Asking this question immediately starts to define ensemble responsibilities. Can I contribute to that? And once this is done, am I still necessary? In the early days of the ensemble, it might be useful to draw on image work for exercises. This allows a large group to work together without difficulty – and without words. One such exercise would be Composing the Image, an exercise which consistently asks improvisers to think about their contribution to the whole.

> **Composing the Image**
>
> An actor goes onto the stage, takes a position, holds it. Another goes in. The two make a picture. Others get up and join in. Actors can also leave at any time. The options are: to enter the picture, to stay where you are, to leave the picture or to change your position in the picture.

For beginners, it's a difficult stance to maintain – this idea of thinking selflessly. It requires operating on a meta-level, holding two things in balance: your own drive and desire to be self-expressive, along with a sense of the potential of that material being explored. You're not just thinking as an actor but also as a director/spectator. Guy Dartnell argues the value of imagining *'What it's like to witness what you're doing.'*

LEARNING THE SKILLS II

The most important skill of all is the attitude and spirit you bring to the ensemble, which is not a skill in any conventional sense of the word. This attitude underpins everything. It starts to unlock a vocabulary for you as the improviser. Characterising this attitude one might refer to generosity, flexibility and courage. It places you in a position where you can begin to access your own emotions and physicality. This means 'knowing yourself', which in turn means having some insight into your

> 'You can learn all the rules in the world but if they're not done with a feeling attitude of generosity, they're worse than worthless . . . they're criminal.'
> Phelim McDermott

different moods, emotions and boundaries. Without this, enacted characters or stage personas remain limited or one-dimensional. The vocabulary for the actor consists of emotions, articulations, words and physicality. The greater the range, the more scope the improviser has.

It's no different for an improvising musician. As the musician Frank Moon pointed out: *'Vocabulary is the key thing there. If you can only say a few words, you can't really improvise anything of any flexibility. With an instrument, the bigger your vocabulary is and the greater your palette of sounds that you can draw on, this gives you more possibilities, and when you're improvising you need all possibilities open all the time. Because if somebody plays something, and you can hear what should go with it, then you can find exactly what that thing is on the instrument.'* This level of ability is only really achieved by putting in the time with colleagues once the initial predisposition to ensemble work is present. You can never force anyone to improvise. It's a vocational impulse.

Once this shared spirit of willingness to adventure is present, the ensemble is in a stronger position. For in performance, it can't be predicted which feeling states will be required from which performer. If, for example, a performer recognises that her character is 'losing' some struggle, then a willingness on her part to 'be defeated' and explore the feelings of despondency, resentment or self-pity becomes necessary. If on the other hand this same actress is the victor, it may be triumphalism and vindictiveness that's required. To develop a real vocabulary of skills, the group has to train by working on the different skills separately. Training in ensemble work is not unlike training for a football team. You spend an hour on passing, an hour on scoring, another hour on working the ball in the air (I'm bluffing here, I don't know the first thing about football). The practice sessions might also involve putting the performers into situations in which they are encouraged into different roles. One scene generates fear and a sense of impotence, another induces sensations of power or eroticism. You can do this in miniature with an exercise called Clint Eastwood, which is devised really for the benefit of one actor. He is she is endowed differently each time the scene is played. The aim is to accept the endowment and feel the consequences.

In Clint Eastwood, a player comes into a bar in which the other players are already drinking and socialising. The scene consists of the one player walking in and everyone else reacting to him. The scene is run several times. Each time, the group is programmed to react differently. Once they applaud, another time they hide under the tables, a third, they all turn their back and talk loudly to each other.

Another way to provoke different feeling states in different actors is to draw on 'stock' or 'archetypal' relationships. These call for specific behaviours from the actor, explored verbally or non-verbally as a game or as a scene. Actor A plays one role while Actor B plays the complementary role. But these are not completely new skills. We already know something of triumph or defeat, what it is to seduce or be seduced, what it is to rage or cower, what it is to fail. Learning the skills means triggering these feelings in one of many possible ways. Here are some role-partnerships that Fluxx has explored both in training and in performance (a fuller list of archetypal characters is given in the lexicon):

- BULLY-VICTIM (Victim loves the Bully so puts up with the provocations)

- SHINY-TINY (Shiny goes out and shines while Tiny stays home and polishes)

- TRICKSTER-INNOCENT (Innocent is naive, gullible and ripe for exploitation)

- MENTOR-MENTEE (Teacher and devoted follower)

- PROTECTOR-INNOCENT (Protector is always on the watch for Tricksters)

- NARCISSIST-ADMIRER (Admirer is the Narcissist's greatest fan)

- CHAMPION-SIDEKICK (Don Quixote and Sancho in a contemporary setting)

These role-partnerships can be explored through games and exercises. We've often started with non-verbal games to develop patterns of interactions. The Bully will gently provoke the Victim who will absorb the bullying by being affectionate. The Bully might just throw rolled-up bits of paper. It's a baiting exercise. Because the Victim loves or admires the Bully, he or she will put up with it, will turn it all to the good. It's painful to watch. For the Champion-Sidekick, the Champion might rush around the space jumping off tables and chairs while the Sidekick rushes around after, trying to prevent the Champion getting hurt. The Sidekick's job, like Sancho Panza, is to pick up the Champion after any disaster, and if at all possible, put him back together. The Trickster will engage the Innocent in apparently innocent play. This might be embodied as a movement game or a game with props. However, there's a secret agenda in place for the Trickster. It's to take advantage of the other's innocence by stealing goods or sexual contact.

Such game-playing also sets up the possibility of natural shifts in the narrative. After the pattern of the initial game has been explored, the scene needs to advance. There are a number of possible ways. The improviser playing the Victim can choose to turn around and confront the Bully. The Innocent can start to become aware of the Trickster's deceits and respond in a new way. The development in the narrative might come slowly as a transformation or quickly as a shift. The Sidekick can choose perhaps to make a shift, and lose his temper, then sit the Champion down and give him a good talking to. Perhaps the actor has started to feel the moment when his patience has been taxed to a limit. These natural shifts create a pathway for the improvisers to travel down. Once the pathways become familiar then digressions, variations or inversions can be explored.

The great advantage of these role-partnerships is that they create a sense of safety for performers. The problem of the Who is defined very clearly through that relationship, and the What is also implied. In other words, the performer inherits a motivation or a drive with the acquisition of the role: the Champion wants to go on adventures, the Innocent likes to explore sensations, the Narcissist is self-absorbed and Shiny wants to go out and be social. If the ensemble uses these roles in training, it may lead to individuals discovering particular affinity with particular roles, as individuals might do with a mask. This in turn means that specialisms can be developed. After all, an ensemble always has to be something like a cricket team with different players able to offer different skills, operating with a shared vision.

> CLOV: I can't sit!
> HAMM: True. And I can't stand.
> CLOV: So it is.
> HAMM: Every man his specialty.
>
> Samuel Beckett, *Endgame*

But this doesn't mean the imposition of orthodoxy with penalties for thought-crime. It means knowing the particular strengths of individuals without sacrificing role flexibility. After all, it's often the individual playing against type, the dancer who acts or the actor who

dances, that brings the improvisation to life. The argument for flexibility and willingness to take on almost any kind of role on stage, is a
hard one to argue against. Each player needs to be as happy playing a
servant as a king, as happy to sing or perform rope tricks irrespective
of the lack of voice or roping skills. It's back to the question of attitude.
Each performer is required to find versatility within himself, even an
incompetent one.

How to achieve that? Thinking about dance improvisation and also
about mixed-art form work, I talked about this with the dancers Rick
Nodine and Gaby Agis, who have both worked within ESP (Experiments in Spontaneous Performance). I wanted them to help me define
something about this spirit of ensemble, and how it is that the best
ensemble players create a sense of playful collaboration on stage, irrespective of the art form. Rick Nodine argued: *'Some people seem to be
achieve that by . . . not hiding anything. By being completely transparent.
And other people seem to achieve it in a different way. By working very
hard to compose the situation. In a very astute way.'* Gaby Agis: *'You see
others who – when the mistakes happen – they relish it. And that's about
being up for it, brave . . . They don't mind making a fool of themselves. It's
the same in drama in a way. In an ensemble you want different people. You
can't have everybody doing the same thing. Some might be athletic, others
sensuous, others angry. They each bring something different.'*

ROLES WITHIN THE ENSEMBLE I

This notion of roles that different individuals take within an ensemble
is a key element in the uncertain game of longevity (or brevity). If onstage personalities complement each other the company has a greater
chance of sustaining itself. Ringo Starr is no master musician but he
brought something to the group that made it gel. In my earlier book
House of Games I explored how a group can be made stronger if there
are both stable and unstable elements operating within it. They tend to
complement each other. Too much instability and the group implodes.
Too much stability and, like a business that ignores growth in technology, the group doesn't allow itself to be influenced sufficiently by
the world outside. Similarly there needs to be a circulation of energy
within the group whereby different individuals take responsibility for
momentum at different times. If, within an ensemble, individuals get
stuck within certain roles, either at the centre of operations or on the

edge of them, there's a danger those roles become atrophied. Individuals may become disgruntled and leave the group. Those on the edge leave because they feel ignored while those in the centre leave because they feel they have to carry too much responsibility. To diminish the chance of this happening, the circuitry of dialogue needs be kept alive. This way any discontents can be expressed. Dialogue and criticism around the issue of roles can function as a kind of acupuncture.

The roles that personalities play within an ensemble are infinitely complex. However, the efficacy of the ensemble will depend probably on a balance struck between different personality types; between thinkers, dreamers, facilitators, drivers and jokers. There will be a balance of introspective and extrovert characters, allowing the group to function effectively when faced with a range of challenges. There will be a mix of both reckless and conservative instincts to ensure both the bottom line is looked after and also risks are taken to ensure the company's onward progression. There will probably be a balance between leaders and followers. There will probably be some distinction and complementarity between different personality types as for example defined in the Enneagram: Reformer, Helper, Achiever, Individualist, Investigator, Loyalist, Enthusiast, Challenger and Peacemaker. This way, each one brings different talents to the party.

ROLES WITHIN THE ENSEMBLE II

When the group moves to the stage, the roles taken there may mirror the offstage behaviours or they may be quite different. The deferential low-status player in life may suddenly take huge risks on stage. The dynamic organiser may simply like to follow others once the location has been set. The driver may become a follower, the follower a driver, and so on. Whatever the pattern, the ensemble will benefit if there are individuals within it who operate differently as improvisers. One way to define how improvisers differ, is by looking at the elements that individuals instinctively relate to first. My perception is that individuals fall into three broad categories, in terms of how they achieve a 'way in':

● The first group is made up of those who look to engage with the IMAGINATIVE MATERIAL, the images emerging within the physicality or the spoken language. This individual listens for imagery in the words that are spoken, or looks at the composition of the space or at the conjunctions of bodies or props.

- The second group is made up of those who like to involve themselves emotionally, who instinctively search out emotional resonances. This individual finds that if FEELINGS don't engage, the dominant sensations are of boredom or disconnectedness. But once a feeling does stir, then passion and intensity become possible.

- The third group consists of those who find themselves looking for orientation through ACTION, through the 'doing' elements in the scene. This kind of performer likes to get busy on stage. Once active, both the imagination and emotions follow and become engaged.

These different types don't exactly fit the NLP typology discussed later under Teaching, but there are similarities especially in terms of image-based and action-based modalities. By recognising such differences between individuals, teachers can understand why an exercise is hard for one, and easy for another. The student who finds a certain kind of 'way in' will probably find a complementary *role* once there. Who's preferring to drive the action forward? Who's trusting to others to do that? It may be that improvisers are not always conscious of their preferred role, they just do what they do.

There's a model of role-playing developed by Jackie Walduck in relation to music improvisation that offers an interesting typology. She writes, *'Role-taking may exist in any interactive situation as a means of exchange or communication. In other words, people in social situations, characters in plays or improvising musicians can interact through roles they consciously or subconsciously adopt.'*[43] The possibility of the role-playing being unconscious is significant. In a theatre context, a preoccupation with 'character' can mean, for example, that the actor concerned doesn't notice that the 'character' is merely an excuse to play a certain 'role'. For example, an actor *thinks* he is being flirtatious and entertaining in the kind of character he likes to play. But to observers, what he enjoys is being able to break into others' personal space. That's the role he prefers. Or he chooses characters who are 'shy'. This means he can avoid accepting offers from others. There's a dysfunction between what he consciously believes and what he's unconsciously carrying out.

A degree of awareness about roles is an advantage. To determine how to assess roles, Jackie Walduck offers this for music improvisers: *'Roles in musical performances exist simultaneously on different levels. They can exist as player-functional roles (solo, countersolo, background), social roles (leader, follower, supporter) or dramatic roles (protagonist, hero, jester).'* [44] There are clear comparisons with a theatre context. From here, there are going to be social roles: one who leads, one who follows, one who gives support, as indicated earlier. Clearly also there are dramatic roles: master, servant, etc. Less evident but perhaps more critical are the roles that improvisers take in relation to each other while on stage. Walduck defines the seven player-function roles that can operate within music as follows:

- SOLO – should be dramatic and worthy of attention in order to draw focus aurally.

- BACKGROUND – should be solid and continuous, and should allow space for solo parts.

- HECKLE AND PUNCTUATION – starts off new phrases or breaks up sustained notes. Can function as a springboard or lift.

- COUNTERPART – should be complementary, e.g. countersolo or counterbackground

- CONTRAPART – are in their own world; simultaneous yet unrelated.

- BLOCK – is a provocative, interruptive role which somehow manages to disrupt the music. *The most extreme block I ever experienced was when a player began to throw chairs around the rehearsal space.*

The word 'block' carries great weight in theatrical improvisation. Jackie Walduck suggests that the block can either be of aggressive intent as in the chairs example, or as something closer to a counterpart where the block is created to force a contrast or struggle with the prevailing instrumentation. It's exactly the same in dramatic improvisation. It's very possible that what may be perceived as a block is really an invitation to struggle.

If I was to devise an equivalent list of roles available within dramatic improvisation, it might run as follows:

- DRIVER – keeps the action moving forward.

- REACTOR – responds to initiatives made by the Driver. Reactor's motivation is less visible. Could be an ally of the Driver. Could also be called Follower.

- RESISTOR – resists the efforts made by the Driver, causing some kind of conflict.

- CHANGER – the one who makes a journey in the piece, through different attitudes, emotions, or both. Could be simultaneously the Driver as in a hero on a 'quest'.

- WITNESS – who observes and in some way represents or carries the 'world' of the piece. Will maybe comment on the action, as a chorus might do.

- INTERRUPTER – who interrupts for comic or other effect, to break the tension temporarily without fundamentally shifting the balance of power.

Different actors will be naturally suited to playing certain roles more than others. Tony may be a natural Driver while Alice is always comfortable being a Witness. However, *A perfectly interacting ensemble with unchanging, always clearly-defined roles would be about as exciting as taking toast and tea,*[45] Walduck writes, even allowing for the occasional excitement at teatime. Her suggestion that an ability to shift into different functional roles can only strengthen the company, applies equally well in theatre. Training therefore has to be about, not just learning the way that each performer tends to tack, but about how to tack different directions as well. Otherwise improvisations are condemned to a dreadful familiarity.

It's also arguable that there's a prime difference in the ways that men and women improvise. Each adopting different strategies within the work. Rebecca Sohn is an improviser and teacher from Chicago who works with Annoyance Theatre: *'Men tend to be more aggressive onstage, i.e. push their ideas harder, and are more comfortable with the "take" part of "give and take". For women it's the opposite, they tend to be more polite and defer to others.'* It's an observation many teachers and improvisers would recognise. It's the reason why exercises like Freeze Tag are so easily dominated by men because the playing relies on impetuous, decisive, risk-taking behaviour. Women improvisers often prefer a waiting game, more desiring of the authentic, less of the immediate. Training therefore can take these different strengths into account. If necessary, performers can be consciously pushed into working outside their default behaviours. Additionally, a certain willingness to tackle any inherent male bias within the improvisation sub-culture may be useful. But does that mean establishing a culture of protest? Susan Messing, another performer and teacher based in Chicago, has commented, *'Don't fight. Just do it. 'Cos that's what improv is about – doing it. It's not about getting off the stage and saying this system is askew – we're all aware that this system is askew. I'll be the first one to tell you, through watching and action, that this is not an equally balanced system. Comedy in general is a man's sport . . . But as a strong, funny woman, I show that women can do it.'*

LARGER ENSEMBLES

As the size of the ensemble increases, issues of power and authority become more acute. It becomes necessary to get consensus around a clear set of rules or protocols, or to solve the problem another way, perhaps by deferring to a director. The establishment of the director role is a clear way to solve the problem of a larger ensemble. The company Rotazaza use a technique with differently-sized ensembles, that employs a directorial offstage voice. This will be played either discreetly to the actors via headphones as in *RomCom*, or transmitted over speakers. In the latter case, the audience as well as the actors hear the instructions, as in *Five In The Morning*. The entertainment lies in watching the actors cope with the demands. It's a convention that solves the problem of ensemble co-operation by establishing a firm authority offstage that is never challenged by the submissives on it. Arguably, while it solves this problem, it reinstates the director function in a way that's more authoritarian than collaborative, mainstream theatre.

There have been other, different initiatives that wrestle with this problem of the director role. With the development of *Lifegame*, Keith Johnstone established himself as the director of the evening. In *Lifegame* the improvisers sit onstage with a 'guest', perhaps a celebrity of some kind. The format involves this guest being interviewed about his or her life, and the stories told being treated as raw material for scenes and sketches. When he devised and directed it, Johnstone would

'Improvised music is more like a conversation which is neither random nor pre-planned. Generally the fewer the individuals involved in that, the more intimate the conversation and the more it will flow ... Working with a large group: you have a lot of people in the room, many of whom don't know each other, some of whom don't necessarily even share the same vocabulary. If you adopt the normal paradigm of a conversation, what happens is that some people will dominate, some will feel excluded, others will find it hard to contribute. All these problems transfer into the musical situation. But the problem also gives us possibilities.'

Simon Fell

periodically stop the interview and call for a particular anecdote to be performed by the company. This way, Johnstone as director established and maintained the run of the event. But when Improbable Theatre began working on their own version of *Lifegame*, they decided to democratise the role of the director and have any cast member call for a scene. When Johnstone came to see Improbable's version, there was something of a heated argument in the green room after the show. Phelim McDermott had to politely point out that this was their version in which there was no place for a supreme director.

There is another example of a rejection of the director role, albeit within a different art form. One of the more interesting musical experiments of recent years is the London Improvisers Orchestra. This ensemble numbers a considerable number of musicians; it includes: reed players (11), string players (11), pianists (3), percussionists (4), brass players (4), along with various members playing electronics, bamboo pipes, and 'objects'. Simon H. Fell plays double bass in the orchestra, and while he's clearly talking about music, his comments would carry across to theatre. He argues that in larger ensembles, the primary problem is not so much the philosophical differences but the practical issue of the communication between relatively large numbers of people.

Before the orchestra existed, Butch Morris came over to the UK in 1997 with his system of conduction by which one individual stands in front of the orchestra and uses signals to cue particular musical states or developments. These need to be learnt and understood by the players so they know how to respond. It appeared to offer a solution to the problem, one not completely unlike that used by Keith Johnstone. Once the Orchestra went on tour however, however, issues of politics came to the fore. Simon Fell told me, *'I think Butch wanted to work with a chamber orchestra . . . but a lot of the musicians booked for that tour were improvising musicians . . . Some of the players found that a bit difficult – but I think any project like that would tend to be difficult where you're taking a group of people out of one routine into another way of working. It's bound to create friction and difficulties . . . I found it valid because I was interested in the problem of structuring improvisation . . . others who were less interested in structuring issues found it more difficult.'* Different improvisers expressed different responses to the strategy. Steve Beresford has written: *'One of the things that you can get with this method is rhythmic unison, which you can't ever get with free improvisation. There are definite parts of the musical language, which become dead simple once you've got a conductor. But you can still get this idea of the music as being the product not just of one mind but of all the minds on stage.'*[46]

Nevertheless, when Morris went back to the States after the UK tour, a more English, liberal tradition reasserted itself. Simon Fell: *'We'd done the tour – and one of the things that made it difficult was that Butch's vocabulary had become quite big. He'd increased the number of signs and gestures . . . Apart from anything else it becomes bloody hard to remember them all. But the increasing amount of information also meant that more and more of what the musicians did was under Butch's control . . . So after the tour finished, I got a phone call from Steve Beresford saying there was a plan to reconvene.'* As a result, the group did come together again, but this time the practice shifted. In particular, it shifted away from any idea of a governing figure. *'There's still not any sense of a clear leader. There are people who regularly conduct and certain key figures without whom the whole thing would evaporate, but they would not consider themselves as leaders in the conventional sense . . . One of the things that has happened with the Orchestra is that it's gone from being quite a hierarchical thing where Butch was very much in charge to being probably one of the least hierarchical orchestras that's existed in music. And what we've found is, fewer signs does not mean simpler music. In some ways, almost the opposite.'* Another significant difference between the old and the new ensemble, lies in how the Orchestra deals with *'the acceptance of the unintended'*, with the disparity between what is intended by the conductor and what occurs. *'If you didn't do what Butch Morris intended you to do, that was a mistake and he was sometimes angry. What has evolved with the British group is that if you do something different to what someone intended you to do, that's OK, let's see what it is. There's not the same sense of right and wrong.'* Fell observes that he himself as a conductor often got too caught up in 'what hadn't happened' – when a sign was misunderstood, for example, rather than looking afresh at what had happened. This will strike a chord with those working in dramatic improvisation. Any piece of work becomes a succession of tiny funerals, often very hard to accept. As Fell observes, the price to pay for having all these radical free thinkers in the room was that *'If you ask them to do BLAT, they're not going to do BLAT when they're told, they're probably going to do BLAT roughly when they feel like it.'* For the orchestra then, the final lesson was to reduce the status of the authority and live with the implications. After all, says Fell, *'Butch's approach was improvisation by the Conductor that was realised by the musicians. In that sense, the only person who was free* was *the Conductor.'*

Perhaps this was a case of the social roles (with Morris as director) being found wanting, because they impeded a more fluid exchange of player-functional roles. So what's the secret of ensemble work? It's elusive and resistant to definition. But the implication of the comments of those interviewed suggests that:

- It's good if people like and admire each other as artists
- It's good if there's a level of trust that springs from this
- It's good if the ensemble is finding their own way rather than feeling obliged to a methodology that is not their own
- A sense of discontent is not necessarily a bar to good, collaborative improvisation
- An indifferent playfulness is probably more useful than 'It's Triumph or Disaster Tonight!'
- A shared ideology or worldview does the work of a hundred rehearsals

CODA

The Scratch Orchestra was set up as a vehicle for anti-authoritarian, conceptualist, post-modern ideas. As Stefan Szcelkun writes, '*The inaugural meeting was held on the 1st July 1969 at St Katharine's Dock next to Tower Bridge, then a complex of cheap studio spaces for upcoming artists. The first concert had already been arranged by Victor Schonfield for November in the same year. From then on the Scratch Orchestra took off like a whirlwind. A high level of excitement, commitment and an extraordinary mixture of skills allowed the orchestra to grow quickly and be putting on almost weekly concerts with 40 to 60 participants within a short while . . . Its activities were open to anyone regardless of ability.*' I myself had the experience of joining it briefly, to play an orange tube at the Royal Albert Hall. I was very young, but I do remember the orchestra members being so impressed by my playing that they all stopped while I whirled this fluorescent toy about my head. Or perhaps it was embarrassment rather than enthusiasm? Stefan Szcelkun describes how another gig by the Scratch Orchestra fused politics, conceptualism, dance, music and performance in its quixotic structure, capturing many of the heady and optimistic qualities (for some, read 'hippy madness') of those times:

'*The Richmond Journey concert, on Saturday the 16th May 1970, followed a route through the landscape designed to compose an allegorical uprising. We began by attempting to break the "claustrophobic spell of capitalist normalcy": Richmond High Street was to be disrupted! We would then pay respects to our ancestors before climbing up through the residential district – recruiting deadened office workers. Our growing ranks would proceed to the top of the hill, to Richmond Park, to celebrate our connection to nature and reclaim the heights. After a break to eat we would descend through the steep Thames meadows and follow the great river on to our destination – that benign archive of the earth's flora, Kew Gardens.*

The allegory consisted of an image of growth, flowering, seeding and dispersal linked to ideas of political renewal. This was to be realised through a series of movements comparable to those in a symphony, which would explore a sequence of moods and emotions. Each stage of the journey was designed by a different individual to meet the overall plan.

The first stage, to start at 11 a.m., was scored by Psi Ellison and Judith Euren. A study of the High Street had inspired 14 optional instructions including such apparently innocuous things as "either shout or whisper in conversation" or "as a group stand and stare in a shop window – hum automatically". But the final instructions were more radical: "Produce imbalance in Dickins and Jones" and: "Sever Marks and Spencer's with a quick march in chain formation holding hands". The "imbalance" was easily produced by such activity as rolling on the floor, and came to a head when a balloon exploded just as the whole staff had reached a state of near hysteric disorientation. Quite harmless but unbelievably dramatic in its effect. Anyway we escaped this excitement to the next stage, which was choreographed by Bergit Burckhardt.

Behind the Magistrate's Court in Paradise Road was an old graveyard through which was a passage called the Vineyard. Bergit had drawn a sort of double helix spiral as a score with musicians in the inner spiral and "dancers" in the outer spiral. As far as I remember there were about 12 to 16 of us at this time.

The next node of the root map was my own: "Awakening the residential area."

"The graveyard of the living?
make enquiries . . . door to door . . .
knock/ring/tinkle/chime/footsteps/
quavers/faces/voices/slam shut/ road . . ."

This was difficult to realise as it threatened to fragment the group, although it worked on a conceptual level. The next stage was a release from the tensions of confronting the city as we entered the old landscape of Richmond Park. "Eating Rites" from the Scratch publication, "Nature Study Notes" and other pieces, were directed by Daphne Simmonds. A complex score by Michael Chant reflected the concentric rings of tree growth.

After our picnic lunch we descended through the terrace meadows towards the river Thames following instructions by Greg Bright, which demanded: "No conversation . . . Remember 3 or 5 things from the journey and say them at any time . . . 3 or 5 hand-claps." This became very magical as we encountered a large group of Orchestra members waiting for us silently in the steep meadow. We went on to play Greg Bright's light-hearted but intense "Field Spiral". His score suggested: 'As each person joins the spiral they should play on flutes, whistles etc . . . Remembering nursery rhymes." '

Stefan Szcelkun on www.stefan-szczelkun.org.uk

3
THE AUDIENCE

'The audience has gotten to be a homebase for us which allows us the freedom to explore.'
Jerry Garcia

'Playing before an audience is always a compromise.'
Paco Pena

'The audience for improvisation, good or bad, active or passive, sympathetic or hostile, has a power that no other audience has. It can affect the creation of that which is being witnessed. And perhaps because of that possibility the audience for improvisation has a degree of intimacy with the music that is not achieved in any other situation.'
Derek Bailey

Mark Long of the People Show clarified very succinctly the role of the audience for me. 'If I get out of bed and walk to the shops and buy a packet of cigarettes, that's life. But if first I find someone and persuade them to stand on the corner of the street and watch me walk along it to buy cigarettes, that's theatre.' The presence of the audience makes theatre possible. It's a truism we know and understand. But who or what are these spectators? Clearly they are ordinary folk – usually – occupying a specific role. But does that change how they behave? How active or passive do they want or need to be, within an improvised theatre? Can they really be changed by watching a show? To what extent does an audience think and feel as one? Should it? Is the relationship between an audience and the performers at an improvised event fundamentally different? How can the performer/s most usefully be changed or informed by the audience? Even after thirty years of meeting audiences – in rooms, theatres, prisons, hospitals and schools – I'm with Derek Bailey when he says 'I've thought about the audience intermittently for years and I know less about audiences now that I did when I first started thinking about them.'[47] Luckily, Peter Brook has also written: 'Today, the question of the audience seems to be the most important and difficult one to *face.*'[48] So there's a respectable group that likes to wobble when asked the big questions. That means I can sidle into another aspect of the enquiry: the standpoint of the questioner. Since this book is concerned primarily with the articulation of practice through the voices of practitioners, their viewpoint has to be considered early. In approaching the problem this way, we can take into account the objectives that performers hold for themselves when meeting audiences, and consider.

Inevitably, there is no uniform view arising from this community either within or across the art forms. Some musicians including Paco Pena and Viram Jasani (both quoted in Derek Bailey's book on improvisation), while aiming for the best possible music, find that the audience enforces compromise: '*I personally feel that with a lot of Indian musicians it's actually at the time that they practise that their best creative powers come out, because they are really free – they're not worried about an audience sitting there, and this is a time when they really let themselves go – a musician obviously will try to put on his best performance before an audience, but he feels restricted. He's very careful.*'[49] It's true that when improvising amongst friends, the most courageous, shocking and beautiful work can be achieved, for the improvisers are not constrained by notions of 'giving the audience their money's worth'. The result is a greater degree of relaxation. And relaxation is often a key predeterminant of successful work. I've seen improvisations in a workshop context that have taken me closer than anything I've seen on stage to understanding what it is to be human. But this private practice is inevitably open to the charge of being no more than singing in the bathroom. It's not the real deal.

The more popular view – against that of Pena and others – was expressed to me by the dancer K.J. Holmes who said that '*If I'm rehearsing an improvisation, it isn't anything until there's a witness.*' It's a view many would recognise and support. Good improvisers who are comfortable with their structures are drawn out by the presence of an audience. 'The audience teaches you' goes the cliché. The audience takes you to new places, that journey created in part by those tensions brought into the room by the spectators. Arguably this is true even when the audience cannot be seen, because the audience still has a presence within the consciousness of the performer at the time of performance. The model with a webcam in her bedroom can't see her audience but her website tells her they are out there. David Blaine in his glass box above the Thames may be expiring from hunger but he knows the fans surround him. It may even be part of the game that the performer pretends there is no audience. This is the conceit of *Big Brother* performers. They enter a game of pretending there is no audience, while all the time they know every move is witnessed. This facilitates an appearance of privacy that is really a sham. The producers' aim is to reveal something of what private behaviour is. By eliminating privacy, the private may be revealed, it is hoped. The participants – because they've signed up knowing, as they think, what they're getting into – nevertheless know they are performing. And as a result, their behaviour will be altered by this knowledge. They may forget at times, but how much they do forget is very hard to tell. Trying to guess is part of the fun of watching.

THE PERFORMERS CHANGED BY THE AUDIENCE I

How much impact does the audience have on the performer? How much should it have? There is a simplistic view that proper theatre shouldn't involve improvisation at all, that the audience should have its impact minimised. In this view, the actors have their moves 'blocked', they learn their moves and then repeat them exactly at each performance. This view of theatre makes an enemy of improvisation. In it, the audience's role is downplayed. We're closer to an idea that the audience is simply required to admire. After all, why interfere with the work of a great playwright? All you require is a strong hand to enforce the correct interpretation. The actor's job is less to respond to the audience than to follow the dictates set by a director. It's a view encouraged by directors such as Annie Castledine who likes to impose her own view on any production she directs. By her own admission she *'gives the actors very little freedom. But I give them the illusion of freedom. I have very pronounced tastes.'*

Adherents to this model of theatre tend to hold the view that any 'deviation' from what has been rehearsed is like an infestation of mice: it's unwanted and the disposal squad will soon arrive. Perhaps one reason for the prevalence of this idea of performance as a *static* entity is because it's necessary for marketing considerations. Each spectator is encouraged to believe he or she is consuming the same product as Auntie Maud did last week. It's about commodification of a process that actually resists commodification. (This is why when the star turn gets replaced by the understudy, the box-office staff brace themselves for

demands for refunds, as happened when Kevin Spacey quite legitimately left the production of *The Philadelphia Story* at the London Old
Vic in 2005.)

This simple idea of theatre is daily found to be wanting. Directors
and actors know this. The truth is the opposite. Actors performing in
scripted plays find moves, intonations and behaviours consistently
altering as their understanding of the text, and their relationships with
their fellow actors, develop. As the production is repeated nightly, the
interpretation alters. The alterations may be subtle but they do occur.
Besides which, the director customarily leaves an assistant director in
charge who may well relax the rules. One factor in this equation is how
an actor's private enthusiasm and support for a show changes. In a run
over a period of weeks or months, the actor's energies inevitably start
to withdraw or become more economical. I had a friend who played a
major role in *42nd Street* for months on end. He said each night he
brought himself to the edge of the stage for his cue, walked on, and
then operated on remote until the curtain call. During this time he
devised shopping lists and planned visits to relatives within the free
mental space that performing allowed. His lines had ceased to resonate
within him. He'd completely zoned out of the project. When this
happens, the actor's moves may stay the same but his emotional and
intuitive energies clearly alter as the run progresses.

Arguably it's the same in dance. A fixed choreography gives little
freedom to the dancers yet, inevitably, improvised elements creep in.
As the relationship between the dancer and the material evolves, the
moves become more fluid or more exact or less fluid or less exact, as the
performance is repeated. The jump in the air is made a microsecond
earlier or later, while the dancer's moment of stillness is microseconds
longer or shorter each night. The challenge to the choreographer is therefore the same as to the director; not to try and fix everything to the point
of impossibility, but to consciously use improvisation to capitalise on
this mutability of form.

This strategy might be as simple as not blocking any moves at all and
allowing actors to follow their impulses each night, as Improbable and
other companies do. It might involve switching roles at short notice as
Jonathan Kay organised in his *Romeo and Juliet* or WNEP What No
One Else Produces (Chicago) did in their production of *Defend Your
Life*. Apocryphal Theatre did something similar with *The Jesus Guy*,
presented at Camden People's Theatre in 2006. The entire cast learned

the entire text of the performance. Who said which lines was decided spontaneously during the performance. Joan Littlewood was notorious for grabbing an actor's attention just before he went on stage and talking about something quite unconnected, just to throw the actor into a different state of mind. Littlewood aimed to reconnect the performer to

> 'Over many years and many trials and errors, we learned that sensitivity at every moment to one another and to the audience is more important than the wish for self-expression.'
> Peter Brook

the liveness of the event, provoking a more spontaneous encounter by him with the material.

When spontaneity is wired into the protocols of the performance, the interpretation of any text will always come closer to the personality of the actor and to that individual's internal life. So there's greater ownership of that material. Not only this, but the presence of the audience, and its character on any particular night, will impact on the ensemble more transparently because the actors know they have the freedom to be responsive. The Wooster Group has developed a particular strategy. In *To You, the Birdie!*, despite the text remaining set, provocations were deliberately made to the actors during the performance precisely to prevent the performance becoming too settled. Video was used offstage as a point of focus for the performers in a convention first explored by Richard Foreman's Ontological-Hysteric Theatre. The Wooster Group show bears examination as an example of how a set text can be combined with improvisational elements to prevent creative atrophy, and to set up questions about the nature of what is or ever can be 'set' within performance. Adrian Heathfield explains: *'If you think about how that work is operating, clearly, it is an intensely precise realisation of a score. At the same time, there are spaces for play inside of it. So in* To You, the Birdie!, *the movement patterns of the live actors are copied from video sources that are in the wings of the space. The audience can't necessarily see them* [the video screens]. *Obviously that live copying is in some ways improvisational. The actors know what video material they are going to watch, but they are encouraged to make new decisions each night about how to copy it. What's really interesting from what they say, is that you're working against your habits. You're attempting to keep your performance of those actions live even though you've done it twenty times previously . . . so you're trying to source something afresh and copy it live.*

At the same time there are other procedures going on within the theatrical event, which are very locked down, very pre-planned. So the question arises "What is improvisation in that context?" What's great about that work is it really problematises what we think of as liveness. So it's constantly asking that question, "What is it that is real now?" "What is it that is live now?" 'What is it that is actual now – in this event?"'

THE PERFORMERS CHANGED BY THE AUDIENCE II

Once American comedy troupes started to improvise sketches on stage, a simple technique was employed. This was the tradition – still practised – of asking for audience suggestions. The question would go out, 'Can we have a theme/location/object, please?' The answer given would in some way be used to inform or define the material of the improvisation. In the USA, this tradition goes back to Paul Sills and the Chicago Compass Theatre. In the UK, Keith Johnstone's Theatre Machine occasionally employed the technique. But Johnstone says they only did it *'out of courtesy'*.

The notion of asking for audience suggestions probably has one or more of the following intentions:

- To demonstrate it's genuine improvisation happening here and that what the audience is witnessing is unique

- To knock the performers away from their 'preferred' material

- To allow the performers to chat with the audience and build a relationship of shared status with them

- To generate some givens for the performance that the performers will work around

- By asking for different material at different points in the show, the company have a greater opportunity of creating variety in their material

- To give the audience a sense of ownership in the performance

As indicated, American improvisers have taken to audience suggestion practice rather more than UK groups, and it fits well with American cultural emphasis on brashness and camaraderie. Traditionally, 'ask-fors' are associated with short-form rather than 'long-form' structures, since they lend themselves to a sketch format. However, many long-form shows also utilise them, such as *Bassprov*, discussed later, in which two questions are asked at the top of the show: 'Could we have a social issue, please?' and 'What is something that you could stick your finger in?' after which the duo, Mark Sutton and Joe Bill, do not return to the audience. The tradition of asking the audience for suggestions is now so well established that any complete list of examples would be very long indeed. So here's a short list:

> *'Could you give me please* a location / household object / date / person from history / time in history / pet hate / something that annoys you / a colour / profession / name of a character / form of death / part of the body / element / title of this show / activity / sport / hobby / sexual position / embarrassing moment from your life / psychological characteristic / vice / secret / member of a family / film genre / literary genre / dramatic genre?'

Other examples of making requests to an audience would be the Dutch group Impromptu's tradition of asking for three musical notes, which are then played to give an initial mood for the dramatic exploration. Improbable's *Animo* involves asking for a number, which gives them a page within a thesaurus then another two numbers gives them a word. Black Sheep have developed a show called Fairly Tales for children, in which words taken from the audience are built into stories involving puppets made out of household items. Dad's Garage ask for any kind of philosophical, psychological or medical question to be written down which the company will then answer (or not) with the aid of *Dr Frapples*. Within Fluxx, we have asked for objects from the audience that have been used in the piece (*The Trickster Show*), and invited the audience to select from a set of cards on which the different characters are represented (*La Ronde Improvised*). We've also asked the audience to vote characters into heaven or hell after they've died and been interrogated about their lives (*Heaven and Hell*). There are parallels here with *Defend Your Life* presented by WNEP in Chicago who invite the audience to make a judgement on the life of their recently deceased central character. Stand-up comedians frequently interact with the audience to ask for words, themes or experiences.

So the practice has been widespread. However, it's increasingly seen as limited in scope and problematic. A primary critic of the practice, as

indicated earlier, is Keith Johnstone himself. Over time he's become
suspicious of both the motives and procedures involved, even though
his own Theatresports relies heavily on suggestions from spectators.
Johnstone's argument is that the use of 'ask-fors' pushes the event
towards a cheapening of dramatic material. The nature of challenges
to the actors is restricted. The questions asked by the actors are banal
and therefore invite banal replies. This leads to the material becoming
trivialised and disconnected from ordinary life. Keith argued to me
that despite improvisation being in some ways, *'the art of the obvious'*,
this didn't mean either serenading or sliding into banality. He wants to
see the audience *affirmed* by the improvisation. He doesn't want to see
the suggestions used by the actors as means to establish themselves as
cleverer or more imaginative than the audience. He argued: *'The problem is, what is innate to the person doesn't feel special to them. How can it?
This is also connected with what's in the mind of the audience. I don't go to
the theatre to "be wrong". I don't go to a movie to be proved wrong. I want
to be right almost all of the time. But improvisers who can't understand this
are desperately trying to do something the audience can't have imagined. So
the audience will think they're original. You should do what the audience
expects almost all the time.'*

When I challenged him that this would rule out the element of
surprise, Keith challenged me in return by asking how many times I
wanted to be wrong. Replaying the tape now, I get a sense that he's
referring almost to a Greek sense of theatre, that what he's arguing to
be shown is the *inevitability* of what has been previously intimated
rather than some *unpredictable* but perhaps more 'original' outcome. He's
suggesting that what audiences want is for the inevitability of consequences to be honoured not shirked. If a shark bobs up out of the
water and notices a passive human floating by, then that human should
be attacked. If the shark gets out a novel and starts reading it instead,
this is a betrayal of expectations created. It's a betrayal of our knowledge of the world in favour of cleverness. His argument is that the
practice of audience suggestions set up a pattern of expectation that is
counter-productive to this investigation of human nature. He went on
to say, *'Basing your work on suggestions, I think, is pointless. I don't see
why we do that. I take one or two a night, just out of courtesy. For variety.
I can explain one of the problems if you like. I had this great idea for
improving American improvisation. We can't stop them asking for
suggestions, even if it wrecks scene after scene. For reasons like: they can*

blame it on the suggestion if the scene doesn't work. I thought we could get them to ask for a suggestion "that inspires us". Because who wants the actors doing stuff that doesn't inspire them? But the actors won't do it. And then I realised why. Because if they say, "Yes, we want to do it, it inspires us" their failure is more cataclysmic if they do then fail . . . Instead, they take things that are funny. And if the suggestion is funny, for God's sake don't accept it, because your scene won't be as funny. Besides, who are the experts? Not the guys in the audience trying to fuck up your work . . . Left alone, the audience will push you towards stupidity. Towards comedy. They can't help that. It may not be what they want. The great thing about Maestro, *where the audience give points for every scene, 1-5, is that they'll give a scene that gets a lot of laughs – a One, and there'll be a scene where nobody laughs and they'll give it a Five. And that's a normal audience, not a university audience.'*

At this point in the discussion I quizzed Keith about his own role. I understood his objection to audience suggestions, and his point that they took the actors away from meaningful play.

But wasn't it the case that Theatresports, the competitive impro game format he invented, was all about having a Lot of Noisy Fun? Wasn't that the point?

'No, it wasn't. That was what those bastards did to it. If you go in and whoop it up and scream and go crazy, you can't do anything . . . Everything has to be kind of squalid and boring. You should be able to do everything on a stage that you want to do. You should be able to challenge the group to make a scene that makes the audience weep.'

'And doesn't maybe even have a single laugh in it?'

'Sure . . . Now they have rules for what you can challenge and stuff . . . dear God.'

'Is that why you don't go and see much of it?'

'It's true, I don't go to improvisation. It's what I told the BBC when they came to interview me, but they didn't put it in the programme. You don't ask the priest to go and watch them shitting on the altar. It's not much fun for the priest.'

THE PERFORMERS CHANGED BY THE AUDIENCE III

There are many other ways, without using audience suggestions, for the ensemble to be informed and influenced by the presence of the audience. The company may not have any dialogue with the audience at all but simply allow for a consciousness of them to provoke and inspire. Arguably this approach is more subtle and more respectful. But some questions follow from it. If there are no formal ways by which the audience informs the event, can't it simply become indulgent? Can't the presence of an audience but the absence of any formalisation of the relationship push the performers into a kind of negative performing? Either a performing that is artificial and showy, or, on the other hand, overly introspective and disregarding. These two negative behaviours could be identified as two opposite vices, each a negative, self-destructive response to the audience's presence.

AUDIENCE PLEASING

In the first case, the performers aim, above all to *please* the audience. They so love the audience that they sacrifices all their internal priorities for their sake. The group tunes in to every laugh, cough and chuckle, every twitch of a chair, to identify precisely the position of the audience's pleasure bone. Once found, the performers go about trying to hit it relentlessly for the length of the show. Most likely the performer in this group will ignore the significance of any content except insomuch as he or she needs it as a weapon.

> 'A lot of it is to make money ... if you're not doing well, you'll cite the thing that elicits the greatest response from the crowd.'
>
> DJ Les Henry

It's not dissimilar in improvised music. As Alain Danielou has noted, *'When the musicians note a positive reaction from the public, they are tempted to reproduce the effect which provoked this reaction and consequently one can understand how the rapid deterioration of the music performed could occur. The musician becomes, little by little, an actor who repeats his tricks when he notices that the public reacts favourably.'*[50]

The question may emerge, why not? Particularly if your goal is comedy. There's no point being moral about this. And it's true that if the performers can consistently generate laughter without cooking up problems for themselves later in the show when some denouement is required, then this is virtuosity put to good use. But the danger referred to by Danielou concerns the possibility that structural or content priorities might be lost sight of. In consequence, the audience may lose their connection with the piece if it emerges that behind the tricks and the jokes, there is really nothing. I asked Sten Rudstrom how he responded to laughter in the audience. Did hearing this response influence his decision-making about material? *'On a good night, no. On a bad night, yes. Attraction to audience response is, I believe, a signal that I don't believe what I'm doing. If I specifically go out to do comedy, that's different. Because then I have an objective in mind: to get them to laugh. But if I'm coming on in an open improvisation – I don't know what the game is going to be. I don't want to know what the game is going to be. And if they start telling me what the game should be – that's a problem. It's a problem for me to start believing that what they're doing is more important than what I'm doing. And that's a very great and wonderful place to work. And that's something that's practised in Action Theatre: the performers getting into that situation and still holding on to their presence, their world. It's very easy and very seductive to give over your world to their world . . . The temptation is to give up on my unfamiliar to join their familiar.'* From a different standpoint, Harold Pinter has commented that to a degree the relationship between the performers and the audience is one of struggle. To give yourselves over to the audience represents a defeat; to win them over to you represents a victory. An improviser such as Maggie Gordon-Walker, who specialises in comedy, knows just how to pull back from the lure of easy laughter and switch the focus of the audience towards more serious material.

AUDIENCE AVOIDANCE

To go the other way and to *ignore* the audience is to risk losing them. When this happens, it acts as a reminder of the unspoken contract that, if nothing else, a relationship to and with the audience is primary. If it happens, it's likely to occur as a result of the performer's focus going elsewhere. For example, the performer might become completely introspective. In a solo performance of my own, I was working with a note to develop narrative. So I did this to the exclusion of almost everything else. The 'everything' in this case included the audience. 'Solipsistic' was the note next time round. When this happens, the performer disappears into a whirling riot of feelings and sensations, chasing each one as it appears like a dog at a carnival. The audience can only stare at this miasmic descent into impulsiveness with a kind of weary despair. Usually the audience suspects there's something wrong but can't put a finger on what it is. Spectators may even blame themselves for the failure of the event. I remember one show performed in an old people's home, years ago in the late seventies. During it, I noticed a kerfuffle in the audience. Some people came from the side of the audience into the middle, then went back out again. I asked the organiser after the show what had happened. *'Oh yes,'* she said, *'that was Betty.'* *'Is she alright?'* I asked. *'Not really,'* came the reply. *'What happened to her?'* *'Oh, she died. I hope we didn't disturb the performance too much.'* Others in the company hadn't even noticed.

Frank Moon is a musician with a particular interest in improvisation who always likes to check out music gigs for himself. *'The gigs I don't enjoy, is when I get the impression the performers are not listening or caring about* [the event] *too much. There was a gig I went to recently, with guitar, drums, bass – and film. And the musicians weren't even reacting to the film, they weren't even watching it. It was some Spunk Meyer shorts. The films would stop and another one would begin, and the musicians were still playing the same groove. They would end something and the film was still going. The drummer was playing a lot – all the way through regardless of what the bass player did. The playing was very good. But it was the level of listening and responsiveness that was lacking. There was too much playing, and too much self-satisfaction from each musician with what they were playing themselves.'*

Of course it's also possible to address the audience directly and still not listen to what they have to say. I remember a performance by the Pip Simmons Theatre Group at the Royal Court in 1971. The performance was based on the book *Do It!* by Jerry Rubin and took the same title. There was a section when the group went into the audience, inciting them to *'Do It!'* I have to say, despite being an exponent of audience participation, I became transfixed with anxiety at this point. Because I was sitting at the end of a row, the girl soon came up to me and gave the obligatory exhortation. *"Do what?"* I asked in reply – because it was genuinely not clear what she wanted. No one else had got up. I still remember the look on her face today. She was momentarily lost. But I could see her mind racing. *'It doesn't matter – just do it!'* Clearly this rejoinder fulfilled the agenda. She looked at me as if I was her new boyfriend too scared to go to her bedroom. I smiled in desperation and slid down in my chair. I felt I'd let down the revolution. But on the night Nick Hern went to the same show, one audience member got up, an American of course, and started taking his clothes off . . .

There are different answers to the problem of performer vices. Some of them have to do with practice. Others have to do with structure, with the use of restrictions, either lifting or imposing them to interfere with the performers' tendency to default to safety. In this chapter we're talking less about the skills aspect than about the structural issues. I talked to the dancer K.J. Holmes about her experience of searching for finding a marriage of personal honesty (interiority) with audience contact (dialogue):

How do your priorities shift, once you have an audience?

An audience makes the work alive . . . It really is the exchange that's important. An audience will focus me. But I don't feel I'm doing it for them. Although there's something about having that outside eye that really brings what is happening out into space a little bit more.

Are you aware that the audience is changing you – in terms of sensations or feelings? And how is that changing your decision-making?

It's a good question because right now I'm looking at how to NOT have that be the big influence on me. I don't really feel I'm doing it for the audience, but I feel it's an event we're doing together . . . If I was making a particular piece and wanted to convey a particular image I may not engage with them visually. If I'm engaged in a really open improvisation, I will. I'll look at the audience, I might even go into the audience and break that fourth wall. I'm working on a project called Body of Truth. *With five other dancers. This is exactly what we were looking at. How do you continue to do a process that is really personal and have people there, without changing what you're doing? But what you're doing is not about just being inside your own personal process. It's about using your personal process to create the theatre.*

So how did you find to answer that?

We did a week last year and we did a showing at the end. During that week we were in process but our timing got very slow and extended because we didn't have any external pressure. But when we did the showing, we just jumped right back into our usual presentation roles. So this time instead of doing a showing, we said we would just allow people to come in during three hour blocks, and they could come and go as they liked. To see how it affected us or not. And in the process of two weeks, I think we started finding a place where we aren't just ignoring them, or not allowing them to affect us, nor are we feeling, 'Oh, they've come to see us so we'd better do something for them.' By the end of the last week, there was a real openness. It really did feel like a performance but without us feeling that pressure . . . I don't know how to define it because it feels really new. I've been improvising for so many years being a singer and also an actress, and there was something about going from the body and being in time and space and staying with it, and allowing something more theatrical to be there – it was really working.

The group solved the problem of being 'defeated' by the audience by altering the time frames and spatial boundaries of the event. It made a difference that the audience could come and go. I was involved in a similar exercise at the London Contemporary Dance School in 2005 with ESP (Experiments in Spontaneous Performance), a mixed art form company who staged a five-hour durational piece allowing the audience similar liberties. We found the benefits achieved in terms of relaxation through absence of time pressure, had to be offset against our own unfamiliarity with these new parameters, suggesting that the time-space co-ordinates, once altered, required a different kind of practice work. Holmes suggests her group took the time to master this. Perhaps unsurprisingly, it was largely in the final hour of the ESP performance that the more effective improvisational material emerged, once the group had attuned to the format and allowed it to impose its own imperatives on the group. What it allowed, and the suggestion in Holmes' replies implies the same, is that the performer, freed from a responsibility to a time-bound short form, can take greater risks, knowing that failure is less likely to involve losing a significant proportion of the time available.

A similar kind of alteration of practice had occurred within Chicago-style improvisation when Del Close initiated a move from short- to long-form structures (pieces of work running over about twenty minutes or longer). Today this idea of a 'long-form' improvisation over half an hour or so, feels less radical than it did. Now the fences around performed improvisations have been pushed back further. As a consequence, different content is associated with these exercises. In the durational work of Forced Entertainment in the UK, abolition of conventional time parameters allows an exploration of content over several hours. In *Quizoola!* one performer asks another a series of questions from a large book, generating supplementary questions as necessary. Tim Etchells observes that in consequence of operating on a radically different set of time parameters, *'We all find ourselves talking about things we didn't expect to get to. I guess one of the things we focus on a lot in those pieces is the importance of "getting into trouble". As a performer one's seeking out the difficult terrain.'* Etchells also notes that despite the difference in format, there is still a shared recognition of the importance of elements associated with earlier, 'short-form' practice. *'In some ways, these durational, improvised pieces of ours are only one step away from the kind of game-like improv set-ups you might find in other contexts like Theatresports. As in those forms, we might use an explicit and to some extent arbitrary frame (a rule, a time limit, an object or phrase or linguistic structure that has to be respected) and the whole thing is being played live, so as a performer/player, your success or failure in following and creating within the rule is always quite exposed. I think we're really drawn to . . . the possibility of the sticky moment, the opportunity for a certain vulnerability and revelation in failure. We like the way that you're always exposed – that there's no way out. So the person who gives very safe moral answers to questions* [in *Quizoola!*] *always looks like they're trying to defend themselves somehow. But even that attempt to defend oneself is visible to an audience. Audiences like the transparency of the system.'* Lyn Gardner in *The Guardian* has observed how these tight formal strictures, combined with a long time frame, change the content. *'Those qualities were forcibly in evidence in* Who Can Sing a Song to Unfrighten Me?, *a 24-hour piece that took place inside the Royal Festival Hall in 1999. Starting at midnight, members of Forced Entertainment told stories without endings, chalked lists of their worst fears on a blackboard, put on skeleton costumes and speculated on the difference between life and death. As the hours passed, the performers' crippling exhaustion affected the structure of the piece so that it became dangerously unpredictable. They took more and more risks, becoming wilder, more inventive and ever more exposed.'*[51] By shifting the time boundaries, a different kind of relationship with the audience is created, one that allows a deeper exploration of material and a more intimate communication within the ensemble. Tony Guilfoyle observed that Pete Brooks, formerly of Impact Theatre

Co-operative, always preferred to start rehearsals around midnight to specifically engender a greater imaginative, risk-taking freedom.

Nor is it simply about time. It's noteworthy that Forced Entertainment is very particular about the siting of any *Quizoola!* performance. It needs to take place in a cellar or disused building or an abandoned chapel – if possible, never in a theatre. Such attention to the location of the event chimes with the community company Word and Action's emphasis on the round theatre space in which it works, and the attention paid to the relative dimensions of the four sides of audience. In both examples, there is clear acknowledgement of the powerful influence that the immediate environment has on the behaviour of the performers and therefore the outcome of the work. Touring with Word and Action in the eighties, I saw how R.G. Gregory would fastidiously organise the seating in ways that confused and sometimes upset outsiders. Despite this, he wouldn't be distracted: he knew that the distances between performers and audience, and between audience and audience, were a major factor in determining whether or not the company could generate the kind of atmosphere it wanted. For these companies, conventional theatre architecture, built to reflect a different set of values, fails to serve the audience-actor relationship that is sought after. It follows that if the improvised theatre experience is to achieve a synergy between its values and aspirations, it has to address issues of space and time parameters not as an incidental issue, but as a fundamental one.

THE PERFORMERS CHANGED BY THE AUDIENCE IV

Over the years, many companies have experimented with ways to involve children as the motors of performance. One of the most successful formats to achieve this, although not particularly designed for children, is Instant Theatre developed by Word and Action, mentioned above. Here, the performers are imposed on by the audience within a format governed by strict rules. The question and answer process initiated by the company generates a story that is taken as the text for the subsequent performance. By rigidly applying the principles of 'no censorship' and 'acceptance of all answers heard'; the group legitimately asserts the primacy of the audience's contribution. Once the story has been developed, it is acted out within the rectangular stage that is created by the seated audience. However, the company alone does not act out the story. The performance is only realised as a collaboration with the audience or with those who are willing to improvise. In this way, the audience again imposes its stamp upon the event. Inevitably, this frightens the socks off those who are fearful of any kind of participatory drama. However, the facilitation by the company, taking both the lead roles and the task of supporting the participants, invariably assuages fears. There are no props or stage furniture; people must represent everything.

For children, it is a particularly magical event. They are so unused to being given free imaginative reign that their participation is usually total. Watching teachers are either worried or delighted, according to their disposition. As discussed earlier, this strategy so profoundly undermines the inherent bias in our culture towards the notion of the superiority of the artist, that it's no wonder the company has aroused the scorn and derision it has over the years. For by means of this democratic inclusiveness the audience is put in the driving seat of the dramatic material in a way no other event quite achieves. The fact that the form is used extensively with young audiences should not be taken as evidence of its inefficacy with older groups. I have seen it work in pub gardens as equally as in schools throughout Europe, as brilliantly in old people's homes as in kindergartens.

Guy Dartnell and Tom Morris' show *Oogly Boogly* involves children in ways that parallel some of Word and Action's approach in that the 'offers' of children (between twelve and eighteen months old) are again taken as the *prima materia* of the performance. As in the work of Word and Action, there simply is no material for the performance before the audience have spoken it, or to be more precise, moved it. *'The premise of it is that parents and carers bring their babies into a safe inflatable space (specially designed by Architects Of Air) and the adults are encouraged to withdraw to the outer limits of the space. So the kids can still see them, but a sense of independence is established. There are four performers in the space. And a game begins where basically they just do what the kids do. So the improvisation is led by the children. The performers don't encourage the kids to do anything in particular; they just follow and copy, even if the children are still and silent. The adults are also asked not to encourage nor discourage their children from doing anything. And there are no toys or objects in the space. So the focus is just on the relationship between the children and the performers.'* Dartnell observes that a pattern involves –

the children initially assume the performers are adults who will soon be giving them instructions, but as the piece progresses and they realise what the performers are doing, this relationship changes into something more playful and reciprocal, until the children feel confident to initiate and repeat things and patterns emerge. And this is all witnessed by the parents, carers and friends who are the audience.

THE PERFORMERS CHANGED BY THE AUDIENCE V

Compagnie Felix Ruckert, a dance-theatre company, began presenting shows within a more traditional audience-performer relationship in which all the choreography was set. Early shows involved Ruckert as choreographer directing the company in rehearsal and following orthodox procedures. Then over a period of ten years, this ex-Pina Bausch dancer moved to creating performances around the responses and behaviour of the audiences. Ruckert explained this transition to me, during which the audience's role became more and more influential. His account tells the story of shifting priorities in response to a growing awareness of the audience's significance, one that practitioners from other art forms might recognise:

'In 1995 I started my company, and there was a lot of improvisation in the rehearsal process. The first performance in '95 was Hautnah, which was a solo performance for a solo spectator . . . I made ten solos with ten dancers. The audience went in one by one, to different spaces. And had to pay for each solo. The pieces were very choreographed. And of course the pieces didn't always work like we thought they would, so the improvisation had to come in. And because these pieces were very successful, I had to ask myself, "Why?" For we had the choreography of course, but in the confrontation with the audience, something new happened – that was perhaps more interesting than my choreography! The audience of one sat on the chair. But when we did this, we discovered that the spectator didn't stay on the chair. He or she sat in the corner or walked around the room, and the dancer was like "Oh, shit . . ." so the dancer turned around or followed the spectator. So next time we took the chair away. Then the dancer adapted. She had some choreography, but she adapted. And this is how we came, step by step, to improvisation . . . And people liked it even more. And the dancers felt more free, more intimate with the spectator. But there was the structure still for the dancer. The consequence was that it became more real. And

sometimes the spectator would touch the dancer. And they were like, "Aha! OK!" But also it was stupid to disallow this completely. So we had to find a solution to that, so we started to choreograph the interaction: giving the possibility to touch or be touched – within a structure, so there was a form. The dancer could choose to skip this if they wanted – if they felt the spectator would abuse this. So the solos became systems with options. We worked on this for four years, until '99.

'After this, I looked for more ways to bring in this unknown element, something that disturbs the choreography. So I took a piece I had choreographed for the stage, Choreographic Project, *and replaced written parts of this with improvised parts. So I said, for example with a duet, you have to keep your choreography in mind but sometimes you can jump out of it. And you can jump back in. So this keeps them connected. There remained an echo, a connection in the improvised section.*

'Then the Ring *show was a recycling of the ideas from the solo show. I wanted to have this intimate one-to-one situation but so it could be seen also from the outside. So I had to structure it differently. I took this circle where you have the same number of dancers as spectators. One to one. Each one had the same choreography, the same material, but with each different spectator it felt completely different; different size of arms and hands, different colour, different smell. Sometimes the dancers proposed a movement, "Come, stand up" and everybody would move together, walk around or be lifted or maybe roll on the floor. This was very successful. And after a while, I used not only dancers. Anyone could learn to take the role of the dancer in the show, it was very simple. So you couldn't tell the dancers from the audience. Local people could learn it. We spent a week with them, teaching. It was very popular, and performed all over the world. In the end I didn't even go myself, I sent some other dancers to teach it. But I became dissatisfied with* Ring *because the audience didn't have so much choice. They had to always be like everyone else.*

'The next step was Deluxe Joy Pilot. *I based the work mainly on duos. In rehearsal, I had each pair of dancers improvise a duet. There were ten dancers so that's a lot of combinations. I looked at these duets, about 45 of them. And where there was something interesting going on, I marked them. Then I repeated all the ones I marked. So I came to this idea, that while some duets are easily resolved in five minutes, in others there is some ongoing conflict or attraction. Things related to family, or relationships. So I picked these ones and composed the piece with these duets. From the 45, I took maybe just four or five that were always good. One dancer had three*

*interesting duos. So while the interaction with the audience was choreo-
graphed, the duets were improvised . . . I had a stage with beds around. The
audience could sit on the beds. If you sat on the bed, you showed your
disposition to interact with the dancers. If you weren't on the bed, you could
sit in the audience and watch. This was the first time that everything the
dancers did was improvised. But the structures were very primitive; I had
no method of improvisation at that time. And it was difficult because of need-
ing to keep it interesting for the audience members who were not involved.
So the action could not fully realise its potential.*

*'After this I wanted to do a piece that was completely focused on the
interaction with the audience. Where there is nothing coming from anything
external. So the spectator would be the subject of the show, the essence, and
the creator.*

'In the show that came to be called Secret Service, *the spectators came
into the space blindfold, one by one. One or two dancers met each one. I
didn't want the interactions to become personal for the dancers but for it to
be personal for the audience. In the show we worked to achieve security but
also to bring sexual and sensual desires into a form. It's about limits. If you
get addressed sexually by the spectator, you can communicate clearly the
limits beyond which you are not prepared to go. But it's also important to be
able to follow your impulses as a dancer. Don't hesitate to go if you want to.
The same was true with rough play. Some people wanted to fight. We looked
at how to fight with people who are blind without hurting them. Also where
to stop if it got dangerous. If someone wanted to fight, we would choose who
he would fight with – man, woman or several. So it wasn't personal against
the dancer. It was important that the spectator meet different dancers during
the performance. Maybe with one they wanted to fight and another one they
wanted to touch and another to play, or dance, and so on. This is why I
needed professional dancers for the show, all of whom had different qualities,
who were able to switch very smoothly. I also wanted the same precision and
quality of touch for every dancer, so the spectator couldn't often tell who was
who and what was what.*

*'It happens in a big space, fifteen by fifteen metres, and there's ten
audience members and ten dancers in at the same time. Every four minutes
someone comes in and someone goes. They stay in for thirty minutes. When
someone comes in, we check their body-mind. To see if they are nervous, for
example, or aggressive. 80 per cent of people are either completely relaxed
so that if you touch them, they lean on you! Or they are very tense in which
case we try to manipulate them so they are receptive without being too*

passive. We might stimulate them for example, by slapping them on the body. Then we walk them so they understand we want them following us without being dead. We try to encourage them to be improvising dancers, to have what a dancer has, so you are present with the tension you need to maintain your body in space. There's a choreographic loop going on. You can get into the loop at any time. There's a part where everybody runs, where everyone is on the floor, another where everybody's free. If someone doesn't want to run, they are taken to the side. So there's a ritual element. Everyone in a way follows the crowd; they feel everyone get calm so they start to get calm . . . But there are these free sections also. And in these free sections, there is improvisation. There is gesture, touch, sound, but not many words. We also have material, for example "symbolic positions". These are positions in which you might be put, and where the shape 'makes sense'. It has meaning. And there are many of those. So in these free sections we make propositions for (physical) dialogue. Some people take these propositions. Others don't. So by getting them to improvise, we find out who they are. The goal is to bring them into action; we don't want them passive. Every spectator can make his personal mark. In terms of interaction, this show, Secret Service, *is the best one I've made.*

'*But some people expressed they wanted to go further – in the pain, the sensuality, the lust. So we developed a second level to the show which is called* Pain and Lust. *So you can choose to go to the second level after the first. So for this we have an agreement with the audience, for example, that they can be touched on the genitals. We ask them to take off most of their clothes. And for the dancers it's the same. About 45 per cent of spectators go on to the second level.*

'*So after* Secret Service, *it was a matter of keeping this freedom of improvisation and also this individuality, but again allowing it to be seen from outside. So the process could be watched. This show was called* Love Zoo. *Like* Ring, *the audience is all around and can go in anytime, stay in or decide to go out and watch. But we had also sections where if you were in, you had to stay in. All actions are improvised but with more formal tools. For example, the dancers create power situations in space. I submit or I dominate – but from a distance. That creates the choreography. But there is a progression: we start with just three spectators only. At this point you have four dancers to each spectator, so there are things we couldn't do in* Secret Service *– lifting the spectators, rolling them, catching them. Then we bring in more spectators so it's three to one, then two to one, then one-on-one. Then the final stage is, the dancers give the spectators propositions to interact with* *other spectators. At that point the dancers start to leave the performance area. So we start with fifteen dancers and three spectators . . . until finally the dancers start pulling out and at the very the end there are only spectators.'*

SHOULD THE AUDIENCE KNOW IT'S IMPROVISED?

Some take the view that advertising a performance as improvisation works as an apology since it covertly signals to the audience that this is low-status work. Others insist the fact it's improvised is the thing that gives it integrity. It's a distinct art form in its own right, they say, and should be advertised as such. Others again argue that the fact it's improvised is just plain irrelevant. It should be marketed simply as dance or theatre or performance.

In the UK, it's difficult to generate audiences for dramatic improvisation as an art form in its own right. So few people have experience of improvised performance outside of jazz or comedy impro that they are somewhat baffled by the idea of it. We have such a literary culture that 'I fancy a night out watching improvisation' just isn't heard that often. UK improvisers would happily support the comment made by Besser at Del Close's funeral, reported by Amy Poehler, that *'Anybody who has a theatre should have Del's picture in it, anybody that improvises should invoke his name, and anybody who says that improv is not an art form should fuck off.'* But having this sentiment accepted in the UK is a little way off, despite the isolated pockets of commercial success that tend to involve either the Comedy Store Players or comics who have made a name for themselves in stand-up.

In a way, these different positions about how to market improvised work are responding to a cultural context in the West where improvisation is considered something incomplete. It would be different if we were performing flamenco in Spain or playing tabla in India. But a performance generated spontaneously is inevitably associated with 'ad-libbing' or 'coping with mistakes'. The holder of this viewpoint doesn't understand why a group should present something unrehearsed. But perhaps it doesn't matter what they believe? Keith Johnstone writes that audiences always assume shows are rehearsed even if they're not. If you tell them about the mechanics, he says, *'They still believe even the worst scenes to have been rehearsed. This is the agony of public improvisation, that on a bad night you are seen not only as untalented, but also as bereft of good taste and any common sense. Why should an audience be expected to lower its standards if they know that a show is unscripted? Would a disgusting meal taste better if the waiter said, "Ah, but the chef is improvising!" The truth is that people come for a good time and nobody cares how the scenes are created except other improvisers.'* [52]

Johnstone's implication is clear, and it chimes with the view expressed by the dancer Julyen Hamilton at Shifti 2006, that the mechanics of creating a piece is not really relevant, and can be a distraction. It may just confuse the audience. Hamilton commented, *'I don't really think about improvisation ever. I just do my work.'* Perhaps it really is better just not to mention how the work is made. A tale of the music group AMM comes to mind, which Walter Horn has written down: *'A few years back, AMM, the venerable English improvising ensemble of Keith Rowe, John Tilbury, and Eddie Prévost, played a concert in Krakow, Poland. At drinks after the gig, a colleague of Tilbury's son Jasper told the trio how moved she had been by their performance. But when this woman learned that, contrary to her belief, the group hadn't memorised a score, but had improvised the entire piece out of whole cloth, the value of the music was destroyed for her. According to Prévost, "She not only doubted our artistic and intellectual integrity, but she had been forced to question her own powers of discrimination. How had it been possible for her to enjoy and admire such work when its practice had been so . . . primitive?" Had AMM "perpetrated some kind of artistic fraud"? Not at all, says the author/musician. The "abiding impression upon us (that is AMM) was that this person could not trust her own sensibilities and that she had chosen a wholly inappropriate paradigm of cultural confirmation to help guide her tastes and aesthetic . . . disposition".* [53]

It seems we're caught in a cultural trap. The prevailing culture is so informed by commodification that when a performance attempts to evade it, the performers run the risk of being misunderstood. Perhaps improvisers need to simply accept this is a gauntlet to be run. In this context, Steve Paxton has a useful observation. He points out that while bad improvisation has helped to give improvisation a bad name, somehow this doesn't happen with dance choreography – however bad the choreographed piece is, the reputation of choreography remains mysteriously intact.

The spirit of these contributions points to a strong argument for minimising the information given to the audience about the birth process of the event. This argument runs that improvisation should be promoted in other ways. More general definitions should be employed.

So the works stands or falls on its own merits, without inviting special attention or any different relationship with its audience. This strategy chimes with developments in jazz, which rarely draw attention to the improvised nature of what is performed. After all, the traditions are now so established that such marketing would appear pedantic and unnecessary. But others find a problem with this in that it gives up on what is distinct and characteristic of improvised work. So marketing performance without reference to this distinctiveness is not just a commercial mistake, it's dishonest.

This alternative view hinges on the identity of improvisation as an *art form in its own right* judged not on its modes of operation but on its ability to function effectively and uniquely as a different kind of event. This argument points to what is distinctive about improvisation irrespective of the artistic medium employed for its vocabulary of expression. It points to an art form that is spontaneous, immediate, flawed and subversive, with its own ethics devolving from its refusal to be made subject to external manipulation or authority. Ansuman Biswas, quoted elsewhere in this book, makes such a case, arguing that improvisation is a distinct and coherent art form that may pick up elements of any number of different art form languages, in order to suit its own purposes.

WHO ARE THOSE GUYS?

If improvisation is defined as an art form in its own right, could it attract a larger audience than it does at present? There are plenty of potential and actual audiences out there. But in marketing itself to a wider constituency, it may be pertinent to consider how the form's integrity and politics are to be retained. The example of improvised *music*, pace AMM, SME and others, is particularly interesting in this context because of the challenges it continues to make to audiences. In other words, it still refuses to compromise on its core aesthetic principles. It makes little in the way of concessions to commercial ethics. For an audience coming to it for the first time, there are no obvious reference points within the practice by which to adjudge quality. There are no 'tunes', 'hooks' or 'riffs'. As a result, it tends to attract largely those who are already familiar with its protocols. Does this mean the form lacks accessibility? Is it an art form condemned to small audiences? When interviewed by Jean Martin in August 1996, the guitarist Derek Bailey, whose career has been spent largely within free music, responded bleakly.

So whenever you play in a concert you are surprised about the reactions of the audience?

I am surprised that they are there. I mean, one obvious thing is that audiences, people generally, don't like freely improvised music, otherwise the audiences would be larger of course . . . It attracts very small audiences.

Why is that?

They don't like it.

Does it take too much effort for them? This music is not nicely prepared in little well structured portions. They have basically to create their own structure in listening to the music, don't they?

These are difficult questions for me. I don't know. To me it is my favourite listening.[54]

In the decade since this interview, audiences have picked up. I talked with Rex Hossi Horan and Alison Blunt, two musicians who work with ESP, about the background to the free improvisation tradition and this business of encouraging audiences to something new. In the past, audiences have often rebelled against new developments in music, as in the case of musique concrete. Rex Hossi Horan: *'They were saying at that time* [the '40s], *"OK, there's an approaching train, that's a bird, that's a jackhammer – this isn't music. Where's the tonal organisation?" That's where the origins of sampling comes from. This was the time when people were questioning what music was, and beginning to say, it's just sound waves that influence what the audience feels. And they've been organised in a certain fashion to have an effect. And if we say this is music, then it is music, because we've organised the sounds.'* Alison Blunt: *'The difference between that and what's happening now in the noise art circles is that it's not directed. A very important thing is that no one is telling you what to do, or how to improvise. So you're not being given choices by someone else.'*

Here, Alison Blunt puts her finger on a key aspect of the unorthodoxy: audiences don't have the comfort of knowing that a master craftsperson is in charge of the event. The truth applies across the field of improvised music, dance and theatre for the most part – at time of performance, the director is not only absent *but significantly without influence.* Mediation of material through the editing of a supervisor/

composer/choreographer is largely absent, with the exclusion of the practice of Zorn, Morris, Johnstone and others discussed previously.

Generally speaking in our mainstream culture, at least in the UK, an audience will rather see a 'known' personality improvise on stage even if he hasn't a clue how to improvise, rather than watch an unknown group who've spent their lives perfecting the art. (The situation is complicated by the fact that a good number of performers who have become media personalities in the UK such as David Baddiel, Frank Skinner and Phil Jupitus *can* actually improvise very well.) Arguably, because of this, such practitioners do help to promulgate improvisatory practice. So this leaves us with a conundrum. It's typified by the success of the television show *Whose Line Is It Anyway?* During the run of the programme, everyone in impro workshops wanted to try and emulate Ryan Stiles, Josie Lawrence, Colin Mochrie et al. I rarely saw anyone come close. The material these amateurs created became grotesque acts of imitation. So the form was popularised but at a terrible price. Additionally the scope of improvisation became limited in the minds of both artists and spectators to understandings based on *Whose Line?*

Improvisation outside such formats has a more elusive identity characterised by playfulness and a desire to undermine consumerist expectations. Once it abandons this essentially subversive role and tries to conform to prevailing notions of what art is and should be, it starts to lose its energies. The struggle to build audiences may suffer simply because the *Whose Line?* format is narrow and not valid outside its own limited terms. How to find a solution to this conundrum can only mean persistence, experimentation and the search for some kind of devil's pact with the society that is its home.

IMPROVISATION'S POLITICS

Live art practice for its part has increasingly ventured into an arena where the orthodox parameters of the live event are deconstructed in the interests of exploring personal/political values – while at the same time hoping to enlist audiences in this project. However, there's no tacit assumption that audiences should be encouraged on the basis that all members of it shall experience the event in the same way. Adrian Heathfield argues that such initiatives are legitimate because while different performance forms have different contexts of reception (historical, material, cultural, spatial), which structure the audience's perceptions, there is nevertheless always room for play in any context of reception. *'Questions around form and meaning – and the relation between the event and the spectator – those questions are not removed from political questions, nor should they be. But this is a very different understanding of the political from the understanding that was dominant in '80s British political theatre. Basically it's the understanding that politics and power rest in information and meaning, and in the micro world of relations. That's the terrain of address in a lot of experimental work: it demonstrates that the form of the event is its politics. It's about thinking about what is political or ethical in a different way. It's not necessarily about the delivery of messages or ideas as such, but believing in the ethical or political force of challenging forms, of opening up ideas. So for me, a lot of my writing has been focused around what the consequences and resonances of that attack on forms, traditions and structures of meaning in experimental work is about – what it does for the spectator and how there is in that de-structuring of meaning, an imperative or agency that a spectator can take away with them and use . . . a tendency to question what is given or naturalised in the culture around you . . .*

'I'm talking about [the performers] *fostering an inclination, rather than performing an idea – an inclination to question meaning, authority and power. Much of the efficacy of improvisation in live art and performance work rests in its shaking up and splitting apart of the audience in terms of their feelings and perceptions. By making the experience difficult, edgy, contentious the work is challenging consensus and traditions of reading, promoting difference and a multiplicity of readings . . . The efficacy of improvisational work is precisely to do with atomising an audience in particular ways.'*

At the time of writing, the audience-spectator relationship is under examination as never before, with a series of innovations testing, challenging and pushing back boundaries. Developing the performer-audience relationship is currently one of the most vital and exciting areas of theatrical experimentation. Examples in support of this claim might refer to a number of initiatives besides those mentioned above: the dance company H2 has recently been presenting a show in which a dance critic, Donald Hutera, sits on stage and intermittently asks the audience for suggestions as to how the dance piece might be developed. Tino Sehgal's recent performance at the ICA, London, involved the performers moving in response to the arrival of the spectators into the space, then repeating and playing with anything the audience said, amongst themselves. Blast Theory's performances have involved them inviting the audience to pursue them through the streets of London while Davis Freeman's show involves each member of the audience being separately photographed, then the photo made into a mask for the performer before he dances for that solo spectator. Gob Squad take over a venue such as a hotel and after seating the audience in front of a video screen, offer them a range of possible forms of interactions. Suggestions include meeting up with one of the characters privately in a hotel room.

Implicit here is the notion that improvised work can make a challenge to an audience that comes in at the level of politics. It concerns itself with the relationships operating within the event, rather than existing as a set of signposts to other events. It does not assume that everyone in the audience 'feels the same way about what they see'. Nor is this necessarily desirable. In fact, the inverse – a multiplicity of understandings – is desirable. It can request a re-examination of some fundamental assumptions about authorship, meaning and authority through both its content and its protocols.

CODA I

Some prescriptive advice offered by different practitioners on how to engage the audience.

'Do not attempt to emotionally affect the audience, unless the work being done at that time demands it. This is not to say that we do not want to affect the audience, but we do not want to hit them over the head with the message. Again, assume their intelligence will allow them to feel for themselves.'

'If you are bored, your audience is also bored.'

'One should always know what the audience knows or has just learned. Playing against this will lead to denial.'

'Try to become a better audience yourself, so that you may begin to understand what makes us appreciate a better performance.'
From the *Second City Almanac of Improvisation* by Anne Libera

'The audience will watch you do anything if you pay attention to what you are doing.'

'The audience loves improvisers who suffer but stay good natured even as those improvisers fail miserably.'

From *Twenty Improv Tips* by Matt Young, Dad's Garage (Atlanta)

'Start "cold", and where will the ideas come from? From you, and then there's a chance that your inner demons may be released, and that's the price you pay for being an artist.'

'Never accept a suggestion that fails to inspire you, or that is degrading.'

'If you accept a suggestion, do it.'

From *Impro for Storytellers* by Keith Johnstone

'An audience can tell whether actors are working well together, they smell it even if it's subliminal.'

'The audience is in the rehearsal from day one. Watching other performers and contributing as an audience is as important as rehearsing.'

'The audience see everything.'

From 'Improbable Principles' on the web site of Improbable Theatre, www.improbable.co.uk

CODA II

'UNCLE ROY ALL AROUND YOU' BY BLAST THEORY

Uncle Roy All Around You *is a game played online in a virtual city and on the streets of an actual city. Online Players and Street Players collaborate to find Uncle Roy's office before being invited to make a year long commitment to a total stranger.*

The city is an arena where the unfamiliar flourishes, where the disjointed and the disrupted are constantly threatening to overwhelm us. It is also a zone of possibility, of new encounters.

The following text describes the work in June 2003 at the world premiere at the Institute of Contemporary Arts, London. The work was changed significantly in subsequent presentations.

THE GAME

Street Players, i.e. the audience, buy a ticket and then are shown to the registration desk. They have their photo taken and hand over all their possessions: phone, purse, bag, loose change, etc. Each Street Player receives

a unique code, which they enter into their handheld computer thus triggering the 60 minute countdown to begin.

Having been told they must meet Uncle Roy within 60 minutes, Street Players take their handheld device out onto the streets. Their device shows a map and the names and positions of Online Players. The map can be dragged around to show other areas and can zoom in or out. A button marked 'I'm lost' is always available. Once outside, they receive a message from Uncle Roy. It says:

'Meet me in the park by the lake. I've marked your map with the location. Click on the "I'm here" button to confirm you've arrived, and I'll come to meet you.' *A red dot indicates the meeting place.*

Online Players are moving around a virtual city which correlates exactly to the real city. They too are sent on a mission to meet Uncle Roy. They can view photos of the real city by going to the corresponding location in the virtual city and clicking on an icon. Initially they can chat with other Online Players but cannot see or contact Street Players.

When the Street Player first declares their position (by clicking 'I'm here' on the handheld computer) their avatar appears in the virtual world at that location. Their card becomes visible to Online Players: it shows their name, their photo and a brief description of their clothes.

Selecting a Street Player's card allows the Online Player to send private messages to the Street Player. The Street Player can record audio replies or ignore these messages. Only the most recent audio message from each Street Player is available: a new message 'overwrites' the previous one. Potentially every Street Player and every Online Player can be in contact: social interaction governs how this actually happens.

After the Street Player arrives at the first location, Uncle Roy sends another message. It says, 'There's something I want you to do for me. Start heading north into the West End. I will contact you as you go.'

When the Street Player declares their position, Uncle Roy replies with context-specific directions, e.g. 'Pay no attention to the street cleaner with long grey hair. Find a dead end and follow it.' *After a time these directions become less context specific and more direct, e.g.* 'Go to 12 Waterloo Place and ring the bell marked Roy.'

Online Players can assist Street Players by matching photos and Uncle Roy's comments and then passing relevant information to the Street Player, e.g. 'The door to Uncle Roy's office has a metal grille.'

THE OFFICE

When the Street Player arrives at the Office, they ring the buzzer. The glass door slides open and gives them access to the deserted office.

Inside the room is an architect's desk, a chair and the rest of a typical executive office of the 1970s. Radio 4 comes from a Roberts radio. A blood-red bin chair sits on the thick brown carpet. Black metal shelves hang on the dark olive-green walls. A model of the surrounding city made of Post-It notes sits on the desk: on a monitor nearby is an Augmented Reality display showing the Post-It note city populated by all current Street and Online Players.

Online Players are informed that the Street Player is in the office and are invited to join them. Once in the virtual office, they see the Street Player on a live web cam. They are asked a series of questions culminating in, 'Some-where in the game there is a stranger who is also answering these questions. Are you willing to make a commitment to that person that you will be available for them if they have a crisis? The commitment will last for 12 months and, in return, they will commit to you for the same period.'

If they agree, the Online Player is invited to enter their postal address. Once they have completed the questions they 'enter' the office and can see the web cam showing the Street Player. On the desk is a postcard with 'When can you begin to trust a stranger?' printed on it. Via the handheld device Uncle Roy asks the Street Player to answer the question and keep it with them as they walk outside to a nearby phone box.

CAR

Once they are in the phone box they receive a call instructing the Player to get into the back of a white limousine parked across the street.

A man gets into the car and asks the Street Player the same series of questions that the Online Player has answered.

If the Street Player agrees to make the commitment to a stranger then they are paired with an Online Player who has also agreed. As the Street Player is dropped off at the ICA, the postcard is posted to an Online Player who has given their address.

Meanwhile the Online Player emerges from the virtual office back into the virtual city. Their experience has no definite end: they can choose to chat with the Street Player, to go into the office a second or third time or to log out.

From www.blasttheory.co.uk

4
THE COMMUNITY

'Contact Improvisation is a way of dealing with the paranoia that gravity is out to get you.'   Jorg Christian

'Play is the device which permits all mammals to have fun, but gives them the means of mastering the skills needed for survival.'   Edward Hall

I have a suspicion that those who are drawn to improvisation find themselves ill at ease with society *out there*. Normal rules are suspended in this complex matrix of decisions and collisions, struggle and impulse, generating an alternative universe where the socially dysfunctional can exist more confidently. I don't exclude myself from this group. Mistakes in this place have none of the consequences of those made in the social world (although performers often attribute to them even greater significance), and risks can be taken (usually) without fear of arrest. Besides, the bonding that can occur between performers can be more intense and intimate than those prevailing within other collaborative forms of artistic production.

This possibility of intimate contact with another individual draws people from all walks of life into the game. Some even come to improvise. As argued earlier, improvisation is a natural digging tool: it gets you in touch with yourself and encourages you to get in touch with others. In the West particularly, many feel drawn to it because they yearn for opportunities to evade the social conventions that separate and contain. Many of us feel we're just struggling along, in close quarters with each other yet still alienated, in a context defined by the absence of creative, democratic, social rituals. In the United Kingdom, our folk culture was largely wiped out – first by the Puritans and then by industrialisation in harness with Victorian idealism – leaving us primed and ready for the advent of mass culture. When it arrived, our habitual forms of collective bonding became limited to sports and

concert arenas, the occasional protest march and the funerals of heroes
or heroines. There has developed little by way of any popular, established interactive language of commu-
nity that is widely acknowledged or

> 'Be suspicious of "mass
> anything".'
> Adrian Heathfield

practised. Perhaps this is a good thing.
Perhaps it validates the thousands of
sub-cultures that exist to combat the
sense of social malaise that is felt to exist
within the mass. Perhaps there is more
richness, vitality and sense of growth within these small occasions than
there is within the large. Perhaps community belongs on the micro scale
of 'great reckonings in small rooms'? If so, it would explain why we
have such a rich culture of groups, societies and clubs that range from
Satanic cults to stand-up comedy, from swing dancing to chess clubs,
from train spotting to studying the battlefields of World War One.

In a sense, we're continuously searching through such pastimes for
a solution to a problem. That is, the problem of the absence of social
contentment. We're searching for a quality of community that might be
found more easily on a small scale than on a large. It can't be legislated
for, this sense of community, although the thousand uses of the word
within government programmes suggest that many believe that possible. Instead, government's relative impotence is only written larger
by these exercises. There's something else required, a kind of alchemi-
cal mixture, a fusion of hearts and minds that is always beyond legisla-
tion or good deeds. It's the admixture of something spiritual, a social,
impulsive, voluntarist flexing of social muscles by people who are
acting not to fulfil a government initiative but to realise a marriage between personal self-expression and the desire to meld into and advance
the interests of the group. It becomes provoked most visibly on the
macro scale in response to disasters or atrocities – 9/11, 7/7 and others.
Throughout the world wars it flourished consistently as the liquid glue
of resistance. Once the threat is removed however or the crisis recedes,
the search for community returns from the macro to the micro level.
It's as if in peacetime, because of the fractures and diversifications
within our society, it can only exist on the scale of the small. If it gets
too big, then it changes, it loses its core energies, and the relationships
of participants become defined instead by anonymity and authority
while the activity itself becomes open to commodification and marketing. For the artist, the journey from small room to stadium is a dream

that necessarily involves the loss of that intimacy so prized in the former location.

OUR LEGACY

This search for an experience that is social, interactive and intense, governed by structure but not dependent on it, became most powerful in the West at a time when a new generation of adults had grown up without the experience of war. Because they hadn't known war, they had less sympathy with the conservative notion that utopias were impossible. My generation felt energised to begin creating those utopias, or at least to dismantle the orthodoxies that resisted their pursuit. Many of today's improvisational art forms have their roots in the counter-cultural energies of those days. The drive to grab the essence of the creative process, to de-mystify it and render it accessible to the ordinary person in the street was understood to be an integral contribution to revolutionary political change. That belief led to a slew of initiatives, some inspired and magnificent, others plainly mad. A list of the best within the UK and the USA might mention community arts, contact improvisation, community drama, breakdancing, hip-hop, African-American dance, experimental music, the happening, the be-in, the festival, the jam, choral singing, underground film-making, play therapy, drama therapy, youth theatre and the schools drama movement. Some of the more significant examples might include Ed Berman's Interaction, Jim Haynes' Arts Lab, Andy Warhol's Factory, the Grand Union, the Judson Church, the Living Theatre, Augusto Boal's Theatre of the Oppressed, Viola Spolin's Theatre Games, Keith Johnstone's work, Steve Paxton's work, Yvonne Rainer's Continuous Project Altered Daily, Cornelius Cardew's Scratch Orchestra, Anne Jellicoe's Community Plays, Charles Parker's Banner Theatre, Cartoon Archetypal Slogan Theatre and Dorothy Heathcote's work with children in schools.

> 'Cornelius enabled us to achieve this unbelievable dream with the Scratch Orchestra. John Cage's notion that all noises, and all silences, can be music was the underlying inspiration. ANYONE who wanted could play and compose music.'
>
> Carol Finer

What unites all these projects is the determination to remove arts practice from the hands of elites and place it into the hands of those who traditionally would be expected to keep their place. Instead of the few, the many. Instead of the exclusion of the untrained, the inclusion of the wo/man on the street. It was about the everyday, and the song of the individual soul irrespective of any judgement on his or her talent. No longer need the exercise be validated by the presence of a consummate artist, the aim was to engage ordinary people. And the fact of the engagement was sufficient to ensure the excellence of the work. Simultaneously, there was redefinition of what 'excellence' really was. It wasn't, by the new creed, a demonstration of extraordinary skill and virtuosity, rather it was evidence of an extraordinary *process*, rooted in communitarian values, which might or might not result in an extraordinary *product*. The switch of emphasis from product to process was central, and has characterised much of the work in similar traditions that we've been part of, in the forty or so years since.

> 'We must reconsider what is meant by "talent". It is highly possible that what is called talented behaviour is simply a greater individual capacity for experiencing. From this point of view, it is in the increasing of the individual capacity for experiencing that the untold potentiality of a personality can be evoked.'
>
> Viola Spolin

Characteristic of this trajectory was the deliberate erosion of barriers that prevented those with disabilities getting involved with arts practice. Practitioners and artists associated with repositioning arts practice recognised that artistry was about a spirit, a willingness to engage, rather than a particular skill. Physical dexterity therefore began to be prized less than expansiveness of imagination and a fearlessness in exercise of the form. A perfect shape was no longer a precondition for participation. Critic Jill Johnston described Steve Paxton's 'Satisfyin' Lover' (1968) as *thirty-two any old wonderful people . . . (walking) across the gymnasium in their any old clothes. The fat, the skinny, the medium, the slouched and slumped, the straight and tall . . . that's you and me in all our ordinary everyday 'who cares' postural splendour.'* [55]

Nabil Shaban formed Graeae, the first full-time professional theatre company for disabled actors in the UK, in 1973 although the name and identity didn't emerge *'until the summer of 1979. I arrived as a business studies student with an obsession for performing . . . I had to initiate drama productions at school and sheltered workshops because there were no theatre opportunities for disabled people in the '60s and '70s – apart from the Theatre of the Deaf which was exclusive to deaf people who had no physical impairments . . . Right at the beginning of Graeae's development, the work was devised and written through improvisation, utilising the personal experiences and perspective of workshop or company members. We wanted to fill a gap. Disabled people who wanted to be actors were being prevented and denied training at every level. The only way to break the barriers was to build our own ramp – i.e. "launch pad" – and prove by example what we as artists can contribute to the development of national and global cultural life.'*[56] The company set out to prove to the acting profession that performance was not simply about physical athleticism; it was rather about the transmission of messages that can emerge from anyone, irrespective of dis/ability.

Community arts projects such as Ed Berman's Interaction also expanded definitions of the creative process, making a point of enlisting individuals from every walk of life into performance creation. John Fox's Welfare State took a similarly non-discriminatory path further north in Cumbria, involving all sections of the community in projects that were celebratory and spectacular. And today there are ten or twenty for each one of these early companies. Why did improvisation play such a key role? Because of its plasticity. If you wanted to cut against prevailing traditions, if you wanted to create something in the moment with those who held no professional arts language, you used improvisation. As Anna Halprin recalls of work in the USA, *'Elements like voice, words, sound, and found objects were introduced. Movement wasn't so pure anymore. Musicians became dancers, dancers became poets, actors and dancers were the same. The possibilities were endless now, and this new release of materials and people sparked a fresh approach to ways we could improvise . . . Improvising was taking us out on the streets, in the aisles, on the rafters – completely free of the restrictions of the proscenium arch. Freedom from preconceptions, boundaries, familiar patterns. Improvisations often led to outrageous and sometimes threatening situations . . . such as taking our clothes off and dancing naked, interacting with automobiles in a parking lot, including audience members as participants. At one university, the head of the dance department accused us of setting dance backwards 100 years. What she meant was there was a total lack of "form".'*[57]

The comment of the department head was not an untypical response. Such work was perceived as failing to respect the traditional structures within which individual or collective expression normally occurred. There was insufficient acknowledgement of prevailing forms. It therefore appeared form-less. Yet it wasn't as if practitioners necessarily dispensed with form in itself. Rather, they searched for new forms by playing into an arena of formlessness to make new discoveries. An example can be found in the work of the radio producer Charles Parker. When he walked out of the BBC in 1958 to record the voices of working people, taking his tape recorder down to the docks and the railway yards, there were no precedents to the work he was doing. There were no existing artistic templates. Admittedly he leant a little on folk music culture through the participation of the singer Ewan McColl who wrote accompanying music for the *Radio Ballads*, but essentially this was pitching into the dark. The resulting form that the pair, along with Peggy Seeger, developed on the BBC was revolutionary because nothing quite so unmediated by 'professionals' had been heard before on the wireless. The *Radio Ballads* finally interlaced McColl's songs with the raw voices of workers from the railways, the docks and the sea. Some forty years later, the National Theatre presented *The Permanent Way*, David Hare's play about the privatisation of the railways, constructed out of the words of workers and managers. The exercise was essentially Parker's. However, it was now 'Verbatim Theatre'. Had Parker still been alive in 2006, he would have appreciated the BBC's new radio ballads of that year, still following Parker's templates. There have been other growings-out from this initial source. Mention should be made of the pioneering work of Peter Cheeseman at the Victoria Theatre, Stoke-on-Trent. 2004 saw Alecky Blythe's show *Come Out, Eli* based on accounts of a siege in Hackney in which actors wore earpieces connected to personal minidisc players, allowing them to speak the words of interviewees who had witnessed the actual events.

There was everywhere an acknowledgement during the '60s and '70s that you had to go not inside your own head but to 'where people are', as R.G. Gregory put it to me. If you wanted to tell the real stories of our society, you had to work with the vernacular of the people. You had to find new forms pliable enough to accommodate the rough voices. You had to improvise your own role as artist, elevating the vernacular of participants to a status equivalent to the words of the professional playwright. Artists therefore became facilitators. Poets became organisers.

Singers became choristers. There was a distrust of the ivory tower; a suspicion that what emerged from it would lack resonance for anyone other than ivory tower dwellers. It was a journey that many resisted. But those who did make it showed that it could lead to extraordinarily powerful work, and a profound sense of ownership by the community in the material it created. Further, it bred a practice that has been profoundly challenging at several levels since, not only to the dominant arts culture but also to widely held views about the place of the artist within it. Within the UK thousands of community-focused projects would not now be taking place, were it not for that upheaval of values in those times.

CONTACT IMPROVISATION

Contact improvisation has been one of the more significant of these developments. In contact work, improvisers use a simple language of movement, triggered by physical contact, to interact with each other in duos, trios and larger groups, in a workshop context that usually eschews any audience focus. If you were to walk into a contact improvisation workshop, you would simply see people moving informally together, often using the floor, pairing off, splitting away, finding other partners, or simply sitting watching at the edge. Some movers will roll together, fall together, and jump together with a contact that might be strong or light. The medium is clearly celebratory and accessible. It requires minimum skill to come in on the first level. It is open to able-bodied and disabled, the seeing and the blind, the old and the young. By its nature, it resists co-ordination or leadership by any authority figure. There's a democracy inherent in the form that comfortably embodies the anti-elitist spirit of its beginnings. After all, its most typical manifestation is the jam, a leaderless, time-unbound party that people can join and leave at leisure. And in contrast to many other dance traditions, it avoids reliance on gender-specific roles for its practice. Instead, roles are defined by abilities to shift gravity and use weight rather than by abilities to lift or carry. By its avoidance of spoken language, the CI practitioner finds himself as comfortable in any part of the world, at home there as in his own back yard. Whether you go to Finland, the USA, the Soviet Union or Wimbledon, it remains essentially the same event. You walk into the room and join in. Robert Anderson, an active organiser and teacher in the UK scene, comments: *'That's something I really enjoy now. I find I have access to people, different cultures, and different languages – because I have this language of contact improvisation. You can go off to Vienna or Israel and you immediately have a language. In that sense, it's an international community.'* So what draws people to contact in the first place? How does it work as a medium of community?

'For me, it's a very enjoyable thing. The amount of physical sensation that's involved. It's about the pleasure of doing it. And experience of the body in motion with another body is quite special. The ability to find yourself disorientated, upside down and falling towards the floor and coming up again . . . I sometimes think of it as akin to swimming almost, in the air, and finding a freedom of movement in the body in relation to gravity and the floor. I used to love swimming. Maybe that's why I'm drawn to it. There's also the fact that you meet people in a dance. And you have these exchanges with these people, and there's something quite nice about that level of contact with people – again, it's unusual in our culture, our society.' So it's accessible and it's pleasurable, but as Robert points out, it's not simplistic. It's easy to enter the room and join in, if you can overcome your nerves, but *'Contact does involve practice, some commitment to learning, if you want to progress.'* Because of this, in contrast perhaps to the Five Rhythms method of Gabrielle Roth, the practice retains the involvement of highly skilled practitioners such as K.J. Holmes, Kirstie Simson, Rick Nodine, Irmela Weimann, Gaby Agis, Charlie Morrissey, K.J. Holmes, Martin Keogh, Scott Smith and many, many others who find within the form a consistently expanding horizon in terms of what can be achieved as a level of skill.

In a way, the relative failure of contact improvisation to spawn an equivalent performance form, bears witness to its effectiveness as a private event. From the early days of CI, the debate has run, with proponents on both sides. Is it a dance form for performance? Or is its value simply as a medium of communication in private? When Steve Paxton and his collaborators first developed the form, they did take it around to venues and galleries for audiences to see. Significantly the show was called *You Come – We'll Show You What We Do*, implying that what the performances were about, was carrying the torch and spreading the flame. They were not about virtuosity. The role of the audience was to observe a process that might well have been going on without them. But please the audiences they certainly did. It had a galvanising effect on the contemporary dance/movement scene. As

Nancy Stark Smith observes: *'To tell you the truth, I don't think there was one performance we did that wasn't enthusiastically received. It was like we had offered something to people as a way of looking at movement and a way of experiencing movement that was very new and healthy, very vital and life-supporting . . . When it was over, there would be a lot of dancing in the audience. People would be jumping all over one another.'* But it would be a mistake not to recognise the clear inference in these comments that this reaction was about recognition of a dance form that projected values the audiences themselves wanted to express. CI appeared to be putting into practice ideas about community, sharing, equality, absence of authoritarianism and gender role similarities that the audiences wanted themselves to espouse. They liked it because it was a celebration of what they believed could be a model of social interaction; further, it refused to conform to a commercial idea of what performance was. The fact that after the show, spectators 'jumped all over one another' suggests that spectators immediately saw themselves as being as good as the performers, as having as much right as they, to access the medium. There was by implication no clear performer/ audience split. So the notion of taking this practice and adapting this practice to make it more commercial to audiences was always going to be anathema to many of its champions.

In Nancy Stark Smith's view, Steve Paxton was creating a form *'that wasn't dependent on a master choreographer telling everyone what to do.'* So, then to start choreographing it would be to undermine a founding principle. However, some dancers did introduce more structural elements. *'I think over time the phenomenal value of it started to shift so it became "Yes, it's exciting to see, but I'd rather see these people do it rather than those people", so a certain level of virtuosity started to kick in which on a certain level was initially weeded out, but inevitably crept back in, especially as people became familiar with it and their tastes started to narrow . . . So as people went off in their own regions, maybe they taught it, maybe they performed it, you'd have people dressing up for it, putting on music, creating special contexts for it, or integrating it with more theatrical improvisation . . . I tended to enjoy the pure form myself . . . Many contact improvisations that were seen in performance somehow actually seemed to lack some of the things I find most beautiful in practice, perhaps because of a desire to please an audience or do something that was spectacular in a certain way. Certain kinds of moves became emphasised, certain other subtleties of communication were eliminated.'*

What happened in respect of the teaching issue was that as the movement expanded, more and more practitioners set themselves up as teachers. After all, it was popular. There was a living to be made. Three years into the practice, there came a fork in the road for the prime movers of CI. Should they rein it in? There were stories of injuries resulting from people doing CI who had misunderstood the extent of training that was required. As a result, an initiative was embarked on to trademark and register teachers in CI and thereby withhold legitimation from those who hadn't trained. The initiative even went as far as drawing up an open letter. This gave the names of six teachers of CI (LaRocque, Little, Paxton, Siddall, Stark Smith and Woodbury) who were the only ones, by a two-thirds majority, able to award permission to teach. *'Any other persons who are now teaching and/or performing under the name Contact Improvisation are requested from this point on to use another name.'*[58] Only Little and Siddall signed the letter before others stepped in and argued that to embark on this policing would be to compromise the essential freedoms that were intertwined with the practice. So the initiative was dropped and you won't find TM appended to the words Contact Improvisation. (But you may find it appended to the terms of Action Theatre, Five Rhythms Theatresports or *Lifegame*. Except that you won't in this book.)

THEATRESPORTS

It strikes me as ironic that the most successful dramatic improvisation format in many communities is one that uses rivalry as a governing notion. Theatresports, Impro Match, Catch Impro and Comedy Sportz all involve variations on the competitive format. On second thoughts, it's not surprising. It makes complete sense. The competitive sports model provides an obvious and familiar point of reference for audiences. Besides, it taps into the traditions of mock conflict referred to in the earlier chapter. Keith Johnstone started Theatresports with Loose Moose Theatre Company in Calgary in response to what he found to be a growing enthusiasm for impro. He did it, *'to cope with so many wanting to go on stage.'* He writes that *'It was inspired by pro-wrestling, a family entertainment where Terrible Turks mangled defrocked Priests while mums and dads yelled insults, and grannies staggered forward waving their handbags (years passed before I learned that some of the more berserk grannies were paid stooges).'*

'The bouts took place in cinemas (in front of the screen) and the expressions of agony were all played outfront. No theatre person could have believed that it was real, and nor could anyone with a knowledge of anatomy. Jackie Pallo explains how he would climb up one of the posts and then crash down on to his prone victim "landing with my knee across his throat". He would go into convulsions, and so would the ladies at the ringside. Everybody would be happy. "But if my knee really had landed on his throat with my weight with the impetus of my jump from the post behind it, the poor lad would have ended up on a slab." Wrestling was the only form of working-class theatre that I'd seen, and the exaltation among the spectators was something I longed for, but didn't get, from "straight" theatre – perhaps because "culture" is a minefield in which an unfashionable opinion can explode your self-esteem.'[59]

> 'Great teams brainstorm to find new challenges . . . set themselves goals like including audience volunteers in every scene, or playing each scene in gibberish.'
> Keith Johnstone

In Theatresports, there are two teams of improvisers, a Master of Ceremonies and a team of judges, although this line-up may vary a little. The MC invites one team to challenge the other with perhaps a mime scene, a scene set in a bathroom, a romantic scene, a scene using props or a one-word-at-a-time scene. The challenges can be many and various. The challenge is accepted, the scene is played and then the other side takes on the same challenge. Then the judges ask the audience to respond and on the basis of the applause given, award points. A number of rounds are played until at the end a winning team is declared.

> 'Three robed Judges cross the stage to sit in the moat that surrounds our acting area. Bicycle horns hang around their necks (these are the "rescue horns" used to honk boring players off the stage). Their demeanour is serious, it being less fun to boo light-hearted people.'
> Keith Johnstone

You could argue that Theatresports is no less than the Revenge of the Audience. At last, spectators win a chance to get up there and play their own madness. And they do so, in considerable numbers. Since its inception, the form has enlisted perhaps thousands of followers, the vast majority amateur performers with little or no professional training. It's taken off in a major way in parts of Europe, although less so in the UK. What it offers to participants is the hustle and bustle of a lively, funny knockabout that provides safety in its team-playing ethic. It gives amateurs a vehicle in which to explore their clubbiness and performer selves without recourse to the occasional deadliness of Amateur Theatre. And as individuals with proper jobs, these activists are able to bring considerable expertise to the business and commercial side of the work organising events, competitions and festivals. The annual festival in Amsterdam would put many professionally run events of similar scale to shame with its hospitality, respect for visiting companies and very full houses. A number of similar initiatives have followed Johnstone's, not excluding television formats of which *Whose Line Is It Anyway?* has been the most prominent within the UK.

What the competitive format does is externalise the fears and anxieties of the performer. You have in front of you the judges, possibly attired with black gowns and wigs whose role is to represent and absorb any negativity buzzing around. If there is booing to be done, it can be directed at the judges. If these figures can be satisfactorily blamed for any failures in the event, the performers are freed up to explore their foolishness. Judgement, after all, is the great demon. These judges function as the 'dictator' in Jonathan Kay's approach, recognition of which (within us all) allows an equivalent recognition of the right of the fool to exist. However, their function is serious. Johnstone writes: *'Judges should be seen as parental figures who are taking their responsibility seriously . . . Unless judges are treated with respect, the quality of the match will suffer . . . They should be in opposition to the players' playfulness, but they should not succeed in stamping it out.'* During the contest, the judges *'are responsible for raising the quality of the game'* and for scoring and managing the event.[60]

The game show atmosphere is intended to generate playfulness and courage. In this way, the format creates both safety – through the use of judges – and playfulness – through the use of mischievous challenges and a lively MC. That's the theory. My own experience suggests that it also limits the range of dramatic material that can be explored. Keith Johnstone's comments suggest that he too has become frustrated with the practice – rather than the theory – of Theatresports, albeit he blames the troupes rather than any limitations of the form. Some of his views were outlined in the previous chapter. The charge remains however that, once the MC starts whooping it up, it becomes difficult to enter any more vulnerable, emotional form of interaction. The emphasis starts to become relentlessly comedic, while any excursions away from this Road to Jollity, while clearly permitted, become unconsciously proscribed.

Training for Theatresports often takes place in the evening or at times that works for community players. The social dynamic of the exercise is immediately apparent. *'The great thing about Theatresports is it's like joining a club. You can go along down the street and sign up for classes and immediately you're hearing about other teams in other parts of the world – Europe, Japan, Colombia – and suddenly I feel I'm part of something. Who knows, I may even get to play against those teams. There are the games, which you can learn, and the format, which you can learn – for many that's enough. What's the point in going further?'* (Sandy Van Torquil.) Theatresports functions similarly to Contact Improvisation in that once familiar with the conventions, you can jump right in anywhere you can speak the language. When Mark Phoenix from Fluxx was filming in Berlin, he tracked down a Theatresports night, offered himself as a player, signed up and played.

Since the format is licensed, groups wanting to use it have to apply to Keith Johnstone's organisation if they want to advertise under that name. A slew of other initiatives, some mentioned above, have followed in the wake of Theatresports, most of which take the central ideas of the format but evade the licensing issue by calling the event by a different name.

COMMUNITY MODELS

What do these two examples of improvisation practice tell us about the art form of improvisation as a recreational model for community? Clearly both are enormously successful in their own right. Neither evades the issue of skill. Neither pretends that skill is not advantageous in any exploration of the form. They both allow for beginners to come in at the ground level. Both have met limitations in their historical development. For CI, many of the more experienced practitioners see it as more of a tool for composition or as a means of training or for meeting others, than for any greater design. Nevertheless, these are still good reasons to participate. Theatresports too has populist appeal, but it's often perceived by professional improvisers as being something of a knockabout, rather than the real deal. Perhaps both traditions are strong in their identity as community forms precisely because they don't encroach into spheres beyond their range. The scope of ambition is appropriate to the level of expertise at which the participants want to engage.

To concentrate on these two is not to imply that other approaches are not also significant. There is the Five Rhythms of Gabrielle Roth, which attracts many followers into its workshops, and can immediately get beginners into action. There are community-based music projects operating within the UK that use improvisation as a means to offer the chance of creative expression to prisoners, hospital patients, schoolchildren and the unemployed. Here, the recognition that 'all sound is music' aids in legitimising the contributions of many who would otherwise be excluded from a music-based process. The Irene Taylor Trust and Live Music Now! are two of the leading organis-ations in this field in the UK. Rex Horan who works frequently for Irene Taylor writes: *'Improvisation can be seen as one of the most effective tools available in terms of getting non-musicians or inexperienced musicians playing. By providing these newer players with the most simple and funda-mental instrumental tools – a couple of chords on the guitar like Em and Am9, the square 4/4 rock beat on the drum kit (even if the hi-hat or snare need be played by another band member) a 'two-finger-style' melodic skeleton on a keyboard, and by pointing out where E and A are on the bass guitar – you have the beginnings of a band and a new piece of music. It doesn't take much to then begin working on aspects of song writing, structure and the building of ensemble playing skills. Improvisation is very much a way in for newer players.'* [61]

Youth theatre offers another route. For young people, the written script is often seen as a document of authority. It may have arrived via the youth theatre director who sees it as educational or purposeful. Improvisation for its part is a more fluid, ambiguous medium. The material generated by it can be interpreted and its meaning defined as well by the young performers as it can by the director. They can devise and perform in their own vernacular. So the young actors may feel more a sense of ownership of that material. The National Association of Youth Theatres has some seven hundred member companies through-out the UK. Many of these are geared to organising performances. But this is not to descry alternative strategies. Often what's valuable for the young people is engagement with a process that has no outcomes, anathema though that may be to educationalists. To let off steam/be expressive/break taboos of behaviour/meet and chat up members of the opposite sex/display tribal allegiances may be more important than making a show. Being able to avoid the obligations of a controlling, ever-evaluating school culture is probably welcomed.

What a process without product lacks is the kind of challenges associated with production. The act of meeting an audience challenges the group to co-operate with each other, develop communication skills, wrestle with issues of form and meaning, and impose self-discipline. Performing validates and confirms the value of what has been excavated. What determines whether the group should perform or not has to be the conditions of the process. Is that what the young people themselves want? Isn't this a decision they can make? Do the conditions of the event lend themselves? That means looking at the aims of the organisers, the nature of the building and the group, and the group's relationship to its potential audience. Friends, families, relatives and staff who see a show in a prison or hospital never expect the production values of the West End. As audiences, they are interested to see the participants use the form as a vehicle to put across something of their worldview. If this is done with energy and courage, the result will be as valued as anything produced in a street of lights.

Improvisation was seized on as a primary tool during the 60s and 70s because of its innate tendency to fracture and shake more authoritarian expressions. Since then, some distinct practices have been nurtured and these now function as (primarily libertarian) value-carriers within communities. Given the way technology continues to permeate social interactions, such communitarian forms of expressions can reasonably be expected to grow further and evolve, amoeba-like, pretty much as long as communities seek ways to fight/play and celebrate/learn together.

CODA I

AN ARGUMENT FOR THEATRE-IN-THE-ROUND

This is an age of sensationalism and dissolution. The Renaissance structures that held Western superiority in place are rapidly disintegrating. There is a fresh multilateral voice trying to be heard. The absolute is being eaten away by the relative. Out of the fear of all this happening there is a taste for the immediate and the shallow. Too much thinking, at any depth, is painful. Celebrity culture, the lauding of the trivial, the giving of too much money to those who, in essence, are like us, has taken over from the awe of the distant and unapproachable. Fashion (the smart, populist and handsomely obnoxious) has taken charge.

It is a very difficult time for the arts, that attempt to reflect the core of the spirit (the ever-shifting zeitgeist) in the deepest of human terms (to touch and interpret the quietest of heartbeats). In the language arts, poetry has been consumed by the flashiness of performance, words wrapped up in colourful accoutrements that don't ask to be dwelt on for too long. Theatre is lauded for being total – that clever combination of all the arts that feeds the eye to the detriment of the ear (and confounds the ear more with the triumph of the worst kind of music). Word is under a constant denigrating bombardment.

Performance means 'through form'. We are victims, even as we accept it as natural, of the raised lit space from which we are addressed, cajoled and manipulated by the representatives of our betters. Who stands in the lit space plays at being master.

Never was there a time when the re-aligning of public communication was more urgently needed; when there should be a going back to basics, to re-imagine the role of the message-giver (the message-searcher), discarding down to its bare boards what the giving and receiving of language has been sucked into, but doesn't require, in order to bring out the real strengths of the creative word at its clearest and strongest.

All is not dismal. Since the death of the Renaissance in the late nineteenth century (to be contentious) feelers and shoots have been daring the bitterly opposed climate in order to voice a different manner of growth. The schools' drama movement (at its clearest) sought to speak to the heart-strings of every young being, saying, metaphorically, no need to bow to the Almighty God above you: let speak your god within. A different kind of language flowed, dependent on nothing but its own sense and others to receive it. Such speakers did not require a raised lit space to speak from, but simply a gathering around them, sharing the ordinary light, able to respond with a like diversity, and willing the central performer to speak both to it and for it. This kind of activity needs no dressing up, no superiority, no professional down-the-nose-looking. It needs no sleight-of-hand or mind, no polished lying. To start it is improvisation, words brought out of the darkness without the intellect getting in the way, an attempt to reveal the untarnished, personally compelled truth. It does not need to be upstaged, cunningly lighted, designerly dressed. It belongs to, draws on the common experience and is provoked by the insights of, those who sit around. Later, holding to its irrevocable values, it can become more sophisticated, inspiring its own plays, in which playwright and actors have learned a different meaning to their trade. It can become Instant Theatre (Word and Action's speciality) which sounds part of the quick and the shallow, but has the ability, over and over, to express its creating audiences at their most mythical.

Improvisation, this different world dependent on equality, can explore itself fully only in the Round, again a slowly growing discovery of the post-Renaissance period, in which truth is allowed at last its three-hundred-and-sixty degrees. All that this quickly-shuttering age yearns for (and the only way in which it will begin to be able to pick its way through its present all-life-threatening dilemmas) desperately seeks a change in its symbolic all-pervasive form. We are being strangled by the symbolic implications of the end-stage, with its all-too-powerful and impenetrable back wall, against which all protocols add up to the one. Inequality breeds uniformity, criminalising difference. Only the Round lauds diversity, absorbs, with an equal seriousness, ideas coming in from all angles.

Neither improvisation, leading to a fresh sense of language, nor the Round, the vehicle of all the world's peoples, are temporary jokes. They are among the seeds from which an environmentally-sound, ecologically-efficient and all-living harmony can attempt to grow.

from *Seeds of a Sustainable Future* by R.G. Gregory

CODA II

6, 5, 4

The American Dance Asylum, Binghamton, NY has performed Contact Improvisation over the past years as part of an improvisational structure we call '6, 5, 4'. '6, 5, 4' is an attempt to wed choreography with Contact Improvisation. It is also concerned with organising contact flow into musical meter. This is the basic 2-dancer structure, from which many variations have evolved:

The dancers agree on a common pulse. Those pulses are felt in measures of 12. Each dancer creates a 6 count movement pattern. They teach them to each other.

Continuing, each dancer creates a 5 ct., 4 ct., 3 ct., and 2 ct. pattern, teaching them to each other.

All the movement is practised and the dancers warm-up their contact improvisation.

The structure begins with the first dancer's 6 ct. pattern . . . the balance of the measure (cts. 7 to 12) is completed with contact improvisation.

The 2nd measure of 12 begins with the 2nd dancer's 6 ct. pattern . . . and the balance of the measure is completed with contact improvisation.

The 3rd measure of 12 begins with the 1st dancers 5 ct. pattern . . . and the balance of the measure is completed with contact improvisation.

The 4th measure of 12 begins with the 2nd dancer's 5 ct. pattern . . . and the balance of the measure is completed with contact improvisation.

Continuing until . . .

The 9th measure of 12 begins with the 1st dancer's 2 ct. pattern . . . and the balance of the measure is completed with contact improvisation.

The 10th measure of 12 begins with the 2nd dancer's 2 ct. pattern . . . and the balance of the measure is completed with contact improvisation.

As the dancer goes along, the choreographic action becomes less and less, and the lines of contact flow get longer. The challenge is in the transition from the mental/physical processes that accompany a dancer's performance of 'learned choreography' to those processes that accompany involvement in contact flow. The final count of each of the phrases becomes the weight situation for the beginning of the contact improvisation.

The contact flow is an energy river that has to be diverted toward the choreography as the 'I' count comes around.

6, 5, 4 . . . was performed by Bill T. Jones, Lois Walk and Arnie Zane of the American Dance Asylum at the Clark Center Festival in the Mally, New York, 1977. Printed in *Contact Quarterly*.

PART THREE

THE WHAT

ELEMENTS

The aim in this chapter is to identify some core elements of improvisation that underpin all practice. These elements might be considered the *prima materia*, the genetic, embryonic plasma that makes up the form. If you took improvisation practice in each of dance, music and theatre and tried to identify a single pure stock, what would you find? I would admit that I've been hopefully looking down the microscope for an image of something distinct. A worm perhaps. Then I can run from the lab shouting: 'A Worm! A Worm! The Secret of Impro is a Worm!' But in fact should I ever see a worm, I find it pretty soon becomes a piece of string and then a barracuda. However, if I cease to care about this riddle and instead try to pick out some fleeting characteristics of what's consistently going on there under the microscope, I can begin to identify within each art form practice some separate active ingredients that appear in each case. I can see these bubbling away, mutating and muttering and trying to find balance or equilibrium with each other. If this starts to be achieved, then as if by magic, some chef-less cookery occurs.

ROLES

In the beginning, there were roles. Improvisers inherited these roles from formal performance practice, and found them wanting. They discovered there was a need to abandon them, or at the very least, beat them up a little. The move from jazz to free improvisation characterises the process clearly. The musician Simon Fell observes how, *'With free jazz, the characteristic roles of the instruments in the ensemble tended to be relatively traditional. The classic example would be a trio of sax, bass, and drums. In a free jazz context, you'd expect (very, very broadly characterising this), for the drums to do a lot of drumming, the bass to plonk away in a bass style and the sax to be the apex of the triangle, dynamically driving down on top . . . A free improvisation definition of that group would be one where the three contributors play much less idiomatically, so the vocabulary which each instrument uses is much less conventional . . . If you play the instrument in the way it's been designed to be played, that tends to put the instrument in a certain hierarchical role because the instrument has been designed to do one or two things very well . . . The saxophone was designed to be very loud and to cut through. A string bass was designed to do almost the opposite, never to cut through, but it has this huge supporting cushion of sound, which goes under everything else. And drums do what drums do. But if you stop doing that – if the sax starts sounding like a cymbal or the drum kit starts sounding like a flute, then straight away that hierarchy disintegrates.'*

Fell elucidates clearly the correlation of role and authority. The player-functional roles, to use Waldrick's term, are fixed. But free improvisation can't necessarily use the roles as ascribed by tradition. To try and work within the old ones, the improvisation dies on its feet. The composer and improviser Peter Weigold has found something similar when he's been called in to get orchestras to improvise. He's found that while on one hand, *'Classical musicians absolutely love to have the pressure taken off'*, in practice it's not easy. The stress induced by being asked to improvise, freezes up the players. In this case, Weigold's strategy might vary. It might be to take away the instruments and give the musicians percussion instead. Or have them swap instruments around. This will help, but *'The real problem with orchestras is they can't hear one another.'* Not only that but, *'from one end to the other they simply can't see each other.'* There may be screens between different sections to protect the ears of those near to the loudest instruments. And getting the musicians to change positions isn't an option because of union agreements. So the musicians are completely dependent upon the conductor. Peter is involved in some sensitive negotiations if he is to dismantle the role structures and release a different content from the group. The fusion of social organisation (form) with traditional classical music (content) is such that he has to tackle both at the same time, if he is to bring the musicians into a new relationship with their craft.

It's not dissimilar in dance. Training encourages a formality of roles, which are inevitably replicated in the larger companies such as the Royal Ballet. Different expectations are made of female and male students that go beyond their natural limitations, being concerned with traditional ideas of masculinity and femininity. Getting dancers to improvise leads to problems similar to those encountered by Peter Weigold. Wendy Houston observes that dancers, for example, are not encouraged to look like *'people making choices (on stage) – you never get asked to do this as a dancer. But the finest dancers are those where you see these decisions.'* Gaby Agis came up against the orthodoxy of contemporary dance when she worked with the Royal Ballet star Ashley Page, in a series of improvised duets. Gaby set herself the task of breaking into Ashley's familiar patterns, helped by the fact that *'Ashley really made himself vulnerable. We had a structure, but we were improvising. So when he would come to me – and I could tell there was nervousness – he would lift me, because that's what he felt I wanted. And what I would do is, I would go dead weight, so he couldn't lift me. So he couldn't do his tricks. And he did those things (that I do) like being still, and rolling, and so in a way it was a real challenge – and I give him credit for making himself vulnerable. For me, it was my territory. But for him, it wasn't.'*

Similarly, if a theatre company operates the star system, and the 'lead' actor expects to get the 'large' parts, improvisations may stall. Things just may not go that way. An ensemble requires a fluid, primitive democracy to operate in which players respond to the needs of the evolving situation and take whatever role is appropriate. Likewise, the role of the director, choreographer or conductor has to be re-evaluated since improvisation is the form least accessible to having meaning determined by an offstage presence. It's in the spirit of ensemble that performers claim the freedom of decision-making. In this they begin to appropriate the tactics and knowledge of directors, choreographers and playwrights instead of being beholden to them. Perhaps any re-conceptualised director role might be limited to composing structures, giving advice and nudging.

But the challenge of self-organisation without directorial authority imposed, and without fixed-player function roles in place, is not inconsiderable. As Joan Littlewood observed, *'To introduce chaos, you have to be very organised.'* Littlewood was a strong director who used improvisation

> 'Joan has talked a lot about developing artists rather than actors through impro – actors who were creative artists who could think on their feet and respond to any given circumstance ... Shows such as *The Hostage* were largely improvised as the company only started with several pages of script. Sometimes shows were changed on a nightly basis as happened with *You Won't Always Be Top*, which led to the prosecution by the Lord Chamberlain.'
>
> Nadine Holdsworth

extensively in rehearsals and always looked for innovative ways to introduce unpredictable elements into performance. She would trust that the company onstage could problem-solve to handle the provocations she introduced.

One strategy for self-organisation lies in a substitution of shared operational values for conventions of status or authority. In other words, performers work to find a shared aesthetic or philosophy that guides their decision-making on stage. The challenge, however, lies in finding a way to accommodate both dark and light, both Dionysiac and Apollonian energies. It's not enough to commit to a set of social values in the way that a political party or interest groups might. To use the stage as a means to promote social idealism in a simplistic way, drains theatre of its essential fire. It can't become about 'demonstrating' ethical behaviour. Mick Napier's comments, quoted earlier, stress how improvisers being *only* 'supportive' simply leads to ineffectual dramatic scenes. *'No, the most supportive thing you can do is get over your pasty self and selfishly make a strong choice in the scene.'*[62] These comments find strong echoes in the world of dance. Jo Blowers: *'Another one of the paradigms is a particularly careful, bordering on precious, very definite etiquette about "taking care" of each other. And sometimes – and I know for myself – it can get over-respectful, and it's not surprising that "release dancers" or "contact dancers" get called the Pyjama People. Because of the softness and the confluence. Because it's so democratic, you just wish someone would get in there and do something obscene . . . Although it's a wonderful aspiration and a fantastic state of being; it is very holistic from that point of view – all of that I entirely applaud, but there are times in performance when you think, "Well, this is an opportunity to bring this to a broader picture and the reality of life . . ." That's when it gets exciting and interesting to watch, when it gets combative, and instinctive. Because that is so much truer to the life we're leading.'*

Improvisation culture has to find a way of incorporating or being able to work with not just conflict but the rough, discordant, baser elements of performance. These colours need to exist on the palette as well as the pastel, harmonious tones. But this isn't an argument for just being selfish.

Rick Nodine: *'I've had the experience of improvising with people who don't do the listening half. They do the action half. You go on stage with them and they're dancing constantly.'*

Gaby Agis: *'And they might be doing really amazing dancing.'*
Rick: *'But I might as well not be there.'*
Gaby: *'Ego!'*
Rick: *'I don't know whether it's ego or fear, but as they whizz past you, you feel like putting your hand out as you might stop a bus and saying "Excuse me, but if you could slow down for a moment maybe we could get on the same bus?"'*
Gaby: *'And you know what they become? They become solo improvisers . . . But to be part of an ensemble – that's tough.'*

Of course the improviser is drawing from selfishness. It's a great source of energy and desire. But unless the selfishness is offered generously, the actor loses the ability to receive information through skin. If the eyes and the skin don't receive, then it's only the blood and nerves pulsing.

The task of redefining roles in this new context must mean several things – one of which is inventing scores that allow performers to bring forward dark energies without a sacrifice of values. Such structures must involve understandings about the restrictions and freedoms of role-playing. The work of Jackie Walduck offers a possible template, based as it is on the mechanics of music improvisation. Andrew St John's development of archetypal characters within dramatic improvisation offers another. Details of this are offered in the lexicon. Shows such Fluxx's *Spitting for England* offer an idea about dramatic character through the use of an evolving chronology, each character having a time line mirroring the audience's own. Within live art, Franko B, Forced Entertainment, Station House Opera and other companies simply bypass any idea of character, finding roles out of time-based or structural procedures. By removing role from character, performers are no longer trapped by any association with conventional understandings of 'what normally happens'.

TENSION

Improvisation is an organised fight. The removal of any element of struggle or rivalry runs the risk of the medium becoming simply a song of praise to the human spirit. In the theatre, the audience is engaged (usually) by the tension created from uncertainty over the outcome of the event. This happens in different ways. In conventional theatre there is *pretence* that the outcome is uncertain. In improvisation, it really is.

Therefore the conflict needs to be authentic if not actually real. Augusto Boal once observed that the sight of two boxers entering the ring on crutches wasn't going to offer much of a spectacle. It's the same here; only a genuine tension makes the audience watch keenly. Who will win? What will be revealed? The opportunity to witness tension, embarrassment and difficulty in others is always engaging. Hanging used to draw huge crowds, a point well understood by reality television producers. This is not an argument for reinstating capital punishment but it is an argument for having something at stake when the drama begins.

Tension is essential. The dancer plays with tension in his body, exploring the submission to and fight against gravity. The exploration is made through movement; leaps, rolls, lifts and jumps that cumulatively realise choreography. It's not the only way: tension may be created through the expression of vulnerability, tenderness or affection. In such acts, the performer opens her or himself up for scrutiny. S/he shares something personal or intimate. There's a sense in the audience of a taboo being broken – because the action is taking place in public. Jo Blowers commented to me about Kirstie Simson's ability to really open herself up to the audience, to be willing to be seen as vulnerable in that moment of spontaneity. Kirstie has said, '*I really try to break down this whole presentational front – where the audience feels separate from what's going on onstage.*'[63] In her performances, you understand clearly that Simson is chancing her arm, you feel for her but also with her. It's discomforting but in some ways also reassuring because the predicament is so recognisable. You feel you are looking into that personality, or through it, to understand something of the person. When two dancers make a duet in that spirit, it's like pointing a flashlight into their relationship. Tension is created by pulling things away; masks, false constructions, layers of skin. It's Grotowski's *via negativa* and Brook's demolition process happening before you. The inevitable flicks of empathy leap from the auditorium to the stage.

Tension is always a staple element in music. In a discussion about this with Alison Blunt and Rex Horan, Horan commented, '*Tension features very consciously – in a variety of ways. There are clichés you can use to build and release tension. For example, if we're doing an improvisation together, as a bassist what I can do is what's called pedal. I can drop down to a certain note that plays a certain role in a key, and I can pedal while someone is going crazy on top with their music. And when I get off that pedal note, and resolve it, there's a great release of tension. It's a fabulous moment. And that tension is caused by the audience expecting it to resolve and it not being resolved. Tension and release in music is about dissonance and consonance. It's about knowing an expectation exists and not allowing it to resolve for a long time.'* This parallels a situation where a dancer consistently and repetitively explores the same routine, refusing to break it. Or within drama, a female character walks provocatively up and down in front of a passive but attentive male character. Who will speak first?

Comedy improvisation relies significantly on tension. It's what makes the joke work. The aim is to build and release tension in short bursts. But even if the joke is only a few lines long, if the *build* isn't there, the laughter doesn't come. If the improviser goes for the gag too early, the whole scene may be jeopardised. This is why a poor joke by a good comedian will work better than a good joke by a weak comedian. For the good comedian knows better how to build the tension, and thereby gets a better response from a weak 'pay-off'. This recognition echoes John Wright's assertion, quoted earlier: *'There are three areas to an action which I think are important to structure: one, the anticipation that something is going to happen – two, knowing where you are in the scene – the relief when it is happening – and three, at the end it's the pay-off. You feel differently to how you feel at the beginning.'*

So how is comedy created improvisationally? Matt Elwell from ComedySportz offered this: *'What I would go back to is the definition of comedy as created when you manipulate surprise in the context of the familiar.'* Comedy is really the defeat of the anticipated in favour of what is logical – but unexpected. The mind (of the spectator) is prompted to make one assumption but gets another instead. There's a surprise element but the pay-off is not ridiculous in the sense of being illogical, having no connection to what came before. Or it can work differently. A hypothesis is established which is bizarre but logical in its own terms. The pay-off comes through the elaboration of the hypothesis. Once Eddie Izzard has established the premise that wolves raised him, everything that follows is logical – in its own terms. It's ridiculous, but not absurd in the way of a sequence of non sequiturs would be. Beginners sometimes think that it's enough to be unexpected, and skip the logic. 'Where shall we go to eat tonight?' 'Cornucopia!' It probably sounded funny in the head. There's no tension built so there's probably no laughter.

Teaching at ComedySportz in Chicago, Elwell uses exercises like the Three Line Scene to teach about comedy. *'Basically, you and I are in a scene. You say a line, I say a line, and you say a line. That's the end. By this time, we know exactly what this scene is about . . . With the three lines, that gives you your familiar. That gives you a playing field. And then, how do you turn this, twist this?'*

But tension doesn't just function as an ingredient of comedy. It can be established early in the drama and rather than be released, it can be maintained throughout. The tension caused by Hamlet's determination to revenge his father's death is established early and concluded late. Alison Blunt outlined how this works musically: *'I'm thinking of Nyman or Reich: there can be a long build-up and the tension created over a long period of time. There can be small tensions between different chords pushing each other, cadences that don't quite resolve, but then there's an overall structure that resolves, like in the sonata form. You can use dynamics to create tension, you can use repetition of an idea, and you can have people playing in unison or in separate parts, more contrapuntally – so many ways. And it's the same in theatre.'* Within dramatic improvisation, long-form pieces tend to rely less on comedic patterns than on the use of narrative tension – how will this end? Keith Johnstone's work is all about story, about encouraging the adventurer-hero into situations of possibly dire outcome. In a context of this kind, re-incorporation plays a greater role as the conclusion of the adventure in some way recalls the beginning. Sherlock Holmes often recalls information gleaned by the private eye at the start of the chase, which suddenly has meaning at the end.

When the improviser's eye is on the longer journey, jokes in the short term can be destructive. They may weaken the bigger pay-off. *'Jokes tend to be employed as a last-ditch measure by insecure players when they are worried that a scene isn't funny . . . Audiences appreciate a sophisticated game player. When a player listens and uses patterns that have developed in a scene, it can elicit cheers from an audience which are much more intoxicating than the laughs that result from a few jokes. Del Close remembers hearing famed comic Lenny Bruce talk on stage for 20 minutes without getting one laugh – and then suddenly tying together several trains of thought with one or two sentences, as the audience erupted in cheers at the brilliance they had just witnessed.'*[64]

The short version of the big book on how to create dramatic tension improvisationally for the audience would probably go like this: There are two ways. By setting up this question – 'What will happen?' or by setting up this question – 'What's the truth?' When the first question is asked, the audience is encouraged to feel the tension generated by the existence of possible multiple outcomes. But to achieve this, the actors need to spend time creating characters, relationships and dilemmas. If they commit to these elements, the audience empathises with the characters so the eventual outcome becomes important to them. There will be a sequence involving establishment, development of what's established, a change point or crisis, and some kind of resolution. That's the orthodox Western story arc. When the second question is asked, there is the establishment of a mystery that needs to be solved. The spectator is invited to speculate around possible multiple interpretations of the truth. The understanding is that one of these will be revealed as the 'real' truth. In a detective story by Agatha Christie, we expect to know at the end 'whodunnit'. (In films and plays less linear in their structure, such as those of David Lynch, there is no absolute definitive truth offered.) From the first model we get epic stories, myths, legends and dramas of conflict. From the latter we get murder mysteries, detective stories, ghost stories, and psychological tales. Improvising the latter is more problematic, because to resolve the mystery requires a more detached mind than is usefully available to the improviser.

There's an art in constructing dramatic improvisation that capitalises on the propensity of performers to create tension between each other. It's possible to instruct players in certain ways by the use of tasks or restrictions:

You meet a woman in a dentist's waiting room. In this scene, all you want to really do is play with her hair.

The point is to set a motivation that establishes tension without verbal argument. Scenes of a sexual or romantic content always lend themselves.

You have a grievance with your lover but you can't say what it is. Leave the expression of this grievance until the last possible moment. Start the scene without knowing what the grievance is.

To avoid the tension being broken, tell the other player not to pursue knowledge of the grievance, but to simply observe it and then get on with something else. Another example might be: 'You really fancy this person but can't express it' or 'You have something difficult to confess to this person, but can't bring yourself to reveal it'. These are effective because they cause tension through establishing a gap between the text and subtext. The performer's preoccupation is with the subtext, yet the actor is 'obliged' to play the surface action on top. So there's a tension in the performer that infects the scene. The audience is drawn to watching what happens. If the scene works well, the audience will be engaged with both 'what the truth is' as well as 'what happens at the end'.

RESPONSIVENESS

If we define reactiveness as what is felt through sensation or emotion, then responsiveness is what the improviser decides to do as a result of receiving this stimulus. Living on the stage moment-to-moment helps make responsiveness authentic. In other words, it more accurately reflects the performer's relaxed use of his or her own reaction as material. In a society that is increasingly preoccupied with either the future or the past – rarely the present – we're conditioned to be always thinking ahead or back. To *be here now* is easier than it sounds. If you listen to soap opera on the radio, you'll be aware that characters are often responding to events that happened earlier or anticipating events to come. This tends to create a reassuring and gentle atmosphere in which difficulties are buttressed by the distance of time. 'Being in the present' in front of an audience can be disquieting for both parties. It's more comforting either to reflect or anticipate. One technique used by improvisers is that of 'disappearing the audience', simply kidding oneself the situation is more private than it is. The good improviser oscillates between registering and disappearing the audience.

> 'To sit inside your own body while you know someone is watching you – the bottom line, that's a really very excruciatingly embarrassing place. Most people start disappearing the audience in order to do what we do.'
> Wendy Houston

'Going into your head' is the phrase used to describe *not* being in the present. In the head, the improviser is looking backwards or forwards. 'How did I get here? Was that a good move? Will it be a good move if

I go there?' Thoughts of this kind take the performer out of the present. 'Going into your head' means that the laser beam of attention is pointed the wrong way. It needs to point back into the physical and emotional dynamics that are occurring in the body. If not in this direction, then to other performers in the improvisation or to other sounds in the event.

Improvisers in different art forms often perceive *listening* as the key to present-time responsiveness. It doesn't mean listening to your thoughts, a process that will lead increasingly to detachment. It means tuning in, kinaesthetically as well as aurally, to what is occurring. Especially in mixed-art form work, *'People think they have to look for something, they have to "think something up". This will generally shift them in the direction of their own art form because their ideas most easily function in that domain. Whereas if you say "Look and hear what's there – and do it", that wouldn't necessarily suggest any particular art form.'* (Guy Dartnell.) Responsiveness therefore begins with noting the auditory, visual or kinaesthetic stimuli that are present. (The comedian Ross Noble is always quick to observe anything distinctive about the audience or the set as soon as he walks on stage.) With these responses, the aim is to trigger the imagination so as to provoke its progenitive ability to spawn its own world within the world of the event. Then responses start to exist within that created, autonomous world. Keith Johnstone always argues that one cannot be held responsible for the content of one's imagination. Accepting this, there need be no concern about the breaking of taboos. Instead, one is looking for an immersion in this emerging material. It's not that detachment doesn't have a place. There are moments during any improvisation when detachment is vital, perhaps to recapture a sense of the whole. At this point the imaginative world is left, temporarily. The original *Commedia* players tended to be so immersed in their playing that, as soon as they came offstage, they'd rush to a list of scenes backstage to reorientate themselves. They needed that detached moment.

To achieve this necessary quality of creative responsiveness may be a matter of 'unlearning' something as much as 'learning' it – rediscovering a level of attentiveness we had as a young child. With that attentiveness came a fearless spontaneity. Johnstone argues that *'You can't teach spontaneity but you can remove the obstacles to spontaneity that have been put in the way of the child.'*[65] One of the learned tendencies to be thrown overboard during this education is the felt need to justify

> 'You have to kill ideas —
> otherwise it would be like
> Salvador Dali's clocks.'
>   Keith Johnstone

everything before you do it. *'Great improvisers justify afterwards. Beginners justify first.'* The actor and teacher Andy Eninger pointed out to me in a workshop that *'You have to treat everything you're doing on stage as being absolutely the most perfect thing you could possibly do in that moment.'* This was a useful tip in finding the mindset that takes the improviser away from judgement and censorship.

Responsiveness, then, is about action that is consequent on awareness. However, the more aware the improviser is, the more the need to choose between different stimuli jostling for attention. At the beginning, at the time when the first chord on the piano is sounded, there's less material available so less need for choice. As material is produced, there is more necessity for choice. The purely reactive improviser who is afraid to choose between alternative elements of material may be driven by the need to make everything 'interesting'. So how do you choose what to respond to and what to ignore? Invariably, practice will bring you confidence to be more completely 'yourself' in making selections, foregoing the superficial desire – out of fear – to give the audience what you think they require. You should seek amongst the material at your disposal that which inspires you the most. Inspiration is profoundly personal. That's how it is.

JOURNEY

'When you meet a partner you might find you're initially listening just through touch, on a light level, so you're exploring the surface of the body. And how you create patterns and pathways through that light touch. Then you might find you really want to sink into a deeper level, into bones and into the centre of the body. And then you're looking at how weight can travel and how you can support each other. From there you might want to jump, find trajectories through space, to get airborne, and help each other find that.' (Robert Anderson.) Recently I was talking to an improvisation teacher who proudly told of how an improvisation started with the actor crying. I wondered how that had come about, and whether those tears weren't coming from somewhere else other than the stimuli of that improvisation. It made me think about journeys and how a more organic process might begin with the actor perhaps doing something

banal, and then making a journey from that point to a later point where a state of heightened emotion is discovered. This seems to me the natural journey, from surface to depth. In this approach, the performer finds engagement through a sensuous connection with the external world, and through this sensuous relationship, to feelings. Robert Anderson in the quote above isn't talking about a dramatic journey but about the journey of two improvisers meeting within contact improvisation practice. However, much of the same applies even though both the vocabularies and the end point are different.

The notion of journey is really an inversion of the idea of form. What the performer experiences as journey, the spectators experience as form. Some improvisers, particularly musicians, reject the notion of their responsibility for creating form except as created out of the dialogue between them. Their responsibility is the quality of that dialogue. They trust the form that emerges. So how does the emerging form have any kind of intelligence or craft about it? How can it speak to the audience if all the emphasis is on the journey? The question is particularly pertinent given the role played by accidents and mistakes that was discussed earlier. Such accidents, rather than swept away out of sight, are given prominence. Michael Ratte attempts to answer this question for music, and the answer might apply to other forms as well. *'What makes the coherence of improvised music actually possible is the fact that its movement depends on a particular kind of concern for what appears and disappears. Such is the concern of the improviser who plays in the full knowledge that each decision taken is irrevocable . . . the concern expressed in the decisions that they throw into the music is reflected in each part as a presence which temporalises that part, and in the whole as a presence which temporalises the whole. It is this temporalisation that destabilises the identities, dissimilarities and differences of the materials and so determines the dialectic of coherence and incoherence in the music . . . How does the irrevocability of decisions make the improviser present to the whole? It first appears through the link between two decisions. An action, which cannot be undone, is greeted by a context that shows up the fragility of the justification for the decision that led to it. This fragility, once registered, motivates a concentration of judgement in the decision taker. The lesson learned from the first decision is already part of the meaning of the second decision. In this way, the irrevocability of decisions makes the improviser . . . responsible to the whole, not by taking decisions that have the whole in mind, but by being present to the whole, and taking decisions informed by this presence.'*[66]

All improvisers require this 'presence to the whole', working with the notion that accidents and mistakes only exist as such if they are *not* treated as 'part of the whole.' In other words, they need to be considered as contributing material that is just as valid, if not more so, as material more deliberately and consciously arrived at. If this is accepted, subsequent decisions allow for acknowledgement and exploration of this 'unintended' subject matter. In this way the unintended becomes part of the fabric of the piece, as comedy, digression or even a central theme. (In dramatic improvisation, a note of caution can be made in respect of the relationship between the journey and the digressions that emerge whether from accidents or some other means. This is simply that too many digressions can render the main journey irrelevant. The kookiness of the accidental material may bring the improvisation alive, but too many kooks may spoil the plot.)

In concentrating on the journey rather than the form, the improviser forgoes some of the formal responsibilities that an actor in a written play has to honour the structure imposed by the playwright. There may well be key moments when attention to the form is required – for example when the *Commedia* player runs to look at the list of scenes, the dancer becomes aware of time constraints or the musician within a jazz context recapitulates the melodic idea. But a defining feature of this kind of dialogue-based improvisation is that normal time is suspended so that the journey happens within a kind of no-time. The paradox of this is that the performer, being 'out of time' hopes to achieve a heightened sense of being 'in the present'. It's no less than what the audience hopes for and expects, this dislodgement of time. By entering into spectating, the audience member puts aside time-bound considerations that dominate most of the day. Both sides hope for an equivalent experience to what Carlos Castenada's Don Juan describes as 'stopping the world'. If the conceit fails, as it often does, the experience drags and everyone feels super-aware of slow time passing.

The use of repetition sets up interesting disconnections that aim to question our perception of time. One might assume that repetition holds a journey up. But this is to forget the changes that spectators go through as the piece repeats, and how their relationship to the material and to their own notion of time, alters. Adrian Heathfield puts it like this: '*One of the things I'm talking about in experimental forms of theatre and live art is this evident use of repetition, which is deliberately oriented towards destabilising the sense of "what is now". And saying, "Is this now a then or a new now?" This problematising of whether a now is really a now is interesting in terms of theatre and the politics of commemoration. Theatre is always an act of remembrance, even if it is an improvisation. It remembers the reality it portrays. The thoughts and acts that a performer brings in the moment of improvisation draw on a history, a personal and cultural reservoir of experiences and references that are remade anew in that moment. All theatre is this in some way. But some theatre unfortunately has an aspiration towards sameness, towards a finished version of reality. The question arises, how does the event close what it remembers, create a fixed rendition of it? This is where improvisation is interesting because it has the capacity to destabilise what is remembered and how it is remembered, to show history being remade, re-invented.'*

If there are obstacles and difficulties within the journey, it may benefit the traveller. Too much ease makes time go slow. Improvisers need to struggle, with themselves and their own limitations, their craft, each other or perhaps the demands of the form. A struggle disarms the traveller and projects him or her, forcibly if need be, into an altered consciousness. *'Sometimes people feel good about a performance when all they've done is articulate their own clichés effectively – when the more interesting performances are the ones where the musicians are ill at ease with the situation and have to work very hard to try and overcome certain obstacles . . . The greatest impro performances – and this is true in all non-idiomatic approaches to group playing – can be where the musicians find it hardest to play with each other.'* (Simon Fell.)

RESTRICTIONS

The notion of restrictions is used across the art forms since, as Nachmanovitch says, *'Limits yield intensity.'* Structure in performance is, after all, simply the imposition of restrictions on performers. The nature of the restrictions may concern space, time, or the performers themselves – but their imposition makes structure possible. This may even be just one rule, as in 'You have to answer the question' in *Quizoola!* Stephen Nacmanovich writes: *'One rule that I have found to be useful is that two rules are more than enough. If we have a rule concerning harmony and another concerning rhythm, if we have a rule concerning mood and another concerning the use of silence, we don't need any more. The unconscious has infinite repertoires of structure already; all it needs is a little external structure on which to crystallise. We can let our imaginations flow freely through the territory mapped out by a pair of rules, confident that the piece will pull together as a definite entity and not a peregrination.'* [67] In *Bassprov* Sutton and Bill decided there would be just the one rule: the two fishing buddies had to stay in the fishing boat. They realised that not having the freedom to get out of the boat created stronger material. The significant single rule in Word and Action's Instant Theatre is that 'every suggestion offered by the audience must be included in the narrative and in the performance'. Betrayal of this rule is seen to invalidate the performance because it introduces censorship. The single rule is like a funnel; it directs the energies of the event down that funnel, and so creates an intensity that is more vivid and elemental.

In jazz, the restrictions might be expressed through adherence to a specific rhythm or key signature that forces the musician to find every possible variation available within that corridor. Players might restrict themselves to no more than slight embellishment of the melody. To do more than that, might be seen as claiming too much freedom. *'Lonnie Hillyer once commented on the combined effect of these practices after hearing a recorded rendition of the ballad "Alone Together" by his late friend, trumpeter Kenny Dorham. Rendering the piece with his warm, intimate tone, Dorham embellished the melody with spare grace notes and varied its phrasing with subtle anticipations and delays . . . Hillyer leaned forward, covered his eyes with his hands . . . then, sighing, he shook his head as if waking from a dream, and softly marvelled, "K.D.! To think he could say all that, just by playing the melody".'* [68]

Free music improvisation eschews restrictions, yet within its own orthodoxy, assumes them through the proscription of rhythm, melody and tonality. Taboos such as these force the sounds to be found through texture and counterpoint. In dance, restrictions might be expressed as lines on the floor as in Trisha Brown's work, or expressed as the wearing of a tight dress, used by K.J. Holmes in her solo performance *'to push it in a certain direction to see what character emerged through the limitations.'* Florence Peake uses rolls of paper in her performances, wrapping herself up and exploring how this restriction creates choreography through the struggle against the restriction.

When jazz musicians pick up a tune, that tune functions as a restriction. All jazz musicians know their way around a host of blues tunes or 'I Got Rhythm'. Musicians hold on to the sense of a tune, its essentials, while pulling these around. It's not dissimilar with comedians and jokes. When comedians or comediennes have a joke to tell, they improvise around it but they need to preserve certain elements or it ceases to be *that joke*. You can see this in the work of comedians Eddie Izzard or Billy Connolly. In a particular set, either might use a certain narrative strand that provides an armatural structure to a monologue, but will pull it around to find different variations each night.

In the joke a man walks into a talent agency and says: 'Have I got an act for you!' The agent chews on his cigar. 'Oh yeah? Tell me about it.' Then comes a lengthy description of an unspeakably obscene act, or the enactment of same, which goes – in most variations – on and on and on. 'My God. Does this act have a name?' asks the agent. The visitor answers: 'The Aristocrats!'

But probably the essential lines will be kept. If a comedian ditches – for example – the punch line of a gag, probably it won't work. In Penn Jillette and Paul Provenza's film about what is considered 'the world's filthiest joke', a host of comedians all tell the same gag. There are many variations. However, very few mess with the punch line: '*The Aristocrats!*' Chris Ayres argues that the best part of the film is when the joke is told at a Hugh Hefner party with many other comedians present – when *'the real laughter is to be found in the endless riffing on the joke's structure – and the insider knowledge of the anti-climax to come.'*[69] The audience already know the punch line – what's interesting is the improvisation.

Neither dance nor theatre have an immediate equivalent to the jazz tune repertoire although the improvising of 'classic' stories might come closest as in Sheila's *Instant Odyssey* or Fluxx's *The Call*. In both these pieces an individual goes on a quest through a series of predetermined stages yet the interpretation of each challenge is consequent upon how the improvisers make decisions on the night. The nature of the challenges along the route might be informed by data provided by the audience. The piece is sectioned, just as a tune is sectioned by a sequence of head-solos-head in the jazz tune. The sectioning would most commonly be scene by scene. Alternatively one might look at 'classic' scenes that recur throughout drama; the goodbye scene, the betrayal scene, the reunion scene. In each case, certain dramatic actions are expected but the interpretation is always unique.

In dance work, you could perhaps find a parallel in the kind of score that has a series of small scores within it, each one timed. To give an example, K.J. Holmes told me about a piece of hers that she toured with Karen Nelson. In this piece, each section had certain obligations that utilised both spatial and temporal restrictions. *'It was a very specific score. We did a duet unison at the beginning, then we split the stage up. She was downstage; I was upstage. And the lights played a big part. They would fade, they would come up on her, and she would do a solo. She was downstage right. They would fade on her, come up on me. I was upstage left. And then we'd come together. And then we'd start playing with this accumulation of imagery. And it was always in a time frame. Knowing how long you're going to do something creates a boundary.'*

It's the pushing against restrictions, while simultaneously being fenced in by them, that makes improvisation fascinating to watch. This relationship between improviser and restriction echoes and comple- ments the constant effort of the performer extending him or herself to externalise imagery, and being reactive to that imagery once created. Some improvisers in the theatre misguidedly argue for a minimum of restrictions in that the freedom acquired will liberate them into a more creative, inventive, spontaneous world. But fit one of those actors into a sleeping bag or lock him in an onstage cupboard, and you will likely see some of his most inventive work.

POETICS

Following the separation of art forms that began probably at the time of our emergence from a hunter-gatherer society, each separate creative medium has developed its own poetics. For any single art form to achieve resonance it largely relies on the exclusion of other aesthetic vocabularies. The narrowness of any one vocabulary permits a degree of precision in the treatment of its subject matter. Arguably, however, artists from different art forms do have this in common: that the vocabulary of each is but a means to an end. This end is a desire to take recipients to an experience beyond the literal appreciation of the art work. A painting invites an experience more than simple ack- nowledgement of how the colours complement each other and the shapes echo life. A piece of dance more than the technique of the dancers. There's a hope that the construction of work propels the spectator/receiver into entering into recognising something greater; a

A Note on ESP and Mixing the Art Forms

The work of ESP (Experiments in Spontaneous Performance), which includes Rick Nodine, Danielle Allan, Rex Hossi Horan, Gaby Agis and Alison Blunt, along with myself in the team, began initially working with quite tight but complex scores in performance. After a year, these were abandoned and the group worked on conventions that could be activated by any artist during the performance. The scoring protocols adapted from separate art forms had proved ineffective in liberating any kind of new vocabulary. They relied instead on juxtaposing separate art form elements, like cake slices from different cakes packed together into one box. There was a recognition that new structures could only be arrived at by dismantling the old. Subsequent explorations were more scary but more productive since it was from a sense of insufficiency and an absence of safety-generating conventions, that more genuinely innovative work emerged. It also became possible then to return occasionally to more 'pure' single art form excursions. Emerging from this was the hypothesis that there were fundamentally two ways primarily for artists from different backgrounds to collaborate. The first, *complementarity*, allows a basis of accompaniment in which either one or other art form is in the ascendancy, or else two or more co-exist. The second, *synthesis*, moves the articulation of an entirely new vocabulary into pole position. Now there are elements of rhythm, movement, use of space and perhaps words or props, operative together but without the norms of their expression identified as belonging to any single art form. This kind of work operates closer to an abstract point on an imagined continuum between concreteness and abstraction, yet aims for accessibility. It involves a hard-to-define kind of rawness.

much bigger, more mysterious goose fair. At such moments, the precise context of the location where the piece is experienced and the precise nature of the time of that experience, become either less significant or resounds differently within the witness. 'Great secrets of the universe', as Del Close might say optimistically, 'are right there to be experienced.'

This is one of the difficulties facing performing artists rooted in any one art form, collaborating across different forms: they know that in their own work, the efficacy of their performed moment depends significantly on the exclusion of other art form elements. To overcome this, the collaborators need to do one of two things: either to work complementarily, so ways are found for dance and music, or music and theatre, to sit alongside each other, or to work a more difficult passage: to boil away the differences between them so that the residue remaining, while emerging without the familiar characteristics of any one art form, nevertheless carries the heady intoxicant of any of them. Either task involves a lot of practice. Inevitably, much of this practice will be given over to the articulation and definition of a shared vocabulary. Just as two spoken languages over time borrow from each other and merge to the point where a new, identifiable language can be named, so too will the artists have to steal from each other while simultaneously pissing on sacred cows. In other words they have to give up the sacredness of some of their own practice, understood as rules or protocols, in order for elements of that practice to become pluralised within the group. As Marshall Soules articulates, *'Both improvising musicians and actors must lose their identities even as they find them, but they do so within a framework of productive constraints – the protocols of improvisation.'*[70]

Inevitably part of this means starting to learn something of the next guy's perhaps quite unfamiliar art form, perhaps from the beginning. *'If you move territory, you start all over again,'* as Wendy Houston argued to me. Not that the achievement of single art form virtuosity should be a target. Rather the opposite. Average fluency is not just sufficient, any more than that might be a hindrance. Once cross-art form improvisation practice is seriously entered into, virtuosity needs to be redeployed away from mastery of the piano, the backflip or the monologue. Instead it needs to move into a different notion of ensemble where skill is employed to make others shine, emphasising the strain of a rough, common language. The skill becomes less about expertise than the craft of collaboration. Performers begin to perform functions that are supportive rather than virtuosic, perhaps even drawing back their default skills. John Miller Chernoff has talked about how African drummers relate to each other, and perhaps there's a point of comparison here. *A drum in an African ensemble derives its power and becomes meaningful not only as it cuts and focuses the other drums but also as it is cut and called into focus by them. Rhythmic dialogues are reciprocal, and in a way that might seem paradoxical to a Westerner, a good drummer restrains himself from emphasising his rhythm in order that he may be heard better.'*[71]

But as indicated above, this means sacrifice, not just of the readiness to display skills but of the very way that you operate as an improviser. Trevor Lines is a bassist working with the mixed art form company, Fence Crossing. He outlined to me something of his learning curve in trying to engage with a dramatic improvisation practice that inevitably relied significantly on an idea of consensus. '*The business of "saying yes"/ not blocking is very interesting, and hard! I suppose in a lot of my improvising activity we move forward by meeting one idea with another, and avoiding creating a flow of acquiescence (but when trying to groove, of course it is the opposite). I thought it would be easier, as jazz rhythm section work is all about supporting and complementing ideas that the soloist presents. It strikes me that I (like many people) am used to a mode of conscious thinking that is essentially dialectical in nature, which means avoiding becoming immersed in someone's idea in favour of critiquing it by applying a counter-idea, and although that may be very good if we are trying to work in a fast-moving scenario it is a better idea to shake that habit, or at least hold it back a bit.*'[72]

In these contexts, congruence of intent must be more important than individual virtuosity, dedication to a shared idea more resonant than the simple act of collaboration. Working together with the ideal of collaboration gets you started, but soon a theoretical articulation about the kind of sacrifices involved will inevitably make the compromises involved in any such process, less painful. Not that they can be quite ever made to disappear.

Does this suggest poetics are dependent on idealism? Not at all, but in terms of ensemble work, to get the car started you need to put some petrol in. Without this the car fights with itself trying to work out what's missing and why there's the sound of screaming metal. When looking at the poetics of cross-art form collaborations, it may be useful to look at how separate practices relate to the idea of abstraction. Dance and music sit comfortably on the end of an imagined continuum. Neither medium needs words or verbal definitions to achieve an enhancement of operating protocols.

A performer moves across the room dragging a chair with slow, stylised moves. A performer plays a series of atonal phrases on a double base.

In these moments of performance, there is no necessity for the spectator to define context or meaning. However, if this was theatre, the performer dragging the chair explains to the audience that this is the last chair in the house, which is being taken outside to the bailiffs.

The player on the double bass is dressed as a clown; she speaks, welcoming us to the circus.

In this way the theatre performer traditionally seeks a reduction of abstraction for which spoken language is the most precise tool. Words and gestures that sign particular meaning open out certain possibilities of interpretation while closing down others.

My own works in cross-art form improvisation practice suggests that collaboration becomes easier within a more *abstract* territory, allowing musicians and dancers to determine protocols. If either comes into theatrical territory, the tendency is for the dancer or musician to fall into illustration or accompaniment. To some extent therefore, in a three-way collaboration it's the actors who need to move sideways and utilise themselves differently, within a vocabulary tending to the abstract. They need to become comfortable operating outside their comfort zone, entering into compacts with other improvisers where the traditional 'who, what, where' categorisations are ineffective or even disruptive. Most concretely, they need perhaps to resign allegiance to notions of character which more than any other convention, ties the exercise to a dramatic frame. This is not to suggest actors are unqualified for the transition since a developed improvisational intelligence can carry them through. Rex Horan: *'Even if people don't have musical training, if they're involved in this kind of action, what they bring with them is their own history of listening. If that history is informed and they've listened to what we accept as being a good improvisation and a solid-sounding thing that's either entertaining or challenging, and if they're a performer of integrity, then what they bring is of great value.'* Perhaps it's ironic that dramatic improvisers have to become the junior partners here, since theatre is traditionally viewed as a house to which other artists seek to gain entrance.

Companies such as La Gata from Colombia and Art and Shock from Kazakhstan, are already better placed for such collaboration given the non-verbal nature of their regular vocabulary. La Gata's use of folkloric performative elements such as the playing of birds, spirits and ghosts, and Art and Shock's drawing from the Russian clowning tradition, mean they are already versed in physical theatre styles. While the influence of Lecoq and other European teachers such as Phillipe

Gaulier has filtered through to devised theatre practice as in the work of Complicite, it has not had a similar impact within the UK tradition of improvised theatre, which largely remains wedded to the Johnstone/Spolin influence. Improvised dance practice for its part, at least in the UK, has started to adopt some more identifiably theatrical elements. Performers stop and talk to the audience or talk to each other, and use props and costumes in a way to signal particularities of relationship. In dance especially, the sense of art form distinctiveness is beginning to dissolve, not least because of the influence of methodologies such as Action Theatre and the Kelman Group. It's for dramatic improvisers to follow.

For the reasons given above, the more heightened development of an improvised cross-art form language of poetics remains largely aspirational except within the territories of a few artists – such as those included in this book, of which Julyen Hamilton, Franko B and E.S.P. might be examples. Work of this kind is a young cat, yet we can talk about the trajectory of a growing up to a leonine maturity as this practice continues. By addressing concerns such as liveness, authority and transparency that are common to all performing art forms, there can start to be a levelling of art form differences. By looking at the protocols of improvisation rather than the art form priorities, the emphasis is switched away from art form definite-ness.

Current live art practice in particular throws everything into the pot for re-examination through an analysis of what actually constitutes performance. This work deconstructs prevailing ideas of what constituent elements ought to be relied on. In so doing, the work starts to define its own relationship with abstraction and definition. This is both its potential weakness and its strength, since the constituent elements have to be deconstructed and reconstructed in the process.

Emerging improvisational structures, informed by live art practice, need not be complex since complexity is characteristic of the higher developments of any one art form. They may involve a reduction, a stripping away to something elemental. They may be about revealing the *story* of the performers themselves, as they wrestle with the challenges of exposition. They also need to function as more than just utilitarian machines. They need to be able to house a poetics. For such work inevitably involves artists being pushed into challenges that reveal not their sufficiency but their insufficiency. In this context we can't ask spectators to be admiring of virtuosity but rather the courage of the performers in their struggle to be transparent. Events may benefit from simplicity of construction since these may more effectively allow for multiple interpretations. In such cases, the performers make no pretence to be in charge of the meaning that is generated. Adrian Heathfield: *'If you looked at a lot of '90s experimental live art and performance, one of the things you'd say was that it was maximalist, that it tended to create density through plurality – lots of different things happening at the same time, lots of clash, lots of collage, a fragmented aesthetics. There's a confusion of playful possibilities. What interests me about this area of performance practice now is that it has returned to minimalist aesthetics. In the sense that it has stripped down the act to a bare set of relations, to a simple set of forms. However, it finds play inside this very minimal aesthetic. It's about the play of the elemental. Franko B's work is a good example of this. It isn't what you would immediately think of as either improvisational or playful. But through the conditions of the aesthetic that Franko creates you enter into an encounter which is, for me at least, incredibly vibrant and vital in its opening of meanings and possibilities. The way he's done that is to strip everything away and focus on the symbolic act, usually some form of wounding, and then the moment of the relation between the performer and spectator. Often in the long durational work, say* Aktion 398 *for instance, where he's in a room for a day and you get two minutes with him, the exchange, whatever that is, is completely improvised and unplanned. There aren't even any rules or structures around the relation. Anything can happen. He just does what he feels like doing in the moment. Often that's very little. But often what the visitors do varies greatly. Improvisation moves down to a very intense micro scale attention so that one is starting to think just about this moment, my eye to your eye, my breath next to your breath, my body next to your body. It's a very simple but complex thing.'*

PART FOUR

THE HOW

I
STRUCTURE

'Nothing exists without structure. Every atom, every identity, every action has structure. Every play, every performance, every presentation has structure. There is no such thing as "structureless" theatre. There are only people who are not aware of perceiving structure.'   Michael Kirby

'As an improviser, I want to throw on to the stage my questioning. I want to expunge some doubts and fears, and through this, celebrate them. For I know that once shared, these excitements or terrors will spread amongst the others there, and my isolation will be decreased. I want to lay out on a tablecloth some of the curious confections that are the product of recipes whose ingredients come from dreams, folk memory and imagination. I want to play a character only if the character gives me permission to do these things more easily than I can do them as myself. I want to talk only if the talking doesn't turn into a web of ropes that tie me into inarticulacy. I want to be honest but only if that honesty is unavoidable.'   Sandy Van Torquil

OPEN AND CLOSED STRUCTURES

The issue of structure or scoring is ever-present. Whether the improvisation takes place in a youth club, a prison drama workshop or on a public stage, the questions are the same. How much structure? What will enable the performers to take flight? What instructions are required? At one end of the scale, there is the notion of the *open score*. In free music improvisation, musicians often rely on an open score, listening and responding to each other, largely avoiding rhythm and harmony, finding structure from the dialogue between them. This enables them to turn up five minutes before the gig, having never met the other musicians, and just start playing. (Derek Bailey argues that there is more playing per cubic unit in free playing than there is in any other kind of music.)

Open structures are also used within dance improvisation. Where dancers know they share a similar vocabulary, performances can be put together with minimal preparation. An open score is all that's required. There is no 'structure' beyond the length of time allocated for the piece. What happens in consequence is that the *relationships* between the dancers become a principal, defining influence on the material. Their level of intimacy, familiarity, how they make each other feel, will be significant. What they 'pull out of each other' generates the material. It's not that strangers can't explore intimacy in performance, but degrees of familiarity will inform the scope of decision-making. When Kirstie Simson reunited with Julyen Hamilton on stage in 2006 after a break of fifteen years, the piece couldn't fail to be about their rediscovered relationship. Rick Nodine and Jovair Longo work with each other consistently. Their mutual familiarity permits explorations based on knowledge of each other. Rick Nodine comments *'You dance in a different way when your "body" knows that the other body can be trusted not to collapse. I think this is quite specific to a form where physical danger is part of what makes the improvisation interesting for audience and performer.'*

If complete strangers meet on stage, it's uncertain how they'll bond. So there's just the technique there as a vocabulary. It might be a triumph or it might just be a triumph of technique. (There are arguably two kinds of chemistry: one that comes from shared vocabulary and practice, and that which comes from a complementary blend of personalities. The greater either quality of chemistry exists, the less need for structure.)

Within dramatic improvisation, there tend to be fewer examples of completely open structures in which nothing is determined in advance. This is partly because the medium relies so much on definitions, in contrast to music and dance that can operate entirely comfortably within an abstract sphere. Mark Phoenix's performance work, rooted in the techniques of Sanford Meisner, might be an example. Here, the actors simply respond to each other without premeditation and build a storyline – of any kind – out of these responses. There are some examples within live art practice. Franko B's work might be mentioned in this context, albeit there is likely to be already some contextual definitions operating. In one of his pieces, *Aktion 38* (for more details see previous chapter), he will sit in a space entered by the spectators one at a time, and what evolves is entirely down to the evolving relationship between the spectator and performer.

There are many more examples of relatively *closed scores* within theatre. A show like *Bassprov* has a complete openness about its narrative development yet Mark Sutton and Joe Bill have a defined location, which is a boat. That location is fixed and immutable. So in a sense, the structure is the boat. In Keith Johnstone's *Lifegame*, there's no narrative structure here either. But as Phelim McDermott has observed, this is because the structure *'is the guest'*. So these examples, where location or orientation or a particular game are involved, are what I would define as closed or part-closed structures. Certain parameters have been set in advance. The more closed structures still would include examples like *La Ronde Improvised* where a certain pattern of scenes is set in advance.

Some of the different ways to define structures for dramatic performance would include:

- LOCATION – where the show will be set defines the 'world' of the piece

- ROLES – perhaps characters developed in advance or archetypal, 'stock' characters or relationships

- NARRATIVE – the performance has a sequence of sections in which different kinds of events are planned

If we know the show is going to be set in a boat or will involve a journey, or is about a champion and his sidekick, or has the structure of two lovers going back in time through their relationship, we can more adventurously get on with the show. Incidentally, these are the structures for *Bassprov*, Sheila's *Odyssey*, *Don Quixote* and *Then Again*, the last being the Andy Eninger/Adrianne Frost vehicle that starts with a relationship breaking up and ends with the very first kiss. As they say on the publicity, the audience get a guaranteed happy ending. Making decisions about structure in advance lets the ensemble off the hard work of making all those decisions on stage. Particularly if the show involves more than two or three players, having no structure at all can be like attempting synchronised swimming in a pool with a wave machine. By creating parameters, the improvisation is oriented around agreed points of reference. This is not dissimilar to organising principles within the jazz tune. Just as the tune has its keynote theme and arrangements for soloing and counterpointing, so too might the dramatic structure.

For an example of a closed dramatic score using clear structural elements, we could turn to one of the first; what became known as The Harold. When improvisers in the US began pushing beyond the sketch format to develop what was termed by Michael Gellman as 'longform'. The Harold was created by Del Close and colleagues. Close described the format as follows: *'The team begins by asking for a suggestion from the audience.'* This will likely be shouted back in the form of a theme such as gay marriage, the war in Iraq, peanuts or the pleasures of bondage. *'They (the actors) then personalise the suggestion and develop an attitude, which is expressed through the opening game.'* An opening game might be the presentation of a series of images on that theme, made quickly by the actors and dismantled just as fast. Or it might be a series of verbal statements on the theme, each actor walking forward and delivering a word, a phrase or a speech. *'Then the players begin the first round by improvising scenes.'* Let's imagine gay marriage is the theme, and the suggestion of peanuts has also been accepted. So perhaps two female actors step out. Maybe one woman would try and persuade the other they should get married. These actors fall back. Someone else comes forward and tries unsuccessfully to open a packet of peanuts. Then there's a family scene with everyone looking at photographs of a happy heterosexual wedding. *'These are followed by a game and then the scenes return for further development.'* After the game, the plots established earlier would move on. The women would now be married, the other actor is still trying to open the packet of peanuts, the family is now arguing and there's a new scene about fish. *'Another game follows, and the scenes are brought back for a third time, though not all scenes will return. The Harold can end with any one of the scenes, or with another game.'*[73] The final scene might bring together some of the characters from the separate plot lines. Finally the guy opening the peanuts gets them opened, and he's at the divorce party of the two gay women. Never mind, he just walked into a room where the family has reunited. Finally a man eats fish, looking at photographs of the divorce party. A concluding game might be an image encompassing some of the different storylines, or it might be a sentence to which they all create a word. At that point the lights come down.

If you were to search for an equivalence with music, Marc Sabatella observes the following: *'Most jazz since the bebop era is based on a form that is actually quite similar in concept to the sonata allegro form from classical theory: an optional introduction, the exposition of a theme (possibly repeated), the development section, and the recapitulation, possibly followed by a coda. . . . In jazz terms, these sections of a piece would be called the intro, the head, the solo section, the head out, and possibly a coda or tag ending.'*[74]

FACILITATING RESTRICTIONS

Drama for its part tends to use closed or part-closed scores rather than open ones. This is certainly the case in performance. In a workshop context, it's also true that directors or teachers will want to lay down guidelines before an exercise. Of course it's possible, and it's done frequently, that an instruction is given to the actors, 'OK, just go on stage and start something,' but this approach works more effectively in the context of an ensemble where conventions are well established. More often than not some structure or *restriction* will be given. The essence of structure is the restriction. It has the function of simply closing off some possibilities and allowing others to remain open. If the scene is set in a boat, then the surface of the moon isn't an option. If it's a scene about brotherhood, student-teacher relations are a distraction. The hypothesis is that the best work emerges from compression. Structure is used not to limit the actor's freedom for its own sake, but to force improvisational decision-making into a tightly confined area where the material will resonate more effectively. Some people think that improvisation is all about 'being free', 'doing what you want', and it is true to a degree, but only if it's understood that an expression of (imaginative) freedom comes about as a result of restrictions. The tighter the restriction, potentially the more inventive the response. John Wright pointed out to me that *'The first restriction was the mask.'* The mask has the effect of denying the use of the face so

> The energy released to solve the problem, being restricted by the rules of the game and bound by group decision, creates an explosion – or spontaneity – and as is the nature of the explosions, everything is torn apart, rearranged, unblocked. The ear alerts the feet, and the eye throws the ball!'
> Viola Spolin

forcing attention on to the body. It encourages the actor into awareness of sensations and frees up physicality.

Restrictions can be used to achieve a number of *results*:

- To create dramatic TENSION
- To create dramatic STRUCTURE
- To create a particular ATMOSPHERE
- To create CONSISTENCY
- To give the director or teacher a greater influence on the FLOW of the action
- To contribute to the performer a feeling of SAFETY. S/he can't be held responsible for the consequences of the restriction – it's the director's fault
- To direct the performer's ATTENTION narrowly, so scene content can emerge more freely
- To create the basis of a CONTRACT for the ensemble

There are essentially only a few *ways* to impose restrictions. Whether the context is a workshop or performance, the options are similar. There are several kinds of parameters that the director or facilitator can establish:

- OF SPACE
- OF TIME
- OF PHYSICALITY
- OF SPEECH

Once imposed, the restriction can always be thrown off. It's not there for all time. If the actor or facilitator times it right, this moment of abandoning the restriction creates a seismic shift in the scene. It's like a rupture of the established order. If, for example, the actors are playing a master-servant scene, and the servant's restriction is always to *obey* the master whatever the consequences, and at a certain point the servant rebels, refusing further orders, it's as if the master's world has suddenly collapsed like a sandcastle under a wave.

It's worth examining in more detail how these different kinds of restrictions might be imposed. Each one might function for a whole play, a scene or even part of a scene. Similarly, a restriction might be imposed on the whole company, a single actor or it may apply to a particular relationship or to a moment in time.

RESTRICTIONS OF SPACE can be used to heighten a sense of location. The floor can be divided into zones. The divisions can be made literally: i.e. into rooms of a house or into features of an archetypal landscape such as castle, quicksand, hovel, desert. In a show with a closed score, the definition of locations is really part of the score. In *La Ronde Improvised*, the stage is divided into pre-chosen locations that help to generate romantic or sexual encounters: a bedroom, the exterior of a club, a park, a toilet, and so on.

Staging for La Ronde Improvised

Toilet	Club Back Door
Double Bed	Neutral Space
Park Bench	
The Audience	The Audience

But space doesn't have to be about location. A company might choose to divide space into different kinds of zones, for example each one representing a different *time*: the past, the present, the future. It might create spaces for different *atmospheres*, following Michael Chekhov's work, with areas for 'panic', 'relaxation', 'creativity' or 'shyness'. When a player moves into the new area, he immediately becomes panic-stricken, relaxed, creative or shy. Props or furniture can also determine space distinctions. I often carry around a suitcase of odd props. Diving into this brings up stones, candles, a teddy bear, a bell, a Ronald Reagan mask, a ship in a bottle, a scrawled letter, a set of keys, a torch or a tape measure. These different props might be placed individually in different zones encouraging actors to develop scenes out of each object in turn.

One tactic is to give different restrictions to different actors. In terms of space, this might be about how to use the space. One actor is given Restriction A, the second Restriction B. The two performers can then be sent into the same scene. Each is obliged to play the scene while maintaining the given restriction. For example, we're going to play a scene set in a bedroom between three friends. The first actor is told that she has to be active within the scene but can't actually enter the bedroom. The second is told to constantly keep moving within the room, never ever sitting down on any furniture. The third is told to be always either lying on the bed or in close physical proximity with another player. These tasks will hopefully trigger inventiveness as the actors work out how to justify their adopted behaviours. A game plan like this one gives the director a chance to structure the improvisation in a certain way, for example to generate a certain kind of tension. It's a way to create relationships without the business of sitting down and working it all out intellectually. If one actor has been told to get close to another and the second is told to dislike it but put up with it, we immediately achieve adoration/flirtation juxtaposed with distaste/stoicism. The instructions form a game and the game creates the relationship. This idea might be taken further so the instructions deal with *events*. In the bedroom scene, for example, if physical contact happens, it has to be held for longer than feels comfortable. Struggling with and against the restrictions imposed, tends to subvert more orthodox kind of acting.

Here are a few space restrictions for individual actors:

- Always try and be in the centre of the stage
- Always break into others' personal space whatever relationship you have to them
- Take the view that you own the space even though you don't belong there
- Take the view that you have no ownership of the space even though you live there
- Play the scene without touching the ground – if possible, float

RESTRICTIONS OF TIME are useful where the improvisation needs to be broken up into sequences, or when a sense of urgency is required. It might be that after a period of time, the next sequence is triggered. Objectives have to be completed before the end of that time period. Competitive games offer a model of a time-based activity. For example, two teams have to cross the room without touching the floor, using only two sheets of newspaper each. The race against time heightens the drama of the event. A classic theatre game that uses time restrictions is Keith Johnstone's Death In a Minute. Two players have to play a scene. One of the two has to die before the end. But – and this is crucial – the whole minute must be used up. Johnstone writes, *'I tell two players that they have one minute during which one of them must be killed by the other, and that "There'll be a five-second fade in fifty-five seconds."* '[75] It's amazing to see this restriction forcing the improviser, if the death occurs early, finding ways to fill up the remaining seconds. There's always some inventive justification for the murderous behaviour found in the dying seconds.

Improvisers' use of time is intrinsically linked to personal rhythm. Some performers like to take it slow and easy. Others want to move swiftly to the emotional core of the scene. Teaching improvisation is sometimes about getting individuals to go against their natural rhythm. In a warm-up for example, everyone might have to play with different rhythms. Then when the group gets to the improvisations, individual performers can be asked to take a rhythm that goes against their natural tendency. One way to help with this is to find a tune for the actor to sing to himself quietly during the scene that helps to maintain the desired tempo.

Examples of time-based instructions to actors might include:

- You're constantly in a hurry (but don't know why)
- You are completely preoccupied, either with something that happened in a previous scene or with something that is going to happen in the next
- You have one minute (or three or five) to achieve your objective
- Conversationally, you're about a minute behind everyone else
- You anticipate everything that is about to happen
- You play as if being constantly struck by small forks of lightning

Sequences of scenes that together form a narrative also operate within a time frame. Actors know they have different tasks to complete before the next sequence is arrived at. Put at its most simple, this might be: Scene One, establish the relationship; Scene Two, introduce a threat to this relationship. More on this later in the chapter.

RESTRICTIONS OF PHYSICALITY   Action Theatre practice contains a significant body of exercises that train participants to cue into physicality. Exercises in this and other physicality-based methodologies help performers to register a greater range of internal, physical sensations. As a result of practice, performers can become more sensitive to internal shifts. This also assists heightened awareness of *feelings* that inevitably are experienced physically. A related learning area is the role of *opposites* within a movement vocabulary. For example, how stillness juxtaposes with movement. How slowness contrasts with speed, directness with flexibility, and so on. Laban movement training offers a comprehensive pedagogy of movement. If short of time, improvisers should study the Laban working actions that have an application well beyond movement practice. Actors are often slower than dancers to discover, for example, the benefits of stillness in performance. It's a similar story with the contrast between sound and silence. The actor loves to move and the actor loves to speak. Learning how to do the opposite is essential practice within any ensemble.

The director can impose restrictions of physicality in many ways: for example, by instructing certain kinds of movement. 'Never move your head' – this will help to create a sense of confidence in the character. 'Move your head a lot' – this will help create a sense of insecurity. 'Move with a shrunken physicality' – this will create low status. 'Open your physicality so you take a lot of space in the room, extend your legs and arms' – this will give the character an aura of high status. 'Never leave so-and-so's side' or 'Constantly look to get eye-contact with so-and-so' will of course generate relationships of dependency or adoration. Less obvious strategies might involve the use of rope, bags, or very tight clothes to create the restriction. Tight clothes immediately induce alternative sensations to which the improviser can respond. High heels very quickly throw the body forward and the counter-balancing exaggerates sexuality.

The secret of restrictions is in the mix. One of the funniest improvisations I ever saw was a scene in which the actor Andrew St John as the boss tried to sack a young, black, female employee. His restriction was that his character was never able to finish his sentences. Hers was different; she was instructed to always to break into other people's personal space. The chemistry of the scene drove the male character mad with frustration as the girl constantly wove around him and subverted his intentions. Another female senior in the firm looked on to heighten the tension. Her restriction was 'three words at a time'. Finally, at the crucial moment, his patience snapped. He abandoned the restriction and delivered the verdict: the girl was fired and should never return to the company again. The effect was extraordinary. The 'rule' of his restriction had been broken at just the right moment to create a fabulous status shift.

Other examples of physical restrictions might include:

- You are constantly throwing yourself around the space impulsively, for no good reason
- You touch yourself constantly throughout the scene
- You play the whole show in a sleeping bag
- You have a very bad itch
- You believe yourself to be naked

RESTRICTIONS OF SPEECH can be imposed to interfere with players accustomed verbal patterns. Dramatic improvisers are usually worrying about which way the scene will go, and they don't think about speech patterns. It's extraordinary how a given restriction, when played, completely alters how the character appears to the audience. I was recently improvising scenes from *Much Ado About Nothing* with the Royal Shakespeare Company. We staged an imagined scene in which the father of a prospective suitor for the young girl Hero came to visit. Hero's father and Beatrice, her cousin, were also present. The two women were both given restrictions. Hero was only allowed to speak when directly asked a question by the visitor or her father. Beatrice was only allowed to ask questions. The women's struggle to maintain the restrictions usefully mirrored the social restrictions operating on women during the historical period in which the play was being set. However, it simultaneously allowed Beatrice, played by Tamsin Green, to subvert good manners while appearing to honour them.

Other verbal restrictions might include the following:

- You only speak in clichés
- You only speak in sporting metaphors
- You never finish your sentences
- You never speak without some kind of physical contact
- You only speak a single phrase, repeating this if necessary

- You speak only in gibberish
- You speak constantly, but when you stop, it's a long silence

COMMUNITY CONTEXTS

Working with young people in workshops, I find restrictions help to clarify the tasks. Young people like to work within rules as long as it feels like a challenge, and the thinking around it is explained. I once ran a project for young offenders in an arts centre. Generally only three young men came along. I don't think the organisers had tried very hard with the recruitment. The three were teenage friends. I tried everything with them, but most exercises just confused them. What was the point of it all? What was the point of drama? When you could do everything, why do anything? It was only when I played Keith Johnstone's The King Game – relocated to a mafia context – that they became energised and involved. The stakes were high, and in ways they didn't understand (nor did I), the game spoke about their own experience of life. The rules of the game were clear and simple: you lived or died by the hand of the Don. You had to please the Don. If he liked what you offered, you joined the gang. If he didn't, you died. I never thought you could play it with just three, but these friends proved me wrong. Week after week. After this, it became easier to enter into more open, potentially elaborate improvisations. Slowly the rules could be left behind.

> **The King Game**
>
> 'If the master is not happy, he snaps his fingers and his servant commits suicide (to be instantly replaced by another servant, ad infinitum). The game is a competition to see which servant can survive the longest, and it makes the players exquisitely attentive to each other.'
> Keith Johnstone

For more experienced improvisers in a community context, I might use an exercise developed from something I saw Jonathan Kay run. The benefit is that the format of the exercise is relatively *open*, but you can make it increasingly *closed* according to the skills of the improvisers. Closing down the score generally makes the playing easier. So what you have is a template that you can adjust, not unlike turning the gas up or down. My version is called Two People Meet.

> ### Two People Meet
>
> Everyone is sat in a circle on the floor. Everyone has a partner across the circle. The facilitator instructs different tasks but each player only works with his or her partner. At the beginning, these instructions might be simple. 'Cross the space with your partner but ensure there are never more nor less than three people in the space at any one time.' These will become increasingly harder, and turn into instructions for scenes. 'Two people meet – they used to have a relationship. One is still in love with the other, while the second has moved on.' Immediately one of the pairs must get up and play the scene. Different kinds of relationships can be defined. Restrictions can be introduced, e.g. of space, physicality or speech. What the facilitator does not decide is *what happens*. Only the context of the meeting is determined.

The restrictions set the challenge in any 'round'. There can be as many rounds as you wish. As it progresses, the restrictions nudge the players into different emotional territories. The players might be called on to explore confessional or intimate behaviour. They might be asked to communicate without words or to play characters far away from their natural playing age. They are always saved the job of 'establishing'; they can instead do what they do best, discovering the narrative of the encounter. The facilitator's task is to establish the rules of engagement and monitor these, ensuring that if rules are broken, they aren't broken so much that the game collapses.

RULE BREAKING

Rule breaking is fascinating in the context of improvisation, because the very act of improvising is about challenging taboos of behaviour. It's one reason why amateurs and community actors, not to mention professionals, get involved because behaviour proscribed elsewhere can here be indulged. Each session is potentially a Feast of Fools when everyone throws off their everyday role and inhabits alternative personalities. It's a chance to be vulgar, arrogant, sexual, flirtatious, morose, mischievous, irreverent, blasphemous, spontaneous, crude, divine, tactile, rapacious, wordy, greedy or vile. Acceptance of the game rules allows breakage of the social rules. But if this is misunderstood, and the principle inverted, improvisers create meandering, chaotic work. The point is to use restrictive structures to support the expression of vulnerability or self-revelation.

Status work is all about the willing enforcement of restrictions. Keith Johnstone's work on status, introduced when he was working at the Royal Court with George Devine, offered a genuine enhancement to the methodologies currently in vogue. *'The actors seemed to know exactly what I meant and the work was transformed. The scenes became "authentic", and actors seemed marvellously observant. Suddenly we understood that every inflection and movement implies a status, and that no action is due to chance, or really "motiveless".'* Nor are the benefits of such work confined to the development of theatre skills. *'Status transactions aren't only of interest to the improviser. Once you understand that every sound and posture implies a status, then you perceive the world quite differently, and the change is probably permanent.'*[76] Status work has application in a range of contexts. There is something extraordinary about the shy girl transforming into the high status Queen while the loud boy becomes the deferential servant. Sometimes the transformation takes even the actors by surprise. (Actors sometimes assume that 'playing status' is largely about 'radiating' a quality of self-importance or respect for others. A more effective approach can lie in *endowing* the other actor – or the space or the object – with particular status high or low. The actor's focus is therefore on the *other* actor/character rather than the *self.* So the rule becomes 'Treat the other as high, and you will achieve low'.)

Once accepted and played, the pay-off lies in the status changes that can be engineered at the moment when the narrative needs a shift. As in the examples given earlier, the restriction can be broken to achieve this pay-off. This is the moment of rebellion / indignity / confession / upset / loss of self-control / the emergence of the truth. The restriction (or game rule) is broken, while respect for the over-arching narrative and improvisational conventions is retained.

FEAR OF RESTRICTIONS

Compromise and vagueness are probably the most deadly vices within dramatic improvisation. This is true whatever the context. Less experienced actors waffle about, are evasive, elusive and like to try everything once. This is sometimes due to fear of restrictions. There is a voice in the back of the head going, 'Don't agree to anything, keep your options open.' Alongside this voice is another, 'Your partner feels the same way. Don't pin anything on her, she won't like you for it.' The truth is, she'll probably be very grateful if the vast acres of improvisational freedom that exist out there are reduced by a square metre or two.

Here are two improvisers fearful of defining what their scene will be about. We're assuming nothing has been given them in advance.

I put the body out the back.

That's good, I never liked her.

We had a hamster, now it's dead, end of story.

Where are we going tonight?

I thought you were going to decide. You said so, after that conversation with your mother.

Never mind, we'll stay in. I know that's what you want really.

No, it's what you want.

OK, it's what I want. Now sit down and help me with the crossword.

We can play strip poker.

Let's sneak out and throw stones at the gypsies!

Yeah, we owe them one.

But what if they fight back?

The exchange drifts because no one is prepared to define 'The About', that is, the primary content of the scene. Fearful of restricting themselves, the actors are constantly opening up new threads. But none of these is developed.

Especially for those learning impro, a useful tool is the *routine*. This is simply a series of actions that repeats. It's used as a staple procedure within clowning where the bucket of feathers is finally replaced by the bucket of water. Routines have application irrespective of the mode of performance. Within live art practice, comedy impro and durational performance, routines represent a powerful means. There are many theatre games that rely heavily on routines: Dog and Bone, in which two teams repeatedly compete for a flag (or bone) in the centre of the space, Grandmother's Footsteps, games that use rhyme like Hi Ho, the King Game and many others. With each repetition, the enactment resonates in a different way in the players. Repeating patterns of action in a dramatic scene build tension and establish character. Simply doing the same action of sweeping the floor, putting on and taking off clothes, kissing someone or laughing for no reason, establish an idea of character in the mind of the audience. Sketch comedy uses repetition as a staple means to project an idea of foolishness or vanity. In *The Fast Show*, the character who emerges from a barn to announce to the camera, 'This week I am mostly . . . (eating carrots/beans/turnips)' establishes in a moment his habitual world. In *Fawlty Towers*, as soon as anyone with a title enters, we know that Basil will employ his bowing and scraping routine. It's default behaviour in response to a certain trigger. At the same time his wife might be employing her conversational telephone routine; 'Oh, I know . . . I know . . . yes, I know . . . Oh, I know . . . '

Once a repetition is established, the improvisers are in a strong position to break the routine to illuminate a different aspect of the character. It's similar to lifting a restriction. It's a moment that can reveal an idea of the 'inner self'. In comedy, often the characters simply don't change. *The Fast Show* actor Paul Whitehouse took the view, when being interviewed by Alan Yentob, that if a character gives up his routine behaviour (complete with catchphrase) he's 'no longer the character'. Arguably the whole notion of character in improvisation is something of a chimera. Given that the medium itself is characterised by fluidity and narrative shifts, this notion of character as something static is probably less valid for improvisation than the idea of character as an evolving combination of characteristics. Furthermore, since character in improvisation is largely a product of interactions, i.e. the relationships *between* performers, it is relationships that deserve a closer

In the *People Show Cabaret*, Mark Long bullied Emil Wolk. Whenever Wolk did something wrong, there was a routine punishment. Long took him upstage where he was beaten and had his jacket pulled back over his head. This pattern repeated itself several times. Finally, Wolk again committed some blunder, saw what was coming, dragged himself upstage, hit himself as hard as he could, and pulled his own jacket over his own head.

attention. Using routines to illuminate relationships can be effective: the fact of repetition indicates how these individuals are tied together and on what this dependency rests. Their fragility is emphasised. When the routine breaks, the responses of both characters to the incident tell us even more. The implication of this is that the issue of character is inseperable from that of structure: character development either *creates* or is *created by* structure.

Let's imagine a woman comes on to the stage and makes a bed. She's dressed as a maid. She opens the drawer beside the bed as if she shouldn't. Then she has a cigarette out of the window. Then she hums to herself. The door opens and a man silently gives her a note. She reads it, laughs, then burns it. She goes out of the door. If this routine is repeated several times (it would really need to be a minimum of three times) and then the man, when he comes in next, speaks to her suddenly – the arc of the drama twists. Our attention is completely focused on what he has to say. The woman's reaction is crucial. The routine has been broken, and whatever happens next feels loaded. It's as if we're drawn into a secret. The break moment also shows us something new about the two characters, the man and the maid. It will give us new information about them. Therefore our perception of them shifts. The improviser can seize this moment to *extend* the prior notion of who that character is, and what drives them.

MECHANICS OF STRUCTURE IN PERFORMANCE

Taking the pattern of *routine /break-in-routine/ new behaviour*, this can be used as a structural template for either a scene or a show. This represents a time-based, narrative form of structuring. It's one of a number of available strategies. Essentially the different ways to struc-ture a long-form improvised show are similar to those available for a scene or an exercise:

- USING NARRATIVE

- USING LOCATION

- USING A GAME STRUCTURE

- USING PREDEFINED ROLES

These elements can also be put together in combination. Fluxx devised a format called *The Visitor* using essentially a *narrative* model of routine/interruption, etc. We had wanted a structure simple enough that it could be explained in a couple of sentences (once played of course, its hidden complexities became apparent). The audience would select two actors from a choice of three to play a central relationship. This might be a parent-child relationship, brother-sister, two lovers or some other close-knit partnership. Again, the audience would choose. In the first scene, the two actors developed routines. They picked the routines that were telling of their attitudes to each other. In addition, they added on top a 'role-set', such as Bully-Victim or Mentor-Admirer. This enabled them to play role-based games whatever the relationships. If the characters were brother and sister, then one of them might get bullied. If two lovers, one might be the admirer of the other.

The second scene would show an interruption of these routines. A third character would enter who had a strong, prior relationship with one of these characters. It was a traditional 'knock on the door' situation as Ibsen defined in *The Lady from the Sea*. The function of the third character was to offer a threat to the existing relationship. The visit upset the patterns of the relationship. Perhaps an old boyfriend returned to claim the sister. Or a secret gay friend would visit one of the lovers, looking for money. Once the routines were broken, the actors could explore the dramatic development resulting. Likely enough the interruption would set up dilemmas. Should the sister go off with the old boyfriend? What if the bully-brother came after her? Would the bisexual man pay off the visitor? Character choices were made and consequences followed through. The third stage would be the finding of a resolution to the drama. Within this, a new set of routines might be established. The old order had died; something new had taken its place. The sister was now living with her new/old boyfriend, and the brother was cruising the clubs. The bisexual man had paid the money but his visitor had wanted more. It had turned into a physical fight; the visitor had been beaten and he'd sulked off.

A structure based on *location* would be *Bassprov*. In this show, two guys played by Mark Sutton and Joe Bill, go fishing. There's no narrative worked out in advance but the men already have an established relationship. So it draws on two structural conventions: pre-identified location, and established roles/characters. The debate within the piece, and it is largely a verbal piece, can go anywhere. There's a love-hate relationship between the two characters and, being stuck on the lake, they provoke each other. As Mark Sutton says, *'We put ourselves in the bear trap and spend the hour trying to get out. There are a couple of hooks that we sometimes use, but there's nothing that has to be used in every show. We take two suggestions from the audience. We usually ask for a social or political issue, and the other suggestion is "Something you can stick your finger into" – just to give it some levity. Then we just start talking – and fishing. We always play the same two guys so then we have the freedom to recall any past information that has come out in any past show that might help us in this show. My character has a son, and his character has a daughter and a son – but the specifics of those children may change to suit the suggested theme. For instance, in one show recently we got teenage pregnancy, so his daughter that time was sixteen.'*

Examples of a *game* structure would be Theatresports in which two teams play sketches, competing for points from the judges, as discussed previously. Another would be *Maestro*, designed for a number of improvisers; perhaps around twenty who will all compete to be the 'Maestro' for the evening. There are two directors sitting in the front row of the stalls (in versions that I've witnessed). It's their task to call for scenes and eliminate performers as the evening progresses. Those scenes most applauded by the audience mean most points to the actors in them, distributed equally. The process continues until there is one actor left who has the most points. This actor is the Maestro – or Micetro – for the evening. The performer Andrew St John commented to me, *'No actor would invent a format like this.'* My experience of witnessing it and talking to participants suggests that actors often find it hard to overcome the competitive (and repetitive) nature of the event. The format treads a tortuous path between scoring that attempts to be 'fair' – marking 'achievement' – and the spirit of comedy impro that is rooted in an idea of ensemble. As an example of a director-led structure however, it remains an intriguing option. It's popular in many countries and audiences still come and cheer for it. And as Johnstone has observed, he was throwing contestants off stages years before *Big Brother* started throwing them out of houses.

Johnstone also developed *Lifegame*, another game format, discussed earlier, which hinges around the interviewing of a guest. As a format, it offers greater opportunities for a more intimate exploration. At any point, the interview might be stopped so an aspect of the story can be improvised around. Some years after it was first developed, Improbable

Theatre approached Johnstone for the rights to perform it and began a relationship with the format lasting several years, culminating in performances at the National Theatre in London in 2004. Phelim McDermott: *'I think* Lifegame *is the closest for me, to experiencing extraordinary impro moments – in front of an audience . . . It is a great format because your structure is the guest, really. Whatever their life is – or whatever he or she chooses to talk about on that night – is the structure. Even if the guest is not very forthcoming, that in itself becomes something revealing. We worked with Keith for five days at the start. His big thing about interviewing was "You're looking for a moment of theatre." '* But of course, once a moment is spotted, you need to know what to do with it – and to that end the company used a range of games to realise the stories as performance. Games, *'like getting the guest to play their grandmother. Or someone plays the thoughts of a character. For example, the last show we did at the National, with Kwame Kwei-Armah . . . it became a show about him discovering and reclaiming his ancestral name. He'd seen* Roots *on television when he was thirteen or fourteen and he was shocked by it. So we did this scene where he was nineteen, surrounded by all these books in his bedroom. He came in and sat down with his nineteen-year-old self (played by Guy Dartnell) and in that scenario, the person playing him becomes an onstage interviewer . . . The moments that really seem to work are where you make an imaginative leap. It doesn't always work if you just say "Act it out." So the guest is seeing that moment himself, from a different perspective.'*

Phelim pointed out that the work is criticised for being on the edge of something therapeutic – however, his experience of getting feedback from guests is that what they find most transformative are the moments of theatre rather than any digging into an uncomfortable area. *'If you try and make it therapeutic, you're stuffed.'* More pertinent for any discussion about issues of authority within structuring is the decision that the company took in relation to the role of director. *'The decision we made – which is where we departed from Keith – is that we wouldn't have an onstage director. So when Keith does it, he sits in the front row of the audience. And he watches. He says you can't interview and direct at the same time. But we decided we would have that as a floating, internalised role. So any performer could suggest a scene . . . For me, having a director takes away from the status of the guest, in terms of it being their show.'*

Forced Entertainment also took a game structure for their durational piece *Quizoola!* In this, there are three performers on stage, one who asks questions one who answers, and one who waits by the door ready to replace either of the first two. Tim Etchells: *'I wrote something like 2,000 questions and you're free to make up new questions. So you can pursue . . . or follow up answers. As an answerer you're obliged to answer, or make up answers. No answers are written.'* What may sound banal on the page, chimes on practical inspection with many of the basic tenets of impro practice: performers attempting to get themselves into trouble, the use of rules, games and verbal patterns, restrictions and transparency. There are certain conventions operating: you need to respect the game. If you 'collapse the game', or cease to take it seriously, you need to 'get it back again'. *'You have to feel that these two people believe there is something in this. That it matters, that it could have some weight . . . Somehow the question, "What have you got behind your rubbish bins?" becomes important that night. It becomes a major source of hilarity. Or annoyance. Or aggression. The performance has the capacity to get fixated on different things. It can have the feeling of an interrogation or two mates having a chat, or a feeling of hysteria, comedy. Some questions are designed to puncture the bubble, such as "Are you acting?", "Do you know some of the people here who are looking at you?" What's interesting is the extent to which you lie. We're very committed to that as a strategy. For example, a question like "Do you fantasise about rape?": a lot of people faced with that question will go – "No!" like that. But a lot of us will go "Yeah!" which is maybe not true. But it's that thing of owning in public unacceptable positions in a way that suggests you don't have a problem with them, so it puts the entire problem on the public. It's a very amoral kind of gaming. It's not self-protecting.'*

Finally, a structure based on *roles* would be *La Ronde Improvised* developed by Fluxx. The MC offers a series of cards to the spectators. On each card is a photograph of one of the six characters. The first card/character picked is the first on stage, the second card gives us the second until the last character is to meet with the first character in the final scene. This pattern exactly echoes that of *La Ronde* by Schnitzler. Fluxx has taken the format back to its roots and made it an exploration of sex, identity and romance as in Schnitzler's original writing. The pattern is therefore as follows: in the first scene we see characters A and B, in the second B and C, in the third C and D – until the last meets the first character A. However, there is additionally an internal architecture that is hidden from the audience. To ensure a range of different kinds of scenes, the actors know the first scene will always be two strangers meeting, the second will be an established couple, the third a couple that have broken up, the fourth an oppressive relationship, the fifth an incipient romance and the last, best friends. Each scene is played out in a different location with the space divided into the playing areas given earlier such as bedroom, exterior of nightclub, etc. Each actor beginning a scene determines the location to be used by walking into it. Often the audience can move around the space, changing positions according to where the action is. Additionally, there are performance games available to the actors associated with each scene, some of which are well known, like the master-servant game, others less so, like the game of remembering the same event differently (in the scene between the ex-partners).

Any facilitator or teacher of improvisation is advantaged by knowledge of how structure is used within the work of playwrights, choreographers

---

A note: holding to a rigid structure can have interesting consequences. I ran a workshop on *La Ronde Improvised* in Tel Aviv with some fine Israeli actors. In one of the paired scenes, sex play between two men in bed led to one 'suffocating' the other. The actor playing the suffocated character decided that he had 'died'. I insisted the next actor play the following scene according to the structure. His journey in the scene became:

Starts in the next room, calling out to the dead man

Makes assumptions that the first character is in a bad mood because he's not answering

Comes into the room; makes assumption that the character is asleep

Becomes confessional

Gets into bed with the apparent intention of having sex

Realises the man is dead

Panics; goes to phone the police

Stops panicking; doesn't phone the police

Realises the potential of making love to his dead body

Makes love to the dead body

Cries

Realises that he might be blamed for murdering the man

Leaves the flat, covering up as best he can, the fact that he was there.

and jazz musicians. Working with the core elements of improvisation, and building structures around core elements rather than what is particular to any one art form, it becomes possible to introduce, absorb or combine different art forms. Role-playing, for example, features in some way in all performing art forms whereas location is usually particular to certain kinds of theatre. Similarly, game structures have been used by musicians such as John Zorn, and dancers such as those associated with the Judson Church, as templates within which to improvise, just as they have by theatremakers like Keith Johnstone. Ability to reference these templates can only help to facilitate cross-art form initiatives that allow imaginative freedom to combine with the discipline of restrictions.

CODA

GAME STRUCTURES IN MUSIC – AN EXAMPLE

In the improvisational system John Zorn devised for his band entitled 'Cobra', the conductor uses a variety of cards to signal instructions to the musicians. These cards might call for, e.g. 'Duos', 'Separate Events' or 'Discord'. They're spread out on a table in front of him, so he can pick them up quickly and show them to the band. By these means is the band directed. However, it's also possible for any musician or musicians to make a challenge to the conductor by putting on a bandana, getting another musician to do the same, and thereby *taking over the power of the conductor.* This new regime remains in place until the conductor is permitted power back again. It's an example of a check on the Director role for which no equivalent exists within impro practice that I've found.

'What I've been working on for the past ten years is game structures. When I started working with improvisers my first thought was: "Here are a series of individuals; each has their own personal music. Each has worked on their instruments on their own, to develop a highly personal language that's often unnotatable." It's often a kind of music that Pierre Boulez would say can't be written down on a staff. So my problem was, how I involve these musicians in a composition that's valid and stands on its own without being performed *and yet inspires them to play their best. And at the same time realises the musical vision that I have in my head.*

What I came up with was the decision, which I think was the most important, never to talk about language or sound at all. *I left that*

completely up to the performers. What I was left with was basically
structure. *I can talk about when things happen and when they stop, but not*
what they are. I can talk about who and in what combinations, but I can't
say what goes on. I can say a change will happen here, but I can't say what
kind of change *it will be . . .*

I came up with a series of game rules like a trading system and an events
system where people independently perform events. Everybody can perform
one event each, for example, but nobody can time it at the same time with
anybody else. [I came up with] *a series of downbeats where changes will*
happen: if you're playing, maybe, you must stop; if you're not playing, you
may come in, for example . . .

I put Cobra together in two basic parts. The first part is a set of 18
downbeats, each of which sparks a different set of relationships between the
player, and sparks it at a sharp point by the prompter who cues all the
information to all the players. Anybody at any time can make a call with a
hand signal to the prompter, who then relates the information to the group.
At the downbeat that call is enacted. Each downbeat sparks extremely
different situations for the improvisers. We stay on that call until someone
else makes a call, which could be two or ten seconds later, could be a minute
later. Often, for a large group, a piece like this will create a more
improvisatory situation than if all the players were left just to improvise on
their own. You have no idea what's going to happen at any one moment.

Then there's a series of guerrilla tactics, in which one or three members
of the group can separate themselves from the regular flow of downbeats and
proceed to attack the other players with different musical strategies to get
other situations happening: situations that are often more complex than
would be possible if I just used a series of downbeats. So my compositions are
usually two-fold, or sometimes three-fold. If something is too simple people
will get bored playing with it. I try to make a balance so that it's completed
enough to be a challenge to them, but not so complicated that they're
completely frightened off and can't play it.

In Cobra there are 18 cards corresponding to each downbeat and the
three guerrilla systems each have a card . . . What you see in one of these
pieces is a really large set up with tons of equipment, everybody really a
mishmash, a really motley group, then a prompter sitting in front at a large
table with a series of coloured cards that are held up at different times and
come down at different times. People raising their hands at times for
different cues, people pointing at their noses, at their eyes, at their ears to
make cues clear; people pointing to each other to make contact between

musicians more clear – if you want to play with someone you've got to get their eye contact so you've to go "Hey, come on, over here" . . . So it's a real kind of circus atmosphere, like a three ring circus where there's so much going on you don't know where to look. The music changes so quickly you don't even know what to listen to sometimes.'

John Zorn interviewed in *Resonance Magazine*, Vol. 6 No. 1

2

TEACHING

'A guru doesn't, or your teacher doesn't, really tell you how to improvise. That is purely up to the student to gain by experience and to intuit the various methods of playing the music. What he directly learns from his teacher is the framework in which improvisation or performance of Indian music takes place . . . He gives you the scope and the field in which to gain your experience and if you're a good student then you take advantage of this opportunity that he gives you and then it becomes something that one develops on one's own.'   Viram Jasani

'The only rules are listen to other people, and do something you've never done before.'   Eddie Prévost, before his music workshop

'What we teach here is all about finding the game, and I think the better you get at it the more you are able to get the game out in the first line and then everybody can relax, 'cos they know who they are and what they're supposed to be doing.'   Amy Poehler

Teaching improvisation is one of the least discussed issues. One reason is that with the possible exception of what happens in Chicago, much teaching tends towards the derivative and the superficial. The dominant approach in the UK has been that evolved from Keith Johnstone. Not that Johnstone ever tried to establish a school but you'd think there was a School of Keith in the UK somewhere, just as you'd imagine there's a School of Viola in the States. Maybe Second City is that school. It's certainly in the right city. Don Hall said to me, *'You can't spit in this city without hitting an improviser.'* But in both cases, there is arguably some comfortable leaning on the past. One consequence is a too-easy acceptance of those tenets established early but more recently losing their relevance. The Johnstone/Spolin axis was born from a desire to liberate performers via game disciplines into a spontaneity that was imaginatively liberating. Perhaps now it's time to move to a stage in which those now-liberated imaginations can dream a science that moves beyond game-dependency. Improvisers from both cities have expressed the need for teachers of impro to bring a little more science to their methodology. We in the UK want clarity around the practice that consistently challenges established precedents while retaining the force of their inventors' passions. There's a clear case for more teaching and more schools.

LEARNING AND TEACHING VOCABULARY

When I first arrived at the House of Improvisation, it seemed essential to get the rulebook. I'd read it, learn it and would know what to do. Coming from formal education, I was confident there was such a book. It would surely have been by wise men. I was told, yes, it had been written, a man called Keith had written it and it was called *Impro*. So I bought it, read it, and like many others, was very inspired. I blagged my way into a workshop and spent a week with him and twenty others in Dorset. I'd read the book so I knew I would be fine. But everything seemed more fluid than I'd expected. At one point during an improvisation, I found myself gibbering complete nonsense about mathematical equations with Phelim McDermott on stage that had no connection with anything. I tried to remember what the rule was for getting out of this particular kind of disaster, failed, and carried on into algebra. I had fallen into a version of the Book-Reality Gap. I had absorbed something of 'the rules', but had little understanding of their application. I was the soldier who was fighting the war with a manual and no combat training. Not that Johnstone had set out to write any rules, but he does by implication outline some, especially through his emphasis on impro vices to avoid.

But even if one agrees rules are a good thing, what kind of terms should be used to describe them? As soon as you start to discuss an intuitive process like impro, you're bringing clumsy vocabulary to bear. Custom and practice have led to terms such as 'offer', 'blocking', 'accepting' and so on being unequivocal. But these terms have been borrowed from adjacent social behaviours, and don't always mean the same thing to different people. So there's a case for looking a bit harder at the vocabulary. Terms such as 'blocking' may have a meaning that's more uncertain than some teachers like to suggest. If the issue of vocabulary isn't addressed, semantic confusions offstage simply lead to accumulating confusions on it.

Now take 'build offers'. OK, but is 'building an offer' like building a house? It's true that Stanislavsky talked about 'Building a Character' but Grotowski's concept of the *via negativa* argues that a character is created not by 'building' but by 'stripping away' and 'eliminating the obstacles'. And Peter Brook says that *'Preparing a character is the* opposite *of building – it is* demolishing, *removing brick by brick everything in the actor's muscles, ideas and inhibitions that stands between him and his part.'* (*The Shifting Point*. My emphases.)[77] So what does this mean for improvisation vocabulary? Surely if we're going to live by rules, or even by *principles*, we have to sort out issues of vocabulary first. In fact, 'building' is a term that sends the brain hunting in entirely the wrong direction. It may be better to use words that have fewer direct associations with specific activities outside performance. It maybe be better to use words that have a general association elsewhere – not for any reason of principle but simply to prevent the mind defaulting to specific mental images such as a man pushing a wheelbarrow full of cement. We need a terminology that is precise yet flexible, relatively free of narrow associations yet doesn't sound like Martian.

If these terms weren't already confusing, I became even more baffled when I worked with improvising dancers and musicians to whom the phrase 'build offers' meant nothing at all. Dancers and musicians each have their own terms that have accumulated over the years. A musician, asked to 'compose the space' by a dancer, might assume 'the space' to be a tune. A dancer, asked to 'play the head' might well start moving from the neck. In the mixed improvisation company ESP, there was nothing for it but sit down and compare vocabularies to find those that resonated across the art forms. This usually meant everyone learning others' key terms, or occasionally inventing new words entirely. In respect of a term like 'building', words like *'developing'*, *'extending'* or *'elaborating'* were found to be much more helpful. The same has proved true in a purely dramatic context.

Teaching becomes a very inexact and confusing science when the terms used are vague or self-contradictory. I found that technical impro terms were dynamite in the hands of those who erred on the side of the Hitlerian. Rather than facilitate, teachers would bandy vocab around as a means to establish their authority. Such practice sits alongside other teaching vices, such as always fixing on the negative, only speaking to one person in the class, refusing to acknowledge a fine piece of work and using the position of teacher as a means to make sexual conquests. No doubt if I founded a School of Improvisation and had many theses written about it, I would standardise my vocabulary and take out an injunction against anyone using it wrongly. If someone used forbidden words like 'building' in my presence, they would get detention. I would write the *Definitive Dictionary of Improvisation* that could be studied and learnt. I would sanction teachers and take offenders to court. I would . . . OK, that's enough. (Hang on; I was just building something there . . .) There is however an unreliable lexicon offered at the end of this book, carrying many of the terms that are currently in usage.

TEACHING BEGINNERS

Of course there are many approaches to teaching dramatic improvisation. But perhaps there are two fundamentally:

- THE SINK OR SWIM SCHOOL

- THE SLOWLY DOES IT SCHOOL

THE SINK OR SWIM (SOS) SCHOOL rests on the idea that you need to throw the child in from the riverbank so that the full impact of water is experienced. The child sinks of course but you bring him out, sit him down and ask 'How was that?' Once he has stopped spewing, you have a discussion about survival strategies. (He may never show up at lessons again, but at least he hasn't been over-protected.) You tell him about different strokes; crawl, breast stroke and so on. You start to bring a conceptual language to bear on what just happened, and discuss the emotions felt. An improvisational equivalent might

> 'The fool is walking around, and there will be something about the fool that the dictator cannot avoid. Which is that the fool loves him. And that is something that the dictator does not understand. So he will want to banish it. For the fool is unrepresented in any hierarchy yet he is represented in every heart. Which is why the fool can talk to everyone. Because the fool talks to the fool in each person. Whereas the dictator talks to the dictator in each person.'
>
> Jonathan Kay

be to put the student in front of the class and ask him or her to perform solo. Jonathan Kay – who does this – has described the process as a 'confrontation with the dictator part of the self'. The argument being: if you want to contact the fool inside yourself, you have to also contact the dictator – the part of you that wants to be in charge, and is frightened of not being in charge. Once identified, you can start to allow the dictator to be somewhere else while the foolishness takes over. When the beginner is put solo out front, all the stock fears are likely to be triggered. That is, fear of appearing foolish, fear of failure, fear of looking incompetent, and so on. These fears, once experienced, can be identified, given names and, over time, held in check or transmutated. The beginner will hopefully get a sharp insight into the mind's defaults at moments of pressure. In particular, the desire for control will be highlighted. As Keith Johnstone said to me, *'Beginners can't have any dealings with a frog carrying an umbrella because they don't know where it will lead.'*

In time, the desire to be in control or to control what the audience will receive lessens and a more foolish, creative, curious attitude is cultivated in which the performer understands that this is a journey embarked on *with* rather than *for the sake of* the audience. Then the frog can be pursued. So the SOS School sets up in the beginner a need to find strategies and tools that will help to avoid sinking. One of these tools will involve the recognition that actually sinking is alright if you enjoy it and start to view it as material for the improvisation. But this is a hard precept to take on board early.

The SOS School tends to eschew rules. It has no time for the gentler, progressive development, preferring instead to move on quickly into doing scenes where the primary challenges can be confronted. Within Chicago, a city with a wide range of educational choices, the Annoyance Theatre would be close to this model. *'At the Annoyance, since we do so many different things, our main focus comes out of our belief that it doesn't matter what form you do, if you can't act the scene then the form's not going to help you. So all our work is based on how you can play the most powerful character and be able to play the best scenes that you can. Our work is scenically based. We teach people how to play characters and improvise scenes. We don't deal a lot with forms, or any sort of devices like that. It's closer to an acting approach than an improv approach . . . The thing that sets us apart more than anything else is the notion that you must begin strongly; and the support notion for us is that the best way to support*

your partner is to serve yourself first. The power of selfishness. Sometimes a
lot of the terminology in improv is confused, so people take that notion of
support too literally. What they end up doing is being a facilitator to their
partner's idea . . .

Our mindset isn't so much about ignoring the rules as working out of a
space of inspiration – rather than obligation. So we try to eliminate as far
as possible all the things the improviser feels "obliged" to do on stage. The
only thing we require is for the improviser to be fearless and to attack the
scene from the beginning, rather than allow the scene to happen to them . . .
It takes a while to get used to the concept. What we found is that it's easier
to push them out there and get them to reach for that, and then pull them
back a little bit, and say, "OK, you've gone this far, that's great, now you
have to recognise what's happening around you" – as opposed to keep
trying to inch them out further and further each time.' (Mark Sutton.)

The advantage of the SOS School is that it's conceptually clean and
simple. It's a 'no nonsense' approach in which learning to swim is both a
prerequisite and imperative for survival. Students aren't mollycoddled
or over-protected. It is close to the European tradition of theatre
training, an example of which might be the Ecole Philippe Gaulier,
where students receive blunt but honest criticism at every stage of their
training. The approach taxes the faint of heart but invigorates the
courageous.

THE SLOWLY DOES IT (SDI) SCHOOL relies more on games and easy
exercises to acclimatise the student gradually to the demands. It involves a slow accumulation of knowledge, working progressively through
basic games to early exercises to improvisations. At risk of putting
artists and teachers into boxes, there are aspects of John Wright's approach that would correspond. *'If I'm training actors . . . it goes through*
a series of different phases. For example, I'll start always with play. Just
straightforward, unconscious play. Which is a bit like doodling or
something.' A fuller account of John's process is given in the chapter on
Ensemble and in his own book, *Why Is That So Funny?* Essentially
what he aims to do is encourage the students to discover in themselves
a quality of *innocent mischief.* This might even involve the use of an
innocent mask. Once the performer has put the mask on, *'I would set*
up various games. And the very first starting point is to stop people thinking.
Stop people making things up and instead get people to react . . . It's
completely mercurial, childlike, although not like a child . . . And then when

they get to conscious play and I've got them doing this for an audience, then they get to realise "This is funny." So once it's funny I get them to do it again. And then they develop this relationship with the audience so it becomes conscious what they're doing. But they're still just being instinctive. And then I take the mask off and get them to play the And Game . . . Working on their own initially, they'd do something and I'd say "And?" and they'd do something else with it, and I'd say "And?" I'm not looking for a planned logic, I'm looking for a stream of ideas. So I'm a provocateur. Provoking unconscious play. Then I might do another exercise to develop that . . . Maybe the same thing in pairs. And this is where the complicity starts to come in.'

The SDI School approach is more reliant upon a methodical pedagogy that introduces students to essential experiences around playing, creativity and openness, slowly building their resilience and courage. Once achieved, the demands can be increased. Action Theatre might be an example of a comparable methodology in which the student engages with progressively more and more challenging exercises. Ruth Zaporah sets out its function in her book *Action Theatre, The Improvisation of Presence*. The book *'presents a month-long training, twenty work days of Action Theatre. Each chapter reflects a single five-hour session of the training. The exercises for the day appear at the beginning of each chapter and are ordered developmentally. I provide instructions for every exercise and discuss their applications and implications.'*[78] Having taken a few short classes in Action Theatre, one does get a sense of this slowly accumulating and heightening series of challenges – the work neither rushing ahead so as to leave participants behind – nor staying still for their benefit.

Of course, these polar opposites are nothing of the kind. There are not really two schools and the teachers quoted here would justifiably resist any such categorisation. But there is a sense of emphasis within the different methods. The best teachers will switch between the two strategies: sometimes throwing out a tough challenge (after all, can a teacher's intuitive sense of a student's ability always be relied on?) and sometimes moving slowly, so individuals don't feel defeated. It's all in the timing. Often it's hard to know which strategy to use. If students underperform they may drift away, feeling insufficiently challenged. But similarly, if a student feels downhearted about recurring failure, he may simply give up. In this case, a combination of wrong exercises and injudicious comments by the teacher might be the cause. I've annoyed a few people. Sometimes constructively, other times less so. I can easily disturb someone with a comment I think is cavalier and jokey, but find out later I've upset that person and she or he (usually she) may not return to the class.

FOCUS AREAS

Especially for beginners, there is a strong case for each class having a clear focus area. This way, the students feel orientated. Sometimes it's hard to work on more than one thing at a time. Besides, the teacher needs permission to say, in answer to a question maybe, 'Yes, that narrative did fall apart but we're not looking at narrative so we can just ignore that (the apparent failing).' What's important is that the *choice* of focus is both broad enough to generate a range of exercises, yet narrow enough so everyone knows precisely what is being explored. It also helps in planning exercises for the class. There are so many games and exercises out there, both established and yet to be established, both invented and borrowed, that knowing *why* each exercise is selected helps the teacher to coach students within it.

Here in this book, focus areas are divided into *Beginners* and *Advanced*. The former would include 'listening', 'responsiveness', 'accepting' and so on. The latter would include 'world', 'conflict', 'reincorporation' and 'risk'. Example lists of focus areas are given later. Now any significant school of improvisation will have far more levels than these two. But this simple division recognises that different students will have differing abilities in different areas. So if you're looking to plan a course, you could start by organising each session to have a clear focus, taken from a list given in the section of Games and Exercises.

LEARNERS' APTITUDES

A lot of teaching comes down to an assessment of the student's aptitude. One way to do this is to look at learning styles or modalities. Each student will probably tend to learn best in a certain way. One pedagogic template is that popularised by NLP (Neuro-Linguistic Programming). Does this individual learn primarily *through visual, auditory or kinaesthetic* means? Does the student tend to achieve in one kind of exercise and not in another? One student is great on composing the space, making images and observing the behaviour of others on stage. Another will pick up nuances in others' dialogues that are usually missed. Another will create great physical characters that kinetically establish a physical rapport. These distinctions suggest three different learning types. Similarly, different performers will find *difficulties* in different areas. They find themselves creatively drying up in scenes where others are flying. One tends to miss seeing things, another doesn't catch what is said and a third is always stationary. Recognition of these different aptitudes can help the teacher identify why problems occur. As Matt Elwell explains, *'Different kinds of learners react differently to stress. When you're in a good scene, you may be fine. But when you're in a bad scene, you may not listen to your partner. Not because you're a bad person but because the hearing centres of your brain shut down in stress. But you can see OK.'*

NLP has attempted to pin down these different ways of operating. A promotional web site writes: *'Most of us learn in many ways, yet we usually favour one modality over the others. Many people don't realise they are favouring one way; because nothing external tells them they are any different from anyone else. Knowing that there are differences goes a long way towards explaining things like why we have problems understanding and communicating with some people and not with others, and why we handle some situations more easily than others. How do you discover your preferred modality? One simple way is to listen for clues in your speech. (Do you often catch yourself saying things like "That looks right to me" or "I get the picture"? Or are you more likely to say "That sounds right to me" or "That rings a bell"? Or again "I like the feel of that" or "I grasp it now"?) Another way is to notice your behaviour when you attend a seminar or workshop. Do you seem to get more from reading the handout or listening to the presenter, or do you prefer "hands-on" activities and group interaction?*

VISUAL PREFERENCE: PEOPLE ARE
neat and orderly / speak quickly / good planners / observant of environmental detail / appearance-oriented in dress and presentation/ memorise by visual association / are usually not distracted by noise / often know what to say but can't think of the right words / need an overall view and purpose.

AUDITORY PREFERENCE: PEOPLE ARE
learners by listening / speak in rhythmic patterns / are easily distracted by noise / can repeat back tone, pitch and timbre / can be eloquent speakers /

have problems with projects that involve visualisation / can find writing
difficult but are better at telling.

KINAESTHETIC PREFERENCE: PEOPLE ARE
learners by manipulating and doing / want to act things out / speak more
slowly / touch people to get their attention / stand close when talking to
someone / are physically oriented and move a lot, gesture a lot / memorise
by walking and seeing / find it hard to sit still for long periods / use action
words / like involved games.[79]

Awareness of these distinctions may be useful for teachers as a means
to assess strengths and weaknesses. Watching a class can be confusing;
there are so many subtle and complex signals given out, not just on
stage but off it. Joe Bill says that, *'When I'm teaching the first class of the*
term, or doing a one time workshop, I'll usually begin with some quick
scenes, or a couple of short, scene based exercises.' The ensuing scenes give
him information about the modalities of the participants. *'The*
kinaesthetic and auditory learners usually go first with the auditory folks
spewing all kinds of exposition in an effort to frame up what's going to
happen in the scene, and the kinaesthetic folks either embodying emotion or
contorting themselves or obsessing on some object work or activity to begin.'
Matt Elwell had actually recommended Joe Bill to me as something of
a proponent of this approach. Talking to Matt, I speculated about the
impro tradition of using *mime*, which personally I have always found
weak and ineffectual. In Chicago it's simply never questioned, having
come down from Viola Spolin. He answered, *'So if this screws you up, as*
far as (for example) holding a (mimed) book, then perhaps you're more
eloquent and can pick out details from what other people are saying: you
may be an auditory learner. As opposed to kinaesthetic. Myself, I'm very
kinaesthetic, you give me a book and I feel safe. You're programmed
differently so you feel like you're pretending, it doesn't make sense to you.
So I think (for the teacher) the thing not to be afraid of is to tell you, "OK,
don't do that." And tell me to do that more. Or – and I think the next step
is – to design exercises that have your modality in mind, but will bridge that
gap. So that maybe it's not the thing you do all the time, but maybe there
are exercises that will not only help you to do that but help you feel more
connected.' This was useful and has wide application, I could see.
However, I still feel Matt has the traditional American myopia around
issues of mime, or working with 'space objects' as it's referred to – now

there's an example of crazy terminology – and doesn't see that the convention holds improvisation in an infantile stage of development. Perhaps because the tradition was started with Spolin, improvisers have a difficulty in casting it overboard.

Joe Bill confirmed to me the point about fear, made by Matt Elwell: *'As a teacher, something that I've come up with is this theory: the way that one prefers to learn – or learns the most efficiently – will also dictate, to some degree, the fears that one will have to confront or manage. And overcoming fear is an essential part of becoming a "good improviser".'* He identifies the fears associated with the different modalities as follows:

- VISUAL – the fear of looking stupid
- AUDITORY – the fear of sounding stupid
- KINAESTHETIC – the fear of not doing enough for the scene or scene partner

Perhaps I should have started this chapter with consideration of arguably an even more fundamental difference: how men learn differently from women. Rebecca Sohn, another performer and teacher based in Chicago observes, *'Generally speaking, men and women have different aptitudes but of course, it all depends on an individual's upbringing. Boy children play differently than girl children and a difference remains through adulthood. But improv tends to attract women who likely had higher aptitudes and didn't play by the "rules" throughout her life . . . Men tend to be more aggressive onstage, i.e. push their ideas harder. For women it's the opposite, they tend to be more polite and defer to others. I make students aware of it when it's an issue for them specifically. I try to get the women to be a little more aggressive and less apologetic while I try to get the men to listen and support more.'* This difference in behaviour has to be an issue for any teacher. Calling for volunteers as a way to start exercises, may play into the hands of the men. If female voices aren't heard in the room, certain subject areas of personal experience may never get adequately heard. Improvisations can become hard-edged and linear in their exploration. There can be too great an emphasis on 'the funny' and insufficient emphasis on the inter-relating of feelings and experiences. A quirkier, abstract sense of humour may start to appear unnecessary and inappropriate whereas if given more space, it might have as much resonance as the joke-driven humour. Women improvisers do in my experience like to take longer to find the depth in scenes. For men it can be a matter of honour to get to the point fast and direct, while women are happy to hang around for a while and see what shows up. If the playwright John Mortimer is correct, men should try to remember, *'Women are better at doing most things than men, except having sexual fantasies.'*

What can't work is any kind of victim stance in the class, any sense that women are disenfranchised by the medium itself and therefore have to be given special treatment. I would argue for sensitive treatment applied even-handedly rather than special treatment. And because I know I can often not recognise my own insensitivity, it's imperative for a male teacher to encourage women's voices in all aspects of the work. Susan Messing, performer and teacher, has added this to the debate: '[A lot of women] *feel very manipulated. And this is an art that you have to manipulate. You have to manipulate yourself through space, and so if you are led through the space, you might be angry about it. I am not angry about it. I never am. I have been given choices, choices have been made for me that I have not cared for, and I have to swallow it, swallow the judgement, and make it work . . . As time and tide and perspective come around, you realise you can play with anything.'*

THE RULES

I did ask Keith Johnstone about rules, and he suggested that they were pretty useful for beginners, and this sounded a good piece of advice. I'm referring here to rules of playing rather than any other kind of rules. *Rules* can refer to different aspects of improvisation work. There are:

- RULES OF STRUCTURE
- RULES OF THE GAME
- RULES OF PLAYING

Beginners can easily become confused.

RULES OF STRUCTURE were discussed in the last chapter.

RULES OF THE GAME are in place not only to make the game work, but also to create certain feelings within the players. Beginners especially, need to be coaxed into some unfamiliar emotional and physical experiences that they would otherwise avoid. Games do this very well.

Everyone has to run around the room, and then get into physical contact with someone else using some unlikely points of contact. The facilitator calls these out. There's compulsion involved. Feet, legs, chest, heads, knees get cosy in unlikely juxtapositions. The rules are there to shoehorn the players into that physical intimacy. If players could choose how to achieve physical contact, they might just hold hands or touch shoulders. Players will naturally try and evade the experience teachers want them to have. Hence the necessity for compulsion. Learners need to start to 'feel different' from how they normally feel when they get up, go to the office or generally live an ordered life. It's necessary to impose the rules pretty strictly. For if you allow them to be broken too often, then you compromise the chance of players having an intense albeit discomforting experience.

> 'The rules defining the exercises are constraints that isolate components of human behaviour. These rules open pathways that lead into unexplored territories where the mind and body rejoin, where there's no disparity between action and being.'
> Ruth Zaporah

For a teacher, it will do well to know just what the benefits are to each game or exercise. The physical contact game is clearly about breaking down personal space boundaries. Many such games are to do with 'making things happen': physical contact, verbal communication, eye contact or heightened emotional states. Others also have to do with ensuring that 'nothing happens' in an area normally over-stimulated, in order that something else can happen in a different area. These games might involve closing eyes or using blindfolds. Sight is cut off in order to provoke the gathering of different kinds of sensory information. Unless the player can 'feel the difference' of how it is to receive the information through skin by means of touch, for example, then he or she won't be able to generate that internal psychic space that allows spontaneous thoughts and feelings to flow into it. She won't be able to respond to feelings generated by later, more complex improvisations. Closing the eyes also helps to open the inner eye, that is the imagination.

Other games and exercises aim to promote courage, persistence or foolishness. They might involve the prohibition of 'offer avoidance' or they might coerce the player into a journey that player wouldn't usually choose to travel. For example, two players link arms and one creates a journey for the other. While both are 'on the journey' across mountains and treacherous rivers, one is clearly the motor for what happens, defining everything, and the other has to agree to everything and engage with all the experiences. This way the passive partner gets to feel fear, anticipation, excitement, relief, elation and pleasure – without taking responsibility. This partner can't say, 'Let's not go there.' Why can't they? That's the rule. It's in place to close those doors that otherwise might let the player out of this experiential journey. The rules say 'Don't Go There – That's a Way Out!'

RULES OF PLAYING simply take these prohibitions into the sphere of dramatic improvisation. They aim to serve the same function by closing off escape routes from the primary *dramatic* experiences that are there to be enjoyed. These rules are used by some teacher to coerce good practice. They include propositions such as:

- Don't block offers
- Don't ask questions
- Always say yes
- Always be energetic
- Build offers
- Don't do transactional scenes
- Don't do teaching scenes

. . . and so on. Once there was a time when these were sacred because they came down from Viola Spolin. And if you consult the book that is closest to the impro bible in that part of the world, you can read: *'Anyone can improvise, but like any game, if the players don't learn and obey the rules, no one will play with them. In childhood games like Cowboys and Indians or Cops and Robbers, if someone is shot, he has to "die". If he is taken prisoner and tied up, he has to remain tied up until someone frees him. A child who doesn't follow these rules won't be very popular in his neighbourhood.'* However, there is a later caveat: *'There are plenty of rules in improvisation, as a quick thumb through this book will show. However, one of the first rules is "There are no rules."'*[80] Nevertheless, core principles are still upheld within much of the American scene. Matt Elwell from ComedySportz told me that in some ImprovOlympic shows – because you're performing a lot to other improvisers – *'you can get booed if you break the rules.'* However, a few years ago along came Mick Napier and Annoyance Theatre, and they said 'rules suck' and there was consternation and muttering in the corridors. Instead, Napier said, *'Proper execution of The Rules in an improv scene does not necessarily yield a good improv scene.'* Further, he said, *'I do not believe one must learn The Rules in order to break them.'*[81]

In his book, *Improvise: Scene from the Inside Out*, Napier argues that the problem with rules lies in their adherents working backwards from the premise that there is somewhere in the sky a perfectly functioning ensemble that is dutifully following 'the rules'. Furthermore, any time a player breaks 'a rule' – about blocking for example – a step back is taken from this ideal ensemble practice. The more rules broken, the faster the ensemble falls out of the sky. Improvisers' choices therefore get assessed according to how they have respected the rules, and teaching becomes a process of negatively attributing flaws. If Jesus had followed this principle, he would have told everyone the reasons why they might go to hell, rather than argue what was necessary to get to heaven. Napier argues that there is a relationship between good improvisation practice and a respect for the rules, but it's not a simple one. He writes, *'Yes, there is a correlation between bad scenes and specific behaviour, but it is not causal. The behaviour is not consequential. Scenes that are bad to begin with often yield such behaviour, but the behaviour itself does not cause the scene to be bad. Correlation does not necessarily equal causality.'*[82]

In other words, one needs to look elsewhere if one wants to find out why improvisers are not making the best of their material. Perhaps these decisions are made because of the performer's attitude which deep down is fearful and destructive. This prior state of fearfulness is more likely to be the root problem, rather than the simple rule-breaking behaviour that is a consequence of the fearfulness. As Keith Johnstone said to me, *'In* Truth in Comedy, *it says that you shouldn't ask questions, but we have to find out WHY the questions are asked. Are they asked out of fear – or not?'* Napier and colleagues might agree with this line of questioning since it argues for a more holistic, visionary approach to teaching and learning. In which case it becomes perfectly legitimate to 'break rules' if the exercise is rooted in adventure and playfulness. It's possible therefore to legitimately block an offer, ask a question or enact a teaching scene; it's the psychological/emotional *context* that makes the difference. We return to the opening notion –

rules are helpful for beginners to help them accumulate unfamiliar experiences. For more advanced students, they might be a more occasional benchmark.

FEAR AND ANXIETY

Because the improviser always feels unprepared, it's an inevitable condition of the work that tension creeps into the body. It's hardly surprising. A measure of tension is desirable because it energises and fuels the imagination. But too much of this floods the engine; the imagination becomes paralysed. In this case, the performer finds it difficult to see, listen and respond. He starts to hear only the braying of internal emotions. Behind this anxiety might be a thought, such as 'I shall be exposed as a failure/ a freak / a hollow person.' This is particularly true for beginners. Not absolute beginners – for them it's a breeze – but for those who have just begun to understand the enormous potential of the form. One way to usefully come to terms with such anxiety is for the improviser to perceive it as just another reaction to what's happening. The body simply acknowledges one more sensation – or thought – in addition to others. Rather than this being felt as the *only* sensation that matters, it can be regarded simply as one of many. The recognition can extend further, acknowledging that this anxiety will pass through the body, especially if it's incorporated. It won't necessarily remain as a felt sensation forever. But the first step is to make the student aware of what is taking place, not categorising these feelings as 'nerves' or 'stagefright' but rather as sensations that exist alongside others; and can be acted on within the frame. The first step to this is awareness. As Sten Rudstrom has observed, *'Without awareness, you cannot craft.'* This is how the musician and performer Ansuman Biswas came to be aware of his own fearfulness and how it operates: *'There's a specific thing that I began to be aware of when I was first learning improvisation, that thing that happens when you're afraid to say something or do something. It could even be word association. And it happens very quickly; sometimes it's not even a conscious emotion. What becomes apparent is we're not always conscious of the choices we're making. Part of the mind goes, "Oh, I can't do that now" – and if that happens enough times, you drive yourself into a cul-de-sac, and eventually you're frozen – that's it. Then you decide you're no good, and a vicious circle is established – of self-deprecation and lack of confidence. Eventually it's impossible to contribute anything. And these impulses have a momentum: they tend to increase themselves. Everyone is prey to these tiny, emotional particles. I don't think it's ever helpful just to react to an impulse, and just go with it, whether that's a negative or positive impulse. It's generally not useful. And if people think that's what improvisation is, I'd say that was a distortion . . . What is important is to notice what impulses happen and to notice them as subtly as possible so as not to be ruled by them.'*

How to deal with anxiety? How to encourage the student to forgive it, and use it? You can't make it go away, but you can incorporate those feelings and sensations associated with anxiety into the piece. The trick is not to think of these feelings as not belonging on the stage. If they exist, they have a place there. When they don't reduce is when they are thought of as unwanted, unnecessary or belonging somewhere else. But you have to be quick to catch them, because they move. Better to knock down that dividing wall in the mind, that separates what is understood as 'acceptable' from 'unacceptable', as soon as possible. The longer left, the more firm and solid the wall. The mind does like to separate things out and put them into departments. This might also include your observations of the audience or your recognition of the carpet. This process leads you to start denying all this 'stuff' as material. In training, the teacher needs therefore to be trying to help the student to be able *'to say yes to more things'*. This may mean stopping the improvisation so any internal feelings not being expressed can be identified. Is there a wall building up? Let's identify what's on either side of it. Sten Rudstrom observed to me how all-important this issue of anxiety can become. It's usually intimately related to judgement of oneself. *'You get obsessed with judgement. Or you believe that your judgement is more important than you . . . I say this in classes all the time. "Here comes this judgement. It's blocking you. Say hello to it, it's a piece of material." The beautiful thing about judgement is it is great energy. It's very powerful. All you have to do to it is add one image to it, and you're off.'*

By 'adding an image', what is meant is that the feeling of anxiety is given an association with a picture from the imagination. It's not unlike drag and drop within computer software. I feel the anxiety but I take this anxiety and place it on an image. So now I'm anxious not about being on stage but that I was caught speeding by the roadside cameras. Or I'm anxious that my girlfriend saw me with another girl. Or I'm anxious I may never walk again after my girlfriend ran me down in her car. What can often be a mistake, and I do see it in improvisers, is the anxiety expressed without any transference into an image, context or scenario. The improviser simply tells the audience about his or her anxiety, not as a character but as a performer. Without a structural frame to facilitate this, the effect can be rather like meeting a stranger at a party who confesses to drinking urine as a health cure straight after saying hello. It's a little too much honesty a little too early. The point of theatre is, it's a distancing medium by design.

I did a solo show recently and there was a moment when I allowed anxiety to close down my inventiveness. There was no transference into an image. I just stressed over the implications of an audience contribution and failed to process it in any way productively. I was playing the character of a boy being brought to his new home. At a certain point, I asked the audience to give me a word. I was in the middle of a scene. In fact I was in the middle of a sentence. I wanted a left-field contribution that would throw me off centre. *'Look, Mum, upstairs in the house is a –* I asked for a word and it came back – *"jockey".* It was a great contribution from a spectator. I joked around with it for a while, rather ineffectually. But in my heart I knew what I should really do: I should embody that jockey. I should be that jockey in the room upstairs, riding imaginary races. I should live again all those triumphs and disasters at Lingfield Park or Aintree. But I became anxious that it would pull me away from material I was already developing. That it would destroy the scene of the boy in the house. That the digression would disrupt the main journey. So I said 'no' to it. And here's the funny thing. I said 'no' to it, even knowing at the time it was a mistake. My overactive rational mind, the one you want to take away and bury at such moments, was telling me that this jockey couldn't *possibly* belong in this house my parents had just bought. It simply wasn't logical. How could a jockey be living upstairs in a house we'd just bought – and we not know about it? Impossible. No fair or reasonable person would accept that. Unfortunately, being fair and reasonable is not what improvisation is about. So the anxiety caused me to freeze up. If I'd simply foregone the jockey altogether and moved

'What fear of revealing, of vulnerability, of being human, grips us so fiercely and above all, why? What is it that, down there in the darkness of the psyche, cries its silent "No" to the longing for "Yes"?'

Bernard Levin

on, that would have been fine, but my 'blocking' of the idea stayed with me as an anxiety – corroding the subsequent scene.

When it's not a soloist but an ensemble, the problem can be magnified. Sten Rudstrom again: *'The bigger the ensemble, the more energy there is. If one person is nervous, everyone feels it.'* Anxiety can ripple through a group faster than the smell of fox goes through a pack of hounds, particularly if the nervous one is determined to share his anxiety.

> *Two players start Scene One. The first is a Champion, the second a Sidekick. The Champion is due to fight a Challenger. Before then, a third character is due to enter, a Guru who will make a prediction about the coming Fight. But the first two players become anxious, cut short their scene – which should be spent establishing the imagery for the world of the play – and call on the Guru too early. Everyone feels their anxiety and it spreads to the third actor quickly. Now it's going to be hard to slow down. The world is never fully created.*

One way to deal with mounting anxiety in a group, if it can't be incorporated, is to go back to basics. To start really listening and watching, and playing every moment for its own sake. Anxiety closes down the listening, so by the group concentrating on it again, helps to diminish the anxiety. They can catch up and perhaps get back into some kind of groove.

Teachers can also introduce restrictions and tasks into scenes to reduce anxiety. This works because the imagination gets channelled into a specific task. The tasks might be impossible. In this way, the thought 'I'm not doing very well here' sits quite comfortably. No one expects anything more than failure. You, the actor, are not to blame. It's the teacher's fault for imposing this ridiculous restriction. Your character is being asked to do something impossible. Examples of instructions like this might include: the actors being asked to move in clothes that are too small for them. They might be asked to levitate. Two actors might be asked to create a scene of Jesus and the feeding of the 5,000 with just themselves and a bottle of milk. Using task-based exercises such as these, the teacher can pull the performers away from their default anxieties. A more creative atmosphere can result. So the tension starts *to go somewhere else*, out of the head and body. It's one of the interests of Wendy Houston, to be pulling dancers away from their preferred behaviours. The imposition of restraints begins to disable the professionalised gesturing, *'so people arrive in unexpected physical places. It's about going outside your own choices, not being wilful but accepting other kinds of suggestions – that's for me what it is about ... Your job as a performer is to make your life more difficult for yourself – to keep yourself alert. It's like driving a nail into your own hand.'*

TEACHING STYLES

A great teacher doesn't have to be a great performer. In the UK two of the most prominent teachers, Keith Johnstone (now based in Canada) and John Wright rarely go on stage. However, other fine UK teachers such as Kevin Tomlinson, Guy Dartnell, Danielle Allan, Jonathan Kay, Mark Phoenix, Timothy Lone, Phelim McDermott and Andrew St John combine both teaching and performing. The advantage of combining both professions is that you know better what the actor is going through. You have a sense of why he or she is doing it because you've done it yourself. In the absence of any 'teacher training', it's a good base knowledge to have behind you.

How does a teacher teach? There are a number of ways:

- BY MODELLING – In other words, acting yourself, joining in as an equal but relying on the students to watch you and to learn by watching.

- BY EXPLANATION – By using words to outline hypotheses, instructions and critiques. It could involve 'side-coaching' – advising while the improvisation is in progress, or briefing afterwards. (Probably the most popular strategy, given Spolin and Johnstone's reliance on the auditory point of view.)

- BY PROVOCATION – This means joining in sporadically around the edges of the improvisation, or perhaps occasionally at the centre, to motor the action in the way you want it to go.

Perhaps these approaches mirror the learning modalities. The visual teacher will expect the students to learn by watching so he or she stands in front of the group and acts out ideas demonstratively. The auditory teacher relies on listening and using explanations. The kinaesthetic type likes to join in on an equal basis, feeling and experiencing what the students experience in order to inspire them.

Of course there are many different roles that go beyond these simple modality preferences. Some have to do with personality, and how the teacher has himself or herself been taught as a student. One of the teachers I had at Drama School was Christopher Fettes, who played high status in the room and could easily cut a student down with a well-timed phrase. He did it often. But he could also build you up just as fast. One day I was 'brilliant', the next, 'absolute shit'. I always wanted to find a way of teaching that was different to this, but sometimes I'd catch myself in some posture that was a distant echo of Fettes. Here are some popular roles I've seen different teachers inhabit:

THE ENTHUSIAST

Runs on a sense of enthusiasm and personal fun. Obviously gets a huge buzz out of working in improvisation and tries to infect everyone else with the same enthusiasm. Uses games and exercises a lot. Has probably created a good few of these.

ADVANTAGES: conveys personal commitment well, and validates the exercise for those who are unsure. Usually prepares effectively and delights in whatever happens. People get a sense of the class as a special event.

DISADVANTAGES: can over-simplify or use vocabulary more casually than others, leaving the group finding it difficult to recreate the same level of work once the Enthusiast has gone.

THE ANALYST

Has an eye for what's happening under the surface. Can pinpoint individuals' strengths and weaknesses accurately. Likes to have something to see before working out where to go. Diagnostic in approach.

ADVANTAGES: good for personal attention, and students feel valued in the receipt of personal information.

DISADVANTAGES: if the diagnosis is wrong, the student may come away with nothing – or with something unhelpful. Less effective at building teamwork or a shared sense of mission. Doesn't tend to address 'what theatre is for'.

THE PARTICIPANT

Likes to join in, deliberately blurring the distinction between teacher and student. Solves problems by participating and working from the inside. Puts emphasis on equality and a shared sense of fun. Always maintains the idea that the teacher is an actor as well.

ADVANTAGES: lessens the sense of fearfulness and anxiety in the room through embodying the playful spirit in their own contributions. Good at building a sense of company. Models a willingness to play any role, and is happy to be seen to fail. Makes teaching look accessible.

DISADVANTAGES: can lack analysis or theoretical perspective. Prefers general discussion rather than analytical critique. Can end up working at a 'base' level that's more appropriate for the least able members of the class.

THE CARER

Likes to look after people. Exudes a warm friendliness and is very reluctant to say anything critical about anyone. Gives lots of positive responses to the work. Good at noticing anyone having a bad time, and addressing that.

ADVANTAGES: people feel looked after. Especially good approach for beginners who are encouraged to believe they can't really make mistakes. Generates a friendly, non-judgemental atmosphere in the room.

DISADVANTAGES: more experienced players can feel patronised. Or they can feel that they are not really being challenged – that the work is being 'dumbed down'. Good work can be perceived by players as indistinguishable from poor work.

THE COACH

Places strong emphasis on teamwork and all working for the good of the group as a whole. Less interested in particular skills or abilities of individuals. Concerned more with the forms or structures of the work, and how best to realise these. Doesn't have a lot of time for those who can't meet the standard.

ADVANTAGES: gets everyone working to the same goal, with a clear, shared understanding of the class objectives. Extends individuals' perceptions of what the group as a whole can achieve, and the value of being part of that.

DISADVANTAGES: can overlook individuals having difficulties. May not be able to give them the personal advice they need. Tends to rely on general advice which is the same for everyone.

THE JUDGE

Is largely concerned with communicating the difference between effective and ineffective improvisation. Works hard to get the group to believe in the judgements given. Tries to be careful with these judgements and supports them with analysis.

ADVANTAGES: can spur the participants to a higher standard of productivity. Conveys well the idea that this is an art form in which extraordinary things can be achieved. Those who succeed get an enormous confidence boost.

DISADVANTAGES: those who don't succeed in the Judge's eyes can come away feeling wretched and discouraged. The difference between a good impro and a bad one can be over-exaggerated. Ignores the subjectivity of the Judge's personal tastes in informing judgement.

Any teacher who is rooted in a particular methodology leans on it for inspiration and sustenance. But there's a danger too, that the teacher relinquishes a right to re-interpret this methodology. There's a need to re-evaluate consistently. If you're teaching improvisation, it's never wise to forget that the teaching itself should be improvised. After all, if students don't see those improvisational skills working in the teacher, they may avoid it in their own performing. The teacher's vices may get mirrored back. To make sure this doesn't happen, the teacher needs to take whatever pedagogy has been learned and subject it to challenge every now and again. I talked about this to Sten Rudstrom, about how he gravitated to teaching and how he found his own style after fifteen years with Ruth Zaporah. *'I think I'm just beginning to spring off from my training. Because I spent so long on the book with her* [as a collaborator] *that I felt such an allegiance to those exercises. It was the way I'd been taught and trained. Only now am I starting to find my own ground and investigate my own material. It's interesting because when we had a teachers training out there in New Mexico recently, a colleague of mine said that one of the things she took from Ruth Zaporah was the idea that in the classes, as a teacher, you're always improvising new exercises. And I thought, I'm not doing that. I'm improvising different focuses, different directions in those exercises, but the core of those exercises remains the same.'*

CONTEXT

How and what you teach is inseparable from the issues of objective and context. What kind of theatre are we training for? Is this training for personal development or preparation for a show? Sometimes teachers are tempted to skip the task of inter-relating theory and practice. They can too easily bypass the theoretical and ideological underpinnings, jumping ahead to a simple idea of recreational play. Improvisation is a subversive, politically loaded medium. It can also be a way to simply let off steam. Pointing the traffic towards a particular objective and creating energy around shared understandings, is part of teaching.

Once objectives and context are correlated, the next task is correctly pitching the level of challenges. This may be helped by knowing your group in advance. A successful workshop is a lot about preparation. Clive Barker would say he only needed one game when he went into a workshop. This was the start game. After that, he'd read the group and plan accordingly. Less experienced teachers might want a few more strategies up their sleeve. Prior information about the group can help with that. What are the group members' ages, backgrounds, experience of improvisation and hopes for the workshops? The success of the teaching may rely significantly on the extent to which it is tailored to the needs of the group. When a group's membership all share a common age or circumstance, you may additionally be able make certain expectations.

1. YOUNG PEOPLE

Young people will eat their way through exercises and want more. It's good to go with more games than you need. Especially because the games that 'don't work' will 'not work' spectacularly badly. The group may not have the patience to wait around for the solution to the problem of an empty ideas cupboard. I found that improvisational work with teenagers was less successful working 'close to the bone', i.e. on themes that you would expect to be critical: sexuality, personal relationships, drugs etc., than themes that were 'further away'. It's not that you couldn't go there, but you wouldn't want to go there before acquiring a level of trust. Instead, working around their sense of humour, or on 'how they tended to see the world', gained better results. With Greenwich Young People's Theatre we devised a show entitled *It's a Mad, Mad, Mad, Mad, Mad, Mad World* set in a Genet-like brothel, where you went to have your socially rebellious and aspirational fantasies realised by actors. The fact of having a frame around the exercise enabled the improvising to be more truthful. It gave a sense of safety and freedom to play expansively with the themes. Impros set in the living room with 'the boyfriend' hadn't been working. This group wanted something more imaginative, further away from everyday experience.

Teenagers have diverse reasons for coming to dramatic improvisation. Many come so they can say 'No' to things – an activity that's a lot cooler than saying 'Yes', which given the event is run by seniors, is a little too close to acquiescing to authority. So expect to explore conflicts and resistance as legitimate subject areas. Be prepared to work with 'no sayers' rather than 'yes sayers', and work with structures that will contain that kind of exploration. It's still improvisation. Roger Hill developed an approach he called 'Drama Nein Danke' that relied largely on players saying 'No' and only stalled if they said 'Yes', which is discussed more fully in *House of Games*.

2. AMATEUR ACTORS

Amateur actors are everywhere. The United Kingdom has a particular breed of amateur actors. These are individuals who elsewhere are pillars of the community, working in banks, building societies, architect's offices and the like. The amateur actor emerges from these bunkers of the establishment to explore his or her 'other side'. (I would distinguish these from actors who are vocationally allied to the performing arts but are using other jobs to generate income.) S/he wants to be 'free' but not so much as to disturb the neighbours or threaten the pension. S/he wants to be radical and naughty, but not reveal anything too personal. S/he wants to be admired for bravery while staying within a conservative frame of behaviour. S/he perhaps wants to be laughed at, because inside s/he knows s/he's really funny. Facilitating such a group of characters can be a blast. There's an atmosphere of a holiday camp for the over-stressed. But you'll struggle if you expect to create the equivalent of a professional ensemble. However, expressing the idea that you are working as a professional ensemble can only help to galvanise the company. What I've found is, you have to identify the individuals who are prepared to make a leap without expecting permission from the rest. Then to validate and approve this risk-taking, hoping that others will follow through the gap in the hedge.

Taking a classic play and turning it upside down can be a good move. Take a Shakespeare play like *Macbeth*, set it in a hospital. Cut it up and put it back together with material from improvisations. The actors feel validated by the fact you have this play in the background even while you're arriving at a whole new piece. Besides, you have a clear anchor for the marketing. Amateur actors often have a foothold in the social or business community, so are able to help build strong constitutional and legal structures around which workshops and performances can take place. Charities can be formed and cheap publicity found.

3. PRISONERS

Prisoners come down from their cells to an improvisation class, looking to escape the boredom. They want to be 'taken somewhere else in their heads' so that the clock becomes quiet for a while. Fierce games and team challenges animate them and get the adrenalin going. They enjoy the experience of a heightened and robust atmosphere. When it comes to improvisation, given half a chance, male prisoners will often choose to simulate successful crimes within a naturalistic style. There's a sense that on stage they can be the successful criminals they haven't managed to be 'on road'. Inexperienced teachers can get led by the nose, as I know to my cost. You can end up acting out bank robberies or kidnaps without much educational benefit. Many offenders do start to recognise performance as offering an equivalent to the act of offending. On stage you get a 'buzz', not unlike the thrill of committing crime. (Jean Genet observed that there was only one thing more exciting than committing a crime – and that was getting caught.) In both situations, you are stretching your muscles, grandstanding your defiance, channelling your anger and asserting your identity. This observation, if an offender makes it, can help effect shifts in his conceptual thinking about where he's going to go next in life.

Those issues aside, it's clear that improvising brings satisfaction because it offers a chance to rule-break. Prisoners can get up on stage, steal or insult people or occupy a factory – and it's all grist to the mill. They find that their initial propensity for rule-breaking – such a disadvantage in life – is actually an advantage here. This impulse to break rules, if successfully transferred, may even give them an edge over the more 'classically trained' improviser. To achieve this successfully, they need to learn to respect the rules of the game. I've found that improvisations that evolve into story are often popular, with narrative lines being remembered for years afterwards. Many prisoners are unfamiliar with theatre practice so their assumptions about drama come from television. There's a case therefore for working initially with a televisual style, at least until the group has settled and is ready to be more adventurous.

4. OLDER PEOPLE

Older people like to take things gradually. A session plan for retired people, coming together in a community centre or home, will look very different to a plan for younger people. While other groups will expect you to take an authority role, old people may have had enough of being told what to do. This is the time of life when they make their own decisions, and if you don't like it, that's tough. Having said that, they usually respect the professionalism that a facilitator brings, in terms of working methods and practices. But they are more likely to expect dialogue around form and content. Taking a plunge is fine, but let's talk a bit first. Let's discuss what we feel about the proposals. And you can be sure to hear very different opinions, some of which just won't shift. Of course these older people may have had very little experience of anything like devising a show. So when you set out how your process will work, they may just plain disbelieve you. They will think you need a playwright. You're trying to pull the wool over their eyes, or you're making a fool of them. Once the project is under way, however, they are likely to bring experiences of great richness to the stage. Old people may be unaware of the contemporary preoccupation with personal confession, but they can still disarm with their frankness. There's sometimes a sense that if these stories aren't told now, it may be too late. Besides, they have less respect for social taboos. I've been stopped in my tracks by what I've heard; stories tossed off casually as if unimportant – but extraordinary in their resonance. I remember a woman in an old people's home, telling me one long story of the death of both her husband and son during the Second World War. Her talking silenced the group. It was delivered with such dignified resignation, as if there was nothing more to be said on the subject. Such disconcerting but powerful material can, if pulled together artfully, facilitate extraordinary performance.

Teaching improvisation is very much about bringing into the room the structures, games and exercises that will animate the group. A facilitator wants as far as possible for rules and protocols to do the hard work. This way the authority in the room lies more with the dictates of the art form, rather than the position or personality of the teacher. The management of the art form provocations is the teacher's responsibility. Rather than imparting wisdom therefore, it's more akin to the job of the boatswoman who stands in the boat, shifting weight from side to side, ensuring the occupants don't get pitched into the water. But ensuring the occupants do some rowing. A hand on the tiller can help.

CODA

MORE ON RULES

An imaginary improvisation in which we test the effect of rule-breaking.

Man (Actor One) comes into the room. Woman (Actor Two) is already there.

ACTOR ONE: Where did you put my divorce papers? (*This is a question, so some might say it's breaking a rule, but really it's a good move. We hadn't determined the relationship in advance and we still don't know it yet, but there's a back-story already.*)

Actor Two doesn't reply. (This is breaking another rule, because it could be construed as a block. However, it's also a good move because it implies something about the relationship through silence. It suggests that the second character is someone who will not be happy for the papers to be found – in other words, it's probably the person to be divorced. Unless they are both of the same sex, in which case it could have other implications. Context is everything, after all.)

ACTOR ONE: Man goes into a pub. There's a crocodile hanging behind the bar. Man says 'Where d'you get a crock like that?' Barman says 'Smoking!' Boom-boom! (*Again this is breaking another rule, as listed in* Truth in Comedy – *Don't Make Jokes, Let the Humour Arise Out of the Situation. In fact this is a good move because it shows us more about the relationship, i.e., that Actor One has reached a breaking point with this relationship, and is becoming wild. Is willing to look stupid, in fact – because the joke is unfunny and desperate. Isn't it?*)

ACTOR TWO: If you make any more fucking jokes about men in pubs, I shall leave tonight. (*Another kind of block, and therefore another rule broken. But in fact a good move because it tells us that this character already has a plan to leave – the threat is to move that plan forward. She continues:*) And don't pretend you're looking for divorce papers because I know you're not. (*This breaks the rule that you shouldn't deny what the other actor has created. In fact it just raises the stakes because it introduces the possibility that the first Character is simply looking for divorce papers as a ruse to spin out the time they have left together. So far, therefore, they've created possibly a very strong scene – by doing nothing except break rules. But there may be a tipping point. One of them soon has to come back within the safe territory, within the circle of expectation, if the constant rule breaking is not to collapse the story. If neither does this, if they carry on in the same vein, it's a risk. However, let's assume they do that.*)

ACTOR ONE: You're a fucking cunt. (*Untempered abuse is not generally seen as following the rules. It's not at all positive.*) You're just acting. (*He's trying to demolish the scene by drawing attention to the theatricality of it all. Again, not usually a good idea – this is objectification. However, it could be saved if the other one rejoined with something like 'It's true. I've been acting for ages. I don't know why. I went wrong somewhere down the road, somewhere where I decided it was finished between us. And now I'm not sure. Pete, I'm not sure I want us to break up.' This would save the scene/it would be a shift/it could generate some action. But let's say she goes:*)

ACTOR TWO: You're acting more than me. This is like a scene in a film in which two people hate each other and destroy each other and it's all bitter and twisted. (*This 'instant conflict' is probably the tipping point – one rule broken too far. From here on it will get increasingly difficult to get back into a groove. If the actors were musicians, they would be so far out of the groove that they would need to stop and start again. There's no rhythm and no listening. I think it's the same with the actors.*)

Actor One is lost, looks confused, and exits.

So . . . rule-breaking worked well for a while but then too many rule breaks collapsed the scene.

3
GAMES AND EXERCISES

This section is devoted to games and exercises that may be useful in dramatic improvisation. This has become a huge field with many games books on the market. What follows are some examples of exercises I've invented, borrowed or stolen. They are chosen either because they are typical of a certain tradition or because they have the capacity to be altered or developed. This is not to dispute the fundamental truth that the success of any game or exercise is down to how and where it's used. The context is all.

I have concentrated on three areas:

- ACTOR AND ENSEMBLE TRAINING
- IMPROVISATION FOR DEVISING
- IMPROVISATION FOR SOCIAL AND LIFE SKILLS

These distinctions imply a greater degree of demarcation than realistically occurs. However, an initial separation may assist those who want some quick ideas for a specific event.

I ACTOR AND ENSEMBLE TRAINING

Clearly each company or school will develop its own approach, which is as it should be. So for this chapter, I'll draw from points of focus in training that Fluxx has explored, procedures with which I'm familiar. Broadly speaking, this training falls into one of two categories: Basic and Advanced.

Focus areas for Basic: Listening, Responsiveness, Accepting, Energy, Extending, Defining, Focus, Image, Props, Driving, Beginnings, Trouble, Endings, the About, Duets.

Focus areas for Advanced: Trios, Quartets, Conflict, Restrictions, Advancing, Subtext, Space, Character, Relationships, Direct Address,

Tension, Journey, Games, World, Style, Routines, Change, Reincorporation, Violence, Entrances and Exits, Absent Characters, Archetypes, Roles, Landscape, Sourcing, Risk, Restrictions, Stance, Commentary.

(N.B. Definitions of the different areas are given in the lexicon.)

ACCEPTING

Getting students to tune in to what's happening on stage and accept everything as potential material, means drawing on games and exercises that have an element of compulsion. The rules of the game are in place to inhibit any desire to hedge or escape the emerging material.

1. THE WEARING

Games in which players have to describe what the partner is wearing can be useful. It can be done with each one sitting opposite a partner. During this, the one who is described can, after a roster of identifications is completed, try and identify items of clothing that were missed by the observer. A variation involves the observer turning away while the observed changes how the clothes are being worn. Then the observer has to identify the changes. Of course there is always the option to guess clothes unseen.

2. WORD-REPETITION GAME

The legacy of Sanford Meisner offers an enormous contribution. His Word Repetition Game is characteristic, perhaps emblematic, of his approach. I've never had direct contact with his teaching, so my interpretation here won't necessarily be faithful. To summarise brutally, two players sit opposite each other. Both attempt to sit still. They don't deliberately make any strong moves. One makes an observation about the other, which is accepted and repeated back. 'You're wearing black shoes.' 'I'm wearing black shoes.' 'You're wearing black shoes', etc. So the same statement is repeated and the same response is given until the other player makes a different observation. Initially the observations will involve purely factual identifications. They concern items of clothing or the way the person is sitting, e.g. with legs crossed or arms folded. *It's mechanical, it's inhuman, but it's the basis for something . . .*

It has connection. Aren't they listening to each other? That's the con-nection. It's a connection which comes from listening to each other, but it has no human quality – yet . . . It's the basis of what eventually becomes emo-tional dialogue.'[83] From this point, extensions to the exercise can be made. The players might move to more subjective assessments of behaviour. These also have to be accepted, allowing for a more emotional dynamic. 'You're smirking at me.' 'I'm smirking at you.' 'You're being very cheeky', 'I'm being very cheeky', etc. This work might be extended further so that actors walk around the room beginning scenes that start with these restrictions then opening out to a more fluid dialogue in which character roles are determined.

3. 'THAT'S RIGHT, BOB'
'That's Right, Bob' was introduced to me by Dad's Garage from Atlanta. I'm unsure if they originated it. Two players speak to the rest of the group about a subject they know something about – or better, something they know nothing about. The subject might be 'cooking fish' or 'playing polo' or 'teaching ravens to fly underwater'. Player A speaks first and when Player B takes over; the first line has to be 'That's Right, Bob' (or Jo which is more clearly either male or female). It might be played with the facilitator indicating when the switch from one player to another occurs, or with the players making their own decisions. I've also developed this for more advanced students where the two presenters start attacking and criticising each other verbally, while still playing the game.

4. 'YES, AND . . . '
'Yes, and . . . ' is a classic game of accepting in which each of the pair accept the other's suggestion with the phrase 'Yes, and . . . ' before elaborating a development on the original notion. Each line of response *must* be preceded by the phrase 'Yes, and . . . ' Actors will seek to find ways to evade the responsibility, such as 'Yeah, OK', or 'Right, right – and – ' It's best to prohibit these variations. Sometimes they like to turn it into a negative, such as 'Yes, and then we can do nothing' which rather defeats the purpose. I've found it useful to start with a very banal statement such as 'Let's have a cup of tea' and then have the actors build the dialogue until finally they are taking over the universe and decorating it with flock wallpaper.

IMAGE

You can also try non-verbal strategies to develop a notion of accepting. One way to do this is to work on image. This work is about using physicality in space, how our place within it forms a composite image for the watcher. It's concerned with what a dancer would call 'composing the space'. Beginners will be unlikely to have much sense of what an audience receives as image, so getting them to alternate with being on stage and then watching has to be a good idea. It helps to develop a sense of what – and how – the audience sees.

I. COMPLETE THE IMAGE

Early image work might start with a classic image game that I learned from Augusto Boal, but the elements of it preceded him: Complete the Image. The group forms a circle or sits facing the stage. A player gets up and makes a shape (what Boal would call an 'autosculpture'), then holds that body position. A second gets up and adds to the picture with a shape of his or her own. It might be a literal, abstract or representational image. After a moment's pause during which the watchers look at the image, the first player exits, leaving the second. Then a third gets up, finding a body shape that matches what the second has created, and so on. The players can be instructed to find a connection between the images or simply not to worry about that. If they don't worry about it, the audience will nevertheless imagine its own connections. The exercise is very differently played in a circle or with the actors sat facing a stage. In the first case, it's more intimate and impulsive, in the second more formal and self-controlled. The facilitator can introduce rules into the playing of the game, e.g. 'You must have at least one point of physical contact', or 'No miming', or 'Always get eye contact'. These rules can be introduced in response to the group's way of playing.

This work can be extended using an end-on stage with players going into the still image, and staying as long as they feel a valuable part of it. So actors only drop out when they feel they've become redundant to the image. The effect is of watching a series of slides that dissolve and morph into each other. A second rule change might mean that actors are allowed to change position *within* the image. As the moving becomes more frequent within the image, the event turns slowly into an improvised scene moving in staccato.

Work on image is not just about the macro image – everyone on stage – but also about the micro: what is held in the hand, the look in the eyes or the shape of a hand. Versatility in creating micro images might be encouraged by introducing props into the image exercises above. By attributing a degree of consciousness to physical gestures, the improviser begins to transmit more effectively. Michael Chekhov writes: *'The will dwells in the legs and feet. Their form expresses their function, which is to move the human body through space, according to man's ideas and feelings. See how characteristic and individual the legs and feet are when moving our bodies through space.'*[84]

Simple games in a circle can develop an awareness of the significance of gestures. Complete the Image can be extended so that each player coming into the circle brings not just a body shape but a repeating gesture. The second player has to find a repeating gesture to match it. Player A beckons to an empty space that is filled by Player B, repeatedly turning his head away. Then Player A sits down. Player C gets up and makes a threatening gesture towards B, an action that repeats.

2. MOVEMENT DIALOGUE

Now two players work consistently together, either within the circle or away from the group. A number of pairs might do this simultaneously. This time, there is no replacing. Player A makes a shape, Player B responds. Player A responds to that response, and so on. After a while, instead of the shape being the focus of the exercise, the movement from one shape into another can become the focus. The intention is not to tell a story or even to be literal, but for the actors to develop reactiveness to whatever the partner is doing. The mood should be impulsive, spontaneous and emotionally generous.

3. A PARTY OF GESTURES

This exercise involves the definition of a location. That location is a room in a house where a party is taking place. This room is designated as a chillout room. Actors enter the space and communicate their feelings entirely through mannerisms and gestures, while sitting or standing in the room. There are no words. Actors can go in, go out and return to explore a different character idea, communicated through a different set of gestures. Additional instructions might be added. For example, there can never be more than one person standing in the

room at any one time but there can be an infinite number lying or sitting. Another variation: everyone in the room has to take on the rhythm
or mannerisms of the person just entering the room, until someone
else arrives.

Working in the language of image helps the actors to think away from
the verbal, to develop their kinaesthetic skills and to intelligently
compose the space.

RESTRICTIONS

By introducing restrictions, actors are compelled both to synthesise
their creative impulses and to employ different aspects of their
expressive armoury. There are games that place restrictions on how the
game tasks might be achieved.

In THE NEWSPAPER RACE each of two teams has to cross the floor of
the room without touching the floor itself. They only have two small
pieces of newspaper. No more than two people are allowed to touch the
newspaper at any one time. The only way to fulfil the rules is for one
player to escort another across the room, and then return with the
papers.

THE WORD AT A TIME GAMES would be mentioned here. The whole
group, following the word at a time rule, tells a story. Or there is
THREE-HEADED EXPERT in which three improvisers play the part of
one expert who answers questions about a subject about which the
actors know nothing. Again, they speak a word at a time. A dynamic game
is that which involves two players linking arms and making a JOURNEY
together, which they articulate and act out at the same time. 'We-fell-
down-a-hole-and-discovered-rats. We-ate-them-to-collect-points-in-
the-competition.'

Within more structured improvisations, it's possible to personalise the
restrictions, in other words to apply them to single performers. This
can be an interesting way to identify and eliminate improvisational
defaults. If for example an improviser always becomes tense every time
a scene begins, this exercise will allow this to be addressed.

1. RESTRICTIONS IN THREES

Let's imagine a group of three improvisers are working together. One
will direct while the other two play a scene. The director will place

restrictions on one of the two actors in response to what she sees. Let's say that a simple mother-daughter scene is to be played in which the daughter tries to get forgiveness for stealing and selling a watch. The director watches the scene and periodically instructs the performer playing the daughter to drop whatever gestural or verbal idea she is relying on. For example, if the performer/daughter uses whining a lot, she might be told to 'stop whining'. Or if she wanders about the stage area aimlessly, she will be told to stop doing that. This way, the performer has to channel her inventiveness away from her defaults (which she may not be aware of), into a new area. Performers are often surprised to discover *just what it is* they do so consistently. Force of habit has caused that player to rely so much on a particular strategy, she or he is no longer aware of doing it.

2. DIFFERENT RESTRICTIONS
Within a scene it's possible to place different restrictions on different performers. One might be told not to speak, or only to speak to the audience. Another might be told to speak only in clichés or in sporting metaphors. Another might be told to consistently break into the personal space of the other characters. Another might be told to contribute to the scene but never enter it. This can be an effective way of directing a scene with many players on stage together. A longer list of options is given in the chapter on Structure.

3. PROPS
Two actors are given a flannel, a light bulb and a cup of water, and instructed to tell the story of the Garden of Eden, without using words. One actor is given an empty beer bottle and a broken doll. She is instructed to tell the story of immigration into the UK during the last 100 years. An actor is given a sheet, a biro and a joker's hat and instructed to tell the story of the murder of John Lennon.

4. THE TRICKSTER
Fluxx developed a performance format entitled *The Trickster Show*. The game/exercise underpinning this involved a Trickster character introducing (real) props into a scene, unasked. The task for the actors was to immediately incorporate the prop given. The simplest version of this is just to sit in a circle and place a prop into the hands of one player who has eyes closed. He or she opens their eyes, looks at the

prop and immediately talks about it, as if it was a treasured or much feared possession. The further development of the idea would be to first get a scenic improvisation going. For example, it's set on a beach. On the beach, a man is sunbathing. Next to him is his girlfriend. As the scene runs, the trickster periodically walks on to the stage and deposits a prop. Perhaps in the hand of an actor or perhaps somewhere nearby. The actor has to immediately incorporate the prop into the scene. Or the scene might involve a pop star and her lawyer discussing financial disaster. Again, the Trickster/facilitator introduces props randomly into the scene, which must be incorporated.

Through research, we discovered there were fundamentally two kinds of interventions – complementary and subversive. The complementary intervention might take place when the lawyer starts talking about figures. The Trickster brings on a pen and paper. The subversive is when the pop star starts crying. The Trickster brings on a banana.

CONFLICT

If asked to select one exercise only to use with actors to encourage flexibility within improvisation practice and understandings around conflict I might be tempted to use:

1. PUSHING

Two players stand opposite each other. Each player holds out their hands and places them palm-to-palm against the other's hands. The aim is to explore pushing and being pushed, both expressing and receiving energy. It's good to use real energy and force while at the same time being responsive to the opposing force. So much is contained in this exercise: will and counter-will, working with conflict (learning how to transmute it into play) and acceptance/acknowledgement of the energy directed against you. The players move around the space, ensuring they don't get physically 'stuck', all the time responding second-by-second to the play of energies between them. To extend the exercise, other points of body contact can be found; back to back, shoulder to shoulder, etc. The extension of this would be one player manipulating the other, who provides a measure of resistance, about the room. This can be extended further by lessening the physical contact and introducing words. So it becomes about using persuasion – with the instruction given that the 'persuader' must always win in the end. There is also:

2. PULLING

Each pair takes a piece of rope or a strong scarf. Now the aim is to pull the other player towards you, being responsive whenever a greater force pulls you the other way. So now both actors are extending great energy yet aiming for a lightness, a flexibility that allows for sudden changes of direction.

3. 'HOW DARE YOU!'

'How Dare You!' again involves actors working in pairs. One begins, 'How dare you!' The other replies, 'I'm sorry!' The first goes again, 'How dare you!', and so on. They play this dialogue, moving about the space, until the 'How dare you!' player makes physical contact with the other. It might be sexual, aggressive, bullying or just demeaning. At that point it switches, and the 'I'm sorry!' player goes, 'How dare you!' The roles are then played in reverse. The exercise can lead on to improvisation based on the same dynamic.

4. COMMENTARY

This exercise is about learning to be in the present, to be attentive always to what is happening right now, not worrying about the future. The players are asked simply to walk about the space and articulate what they are doing. There are three stages to the exercise. Each stage invites the performer to tune in to a different kind of self-awareness. The first refers purely to action. Every action is described. 'I am walking along the floor. My walk is rhythmic. I am making larger and larger strides. My arms are swinging. Now I'm raising up my arms.' Movements can be a combination of both willed and involuntary movements. All are observed and commented on. The second stage involves awareness of feelings or moods. 'I feel bored . . . ' 'Now I feel aggressive, determined.' Meanwhile the physical actions continue. Thirdly, the eye of awareness turns to thoughts. This is more difficult to achieve. 'I'm wondering how long this will go on for. I'm wondering what I look like. I'm thinking that this other actor here is really going over the top with this. He's getting it all wrong . . . ' The fourth stage takes the action of observation outside the body – on to the external environment. After the others, it's comparatively easy. 'There's a brick wall there. A lamp. A window. A woman, laughing . . . ' etc.

As each sensation or feeling or observation is identified, it is spoken about. This closes the gap between what is experienced and what is expressed. Inevitably this involves an element of selection, so the aim is to be consistently doing an inventory of what is being experienced through the senses, thoroughly but quickly. Once the performer has spent some time articulating different levels of awareness, they can be combined. 'I feel restless. My feet are just lightly kicking the floor. The toe points up sharply. I feel stronger now, more determined. I look straight ahead and I'm frowning slightly. There's someone just crossed my vision.' Then the actor can be instructed to *act* on the feelings that are identified. 'I feel resentful but I don't know why. I'm pointing around the room, trying to find a target for my anger. Now I'm going in search of something to kick. Aha, a waste paper basket!'

Then actors can be brought together into a group. The task is to all move and commentate at the same time. It's easier to concentrate on actions only. Every sentence (more or less) starts with 'We'. 'We – are – walking – along. We – are – sitting – and – rolling. We – are – jumping – up.' As with similar exercises such as MIRRORS where one individual copies another, mirror-like and the pair try to find a leaderless movement, here the group is aiming not to be led by any one individual. The group is trying to find a collective leadership, through everyone contributing. The instruction is, 'If you feel you're leading, then pull back, if you feel you're being led, then pull ahead.' This way the group moves around the room, as far as possible moving and speaking at the same time.

The session might then return to individuals working on their own. Now the task is different; it's to articulate the opposite of what you are doing. This is to encourage a sense of achieving awareness at a meta-level. It might if necessary be preceded by a POINTING exercise in which individuals point at objects in the room and call them by the wrong names. Here, the individual walks around but says out loud, 'I am sitting down; I am moving my bum from side to side. I am rolling over and lying down.' The aim is to find opposites between what is said and what is acted. This might be continued with different levels of energy. Imagine the actor runs. Then the lines might be 'I am lying down, relaxed, completely at ease, drifting away . . . ' Through this work, one gets a sense of the opposite activity always existing in shadow from the driven, visible activity.

This work can then be taken into a group situation, where the whole group attempts to articulate opposite actions from those that are performed. The final stage of the sequence involves pairs of performers presenting to the audience. One walks on to the stage and articulates as much as possible of what they are doing, feeling and thinking. 'I'm feeling nervous in my stomach. I notice that my foot is tapping but I don't know why. I'm aware that I'm frightened to look at the audience. OK, I'm going to look at the audience.' (She looks at the audience.) The other actor offstage: 'I'm waiting, wondering when I should come in. I'm looking for a moment but not seeing it. I'm enjoying the discomfort of the first actor. I'm taking a pace forward. I'm alarmed because the first actor is not paying any attention . . . ' and so on. The other benefit to this work is it brings to the surface those thoughts and feelings not thought to be 'appropriate' for the improvisation. These become the subject matter of the exercise.

2 IMPROVISATION FOR DEVISING

Comparing some of the devising practices indicated during the course of this book, it will be clear how they vary between companies and traditions. I can only list a few that I've used, in different situations. With devising, it's useful to have clarity around the objective of any particular session. If you are looking for a central idea or frame for the piece, this can invite quite different exercises from an objective to fill in an existing frame. Essentially the stages would be:

- FIRST DIGGINGS (RESEARCH); looking for resonant ideas or threads on which to base the work (assuming there's no pre-existing material)

- ELABORATING the central thread or improvising within the restrictions implied by it

- EDITING down this material

- REHEARSALS

Most exercises given here would take place within an early stage of devising. The aim is to answer the question 'What will the piece be about?' without resorting to discussion. It's not that discussion isn't one way, but some companies, especially those newly formed, might want to experiment with lines of enquiry that are more intuitive or theatrical in their elaboration. By asking the question within the language of performance, different answers emerge.

1. QUESTION AND ANSWER

A single performer is asked to go on to the stage area and take up a position there. That position creates an image on the stage. (If thought useful, a second performer could be added to the image.) Then the facilitator asks questions about the image that are answered by the rest of the group. (See the chapter on Research for an example of this in action.) The purpose of the questioning is to build up the imaginative world implied by this image. Early questions would deal with the issue of location, and go on to consider, for example, the relationship between any two characters, recent events that had brought them to this moment, what each is thinking or feeling, and so on. As far as possible, all answers have to be accepted. If there are contradictions, these are fed back as new questions to the group. 'You've already told me that the woman in the scene hates the man, and would go to great lengths to avoid him. Now you're telling me she's pleased to see him. How is that possible?' Or 'You said this scene is taking place in a school. Now someone else has said it's in an army barracks. How is that possible?' The answers might be, 'She's been told he's going to give her money' and 'The scene is set in a training room in the barracks.'

Improvising this material is clearly possible. What is usually very difficult is improvising the dramatic moment that has been set up and discussed. The situation may be already too loaded for the actors to do it justice. Better usually to explore the backstory through improvisation. Alternatively, sub-groups can take on the task of inventing/devising subsequent scenes.

2. THE MODEL SEES

Actors get into groups of three. One is a sculptor, one a model, one a questioner. The sculptor moves the model into a shape. The aim is to find an expressive shape that generates feelings within the performer. A classic shape, such as pointing at something, or curling up on the floor is more likely to achieve this. The questioner then asks 'Do you feel (emotionally) connected to the image?' If the model feels nothing in the shape, is not inspired either imaginatively or emotionally, the answer given is 'No'. So the sculptor changes the shape and asks again. This can be carried out several times if necessary. In the next stage, once a 'Yes' is given, then the questioner asks a series of questions of the model to build up the reality of their imagined situation. It's useful to start with 'What can you see?' So the invitation is to talk about where the eyes are falling. Later questions will elucidate information about the landscape within which the character is situated. There is no assumption that what is 'seen' has to be literal or naturalistic. The actor might see herself surrounded by gnomes, or alone in a desert, or balanced on a cliff. Once the landscape is established, then questions can range into backstory – how she got there – and feelings about the fix she's in. The questioner should avoid asking 'What are you thinking about?' or 'Why are you here?' These questions take the improviser into thinking, rather than imagining. Better questions are 'What just happened?' Or 'Describe your feelings towards (a person or an aspect of the landscape)'. If appropriate, the still image can be taken into an improvisation, either by the actor alone or with another. It is possible finally to ask the actor to animate the image, to improvise a conclusion to the scene.

If several groups of three have been using the exercise simultaneously, the results of this research can be pooled. As in much devising work, to chart the accumulation of imagery and ideas can only help in a later selection process.

3 · NARRATIVE IMAGES

The group divides into groups of four or more. Each group makes a sequence of eight still images, without discussion. It's understood that these eight images are sequential. They make up a story. Image Number One is sculpted entirely by the first actor, Image Two by the second, and so on until each actor has made two within the sequence. There must be no discussion about content whatsoever. As far as possible, the exercise should be conducted in silence. Then the eight pictures are rehearsed in sequence. The sequence is presented to the rest of the group whose task it is to make sense of the story. They cannot be wrong in their speculations because the makers themselves have no idea what the story is.

The watchers are encouraged to respond in one of two ways. First, they might respond by talking about the theme of the story. 'It appears to be about betrayal' or 'I think it's all about men and women not getting along'. Second, they might go further and give an account of the story that has been told. 'At the beginning, Jen and Asif are lovers. They have a fight and Asif steals her clothes and burns them in anger . . . ' and so on.

These themes or threads, produced by the different sub-groups, can be compared. Any common or interesting themes, stories or characters can be taken through to the next stage of devising.

4· PHYSICAL DIALOGUES

If the actors have characters they'd like to develop, the director might run a series of shorter exercises leading to Physical Dialogues. In the preface work, the director might set a number of tasks for the actors to complete individually – yet simultaneously – to help them towards finding a physical/emotional life for the character. The actors would walk about the room initially. Then tasks would be given that might include:

- Finding the walk of the character
- Finding the physical stance of the character
- Finding the internal monologue of the character, in particular a key phrase
- Finding a song for the character
- Painting a self-portrait (mimed or actual)
- Telling a best friend about a secret (each actor gets two chairs that are placed facing each other so each actor sits facing an empty chair)
- Running away from an adversary (imagination will tell you who that is)
- Finding three key gestures for that character
- Taking a shower then choosing clothes to wear; at the end choose a facial expression to wear when leaving the house

Finally the characters meet each other within a large open space, interacting in pairs but without verbal dialogue. There is no location or defined context for these meetings. The aim is to simply discover what each actor 'feels' about the other characters. Actor A (male) therefore meets Actor B (female) and presents himself through gesture or some other behaviour. Actor A discovers that he feels mischievous in this woman's company. She shows she feels the same way. There's no sexual attraction but instead these two bring out a sense of mischief in each other. So they find themselves becoming childlike in the space. Actor B moves on and meets Actor C (female) whom she finds irritating. The two fall into a mistress–servant relationship. In this way, all the characters meet all the other characters.

Once the exersise has been stopped and the actors are seated, the director might ask each participant which of the relationships proved most affecting or most intense. This intensity might be either positive or negative. Both are useful to identify. Either way, the director is looking to identify the most powerful relationships as these might be worth spending time on. Improvisations can then be set up with those pairings, and a context found for them. 'He felt like he might be my father,' one would say, 'and while I respected him, I also wanted to provoke him and make him angry.' The director might then use comments like these to explore a father-son relationship between these two actors. If it works, it might become a plank within the narrative for the devised play. The strong, intense relationships might generate the main plotline for the story while the less potent relationships, the subplots.

5. THE WORLD

Once there is a sense of a narrative thread, a relationship or a theme, it might be useful to do an exercise to develop the *world* of the piece. For this to work, there needs to be a location defined. For example, we know that this character Pete Burns works in a greasy spoon café. At night he goes home to his mother's house where he still lives, even though he's in his thirties. We might therefore develop either the café or his mother's house. Let's imagine we take the house.

First, the group gets hold of as many props, items, bits of furniture and so on that are available. Then they construct the house. (You need a good-sized space for this exercise.) One part of the space is given over to the ground floor, another part to the first floor. Rooms are divided off, and as much as possible the house paraphernalia is represented. There is something marking or indicating where Mum sleeps and where Pete sleeps. There is a kitchen table, probably. There is a front door.

Once the house has been 'built', the group is instructed to give it a history. Every member of the group takes pieces of paper and a pen. They are invited to create Secrets, Rumours and Facts. On each paper will be written a secret, a rumour or a fact. Each paper will then be placed in an appropriate part of the house. For example, an actress in the group decides that it's a *fact* that Pete's Dad died in the living room from a heart attack. She marks the spot with a paper saying that. She also decides that it's a *secret* that Pete's Mum hoards money in a top kitchen cupboard. She places a paper accordingly. Finally, she decides that it's a *rumour* that the ghost of Pete's father sits in the garden on moonlit nights. The person who claimed this was Pete's uncle who claimed he saw this occur when he was a houseguest.

Once a paper is down it becomes part of the social or historical fabric – unless it contradicts or is incompatible with facts that have already been established. So it's important when papers are put down, that group members are constantly checking to see what is already there. But multiple truths are possible. If Pete has a secret smoking place, he might have another one. If his Mum once cried her heart out in the kitchen, that's not to say the kitchen isn't also the place where she feels happiest.

The next stage is improvisation. Now that the house has been brought to life, scenes can be set up. Any scene between Pete and his Mum, for example, when they talk about the father, are critically informed by their shared knowledge, not only of the father's life and death, but also of where these events happened. When a visiting salesman persuades the mother to buy kitchen utensils, we know from which kitchen drawer she'll take the money.

3   IMPROVISATION FOR SOCIAL AND LIFE SKILLS

These exercises are for use with non-actors in contexts where the aim is for participants to extend their social, communication or thinking skills. My own experience of using these exercises is primarily within young offender institutions.

Characteristic of these exercises is the emphasis on process rather than output. There is much less in the way of performance. There is no presupposition that the facilitator is encouraging the participants to be actors except in a social sense. However, an element of play is intended. It's the enlisting of this element of structured play that marks the work out from more orthodox teaching practice.

1. KIM'S GAME

I used to play this in the Scouts. A range of small objects is gathered together and placed on a tray. Then a cloth is placed over the tray without the group seeing what's on it. The collection might include a drawing pin, a stamp, a button, a piece of string, etc. The group is divided into pairs and each pair given a pen and paper. The cloth is taken off the tray for sixty seconds and everyone has to remember what he or she can. The cloth is replaced and there are three or five minutes for each pair to recall what they can. The pair who recalls the most are the winners.

2. PHOTOGRAPHS

The group is divided into two teams. Team B is given a photograph (perhaps from a newspaper) to study for sixty seconds. Then the photo is passed to the other team to retain. Team A then quizzes Team B about the content of the images. There are perhaps five questions. Five good answers out of five would be a maximum score. Then Team B quizzes Team A about their photograph, once it's been shown, asking questions such as 'How many people are in the picture?', or, 'What is on the table at the back?' The team with the most correct answers is the winning team.

3. OBSTACLE COURSE

Again in teams, each team devises a puzzle for the other team to crack. The puzzle is in the form of a journey. The journey involves a book, a table and a chair. The journey has to involve passing around, over or under each of these. So Team A might decide, for example, that the journey involves going round the book, then under the table then to the right of the chair. Once determined, Team B has to work out the journey by asking Yes or No questions. 'Does the journey start with the book?' 'Yes.' 'Do you go over the book?' 'No.' And so on. The team that discovers the correct journey with the fewer questions, is the winner.

4. HIDDEN OBJECT

An object is hidden from the sight of three players. These three players have to identify what the object is, by asking a series of Yes or No questions. The team that gets to identify the object correctly in the least number of questions, is the winner.

5. THE DON GAME

'The Don' wants people to join the family. He or she sits apart from the rest of the group, and then invites participants to approach one by one. He or she accepts or rejects people according to a secret system (that has been agreed in advance with the facilitator – but the players don't know it). For example, if a player begins with a bow, that player is allowed in whatever happens. Or if a player makes a gesture to touch his or her face, then they get in. The task of the players is to break the code by watching who gets in and who doesn't, and why. It's necessary to establish a code that is unostentatious, and is likely to go unnoticed except by the more observant. The code can be changed for each round.

6. CHINESE MIME

Player 1 invents a story. The story should revolve around a central character. This player tells the story in words to Player 2 without the rest of the group hearing it. Player 2 then has to act out the story to Player 3 without using words and *without the rest of the group seeing*. Player 3 then has to act it out to Player 4, and so on. Finally the last player tells back the story. Usually this story is significantly different. The fact of working in a visual, mimetic language has meant that story elements have been lost and others have been misinterpreted. The subsequent discussion can focus on which elements remained and why, and which were lost and why. The mind tends unsurprisingly to identify more easily those acted elements that are recognisable, while more abstract expression leads to confusion.

7. FORGIVENESS

Working in pairs, it's imagined that one player is asking forgiveness for another. The transgression is defined. For example, Character A took a personal item from Character B without permission, and then damaged it. Now Character A has to ask for forgiveness. The two players stand a room-length apart. Character A starts to ask for forgiveness. If Character B is persuaded, then he or she starts to cross the floor towards Character A. If not, Character B stays still – or might even move backwards.

8. 'I'M A CELEBRITY PRISONER, GET ME OUT OF HERE'

This was devised for young offenders but might have application in other contexts. The group is divided into pairs. In each pair there is an A and a B. A has to explain what he or she was convicted of, and why he or she should now be released from prison. The group is asked for these to be true stories and real arguments. B is going to present these arguments to the group. Once the first stage is completed, each B, the 'persuader' presents the case. The group, guided by the facilitator, decides which case was best presented, and why.

9. ANIMALS, DRINK, SPORT

The group is divided into two teams. Each team needs to have at least three members in it, preferably four. Each team is going to take a challenge in which items of information are communicated between them, using non-verbal language. The team selects two members as

Communicators. When they are ready, these two receive from the facilitators a list. On the list is written down an animal, a sport, a drink, a job, a hobby and a kitchen implement. The Communicators have to communicate these, one by one, to the other members of their team without using words. It's something like Charades. However, the team is working against the clock. When the task is completed, the other team steps up and tries to do the same task with a different animal, sport, drink, etc. – and to beat the time achieved by the first team.

10. PROBLEM SOLVERS

Two participants are invited to step up and play an improvised scene. Their task is to solve the problem that is given to the characters in the scene. They have to achieve this by finding a compromise solution that doesn't overtly favour one party or another. For example, one character is a decorator and the other has employed the decorator. The decorator has just finished painting the room as instructed. It's been painted red. However, the employer comes in and insists that the instruction was to paint the room blue not red. The two players have to find a compromise solution to the problem. Another example: two characters arrive in a room above a pub. Each believes he has hired the room from the landlord, one for a funeral wake, the other for a wedding party. A third example: a taxi is arriving at the end of the journey. At the outset of the journey, the taxi driver had said the journey would cost ten pounds. Now the taxi drivers says it costs £15. But the rider only has £10.

11. THE CHAIRS GAME

A number of chairs are scattered throughout the room. There should be one chair per person playing the game, assuming one player is the facilitator of the group. Everyone bar the facilitator sits on a chair leaving one free. Then the group leader tries to sit on the one empty chair and the group try to prevent her. The only way this can be done is by the group moving from one chair to another, rather than wrestling that group leader to the ground. Each move by one group member to an empty chair obviously creates a new empty chair. To ensure fairness, the facilitator moves slowly, while the group members can move as fast as they can. The aim for the facilitator is to challenge the group to develop teamwork, communicating between group members to ensure a swift and effective distribution of bodies around the space.

12. STATUS GAME

After the facilitator has demonstrated different levels of status through acting, a stock situation is set up. Within this, the participant is given a role and a status to play. The audience assesses whether that status is achieved. For example, the task is to get a possession back from a bullying character to whom it has been loaned. The instruction is to play low status. Or at closing time in the pub, the task is to play the barman high status in clearing out the remaining drinkers. The audience adjudge how well the status playing came close to what was intended. The tasks can be set so they represent appropriate challenges for the individuals taking them.

AN UNRELIABLE LEXICON

ABOUT, THE

The found content of the scene that is the essence of the Who, What, Where. It's the answer to the question, 'What's the scene about?' 'Well, it's about sharing our first sexual experiences.' 'It's about getting a rat out of a hole.'

ACCEPTING

Usually talked of by reference to 'accepting an offer'. It means agreeing to work with the inventions of the other player/s. It means not denying the truth of what others have created. To accept something doesn't mean you can't literally say 'No' to it. It means you accept the existence of that person/thing/event. Accepting means acknowledging visibly or audibly what is happening, even if you don't know yet how to respond to it emotionally. Following acceptance comes the task of how the actor develops or extends what is accepted.

ADVANCING

Moving the story on. In my observations, the best improvisers understand intuitively about moving the story on. They accumulate information, wait, and then leap forward. Rather than, for example, moving it forward at a consistent tempo. Regularity of rhythm can send the audience to sleep. It's about surprise. Peggy Ramsay, the famous writer's agent, told Alan Plater, *'Drama is a lot of small surprises, darling, and then every so often, one big surprise.'* Some moments of improvisation deserve an exploration downwards or sideways rather than continuously forwards. But the good improviser doesn't forget about the necessity to move stuff on. Lisa Nelson, in her Tuning Score for dancers, uses video vocabulary. So within that analogy, the piece would move frame-by-frame, then slow, then frame-by-frame, then fast forward.

ANXIETY

'I walk on stage. There's no one there. I can't see anything, only the audience. Especially their eyes. Their eyes are looking at me. I know that's true even though I'm not actually looking at them. Already that's a mistake, to be thinking about the audience. I mustn't think about the audience, I must be involved with something else. Aha! There's a chair on stage. Thank God! I can sit down. That solves that problem for a while. Everyone knows that chairs are to be sat in. The audience will like me sitting in a chair. They would surely be disappointed if I hadn't sat on it because they'd be thinking 'There's a chair and he hasn't sat in it.' But now I'm sat in the chair I'm thinking, 'That isn't really enough, is it? Maybe I should get up. If I get up, that's ACTION *and theatre is all about action. So I get up. I quite liked my getting up, it appeared quite spontaneous. But – I should have worked out a plan before I got up. Now I just look stupid because I've got up and* I DON'T KNOW WHAT I'M DOING. *Fuck! Another actor's coming into the scene. I know! I'll start an argument. That's good because that's* CONFLICT.' And so on.

ARCHETYPES

Andrew St John writes: *'Archetypes are best understood as different qualities and directions of energy and their relationships to space. They appear and reappear in stories in different times and different cultures. Within any given story they transform. There are twelve archetypes that I have found useful to work with, drawn from John Wright's maskwork and developed in Tellers and then Empty Space Theatre Company. I find it easiest to see their energy and direction if I imagine them at a nightclub:*

THE KING *rules space* (*The nightclub owner*)

THE DEVIL *pursues his or her own desires with no awareness of others* (*Using date-rape drugs to take what they want*)

THE SAGE *accepts situations in pursuit of a greater truth* (*A monk praying in the corner, there and aware*)

THE INNOCENT *is always moving into new space* (*It's his or her first night in a nightclub*)

THE MOTHER *nurtures within the space* (*Cares for the friend who has had too much to drink. Again*)

THE MISTRESS *draws you towards them* (*He or she is gorgeous and everyone wants to buy them a drink*)

THE HUNTRESS *is about the joy of the chase* (*Pursues the person fancied and enjoys the pursuing*)

THE FOOL *is at the mercy of the universe* (*Spills drink, loses the phone number they have been given, is sick on their new shoes, etc . . .*)

THE CRONE *keeps himself to himself* (*In the corner grumbling*)

THE VIRGIN *holds a secret that will be released* (*This is a special night where something extraordinary is going to happen*)

THE HERO *makes a quest for something other than personal gain* (*Is present to protect, or to make a declaration of love*)

THE TRICKSTER *approaches situations tactically for personal gain* (*Ripping off the owner, or the guests, etc.; impressing others through lies, etc.*)

As I understand them, Archetypes are neither male nor female. In any given society in any different time they can express themselves in different ways through women and men. I find it helpful to think of he/she archetypes as in he/devil or she/devil, the he/mother and she/mother. He/mothers have become more common in Western society in the last twenty years. People are not archetypes. People's bodies express archetypal energy. They are always evolving. Archetypes, like chemical elements, can be put together e.g. a fool/hero. A fool/hero is different from a hero/fool. Finally, archetypes have playing ages: a spring/virgin is very different from an autumn/virgin.'

ASK-FORS

Refers to the practice of inviting the audience to contribute material, perhaps by way of a suggestion that will inform the course of the improvisation. Might also be referred to as 'randomisers'.

ASSUMPTIONS

Rather than ask questions, improvisers move further forward – and deeper – when assumptions are made about the imaginative reality that constitutes the improvisation. If at the beginning of an open impro, Player A makes the assumption that Player B coming in is a fellow thief returning empty-handed, and makes this plain through dialogue, we as the audience have our connection to the scene established. If, during the subsequent scene, Player B makes the assumption that they both have a van with dodgy plates, and refers to it, the assumption strengthens the fiction.

ATMOSPHERES

Although Michael Chekhov is here referring to the production of written work, the points have application for dramatic improvisation: *'Atmospheres enable the actor to create the element of the play and the part that cannot be expressed otherwise. For example, imagine Romeo speaking his words of love to Juliet without the atmosphere of love. Although the spectator may understand the sublime text and enjoy the beauty of Shakespeare's verse, he or she will still miss something of the content. And what is this content? It is love itself. All feelings require a specific atmosphere to be conveyed to the audience. Without these proper atmospheres radiating from the actor, Shakespeare's words of love, hate, despair, and hope reverberate meaninglessly in empty psychological space. Atmosphere reveals the content of the performance.'*[85]

ATTENDING

Listening, watching, observing, following what happens on a moment-to-moment basis. Not 'going into your own head', not speculating. To use this skill involves a sacrifice of something, your 'better ideas', your 'grand schemes', and your 'practised stunts' from wherever they come. Interestingly, dancers use the term 'listening' as much as they do 'observing' while what they mean is both.

AUDIENCE

Jonathan Kay observed to me that *'All the world is not a stage, all the world's an audience.'* Socialised into an awareness of others, many of us are super-conscious of the audience around us, much of the time. We speculate constantly about how we might be appearing to others. We try to engineer a good result. But we're usually wrong about how we're being received – it's almost impossible to create the impression we would like. Those coming into performance often spend time making a similar mistake: trying to fix the performance so that the audience receive precisely the message the makers intend. Even educational or agitational theatre, concentrating on communicating simple truths, cannot be sure of a guaranteed result. The reason is that there are too many subjective, slippery, uncertain processes governing the responses of the audience. Better then to be true to oneself (as far as possible), and make a journey within the frame of the exercise, allowing the audience to make up its own separate minds.

BACKSTORY

Everything that has taken place prior to the (first) scene opening. Within long-form improvisations, the existence of a previously explored backstory can heighten the tension in the opening moments. If it hasn't been created in advance, the backstory might be created on stage.

BLOCKING

Blocking within improvisation usually refers to the inhibition of a dramatic idea. In theatre elsewhere, the term refers to the patterns of movement given to the actors across the stage. Blocking can be a contentious issue within dramatic improvisation. Sometimes regarded as a kind of sin, it's the equivalent of saying Che Guevara was neither handsome nor revolutionary. An improviser who 'blocks' another is essentially refusing to accept or develop the 'offer' which might relate to elements of story, character or location.

Some examples of 'blocks' (by Player B):

Player A: Welcome to my greenhouse!

Player B: I can't see anything.

or

Player B: That's not your greenhouse!

A mitigating block – because it doesn't confound the reality – might be something like:

It's not exactly green, is it?

or

But you don't own it as such, do you?

or

So why is it red?

or

You said you'd take me to your bedroom!

Less experienced improvisers may find blocks discouraging. A good improviser will always take a block and work with it, treating it as conscious resistance rather than unconscious blocking. In the case of resistance, the responding performer accepts the block as an invitation to explore conflict.

Player A: Welcome to my greenhouse!
Player B: That's not your greenhouse!
Player A: I paid you the money in good faith. It wasn't my fault if
you were drunk and can't remember!

CANCELLING
Negating an idea, killing it. 'Let's go fishing!' 'That's a terrible idea!'

CHARACTER
Elusive, slippery, transient, the idea of character is much more problematic within dramatic improvisation than it is within written plays.
It's a tenuous construct that may benefit from being carried lightly.
More experienced improvisers understand that what needs to be developed on stage is relationships, and that characters come, if necessary,
on the back of this work. Character is what the audience perceives as
the performer engages with the themes of the piece.

CHART
The sequence of chords and notes that will be drawn up for musicians
to improvise around.

CIRCLE OF EXPECTATION
This is a term coined by Keith Johnstone to describe the arena of
reasonable possibilities that exist once a scene has begun. Once a scene
is set, for example in a desert, there's a circle of expectation within the
audience about the kind of events that could happen there. If a man
walks in with a clipboard to check the fire extinguishers, this may be a
great gag, but it's probably outside the circle, so the consequence is the
sense of location will diminish or be destroyed. It's not an argument for
an expression of normal behaviour; it's about how to legitimately
extend the original premise.

CLICK, THE
The moment when the performers bed in to the scene. The point when
they get into the groove and can start laying back, rather than worrying
where it should go.

COMPLICITY
The sense of affinity between performers which allows narrative or
conflict to be explored. Complicity is largely based on trust. This

doesn't mean that the performers have had to be working together for years, rather that they share a commitment to the working conventions. They are prepared to take risks and they assume that the other/s will go along with whatever is created.

COMPOSING THE SPACE
Dancers use this term to describe how their decision-making is informed by the length, height, and depth of the space. Decisions are taken to juxtapose physicality with the immediate architecture.

COMPOSITION
Used by musicians primarily to describe the act of defining a tune or score, possibly using improvisation. There is a debate around whether or not improvisation in performance represents an act of composition. Most of those involved in the free music movement argues that it does, making traditional composition practice vulnerable to charges of irrelevance.

DEFAULT
The behaviour, pattern or subject matter that's used time and again by an improviser. Often the default choices are unconscious. They are easy to make: the pattern is familiar, trusted and safe. It's like there's an unlocked cupboard of much-loved toys. There can be a correlation between defaults and practice work. If practice work, in movement for example, circles around a particular set of moves, it's not surprising these re-emerge easily in performance.

DEFINING
The action of publicly establishing with words or gestures a location or a relationship within a dramatic scene. Paul Sills allegedly insisted on the performers always defining the location first, prior to any consideration of characters or relationships. If improvisers go too long without defining, it becomes hard to do it late in the day.

DEVELOPMENT
In which performers remain with the same idea, but elaborate and extend it, so what they are doing comes into clearer focus. The spectator might notice that the location, the character or the character's desire becomes more evident through the development.

DEVISING
The term given to the process by which improvisation is used to create and then set a production. In other words, the performers, perhaps with a director or writer, create the piece from scratch, possibly drawing on raw material. Selections will be made from the material improvised, then shaped, edited and constructed into a piece that will remain largely fixed.

DRIVE
Another word for a motivation or an objective. The word 'drive' sits more easily in improvisation than the Stanislavskian 'objective' because it suggests something less definite. You might have a drive to be successful, or to get the upper hand, or to seduce someone or to have your worth recognised. The 'driver' or 'motor' in the scene is one whose pursuit of their drive is moving the action forward.

DURATIONAL
Refers to a performance that will run longer than the traditional one or two hours. A durational performance will probably run at least five or six hours, and will often assume that the audience might come or go as they please, implying a structure that uses repeating patterns or cyclical structuring.

ELIMINATION GAMES
In which a large group is whittled down to a small group by means of a process in which those who 'fail' or 'make a mistake' are removed from the field of battle.

ENDOWMENT
Involves the act of consciously attributing certain characteristics to another player, an object or a space. This attribution goes beyond what is evident to the ear or eye. Keith Johnstone has an exercise in which three people have a picnic. Character A is endowed with having a bad smell, Character B with being rather sexy and Character C with being stupid. By playing endowments in this way, the performer acquires characteristics from the others without having to project them.

ENSEMBLE
Another name for 'company' where the emphasis is on a democratic spirit of collaboration and shared leadership.

FORUM THEATRE

The participatory theatre form developed by Boal and his colleagues that allows for an issue of oppression to be acted out and challenged by the players along with the audience. Usually the format is as follows: a short play is presented where the outcome is a defeat for the protagonist. The debate offered to the audience is around how the protagonist might fare better by adopting different tactics. Then the play is begun again with spectators ('spectactors') invited to take the part of the protagonist to explore those different tactics. There is no assumption there will be a definitive 'solution' found, rather that a number will be explored in preparation for a return to the real world outside.

FUCK-AROUND GUY

A player who rather casually blocks, shrugs off offers, fails to amplify, wanders into scenes without anything worthwhile to offer, or just generally fucks around instead of trying to create a good scene. Most teachers will encourage the fuck-around guy to get offstage.

GAMES

A much used term. You'd think it would be obvious what a game was. Certainly children have little problem. But once you write a book or stay a long time with 'theatre games', the dividing line between games, exercises and impros start to disappear. Whatever distinctions you choose, there will be alternative viewpoints. I refer to theatre games and performance games. A theatre *game* is like a children's game in as much as you can run it easily, it kind of runs itself, the facilitator simply keeps the wheels on the track. It's used for training (as in Clive Barker's work) or developing teamwork or other skills, or sometimes for exploring themes (as in Boal's work). Whereas an *exercise* involves the facilitator becoming more actively engaged in directing what's occurring, giving instructions, managing the players. A *performance game* is a repeating pattern of behaviour within an improvisation, usually playful and consciously driven. It's like a *Commedia* lazzi, except probably improvised rather than prepared beforehand. It doesn't drive the action forward so much as hold it up, to reveal something about the characters, the relationship or the world. These games can be pushed to the edge till they collapse or are stopped while the audience is still captivated by their silliness, or again dropped and picked up again later. An *improvisation* might have no structural elements at all.

GROOVE
In music, a shared sense of the beat incorporating intensity, stability and swing. In drama, a shared sense of riding the same dramatic idea or pattern.

GROUP MIND
The idea that everyone in the group is acting in concert, tuned to each other, all serving the same end as if by some miracle of psychic tuning.

HAROLD, THE
The Harold is the influential long-form developed by Del Close and colleagues in Chicago, as a solution to the problem of a) giving audiences something more than just sketches, and b) involving a larger number of improvisers than you'd get in a sketch show. Big claims are made for the Harold. In *Truth in Comedy* there is the following: '*The Harold is an incredible tool for teaching improvisation, but it teaches other lessons, as well. The nature of life and the nature of improvisation are similar — such as order out of chaos, anything can happen, the natural occurrence of cycles and patterns. Understanding this makes life a bit easier to understand. We learn lessons from the patterns in our lives and start to believe that there are no coincidences. Improvisers are trained to notice the connections in everything. The connections are always there; they run through our work and through our lives. When you notice the richness of connections in a Harold onstage, you can go out and live your own Harold.*'[86]
A fuller description of the Harold format is given in the chapter on Structure.

IDIOM
'*When I put the book* Improvisation *together, I found it useful to consider these things in terms developed in the study of language. And the main difference I think between freely improvised music and the musics you quoted is that they are idiomatic and freely improvised music isn't. They are formed by an idiom, they are not formed by improvisation. They are formed the same way that speech vernacular, a verbal accent, is formed. They are the product of a locality and society, by characteristics shared by that society. Improvisation exists in their music in order to serve this central identity, reflecting a particular region and people. And improvisation is a tool — it might be the main tool in the music, but it is a tool.*'[87]

INSTANT THEATRE

Developed by Word and Action (Dorset). The audience sits on four sides of the stage space. There might be a short scene to start. Then the Questioner asks questions of the audience about how the story might go. All answers are accepted. Then the company acts out the play, inviting the audience to participate. This is the form of Instant Theatre I know.

INVISIBLE THEATRE

Within Theatre of the Oppressed, this theatre form involves actors going into a space where members of the public are, in order to covertly trigger a debate about a particular social theme or injustice. The actors pretend to be regular members of the public. In this role they will, through their scenario, try to draw into discussion the unknowing members of the public. For example, in a restaurant, a couple eat a meal and then refuse to pay for it, citing an age-old law that says the poor should be fed by the wealthy. Rather than leaving the restaurant the actors hope to draw the other diners into the argument.

JOURNEY

The performer starts in one place with a particular viewpoint, then travels through time or space and ends in a different place with a different viewpoint.

LAZZI

Pieces of stage business, usually referred to in the context of *Commedia dell'Arte.*

LISTENING

The one key skill cited by improvisers right across the art form spectrum. Doesn't mean just listening. Instead, it means a level of concentration and attentiveness to everything that's happening. The sine qua non of improvisation skills.

LONG-FORM

The term is credited allegedly to Michael Gellman of Second City. It's a term coined to describe an improvisation in performance, which by its use of a thematic or narrative structure, runs longer than ten minutes or so. 'Short-form impro' would refer probably to a series of sketches that are not particularly linked in theme or content.

MODE
A way of communicating to the audience, for example, telling a story, playing a character, using abstract movement or singing.

MYSTERY
A mystery created at the top of a scene draws the audience in. Good improvisers are happy for mysteries to be created, knowing that there is time available for their solution.

NEGATIVE SPACE
In dance, it's the space between the dancers. It doesn't imply negativity. The term is drawn from visual arts when it refers to space around the object that is the subject of the painting.

OFFER
A much-used term in dramatic improvisation. Essentially an offer is anything that is perceived or imagined as a possible stimulus to action. So an offer could be a spoken statement or phrase, it could be a physical action, a gesture, or it could simply be a look. Good improvisers create or imagine offers even when they're not intended. Such an improviser will enter a completely empty room and the very emptiness is perceived as an offer.

OPPOSITE CHOICES
This notion, referred to by Mick Napier in his book *Improvise*, refers to the jump an improviser makes in her or his head, away from an obvious, perhaps 'default' choice to one that is the complete opposite. It has the effect of throwing the trajectory of the action into a different gear. It's possible to set up exercises that have this function of compelling the performer to make opposite choices at short notice, perhaps even during a line of dialogue on stage.

PASSENGER
The improviser who rather than drives the scene forward, prefers to take the back seat, allowing the other to define and take responsibility.

PATTERNS

A recurring sequence of action that is not routine-like. Routines imply a conscious organisation of behaviour whereas a pattern might emerge and then recur without deliberation, perhaps becoming a routine.

PHRASING

Within improvisation, used primarily by dancers or musicians to indicate a short passage of movement or music that has an integral coherence or unity. Oliver Scott writes: *'Once a performer can see and anticipate or feel the end of a phrase approaching, they are presented with a number of choices, particularly if they are offstage and about to enter, where the transition will be more marked. I liken the transitions to editing in film. You can have a straight cut – one stops the other starts – a cross fade where one phrase dies out as the other performer enters to start. Or an additive dissolve, for want of a better term, where the new phrase starts some time before the old one ends and gains strength to pull the audience's focus. Of course there are many other kinds . . . A "wipe" for instance – where the phrase ends with the performer leaving say stage left, and the new phrase starting with the performer entering stage right "wiping the stage across". The key thing for me about phrases – particularly evident with movement – is they don't end when the performer is still – that is a pause. I find there is a combination of the cerebral watching and instinctive feeling to notice when a improvised phrase ends, consequently influencing when to enter the composition and what type of transition will occur.'* Similarly, musicians will refer to a phrase as being a complete unit of melody or a sequence of notes that can be sung or played within a few seconds. In dramatic improvisation, it has the more literal meaning of a series of words that sum up a situation, a feeling or an attitude.

PIMPING

An offer that forces another player to do something difficult or unpleasant which you probably wouldn't do yourself. Used sparingly and playfully, it can be quite entertaining. Good pimp: 'I'd sure like to see you do that back flip again,' knowing that the other player *can* do a back flip. Bad pimp: The same line knowing the player *can't* do a back flip.

PLATFORM

The who, what and where of a scene. Some argue the success of a scene depends on having a solid platform.

PLAYBACK THEATRE
In a performance setting, the actors invite stories from the audience then literally 'play them back', providing a dramatic interpretation, more often than not in a metaphorically imaginative way. While not avowedly therapeutic, Playback does aim to have therapeutic impact. It is intended as a transformative and healing tool.

P.O.V.
The viewpoint of a particular character or performer on the action. Holding fast to this creates a strong sense of character with minimum amount of effort.

PROJECTED IMAGE
An image created on stage that is deliberately a projection, that is, rather than conveying in any way the objective reality of something, it objectifies what the performer 'feels' about that subject.

PROPS
Any material objects used in the improvisation.

PROTAGONIST / ANTAGONIST
These are terms used by writers and practitioners such as Augusto Boal within Forum Theatre to denote the central character, and the character who is pitted against her or him. In Forum, the audience is invited to side with the protagonist, examining through play how that character might find resources to bring against the antagonist.

REACTION
What is felt or experienced as a result of the actions of others.

REINCORPORATION
In jazz, the head is the theme stated at the outset of the piece and reprised usually at the end. Its use gives a kind of 'bookends' feel to the piece, and anchors the improvisation. Reincorporation is a dramatic equivalent in which elements discovered early in the piece are brought back, usually at the end but it could be earlier. These elements might constitute a piece of dialogue, some information, a story, a joke – almost anything. The use of reincorporation is not a formal structuring element like the head, but its use helps to give a sense of crafted unity

to the improvisation. Keith Johnstone has placed great emphasis on the two central elements of improvisation – one is free association and the other is reincorporation.

RESPONSE
What is expressed in reply to the actions of others.

RESTRICTIONS
Rules imposed on the performers to deliberately inhibit words, speech or interactions.

RHYTHM
The three art forms which use improvisation most extensively in performance – dance, music and theatre – are united by the use of rhythm. It's no more possible to extract the element of rhythm from these art forms than it is to extract the skeleton from a fish and still expect it to swim around. The rhythm is happening whether you like it or not because the event is taking place in time. You can ignore it but then you default to a rhythm that you haven't chosen. Gabrielle Roth's Five Rhythms *'comprise a simple movement practice designed to release the dancer that lives in every body, no matter what its shape, size, age, limitations and experience.'* As defined by Roth, the five rhythms, trademarked (by the way) if you want to refer to them, are flowing, staccato, chaos, lyrical and stillness. *'They come together to create the Wave, a movement meditation practice. Rather than having steps to follow, each rhythm is a different energy field in which you find your own expression and choreography, thereby stretching your imagination as well as your body. Each rhythm is a teacher and you can expect to meet different and sometimes unknown aspects of yourself as your dance unfolds and your practice of the rhythms deepens over time.'*[88]

ROLE
Role is different from character. Role is about the function of the performer in the scene – in relation to other characters. A role might be that of Questioner (to another's Answerer) or Bully (to a Victim).

ROUTINES
A routine is simply a repeated pattern. It can be a repeated phrase in music or repeated action in drama. Repetition has a particular and

almost magical effect on audiences, because it mirrors back the body's own functioning patterns: the rhythm of the heart, the movement of the blood. Trance states are induced through a use of rhythm. The conscious mind closes down temporarily in favour of a semi-hypnotic state. Within improvisation a routine establishes a context in which surprise, the breaking of the routine, is possible. It's like a production line in a factory. We watch the machines working, the workers lifting, placing, marking and dressing the pies. The drama begins when there's a break in the routine, when a worker catches their hair in the machine. Or when someone of higher status walks in and the machine is stopped.

RULES
Rules are generally taken as referring to basic good practice in dramatic improvisation. For example, you don't ignore or disbelieve an idea invented by another player. You try to co-operate. You say 'yes' to things. The danger with too great an emphasis on rules is that teaching becomes an assessment of the degree to which rules are adhered to, a practice that belies the spirit of the exercise. Rules can also refer to very concrete instructions that are given to validate or support a particular score. In Rotazaza's *Five in the Morning*, there is only one rule: actors must obey the offstage voice.

SCENARIO
A predetermined sequence of events that the improvisers will use as an armatural structure around which to improvise. The usefulness of having a scenario in place is that it allows the performers to work against it, much as a jazz musician will take a tune and stretch it far away from its familiar pattern, while holding it always in the background. The scenario of Adam and Eve, if used as a structure to improvise, might involve a reworking of the traditional outcome much as Angela Carter has reworked traditional folk tales like *Little Red Riding Hood*.

SCORE / STRUCTURE
The (usually predetermined) factors that the players have agreed will limit the boundaries of their decision-making.

SELECTION
The notion that improvisation is entirely about spontaneity has limited value. It's useful for the beginner. Keith Johnstone emphasises the

value of working with 'the first idea' as a means to liberate the imagination. It's a better approach than casting around for 'the best idea',
which will probably never come. The more experienced performer can
appreciate that there is always an element of choice involved. This is
not so much about searching for the best idea as about selecting an
option which is true to the journey you're on. *Always work at the top of
your intelligence . . . Try to skip your first impulse to respond, and move on
to the next, less obvious one. This is contrary to most academic advice that
the first thought is the best one. It just isn't. Sometimes, it's the third thing
you think of.'* (Del Close.) However, there's only so much that can be
held in the conscious mind simultaneously without the practice
becoming self-conscious. It's a small room in there, like a tiny upstairs
room above a vast cathedral. Stuff gets sent up from the cathedral
unprompted and fills up the small room. Then it disappears. So the
selection process is very fast and as soon as choices are made, other
options are best forgotten because soon enough they'll blow out of the
window.

SHELVING

The improviser puts an idea on an imaginary shelf for later use. Instead of speaking or showing it the moment it's conceived, the improviser stores it. Then it can be drawn from at a later time. It may be an
observation, a joke, a narrative idea, some information or an action. It's
a great way of dealing with the problem of suddenly being swamped
with ideas for possible reactions to a situation. One is selected, the
others stored. Or they are all stored and the emphasis remains on just
playing moment-to-moment, taking from the shelf as necessary.

SHIFT

The qualitative change in what's occurring. A performer suddenly
stops doing what he's doing – bragging, for example – and starts doing
something completely different: apologising, for example. If the shift
occurs organically out of what came before, although it's a radical
departure, the audience understands the logic of development.
Cumulative shifts enable a journey.

SHORT-FORM

The format of an improvisation where a series of unconnected scenes or
sketches are played consecutively. Usually associated with comedy impro.

SIDE COACHING

The art of helping players while an improvisation is running by making verbal suggestions from offstage. I've heard some dumb interventions in which the facilitator's use of words was so crass the improvisation seized up. I've been responsible for a few of those myself. Unless it's established as a convention early, actors may get taken by surprise. Vague exhortations to 'raise the stakes' or 'push on through' may simply confuse and irritate. Far better are very specific instructions such as 'Pick up the glass now', 'Kiss her', 'Get into bed', 'Light a match and start a fire now', and that trusted favourite, 'Leave the stage'. Side coaching is particularly useful in nudging actors towards what they are keen to do, but have insecurities about. If you nudge them, and it doesn't work, they can blame you afterwards.

SOURCING

Consciously identifying elements within the improvisation to use as material. Particular elements might be sourced in order to generate responses. You might source:

- Yourself – your own feelings or sensations
- Other players around you:
- The space you're in – which would include the look of it, the smell of it, the expansiveness of it, the nature of the materials in it
- The audience, including any material they have given you. Consciously choosing what to source gives you a strategy to avoid just being a hopeless blob riven from moment to moment by a series of competing impulses

'I recently ran an exercise in which the given was a young woman crying at a table. I asked the performers to come into the space and start improvising. The first six performers all responded to the girl, they "sourced" her feelings by coming over, comforting her, talking to her, getting angry with her or crying with her. They all responded exclusively to one element only within the scene. Finally an actor sourced the space instead. He simply came in, rolled up the carpet and carried it out. Immediately a more interesting story began to be told. The young woman was being evicted.' (Sandy Van Torquil.)

SPECTACTOR

The spectator who becomes an actor within a Forum Theatre session.

STANCE
This is the view of the world taken by a character. For example, a character may be very embittered by experience, or very naive or very gung-ho. Whatever it is, once found, it can give the performer a sense of rootedness for that character. Stance is somewhat similar to what is referred to as P.O.V. (point of view).

STARTING BACK
By starting a long way away emotionally from the point you expect to arrive at, you create a greater sense of journey. To use an analogy, if you're travelling to London and you start at Watford, there's less of a transition than if you leave from Budapest.

STATUS
A way of acknowledging the relative importance of characters (or objects or environments) on the stage. A 'high' status might be achieved by players acknowledging a character's superior job, place in society or achievements. A 'low' status might be achieved by players responding to a character's menial job, low character or despised behaviour. A sense of status is often best achieved through it being projected on to the high or low status character, rather than by that character 'playing it' him or herself. Keith Johnstone has used awareness of status extensively as a means to initiate improvisations.

STOCK RELATIONSHIP
An archetypal relationship that occurs in human society and is written up in plays, stories, novels and myths. Examples might include Bully-Victim or Innocent-Trickster. These are useful for creating scenes and stories in a way that grounds the playing. Their use might give the actors more substantial imaginative resources than social or familial relations such as brother-sister or husband-wife. Of course a husband–wife could itself be either a Bully-Victim relationship or a Trickster-Innocent relationship.

TENSION
A sense of something unfulfilled while the possibility of its fulfilment hangs in the air.

TILTING
The action of tipping the scene on its head without undermining it. Getting the audience to look at it from a different point of view.

TIME

What sets improvisation apart from other kinds of performance is its relationship to time. Keith Jarret said, *'Jazz is there and gone. It happens. You have to be there for it. That simple.'* Because of this relationship, improvisation has the capacity to carry to the surface all the elements that are floating around in the space, at that moment. The corollary of this is that the performer needs to be alive in that moment to the sensations of the present, rather than operating according to dictates that were operative before or might be operative later.

TROUBLE

The idea of 'getting yourself into trouble' refers to situations where the improviser finds herself vulnerable or defenceless. It's often a strategically valuable aim to engineer this situation, since in that moment the individual becomes more revealed, more human, more interesting. Scenarios can be deliberately constructed in order to 'get a performer into trouble'. Imagine a gift has been made by A to B, but the gift has been abused, destroyed or given away. Then A comes to visit B to find out how the gift is working out. The classic master-servant relationship can be used to explore situations of trouble, such as when the servant is caught out. If done with good humour, 'getting your partner into trouble' achieves similar results.

WIMPING

Wimping is considered to be taking a lazy short cut that avoids having to engage more riskily. Implying that your partner is drunk, stoned, stupid or insane would be a major wimp. Some wimps are common to certain games, like looking for your contact lens or being stuck together with crazy glue during games like Freeze Tag.

WORLD

The world of the scene or the play is a notion that embraces everything really significant about it that isn't the narrative. It's the invisible culture of the location. The world might be informed by any number of notions: hierarchy, idealism, tradition or creativity. These notions inform the behaviour of the characters within it. Shakespeare often juxtaposes two worlds in order to throw up questions about the values of each: town and country, city and court, spirit and human.

INDEX OF
CONTRIBUTORS AND ARTISTS

GABY AGIS is a dancer, one of the pioneers of collaborative performance in Britain. She has improvised and performed with leading artists of her generation from other disciplines in galleries, museums and theatres. She choreographed a piece for the opening of London's Millennium Bridge in 2001.

DANIELLE ALLAN is an actress, performer and teacher who has performed extensively with Fluxx, Tellers and other companies. She has a special interest in flamenco dance. She also performs with ESP (Experiments in Spontaneous Performance).

ROBERT ANDERSON teaches and performs dance improvisation in Britain and abroad in a variety of settings with adults, children and mixed-ability groups. His work is strongly influenced by contact improvisation which he has studied since 1996 with leading teachers from the US and Europe.

DEREK BAILEY, 1930-2005, was a guitarist and a significant influence within free improvisation practice. His collaborations were many and involved musicians such as Gavin Bryars, Evan Parker, Anthony Braxton, Tony Oxley and John Stevens. His book *Improvisation* has been a consistent source of inspiration to many.

JOE BILL is a Chicago-based performer and teacher who was a co-founder of Annoyance Theatre in 1987, working on many productions since. He has also worked for several years with Mark Sutton on the production, *Bassprov*.

JO BLOWERS is a dancer and teacher. She performs with Liverpool Improvisation Collective with Andrea Buckley, Paula Hampson and Mary Prestidge. She teaches at Liverpool Institute of Performing Arts.

ALISON BLUNT is a musician who has worked in a wide variety of styles, genres, art forms and environments, both nationally and abroad.

Recent credits include regular gigs and recordings with improv duo *Songs That Hum* and touring her music and stories for the under-fives. She is a member of ESP.

SALLY BROOKES is a theatre director and facilitator, and former Director of Geese Theatre (UK). She is also a mask-maker who works extensively in prisons throughout the United Kingdom.

DEL CLOSE was a teacher, performer and co-author of the book *Truth in Comedy* which outlines techniques now common to longform improvisation and describes the Harold. His favorite framework for comedic storytelling was allegedly the structures of Wagner's Ring Cycle.

JULIAN CROUCH is a member of Improbable Theatre who also works as a theatre designer on shows such as *Shockheaded Peter* and *Jerry Springer – The Opera*.

GUY DARTNELL is a performer, director, writer, collaborator and teacher whose work spans the realms of theatre, music, dance, circus and film. He has created a series of one-man shows and regularly collaborates with Improbable Theatre in productions such as *Lifegame*.

JENNIFER ELLISON is a writer and performer based in Chicago who works with WNEP (What No One Else Produces).

MATT ELWELL is a performer and teacher based in Chicago. He is Director of the Training Centre at ComedySportz and also teaches for Second City.

TIM ETCHELLS is a member of Forced Entertainment, a company based in the UK but performing internationally. He creates the texts for many of their productions.

SIMON FELL is a composer and double bassist active in free improvisation and contemporary jazz and chamber music. He is a founder member of London Improvisers Orchestra. His discography includes over one hundred recordings.

KEVIN FINNAN is the Artistic Director of Motionhouse Dance Theatre, based in Leamington Spa in the UK. Motionhouse have been running residences and touring dance performances since 1988.

MARTIN GLYNN is a director and teacher, currently involved in a research project looking at African Religious Traditions as a Resource for a 'Rites of Passage' for Black Men in Prison, the Black Church, and Community.

MAGGIE GORDON-WALKER is an actress and comedy performer based in the UK who is a founding member of Fluxx and who works with Black Sheep Theatre Company amongst others.

R.G. GREGORY is a poet, writer and theatre maker who worked initially within the education system before developing new approaches to teaching in Africa, after which he returned to the U.K and set up Word and Action (Dorset). He has now retired from the company and is writing plays and poetry.

TONY GUILFOYLE is an actor trained at the Drama Centre, London and has since performed widely with the Royal Court Theatre, the BBC, Insomniac Productions and with Lepage's company, Ex Machina.

DON HALL is a musician and performer based in Chicago. He is the Director of WNEP (What No One Else Produces) which presents 'the grotesque as beautiful and the mundane as unexpected'.

JULYEN HAMILTON has been making dances, directing and teaching for the past thirty years, and has been hugely influential on the international dance scene. He is now based in Girona, Spain. Trained in a period of experimentation in London in the mid-'70s, he has constantly made work from a radical point of view.

ADRIAN HEATHFIELD is a teacher, maker of, and writer on performance. His research investigates the cultural, political and philosophical resonances of contemporary performance and live art. It is conducted through critical examinations in publications, curatorial interventions and creative practices.

SAUL HEWISH is a former director of Geese UK and a current co-director of Rideout (Creative Arts for Rehabilitation) with Chris Johnston. He works extensively within prison and probation contexts, creating performances and workshops.

K.J. HOLMES is an independent dancer, singer, poet and body worker who has been exploring improvisation as process and performance since 1981, as a soloist and in her collaborations with other artists. She is based in the United States.

REX HOSSI HORAN is a multi-instrumentalist musician. His work in London's R'ai bands Yusef and the Halal Joint and Cheb Nacim has seen him on the European festival circuit and performing at the Queen Elizabeth Hall. Rex also performs with ESP (Experiments in Spontaneous Performance).

WENDY HOUSTON is a London-based artist who has been working with movement and words for twenty years. She has collaborated widely as well as touring her own solo work in Europe, USA and Australia. Wendy creates work which exploits the tension between language and movement. She creates work in many formats (theatre, video, site-specific).

KEITH JOHNSTONE is a teacher of improvisation whose most celebrated work began at the Royal Court Theatre in London as part of the Writers' Group. This led to the formation of Theatre Machine. He later moved to Calgary University from where he developed Theatresports, *Lifegame* and other formats.

JONATHAN KAY is an improviser and teacher, based in Winchester, whose work on discovering 'the fool' in each person has set a benchmark for originality and distinctiveness within the world of improvisation.

ROBERT LEPAGE is a performer and director based in Montreal, Canada whose company Ex Machina performs throughout the world. Lepage is also the director of a number of films and other performance-related projects.

TREVOR LINES is a musician and composer with special interests in improvisation, folk and related musics. He is active in community music work and also teaches Cultural Studies and Jazz History at Birmingham Conservatoire.

TIMOTHY LONE is an improviser with the Improfessionals based in Paris and Fluxx based in London. He teaches improvisation and other theatre practice in Europe and the USA.

KATE MCCOY is a former member of TIPP (Theatre in Prisons and Probation), now running a range of projects as a freelance drama worker.

PHELIM MCDERMOTT is a performer, writer and director with Improbable Theatre who was a co-creator of *Shockheaded Peter* and many Improbable shows at the National Theatre and elsewhere. He also performs with the Comedy Store Players.

SUE MCLENNAN is a dancer and teacher now based at the London Contemporary Dance School in Euston, London.

FRANK MOON is a musician and teacher who recently worked at Coventry University and now freelances, combining with a range of other musicians to create events using free and structured improvisations.

NEIL MULLARKEY is a founder member of the Comedy Store Players who also performs in a range of contexts. He runs training sessions for business folk using improvisation techniques and tours his one-man shows.

MICK NAPIER is a performer and director based in Chicago. He is the co-founder and Director of Annoyance Productions and regularly directs shows by Second City Theatre Company.

RICK NODINE is a teacher, dancer and staff member at London Contemporary Dance School. He performs extensively with Jovair Longo and also with ESP.

MARK PHOENIX is an actor and improviser who works with Fluxx. He also teaches improvisation in a range of contexts and appears in films, advertisements and other media.

JOYCE PIVEN is the founder of the Piven Theatre Workshop in Evanston, Illinois that 'aims to preserve a process of creative exploration that celebrates each individual's unique voice through an ensemble-based, community-oriented approach to theatre training and performance'.

EDDIE PRÉVOST founded AMM with Lesley Gare and Keith Rowe. He is a drummer who has since worked with many bands including GOD, Main and Ear. When he isn't performing, Prévost conducts workshops, gives lectures, and writes about improv for several magazines. He also runs his record label, Matchless Records.

KEITH ROWE is a musician who uses guitar and radio amongst other sources to create improvised performance. In his early days he worked with Mike Westbrook then later with the Scratch Orchestra and AMM. He is currently resident in France.

FELIX RUCKERT is a dancer and choreographer who formerly worked as a member of Pina Bausch's company. He now leads his own company based in Berlin and has established an international reputation with a range of productions, many of which have explored the use of improvisation in performance.

STEN RUDSTROM worked extensively with Ruth Zaporah, developer of the improvisational performance training process Action Theater™, and was editor of her book, *Action Theater, The Improvisation of Presence*. He teaches and performs throughout the United States and Europe.

PETER SANDER is a pianist and composer who was born in Budapest, came to London and trained at the Guildhall School and has since composed music within both the serious and commercial music fields.

OLIVER SCOTT is a dancer and movement teacher who has performed with Fence Crossing, based in Coventry, and who leads his own company, Mercurial Dance.

LEE SIMPSON is a performer, improviser and founder member of both the Comedy Store Players and Improbable Theatre.

KIRSTIE SIMSON studied ballet and modern dance at the Laban Center, London. Over the course of the next twenty years she has worked extensively, performing and teaching throughout England, Europe and the USA.

REBECCA SOHN is an improviser, performer and member of the Annoyance Theatre based in Chicago, USA. She also performs with Second City and Switchboard, her own company.

ANDREW ST JOHN was the founder of Tellers theatre, creating improvised and other shows in community contexts in the UK. He is currently a member of Fluxx.

MAX STAFFORD-CLARK is the former director of Joint Stock Theatre Company and the current director of Out of Joint. He has become known in particular for his powerful productions of contemporary plays, sometimes developed collaboratively with the writer, which have toured extensively throughout the world.

NANCY STARK SMITH was an early developer, with Steve Paxton and others, of Contact Improvisation. She is a dancer and teacher based in the U.S.A. who is now in demand as a teacher and workshop leader.

MARK SUTTON is a Chicago-based improvisation teacher and performer with Annoyance Theatre. He also developed a two-man show with Joe Bill entitled *Bassprov* that has toured extensively within the USA.

SANDY VAN TORQUIL was born in Venezuela and later moved to the UK where she trained with Mark Phoenix and created a number of improvised, participatory shows including *Have You Got Your Lunchbox?*

JACKIE WALDUCK describes herself as a 'collaborative composer', working with a range of different groups to create music through improvisation. She is a partner with Alison Blunt in Songs That Hum.

PETER WEIGOLD is a composer, conductor and music teacher. He founded and directed the chamber music ensemble Gemini, performing and broadcasting twentieth-century repertoire and pioneering participatory workshops. His compositions have been widely commissioned, including works for the London Symphony Orchestra.

KEITH WHIPPLE has worked for prisons, probation services, and international refugee centres. He learned improvisation and *Commedia dell'Arte* with Geese Theatre travelling across the United States and the United Kingdom. He now works with ComedySportz and as a drama therapist in Chicago.

JOHN WRIGHT co-founded Trestle Theatre, a company that tours mask-based performances extensively within the UK and beyond. He later co-founded Told by an Idiot with Hayley Carmichael and Paul Hunter. He also teaches extensively and creates productions with different theatre companies and organisations. He is author of *Why Is That So Funny? A Practical Exploration of Physical Comedy.*

RUTH ZAPORAH is a teacher, performer, and director. She travels widely in the United States and abroad, performing and teaching in theatres, dance and theatre studios, on college campuses, and psychological training programs. She has twice been the recipient of a National Endowment for the Arts Choreographer's Fellowship.

ENDNOTES

PART ONE: THE WHY

1. Keith Johnstone, *Impro*. Faber and Faber, 1979.
2. Haruki Murakami, *Kafka on the Shore*. Vintage, 2005.
3. R.G. Gregory, *Spring at the Crane Stream*. Wanda Publications, 1994.
4. Edwin Prévost, *No Sound is Innocent*. Copula, 1995.
5. Viola Spolin, *Improvisation for the Theatre*. Northwestern University Press, 1963.
6. Victor Turner, 'Body, Brain and Culture' in *Performing Arts Journal* Vol. 10, No. 2, 1986.
7. www.jam2dis.com
8. Ted Goia, *The History of Jazz*. Oxford University Press, 1997.
9. Augusto Boal (trans. Adrian Jackson), *Games for Actors and Non-Actors*. Routledge, 1992.
10. www.rspopuk.com
11. www.improbable.co.uk
12. www.inplaceofwar.net
13. James Thompson, *Digging Up Stories*. Manchester University Press, 2005.
14. Interview with Viola Spolin, published in *Los Angeles Times*, 26 May 1974.
15. Rob Kozlowski, *The Art of Chicago Improv*. Heinemann, 2002.
16. Sam Brenton and Howard Cohen, *Shooting People*. Verso, 2003.
17. Ibid.
18. Ibid.
19. David Wilson, 'Big Brother Damages in Our Health' in the *Guardian*, 13 August 2005.
20. Sam Brenton and Howard Cohen, *Shooting People*. Verso, 2003.
21. *A Short Film About SHIFTI*, DreamTime Productions, 2006.

PART TWO: THE WHO

22. In Paul F. Berliner, *Thinking in Jazz*. The University of Chicago Press, 1994.
23. Ibid.
24. *A Short Film About SHIFT1*, DreamTime Productions, 2006.
25. Edwin Prévost, *No Sound is Innocent*. Copula, 1995.
26. Antonio Domasio, *The Feeling of What Happens*. Vintage, 2000.
27. Ruth Zaporah, 'What's on my Mind Now?' in *Contact Quarterly*, Winter/Spring 2002.
28. Ibid.
29. *Amplify* DVD, 2002.
30. Mick Napier, *Improvise: Scene from the Inside Out*. Heinemann, 2004.
31. Ibid.
32. Paul F. Berliner, *Thinking in Jazz*. The University of Chicago Press, 1994.
33. Ibid.
34. Ruth Zaporah, 'What's on my Mind Now?' in *Contact Quarterly*, Winter/Spring 2002.
35. Keith Johnstone, email to the author, April 2006.
36. Rob Kozlowski, *The Art of Chicago Improv*. Heinemann, 2002.
37. Stephen Nachmanovitch, *Free Play*. Jeremy P. Tarcher, 1990.
38. http://proximity.slightly.net
39. Edwin Prévost, in Derek Bailey, *Improvisation*. The British Library National Sound Archive, 1992.
40. Derek Bailey, *Improvisation*. The British Library National Sound Archive, 1992.
41. Ibid.
42. www.improbable.co.uk
43. Jacqueline Walduck, *Role-taking in Free Improvisation and Collaborative Composition*. City University, 1992.
44. Ibid.
45. Ibid.
46. Steve Beresford 'Reshaping the Sonic Landscape', in *Resonance Magazine*, Vol. 6, No. 1.
47. Derek Bailey, http://efi.group.shef.ac.uk/fulltext/mbailin2.html
48. Peter Brook, *The Empty Space*. McGibbon & Kee, 1968.
49. Derek Bailey, *Improvisation*. The British Library National Sound Archive, 1992.

50. Ibid.
51. Lyn Gardner, 'The Crazy Gang' in the *Guardian*, 25 October 2004.
52. Keith Johnstone, *Impro*. Faber and Faber, 1979.
53. Walter Horn, in *Paris Transatlantic*, July 2004.
54. Derek Bailey, http://efi.group.shef.ac.uk/fulltext/mbailin2.html
55. Jill Johnston in *Contact Quarterly*, Fall 1987
56. Nabil Shaban, email to the author.
57. Anna Halprin in *Contact Quarterly*, Spring/Summer 1987.
58. Letter reprinted in *Contact Quarterly*, Winter/Sprint 1998.
59. Keith Johnstone, *Improvisation for Storytellers*. Faber and Faber, 1999.
60. Ibid.
61. Rex Horan, email to the author.

PART THREE: THE WHAT

62. Mick Napier, *Improvise: Scene from Inside Out*. Heinemann, 2004.
63. *A Short Film About SHIFTI*, DreamTime Productions, 2006.
64. Charna Halpern et al, *Truth in Comedy*. Meriwether Publishing, 1994.
65. Keith Johnstone, *Impro*. Faber and Faber, 1979.
66. Michael Rattle (trans. Tim Hodgkinson) in *Resonance Magazine*, reprinted in *Musicworks 66*.
67. Stephen Nachmanovitch, *Free Play*. Jeremy P. Tarcher, 1990.
68. Paul F. Berliner, *Thinking in Jazz*. The University of Chicago Press, 1994.
69. Chris Ayres in *The Times*, August 16 2005
70. Marshall Soules, 'Improvising Character: Jazz, the Actor, and Protocols of Improvisation' in *The Other Side of Nowhere* (ed. Daniel Fischlin and Ajay Heble), Wesleyan University Press, 2004.
71. John Miller Chernoff, *African Rhythm and African Sensibility*. University of Chicago Press, 1981.
72. Trevor Lines, email to the author.

PART FOUR: THE HOW

73. Charna Halpern et al, *Truth in Comedy*. Meriwether Publishing, 1994.

74. Marc Sabatella, *A Whole Approach to Jazz Improvisation*. ADG Productions.
75. Keith Johnstone, *Improvisation for Storytellers*. Faber and Faber, 1999.
76. Keith Johnstone, *Impro*. Faber and Faber, 1979.
77. Peter Brook, *The Shifting Point*. Methuen, 1987.
78. Ruth Zaporah, *Action Theatre: The Improvisation of Presence*, North Atlantic Books, 1995.
79. www.new-oceans.co.uk
80. Charna Halpern et al, *Truth in Comedy*. Meriwether Publishing, 1994.
81. Mick Napier, *Improvise: Scene from the Inside Out*. Heinemann, 2004.
82. Ibid.
83. Sanford Meisner and Dennis Longwell, *On Acting*. Vintage Books, 1987.
84. Michael Chekhov, *On the Technique of Acting*. Harper Collins, 1991.
85. Ibid.
86. Charna Halpern et al, *Truth in Comedy*. Meriwether Publishing, 1994.
87. Derek Bailey, *Improvisation*. The British Library National Sound Archive, 1992.
88. www.acalltodance.com/5rhythms.htm

BIBLIOGRAPHY

Bailey, Derek, *Improvisation: its nature and practice in music* (London: The British Library National Sound Archive, 1992).

Baim, Clark, Brookes, Sally and Mountford, Alan, *The Geese Theatre Handbook: Drama with offenders and people at risk* (Winchester: Waterside Press, 2002).

Bergman, John and Hewish, Saul, *Challenging Experience: An Experiential Approach to the Treatment of Serious Offenders* (Oklahoma City: Wood 'n' Barnes, 2004).

Berliner, Paul F., *Thinking in Jazz: The Infinite Art of Improvisation* (Chicago: The University of Chicago Press, 1994).

Brenton, Sam and Cohen, Reuben, *Shooting People: Adventures in Reality TV* (London and New York: Verso, 2003).

Boal, Augusto (trans. Adrian Jackson), *Games for Actors and Non-Actors* (London: Routledge, 1992).

Brook, Peter, *The Empty Space* (London: McGibbon & Kee, 1968).

————— , *The Shifting Point* (London: Methuen, 1987).

Chekhov, Michael, *On the Technique of Acting* (New York: Harper Collins, 1991).

Chernoff, John Miller, *African Rhythm and African Sensibility* (Chicago: University of Chicago Press, 1981).

Domasio, Antonio, *The Feeling of What Happens: Body, emotion and the making of consciousness* (London: Vintage, 2000).

Frost, Anthony and Yarrow, Ralph, *Improvisation in Drama* (Basingstoke: Macmillan Education, 1990).

Goia, Ted, *The History of Jazz* (Oxford: Oxford University Press, 1997).

Gregory, R.G., *Spring at the Crane Stream* (Wanda Publications, 1994).

Halpern, Charna and Close, Del and Johnson, Kim, *Truth In Comedy: the Manual of Improvisation* (Colorado Springs: Meriwether Publishing, 1994).

Heathcote, Dorothy, (ed. Liz Johnson and Cecily O'Neill), *Collected Writings on Education and Drama* (London: Hutchinson, 1984).

Hodgson, John and Richards, Ernest, *Improvisation: Discovery and Creativity in Drama* (London: Methuen, 1966).

Johnston, Chris, *House of Games: Making theatre from everyday life* (London: Nick Hern Books, 1998).

Johnstone, Keith, *Impro: Improvisation and the Theatre* (London: Faber and Faber, 1979).

Johnstone, Keith, *Improvisation for Storytellers* (London: Faber and Faber, 1999).

Kirby, Ernest Theodore, *Ur-Drama: The Origins of Theatre* (New York: New York University, 1975).

Kozlowski, Rob, *The Art of Chicago Improv: Shortcuts to Long-Form Improvisation* (Portsmouth: Heinemann, 2002).

Libera, Anne, *The Second City: Almanac of Improvisation* (Evanston: Northwestern University Press, 2004).

Meisner, Sanford and Longwell, Dennis, *Sanford Meisner on Acting* (New York: Vintage Books, 1987).

Mindell, Arnold, *Sitting in the Fire: Large group transformation using conflict and diversity* (Portland: Lao Tse Press, 1995).

————— , *The Leader as Martial Artist: An Introduction to Deep Democracy* (Oakland: Lao Tse Press, 1992).

Murakami, Haruki, *Kafka on the Shore* (London: Harvill, 2005).

Nachmanovitch, Stephen, *Free Play: Improvisation in Life and Art* (Los Angeles: Jeremy P. Tarcher, 1990).

Napier, Mick, *Improvise: Scene from the Inside Out* (Portsmouth: Heinemann, 2004).

Novack, Cynthia J., *Sharing the Dance: Contact Improvisation and American Culture* (Madison: The University of Wisconsin Press, 1990).

O'Connor, Joseph and Ian McDermott, *The Way of NLP* (Thorsons, 2001).

Prévost, Edwin, *No Sound Is Innocent* (Harlow: Copula, 1995).

Ronen, Asaf, *Directing Improv: Show the way by getting out of the way* (Yesand Publishing, 2005).

Rudlin, John, *Commedia dell'Arte: A Handbook for Troupes* (London: Routledge, 2001).

Sabatella, Marc, *A Whole Approach to Jazz Improvisation* (ADG Productions).

Spolin, Viola, *Improvisation for the Theatre* (Evanston: Northwestern University Press, 1963).

Stevens, John, *Search and Reflect* (London: Open University Press, 1985).

Sweet, Jeffrey, *Something Wonderful Right Away* (New York: Limelight, 2004).

Szczelkun, Stefan, 'Exploding Cinema 1992–1999: Culture and Democracy' Ph.D. thesis (Royal College of Art, 2002)

Thompson, James, *Digging Up Stories: Applied theatre, performance and war* (Manchester: Manchester University Press, 2005).

Turner, Victor, 'Body, Brain and Culture' in *Performing Arts Journal* Vol. 10, No. 2, 1986.

Walduck, Jacqueline, *Role-taking in Free Improvisation and Collaborative Composition* (City University, 1992).

Wright, John, *Why Is That So Funny?* (London: Nick Hern Books, 2006).

Zaporah, Ruth, *Action Theatre: The Improvisation of Presence* (Berkeley: North Atlantic Books, 1995).

INDEX